Praise for
Improving America's Schools Together

"This volume provides remarkable perspective on the power of districts and universities learning together—in partnerships and in community—to do more for more students than either could possibly do on their own. It serves as both a call and a blueprint for action, with the contributing authors inviting district and university leaders to follow in their footsteps to forge institutional change." —**Donald J. Peurach, Marsal Family School of Education, University of Michigan**

"This volume brings together a dream team—a mix of scholars and scholarly professionals with complementary research and practice-based expertise who have figured out how to work together in research-practice partnerships. Their contributions provide inspiration and concrete guidance for educational leaders in schools, districts, and institutions of higher education. This book is on the cutting edge of the continuous improvement movement in education and is a must-read for educators seeking to transform US education and create more equitable learning opportunities for students." —**Jennifer Lin Russell, Peabody College, Vanderbilt University**

"Here's a must-read volume for those building new disruptive relationships between institutions of higher education (IHEs) and local education agencies (LEAs). Case studies tell examples of intentional, sustainable partnerships. They are held together through the mutual use of and belief in improvement science and continuous improvement; a leadership network; and efforts to develop mutualism through boundary spanners and braiders." —**John Q. Easton, University of Chicago, UChicago Consortium on School Research**

"Gomez, Biag, Imig, Tozer, and Hitz bring together powerful examples of how—through thoughtful and deliberate continuous improvement processes—partnerships can be formed to address complex problems of practice in our schools. This text will quickly become a go-to guide for those seeking to engage in equity-focused and contextually relevant collaborations designed to address public school challenges and to develop sustainable and impactful solutions." —**Karen L. Sanzo, Old Dominion University**

"These cases provide wonderful examples of how district-university partnerships for continuous improvement can benefit both school districts and schools of education. Anyone interested in engaging in such partnerships should read this book, especially to identify the benefits but also to get a sense of the challenges such partnerships face." —**William Firestone, Rutgers University, Graduate School of Education (retired)**

"This book demonstrates how improvement science is a rigorous but user-friendly way to get stakeholders on the same page to do research in the name of making schools better. Each case is co-written by a university faculty member and educational practitioner, which supports the notion of university-district partnerships and decolonizes who owns and produces knowledge. This book is a useful contribution to practitioners—both K–12 and university—as they consider venturing into similar work." —**Jill A. Perry, PhD, Carnegie Project on the Education Doctorate**

"This text is compelling in that it presents varied, well-documented examples of effective, enduring partnerships and provides a concise and clear conceptual framework for those cases. Readers seeking to evaluate or create similar inter-institutional partnerships have the proof of concept and the conceptual guidance needed to do so. It is both an ideal leadership and policy course text and a very practical guide for those involved in the work of partnerships." —**Mark LaCelle-Peterson, president and CEO, Association for Advancing Quality in Educator Preparation**

"If you've wondered what 'mutually beneficial and co-constructed partnerships' look like in practice and how they can be authentic and sustainable over time, this book is for you. With one fell swoop, it silences those resistant to change who wield the argument that 'it can't happen here' as their justification for not innovating." —**Sean Kottke, PhD, Office of Educator Excellence, Michigan Department of Education**

"This book is a two for one—it discusses improving the content of the leadership development programs as well as the outcomes of the school-university partnerships required to make leadership development effective. I highly recommend this book for people working on improvement in the field of education from both practice and research roles and organizations." —**Laura Wentworth, director of research practice partnerships, California Education Partners**

"This book captures multiple stories of how institutions of higher education can come alongside school districts to tackle complex problems of practice. Each case provides insight into how diverse actors and partners negotiate and engage in the trading zones and boundaries of policies, practices, programs, and processes to reimagine not only how we continuously improve schools but how we prepare educators and educational leaders to lead and work together." —**Edwin Nii Bonney, Radford University**

"This important text provides a multifaceted examination and discussion of partnerships between PK–12 school districts and universities using real life examples from existing impactful partnerships across the United States. The stories and lessons shared in each chapter can serve as a blueprint for others interested in forming similar partnerships with the aim of transforming their surrounding PK–12 educational community." —**Christopher Benedetti, Texas A&M University–Corpus Christi**

"This volume brings together some of the most important applied thinkers and doers about complex education partnerships active today. The editors are seasoned education researchers who also share an extensive background in the use of improvement science. Their necessary communication to co-create this volume has proven to be highly generative, with each sharing innovative insight and imperative detail, to the benefit of the reader." —**Edmund "Ted" Hamann, University of Nebraska-Lincoln; chair, Carnegie Project on the Education Doctorate (CPED) Council of Delegates; AERA Fellow**

"I highly recommend this text for school districts and institutions of higher education that want to form a partnership through the lens of improvement science. All IHEs should be training their candidates in school district administration on improvement science and how forming these partnerships not only improve outcomes for students but also create equitable leaders that will be transforming schools and communities in which they are employed." —**Tori L. Colson, EdD, University of Southern Indiana**

"Blending the expertise of researchers and practitioners with the use of case studies, this book will be valuable for universities and school districts who want to deepen their partnership work and to see what this work looks like 'in real life.'" —**Corrie Stone-Johnson, University at Buffalo, The State University of New York; editor-in-chief,** *Journal of Educational Change*

"This text is full of pragmatic and versatile lessons on continuous improvement in education. I'm not a believer in 'one size fits all' methodologies, so improvement science cannot be a panacea. But where evaluation and other social science research methods stop short of fixing problems, improvement science can indeed transform practice through innovation, collaboration, and learning from data. Just as healthcare and other vital human service fields have embraced it, education must as well." —**Dane Joseph, George Fox University**

Improving America's Schools Together

How District-University Partnerships and Continuous Improvement Can Transform Education

Edited by
Louis M. Gomez
University of California, Los Angeles

Manuelito Biag
The Carnegie Foundation for the Advancement of Teaching

David G. Imig
University of Maryland, College Park

Randy Hitz
Portland State University

Steve Tozer
University of Illinois Chicago

Foreword by
Anthony S. Bryk
Ninth President of The Carnegie Foundation for the Advancement of Teaching

ROWMAN & LITTLEFIELD
Lanham • Boulder • New York • London

Associate Acquisitions Editor: Courtney Packard
Assistant Acquisitions Editor: Sarah Rinehart
Sales and Marketing Inquiries: textbooks@rowman.com

Published by Rowman & Littlefield
An imprint of The Rowman & Littlefield Publishing Group, Inc.
4501 Forbes Boulevard, Suite 200, Lanham, Maryland 20706
www.rowman.com

86-90 Paul Street, London EC2A 4NE

Copyright © 2023 by The Rowman & Littlefield Publishing Group, Inc.

All rights reserved. No part of this book may be reproduced in any form or by any electronic or mechanical means, including information storage and retrieval systems, without written permission from the publisher, except by a reviewer who may quote passages in a review.

British Library Cataloguing in Publication Information Available

Library of Congress Cataloging-in-Publication Data

Names: Gomez, Louis M., 1950– editor.
Title: Improving America's schools together : how district-university partnerships and continuous improvement can transform education / edited by Louis M. Gomez, University of California, Los Angeles, Manuelito Biag, Carnegie Foundation, Center for Postsecondary Innovation, David G. Imig, University of Maryland, College Park, Randy Hitz, Portland State University, Steve Tozer, University of Illinois Chicago ; foreword by Anthony S. Bryk, Ninth President of The Carnegie Foundation for the Advancement of Teaching.
Description: Lanham, Maryland : Rowman & Littlefield, [2023] | Includes bibliographical references and index.
Identifiers: LCCN 2022061411 (print) | LCCN 2022061412 (ebook) | ISBN 9781538173213 (Cloth : acid-free paper) | ISBN 9781538173220 (Paperback : acid-free paper) | ISBN 9781538173237 (epub)
Subjects: LCSH: School improvement programs—United States. | School management and organization—United States. | Educational evaluation—United States. | Educational change—United States. | Teacher effectiveness—United States.
Classification: LCC LB2822.82 .I465 2023 (print) | LCC LB2822.82 (ebook) | DDC 371.2/070973—dc23/eng/20230118
LC record available at https://lccn.loc.gov/2022061411
LC ebook record available at https://lccn.loc.gov/2022061412

Brief Contents

Acknowledgments	xviii
Foreword	xx
Anthony S. Bryk	
Introduction: Getting to Mutual–Benefit Partnerships	1
Louis M. Gomez and Manuelito Biag	

SECTION I: IMPROVEMENT METHODS, EQUITY, AND PROBLEMS OF PRACTICE IN LOCAL CONTEXT — 27
STEVE TOZER

1. Braiding Improvement into the Fabric of District Leadership Preparation and Practice — 30
   University of Virginia and Chesterfield County Public Schools
   David Eddy-Spicer, Tinkhani Ushe White, and Michelle M. Beavers

2. A University–School District Collaboration to Improve Equity- and Inquiry-Driven School Leadership — 52
   Fordham University and Bronx School Districts 9 and 11
   Margaret Terry Orr, Kris DeFilippis, Meisha Porter, and Elizabeth Leisy Stosich

3. Moving a Partnership from Itinerant to Integral: Using Improvement Science as a Catalyst for Change in Leadership Preparation and Induction — 74
   George Mason University and Fairfax County Public Schools
   Samantha Viano, Farnoosh Shahrokhi, Regina Biggs, Natasha Saunders, Claire Silva, and Paige Whitlock

4. Using Improvement Science Principles for New-Teacher Support — 97
   High Tech High and High Tech High Graduate School of Education
   Julia Jacobsen and Diana Cornejo-Sanchez

SECTION II: A NEW KIND OF PARTNERSHIP: CONTINUOUS IMPROVEMENT AS AN ANIMATING FORCE 123
DAVID G. IMIG

5　From a Transactional Relationship to a Transformational Partnership　126
University of Maryland College Park and Prince George's County Public Schools
Segun Eubanks, Jean Snell, Douglas W. Anthony, Charoscar Coleman, Felice Desouza, Kara Miley-Libby, and Christine M. Neumerski

6　Redesigning School Staffing Models through Team-Based Residencies　149
Arizona State University and Avondale Elementary School District
Betsy Hargrove, Christina Flesher, Nicole L. Thompson, and Carole G. Basile

7　District-University Partnerships for Continuous Improvement: How Can UM Help?　174
University of Mississippi and Oxford School District
Denise A. Soares, Mark E. Deschaine, W. Bradley Roberson, David Rock, Marni Herrington, and Brian Harvey

8　Equity-Focused Improvement Science　192
Portland State University and Portland Public Schools
Susan P. Carlile, Deborah S. Peterson, and Tania McKey

SECTION III: PARTNERSHIPS AIN'T EASY: LEARNING FROM SHORT-TERM EFFORTS AND LONG-TERM SUSTAINABILITY　217
RANDY HITZ

9　Shared Goals, Methods, and Learning: Partnering for Equity-Focused, Systems-Level Improvement　219
University of Denver and Denver Public Schools
Erin Anderson and Sandra Lochhead

10　Organizational Changes' Impacts on University-District Partnership Development　240
University of South Carolina and K–12 School District
Kathleen M. W. Cunningham, Peter Moyi, and Barnett Berry

11　Preparing Principals for Urban Schools: The Challenge of Equitable Outcomes at Scale　262
University of Illinois Chicago and Chicago Public Schools
Steve Tozer, Peter Martinez, Cynthia K. Barron, Shelby Cosner, Zipporah Hightower, Janice Jackson, David Mayrowetz, Sam Whalen, and Paul Zavitkovsky

Conclusion: Evolving Tethers That Bind School District to University　298
Louis M. Gomez and Manuelito Biag

References　311

Index　327

About the Contributors　345

Contents

Acknowledgments	xviii
Foreword	xx
Anthony S. Bryk	
Introduction: Getting to Mutual-Benefit Partnerships	1
Louis M. Gomez and Manuelito Biag	
Navigating the Tangles of Inter-Organizational Work	2
"It Takes a Village" to Redress Inequities	3
The Improvement Leadership Education and Development (iLEAD) Network	3
Social Learning Theory and Culture	5
Moving Beyond Transactional Relationships	6
Trading Zones and Boundary Objects	6
iLEAD's Developmental Progressions Framework as a Boundary Object	8
The Desiderata to Sustain Trading Zones	20
Continuous Improvement	20
Equity	21
Coordination	22
Capacity Building	23
Conclusion	23
References	23

SECTION I: IMPROVEMENT METHODS, EQUITY, AND PROBLEMS OF PRACTICE IN LOCAL CONTEXT 27
STEVE TOZER

1 Braiding Improvement into the Fabric of District Leadership
  Preparation and Practice 30
  University of Virginia and Chesterfield County Public Schools
  David Eddy-Spicer, Tinkhani Ushe White, and Michelle M. Beavers

Partnership Context	31
University of Virginia	31
Chesterfield County Public Schools	32
An Educational Leadership Preparation Partnership Emerges	32
The "Improvement Sandwich": Cooperation into Coordination	33
CCPS Strand: Focus on Programmatic Equity and School Improvement Planning	35
UVA Strand: Redesigning the M.Ed. Program	37
Field–Based Learning as Boundary Infrastructure	38
Securing the Braid: Coordination into Collaboration	40
Deepening Coordination Across School Levels and With Central Office in CCPS	40
Collaborating across School Levels in CCPS	41
Collaboration in Teaching and Learning at UVA	42
Results: Organizational Practice and Partnership	43
Conclusions and Lessons Learned	44
CCPS Lessons Learned	44
From Professional Development to Intrapreneurial Collective Learning	44
UVA Lessons Learned	46
A&S Faculty Collective Learning	46
Partnership Lessons Learned: Co-Development of Leadership Pedagogies	46
Essential Lessons of Partnership Work	47
Questions for Discussion	48
References	49

2 A University–School District Collaboration to Improve
  Equity- and Inquiry-Driven School Leadership 52
  Fordham University and Bronx School Districts 9 and 11
  *Margaret Terry Orr, Kris DeFilippis, Meisha Porter, and
  Elizabeth Leisy Stosich*

Context	52
Problem	56
Challenges, Solutions, and Evidence	57
Development	58
Advanced Leadership Preparation	60

Redesigning Fordham's EdD Program	60
Creating a Bronx EdD Cohort in Equity-Focused Improvement Science	62
Leadership Development	65
Assistant Principal Math Networked Improvement Community	65
Creating Positive Change through the Bronx Academic Response Team Initiative	67
Principal Equity Improvement Networked Improvement Communities	69
Conclusions and Lessons Learned	70
Questions for Discussion	72
References	72

3 Moving a Partnership from Itinerant to Integral: Using Improvement Science as a Catalyst for Change in Leadership Preparation and Induction — 74

George Mason University and Fairfax County Public Schools
Samantha Viano, Farnoosh Shahrokhi, Regina Biggs, Natasha Saunders, Claire Silva, and Paige Whitlock

Context	75
EDLE Program at GMU	75
FCPS	77
FCPS and GMU Partnering Prior to iLEAD	77
Joining Together as iLEAD Partners	77
Problems	78
Stagnant Progress on School Improvement	78
Mismatch Between EDLE Leadership Preparation and FCPS Practice	79
Challenges, Solutions, and Evidence	79
Improvement Science as Our Catalyzing Agent to Come Together	80
Making Improvement Science EDLE's Signature Pedagogy	81
EDLE Faculty's Introduction to Improvement Science	81
Commitment to Improvement Science through Curriculum Development	82
Diverse Approaches to Supporting the Use of Improvement Science in FCPS	84
Professional Development Opportunities	84
School-Based Leadership Induction	85
Title I Comprehensive Needs Assessment	87
Our Partnership-Driven Initiative: Piloting an Improvement Science Approach to School Improvement	88
Phase 1: Cultivating Cultures of Continuous Improvement, 2019–20 School Year	89
Phase 2: Redressing Inequities, 2020–21 School Year	91
Phase 3: Spreading What Works, 2021–22 School Year	91

Showcasing Our Joint Efforts	92
Synergy between Leadership Preparation and School Improvement	92
Conclusions and Lessons Learned	93
Starting with a Foundational Relationship to Build upon	93
Garner Immediate Excitement about Improvement Science	93
Leverage Eagerness and Capacity to Make Time for Collaboration	94
Concluding Thoughts	94
Attending to the Mission of our Partnership Work	95
Questions for Discussion	95
References	96

4 Using Improvement Science Principles for New-Teacher Support   **97**
High Tech High and High Tech High Graduate School of Education
Julia Jacobsen and Diana Cornejo-Sanchez

Context	97
High Tech High & the High Tech High Graduate School of Education	97
Problems	98
Induction as a Lever for Teacher Retention	100
Experimenting with Improvement in Teacher Induction	101
Challenges, Solutions, and Evidence	104
Challenge #1: Entry Planning that Incorporates Continuous Improvement	105
Root Cause Analysis	105
Plan-Do-Study-Act Cycles	106
Sharing Learning	108
Challenge #2: Operating in a One-Year Time Frame	109
Challenge #3: Developing the Capacity of Improvement Coaches	110
Deficit Thinking	111
Compliance Orientation	112
Improving Coach Development	112
Facilitating Continuous Improvement for Equity	113
Induction Improvement Coach Summit	113
Impact	114
Conclusions and Lessons Learned	114
CI Can Be an Effective Framework for Adaptive Learning	114
The Importance of Improvement Science in Our Own Program Processes	115
Developing New Organizational Capacity for Continuous Improvement	115
Teachable Moments	117
How Might Improvement Processes Foster Connection and Belonging?	117

How Can Both the Process and the Outcome of Improvement
   Efforts Support Equity? 119
How Can We Develop Sustainable Improvement Efforts? 119
How Can Improvement Science Help Organizations Grow Toward a
   Common Mission and Develop Concrete Understandings? 120
Questions for Discussion 121
References 121

SECTION II: A NEW KIND OF PARTNERSHIP: CONTINUOUS IMPROVEMENT AS AN ANIMATING FORCE 123
DAVID G. IMIG

5 **From a Transactional Relationship to a Transformational Partnership** 126
   University of Maryland College Park and Prince George's County Public Schools
   Primary authors: Segun Eubanks and Jean Snell
   Additional contributors: Douglas W. Anthony, Charoscar Coleman, Felice Desouza, Kara Miley-Libby, and Christine M. Neumerski
   Context 126
      Not Your Father's MOU 127
      The Back Story: People Building Trust, Institutions Leading Change 128
         A Change in Perspective 128
         PGCPS Initiates a Catalyst for Change—the EdD in School
            System Leadership 129
         UMD Initiates a Catalyst for Change: The CEii 130
         iLEAD Initiates a Catalyst for Change: Getting to the Work of
            Improvement 131
         Getting to Work: Our First Problem of Practice 132
   Problems 134
      A Shared Problem of Practice: Putting the "Improvement" in the
         School Improvement Process 134
      Leveraging the New Strategic Plan 135
   Challenges, Solutions, and Evidence 136
      Improvement Science as a Shared Methodology and "Solution" 136
         The Partnership "Solution" to the Challenge of District Capacity
            Building with SPPing 137
      Looking Forward to Future Work: The Launch of 2 Partnership
         Networked Improvement Communities 138
      Showing Evidence of Partnership Impact 138
         Evidence of Engagement and Commitment Is Strong and Growing 139
         Growth in the iLEAD Developmental Progressions 139
         Emerging Data of Change in Systems Practice 139

	Lessons Learned	140
	Key Learning #1: Building Strong Relationships Is the Starting Point	140
	Key Learning #2: Focus on Problems of Practice and Stay Prepared for Change	140
	Teachable Moments	141
	You're Not Really Married if You Don't Have the Paper	141
	Adapt, Don't Abandon	141
	Shifts Happen	142
	Just Do Something	142
	References	142
6	**Redesigning School Staffing Models through Team-Based Residencies**	**149**
	Arizona State University and Avondale Elementary School District	
	Betsy Hargrove, Christina Flesher, Nicole L. Thompson, and Carole G. Basile	
	The Next Education Workforce: A Growing Idea	150
	Context: MLFTC and AESD Partnership	151
	Challenges, Solutions, and Evidence-Based Teacher Preparation	153
	Challenges for AESD	154
	Changes and Vision at MLFTC	154
	A Renewed Partnership	154
	Serendipity and Early Models	156
	Improvement Science: Planning, Doing, Studying, Acting	157
	Residents	158
	Lead Teachers	158
	Site Lead	158
	Instructional Configurations	158
	Studying the Innovative Approach	158
	Lessons Learned	162
	Invested and Involved Leadership	162
	Systems and Structures	163
	Challenges of Teams	164
	Developmental Progressions and Growth in Collaboration	165
	Characteristics of Successful Teams	168
	Conclusion	168
	Afterword: Beyond Teacher Preparation	170
	Questions for Discussion	171
	References	172
7	**District-University Partnerships for Continuous Improvement: How Can UM Help?**	**174**
	University of Mississippi and Oxford School District	
	Denise A. Soares, Mark E. Deschaine, W. Bradley Roberson, David Rock, Marni Herrington, and Brian Harvey	
	Context: Beginning the Partnership Work	175
	The Achievement Gap Project	175

Chronic Absenteeism PDSA Cycle	178
Plan	178
Do	178
Study	179
Act	179
Building Capacity	181
Spread and Scale Progress	182
OSD Improvement Science Problems of Practice	182
Passion Professional Development PDSA Cycle	183
Plan	183
Do	183
Study	183
Act	183
Youth Truth Survey PDSA Cycle	183
Plan	183
Do	184
Study	184
Act	184
UM-SOE Improvement Science Problems of Practice	185
Graduate Studies Office PDSA Cycle	185
Plan	185
Do	185
Study	186
Act	186
UM-SOE Dean's Office Staff PDSA Cycle	186
Plan	186
Do	186
Study	186
Act	187
UM–Developmental Progression	187
The "How" of Partnerships (Partnership Mechanisms)	187
Expectations, Sustainability, Norms, & Routines	187
Vision for the Future	188
NCSUP Mission	189
Lessons Learned	190
Questions for Discussion	191
References	191
8 Equity-Focused Improvement Science	**192**
Portland State University and Portland Public Schools	
Susan P. Carlile, Deborah S. Peterson (co-first authors), and Tania McKey	
Key Leaders	193
Professor of Practice Susan Carlile	194
Associate Professor Emerita Dr. Deborah S. Peterson	194
Assistant Professor and Senior Director of Humanities	
Dr. Tania McKey	195

Context of the PSU–PPS Partnership 196
   Portland State University 196
   Portland Public Schools 197
Chronology of Improvement Science Efforts 198
Networked Improvement Communities 202
   Partner Districts 202
   Newberg School District (NSD) 202
   Changes in the Partnership with the Newberg School District 203
The New District Partnership: Portland Public Schools 204
Challenges and Solutions 205
Tools to Identify Next Steps 207
   Progress (Strengths) at the Partnership Level 207
   Progress (Strengths) at PPS 207
   Progress (Strengths) at the PSU Level 207
   Areas of Focus (Challenges) at the Partnership Level 207
   Areas of Focus (Challenges) in PPS 208
   Area of Focus (Challenge) in PSU 208
Contextual Complexities 208
Theory of Improvement 209
   Program Redesign 209
   Redesign PPS Practices for Principal Support 210
   Hire Scholarly Practitioners as Principal Preparation Cohort Leaders 211
   PPS Hires PSU Principal Licensure Completers 211
Lessons Learned 211
Next Steps 212
Conclusion 213
Questions for Discussion 214
References 214

SECTION III: PARTNERSHIPS AIN'T EASY: LEARNING FROM SHORT-TERM EFFORTS AND LONG-TERM SUSTAINABILITY   217
RANDY HITZ

9 Shared Goals, Methods, and Learning: Partnering for Equity-Focused, Systems-Level Improvement   **219**
University of Denver and Denver Public Schools
Erin Anderson and Sandra Lochhead
   Context 220
   Problem 222
   District Context 223
   Sustainable Improvement in the District 225
   Challenges, Solutions, and Evidence 227
      Shared Goals: Embedded Process Over External Program 228
         Where Did We Start? 229
         What Steps Happened Along the Way? 229

Where Are We Now? ... 230
　Shared Methodology: The Design Improvement for Equity (DI4E)
　　Model ... 230
　　　Where Did We Start? ... 231
　　　What Steps Happened Along the Way? ... 231
　　　Where Are We Now? ... 232
　Shared Learning: Shared Research Agenda in a Research–Practice
　　Partnership ... 232
　　　Where Did We Start? ... 232
　　　What Steps Happened Along the Way? ... 233
　　　Where Are We Now? ... 233
Summary of Impact ... 234
Conclusions and Lessons Learned ... 235
　Lesson 1: Be Clear About your "Why"—Your North Star Guides
　　the Way ... 236
　Lesson 2: Create a Shared Theory of Improvement for your
　　Partnership Work and Use It as a Map to Reach your Destination ... 237
　Lesson 3: Interdependence Was Essential to the Partnership and to
　　Increasing Equity in the System ... 237
　Lesson 4: Be Disciplined about a Shared Learning Agenda or
　　Research Plan ... 237
　Lesson 5: Despite Shared Values, Norms, and Goals, There Are Still
　　Organizational Values and Conditions That Will Limit Systems
　　Change ... 238
Questions for Discussion ... 238
References ... 239

10　Organizational Changes' Impacts on University-District Partnership Development ... 240
University of South Carolina and K–12 School District
Kathleen M. W. Cunningham, Peter Moyi, and Barnett Berry

Context ... 241
　University of South Carolina College of Education ... 241
　　Myrtle Creek School District ... 242
　The Partnership Between CoE/EDLP and MCSD ... 242
Developing and Sustaining a District-University Partnership ... 244
　Two Partnership Frameworks: iLEAD's Developmental Progressions
　　and the Stage Model ... 245
　　Developmental Progressions (Carnegie Foundation for the
　　　Advancement of Teaching, 2020) ... 245
　　Stage Model (Trubowitz, 1986) ... 246
　Partnership Journey ... 247
　　Improvement Work Begins ... 247
　　Establishment of a Core Improvement Team ... 248
　Organizational Progress: Partnership ... 252

Organizational Progress: USC (i.e., CoE and EDLP)	252
Challenges	254
Challenge 1: Multiple, Evolving Goals	254
Challenge 2: Logistics (Distance, Funding, Time–Competing Priorities)	255
Challenge 3: Personnel and Leadership Transitions	256
Challenge 4: COVID-19 Pandemic	256
Conclusions and Lessons Learned	258
Consideration 1: Clearly Defined Goals and Expectations	258
Consideration 2: Core Partnership Team with Consistent Membership, Leadership, and Active Commitment	258
Consideration 3: Lean on a Continuous Improvement Mindset to Reflect and Learn	259
Questions for Discussion	260
References	260

11 Preparing Principals for Urban Schools: The Challenge of Equitable Outcomes at Scale 262

University of Illinois Chicago and Chicago Public Schools

Steve Tozer, Peter Martinez, Cynthia K. Barron, Shelby Cosner, Zipporah Hightower, Janice Jackson, David Mayrowetz, Sam Whalen, and Paul Zavitkovsky

Partnership Context: Chicago School Reform and UIC's "Urban Mission"	263
Chicago School Reform and State Legislation	263
The Principal Preparation Program Design and Re-design: 11 Key Components	264
Impact of Program Design and Re-design	268
"We Want to Be as Good as People Think We Are"	272
Using the Developmental Progressions to Tell the CPS/UIC Partnership Story	273
From MOU to Vendor Contract	276
A Missing Objective?	277
Preparation of CPS Principal Supervisors (Network Chiefs) and Central Office Personnel	278
A Next Edge of Growth	278
Summary of *Partnership* Development	279
Developing Capacity as a District Partner: The UIC EdD Program	279
Elaborations and Qualifications on the IHE Narrative	281
Vision, Systems, and Above All, People	281
Our First Targeted Program Hire	282
Building the Team	283
Leadership Coaches as Boundary Spanners	284
Creating "Boundary Objects"	284
Next Edges of Growth	285
Need for New Resources	285
How Did the District Sustain Its Share of the Partnership for 20 Years across Nine CEOs?	286

Conclusions and Lessons Learned	288
1. Equity	288
2. Partnership	289
3. Leadership Development: Vision, Systems, and People	290
4. Continuous Improvement	290
Questions for Discussion	291
References	292
Conclusion: Evolving Tethers That Bind School District to University	**298**
Louis M. Gomez and Manuelito Biag	
Tightly Tethered Mutuality	298
Attending to the *How* of Partnerships	300
The Role of the Carnegie Foundation for the Advancement of Teaching	301
Building a Strong Field: Infrastructure that Recasts Partnerships	302
Creating Social Infrastructure for Collective Action	303
Looking Forward: The Sustainability of Mutually Beneficial Partnerships for Leadership and Continuous Improvement	306
References	308
References	**311**
Index	**327**
About the Contributors	**345**

Acknowledgments

This volume would not have been possible without the hard work and commitment of the iLEAD community. The book came to life because of the longstanding support of the Carnegie Corporation of New York and the tireless effort of Carnegie Foundation staff and senior fellows.

We are grateful to the chapter authors for their persistence and unwavering dedication to continuous improvement, the iLEAD network, as well as their partnership despite the challenges and turbulence that have become commonplace for most educators in these uncertain times. We appreciate the authors' responsiveness to our check-in calls and email reminders, and for their general openness to critique and revision. We thank them for sharing their stories, strategies, and reflections, so that others in the field may learn from their efforts.

We offer special thanks to the following colleagues, without whom iLEAD and this book would not have been possible. Thank you to Anthony Bryk and Ash Vasudeva for their vision and ongoing leadership and guidance of the iLEAD community. We are grateful to Al Bertani for modeling how to listen and support in meaningful ways; his masterful facilitation skills helped foster trust, vulnerability, and learning in our network. We extend our appreciation to Mike Hanson for his expert coaching of our members and unwavering belief in the power of our community and the work that we do. A big and special thanks to Jennifer Au for her kindness, graciousness, and expert coordination of various project activities including our network-wide convenings, Steering Committee meetings, and virtual town halls, among others. Thank you to Patrice Dawkins Jackson for her insights and support in designing and facilitating our iLEAD events; she helped create spaces for everyone to feel welcomed, seen, and heard. We are singularly indebted to Katharine Bartholomew for her patience and skillful management of the endless number of moving parts that come with managing a large network and putting together such an ambitious publication. We appreciate Mark Kerr, Courtney Packard, and Sarah Rinehart at Rowman & Littlefield for responding to our questions and requests, guiding us through the production process, and cheering us on at each step.

We also wish to thank the below reviewers whose thoughtful comments and expertise guided our writing and revisions for the development of this book. As always, any errors and omissions are our own:

Paula Arce-Trigatti, *Rice University*
Christopher Benedetti, *Texas A&M University–Corpus Christi*
Tori Colson, *University of Southern Indiana*
Benjamin Cooper, *Walton Family Foundation*
John Q. Easton, *University of Chicago Consortium on School Research*
William Firestone, *Rutgers Graduate School of Education*
Joe Flora, *University of South Carolina*
Edmund Hamann, *University of Nebraska–Lincoln*
Dane C. Joseph, *George Fox University*
Christopher Koch, *Council for the Accreditation of Educator Preparation*
Sean Kottke, *Michigan Department of Education*
Mark LaCelle-Peterson, *Association for Advancing Quality in Educator Preparation*
Maritza Lozano, *California State University, Fullerton*
Jill A. Perry, *Carnegie Project on the Education Doctorate (CPED) and University of Pittsburgh*
Donald Peurach, *University of Michigan*
Jennifer Lin Russell, *Vanderbilt University*
Corrie Stone-Johnson, *State University of New York at Buffalo*
Megan Tschannen-Moran, *William & Mary School of Education*
Laura Wentworth, *California Education Partners*

Finally, we express our gratitude to those who read and share this volume with their colleagues and professional networks. We hope that you will be inspired and see yourself and the power and potential of your work in these stories. May the partnerships you cultivate improve the lives of the most vulnerable children and youth in the communities you serve.

Louis M. Gomez
Manuelito Biag
David G. Imig
Steve Tozer
Randy Hitz

Foreword

Anthony S. Bryk

The accounts offered in this volume represent the culmination of a five-year effort by the Carnegie Foundation for the Advancement of Teaching to strengthen the preparation and practice of education leaders to advance improvements on longstanding inequities in student outcomes. This effort grew out of multiple independent streams of working dating back numerous years.

I first met Louis Gomez in the mid-1990s. Louis and I were kindred spirits: we shared a belief that good scholarship could and should contribute more productively to improvements in educational practice than was the case at that time. We were both exploring ways to form partnerships with school and system–based educators in Chicago toward this end.

Based on these experiences, we co-authored a paper in 2008 that argued for the need for a new infrastructure in education focused on practical educational problem-solving (Bryk & Gomez, 2008). This was followed by a second paper, with another colleague Alicia Grunow, that set out the underpinnings of networked improvement communities (Bryk et al., 2011). These two papers anchored conceptually the work of the Carnegie Foundation for the Advancement of Teaching during my tenure as president from 2008–2020.

As the Foundation moved to bring the discipline of improvement science and the organization of improvement networks into education, we had occasions to meet a number of faculty from colleges of education who were now interested in bringing these principles, and associated tools and methods, into their own teaching and research. In response, Louis Gomez, with funding from the Foundation, organized the Higher Education Network (HEN) to support their efforts to develop a curriculum and learn to teach improvement science. While their situations were varied, many like Louis were focused on strengthening the preparation of school-based educators as improvement leaders. Both Louis and I had experienced firsthand in Chicago the key role that school leaders played in advancing local improvement efforts. (Our practice-based observations were subsequently strongly affirmed in numerous research studies carried out by the Consortium on Chicago School Research.) Louis's own teaching was centered here, and he invited his HEN colleagues to observe his classes as a context for their collegial conversations. The HEN community became a primary root for what eventually grew into the Improvement Leadership Education and Development (iLEAD) network whose work is reported on in this volume.

Initially separate from this, a few years after arriving at Carnegie, David Imig invited me to participate in a convening of faculty leads from the Carnegie Program on the Education Doctorate (CPED). David had collaborated with my predecessor at Carnegie, Lee Shulman, in advancing efforts to design, develop, and institutionalize the professional practice doctorate in education. This degree program now exists in over 125 colleges and universities around the US. The main topic on the agenda for that convening was the design of the capstone project for this new professional practice doctorate. The traditional culminating task of producing original academic scholarship to earn a PhD was ill-suited to the ambitions of a professional practice degree. What should take its place?

After listening for a while as these conversations proceeded, I asked "Well, what do these individuals do upon graduation?" I learned that most were leading some educational organization and intent on helping that organization get better at doing its work. So, I shared, "If organizational improvement is a priority in their professional practice, and given that they are earning a professional practice degree, might not a demonstration of competence in leading improvement be the basis for designing the capstone for such a program?" And this quickly led to a follow-up question: "What also are you doing in your programs in terms of both classroom instruction and apprentice-based experiences to help your students learn *how* to lead improvement?" While students were receiving deep theoretical training on important educational topics, little methodological preparation on the principles, tools, and methods of improvement science was being offered then in most programs. Under David Imig's leadership, these conversations continued post the CPED convening, and another root began to grow. So, through these two different paths, David and Louis came naturally to co-lead the Foundation's efforts to grow the iLEAD community.

iLEAD sought to build on HEN's efforts to bring improvement science into educators' professional preparation and anchor their development in the practice improvement research partnerships that HEN faculty were forming with local school districts. In addition, as district leaders signed on to iLEAD, they added priority to advancing the improvement expertise of existing school and district staff as well. iLEAD would now encourage Ed Leadership program students to undertake capstone projects focused on district-identified improvement priorities, and ideally undertake these as part of an improvement network with other students and district staff rather than as an idiosyncratic culminating project. Such collective activity offered promise for developing valuable practice improvement knowledge. While this has been long noted as a need in the education field (Hiebert et al., 2002), neither the organization of school districts, the traditional incentives in the academy, nor the market forces in the commercial sector have supported such developments. This connects back to one of the key arguments that Louis and I made in that 2008 paper.

From the outset, iLEAD was designed as a learning community for both district and higher education partners. To initiate and sustain this community required the development of a hub infrastructure to offer social, intellectual, and technical support. I recruited a group of senior fellows to join David and Louis. Randy Hitz joined and allowed us to expand the connections to CPED institutions and other faculty in Ed Leadership programs more generally. Al Bertani brought his extensive experience and superb skills in facilitating and supporting professional learning communities both domestically and internationally. To deepen the bench on improvement efforts in urban school settings, I recruited Steve Tozer who had advanced innovative work on leadership preparation and was engaged in a longstanding partnership with senior system leaders in Chicago Public Schools. Complementing Steve on the district side was Mike Hanson. Mike had recently stepped down as superintendent in Fresno Public Schools where he had led the development of an improvement capacity internal to that district that resulted in notable gains in students' high school success and college going.[1]

Joining this group of senior fellows was core Carnegie Foundation Staff. Senior Associate Manuelito Biag, who took on the role of project director, brought an extensive background in both the practice and scholarship of improvement science. He was supported in turn by Associate Patrice Dawkins-Jackson, experienced in practice improvement efforts in urban school settings, and Coordinator Jennifer Au who ably managed the complex logistics of running a national network. Taken together, this assembly of Foundation staff and Senior Fellows formed a colleagueship of expertise; each had been recruited for a particular purpose; each brought different relevant experiences and expertise domains needed to support the development of the iLEAD community.

The North Star for the iLEAD community is a shared aim to develop and support educators capable of leading continuous improvement efforts that strengthen schools and school systems to redress longstanding inequities in educational opportunities and outcomes. To advance on this aim, members focus attention on five strategies: 1) integrating the discipline of improvement into the preparation and development of school and district leaders; 2) catalyzing practice-improvement-research partnerships to target high-leverage problems; 3) developing and sustaining mutually beneficial district-university partnerships committed to educational equity; 4) growing a thriving, collaborative learning community who share responsibility for achieving jointly defined goals, and 5) documenting and sharing widely the processes and results of their collaborative work for others to learn.

This volume is the story of what subsequently emerged. An enormous amount of effort has been committed by iLEAD partners in pressing on these transformative aspirations in their local contexts, amidst diverse constraints and often rapidly changing local circumstances. iLEAD participants came into the work as individual researchers and district leaders. Developing trust relations and building up shared local understandings consumed much of the early efforts in each of these partnerships. Productive work eventually emerged in each context, and a genuine professional community subsequently grew across them.

This volume offers a lens into the vitality of this community in action—how it began, evolved, and the work still ahead.

Anthony S. Bryk
President Emeritus, The Carnegie Foundation for the Advancement of Teaching

Note

1. For a discussion of these developments, see the "Attacking inequities in postsecondary opportunities: Fresno Unified School District" chapter in Bryk, A. (2020). *Improvement in action: Advancing quality in America's schools.* Harvard Education Press.

References

Bryk, A. S., & Gomez, L. M. (2008). *Reinventing a research and development capacity.* In F. M. Hess (Ed.), *The future of educational entrepreneurship: Possibilities for school reform.* Harvard Education Press.

Bryk, A. S., Gomez, L. M., & Grunow, A. (2011). Getting ideas into action: Building networked improvement communities in education. In M. T. Hallinan (Ed.), *Frontiers in sociology of education* (pp. 127–162). Springer.

Hiebert, J., Gallimore, R., & Stigler, J. W. (2002). A knowledge base for the teaching profession: What would it look like and how can we get one? *Educational Researcher, 31*(5), 3–15.

Introduction
GETTING TO MUTUAL–BENEFIT PARTNERSHIPS

Louis M. Gomez and Manuelito Biag

Three key assertions guide this volume. First, to build and sustain equitable and first-rate education as a regular and reliable experience for all students, local education agencies (LEAs) and institutions of higher education (IHEs) have an extraordinary opportunity to improve through working together in what this volume calls mutual benefit partnerships. Second, continuous improvement thinking (e.g., Bryk et al., 2015; Hinnant-Crawford, 2020; Langley et al., 2009) can serve as philosophical and methodological guard rails to help siloed actors, like universities and school districts, learn together and not lose sight of the public good that practical inter-organizational work can achieve. Finally, the narratives presented here demonstrate how formal and informal leadership is essential in creating partnerships that benefit both IHEs and LEAs. Taken as a whole, stories in this volume underscore that knowledge for vitalizing leadership comes in equal parts from LEAs and their university partners.

Chapter authors describe how LEAs and IHEs in different settings and circumstances are learning to create public-sector and student-centered partnerships that address shared educational aims. They demonstrate how historically separated institutions can come together to lay the groundwork for what leadership for mutual benefit means both in theory and in practice. Mutual benefit, as we mean it here, entails shared commitment to all organizational actors being better off for the experience. For instance, in many of the chapters, the reader will encounter LEAs making current problems of practice visible to their IHE colleagues in as unvarnished a manner as possible. This is an act of inter-organizational trust. Readers will encounter several acts like this that set mutual-benefit cycles in motion. This cycle might unfold with IHE members inserting the LEA problems of practice in current course structures for leaders or in the creation of new classes where the problem of practice serves as the organizing centerpiece. When it works, the mutual-benefit cycle accelerates the reinvigoration of IHE programs as well as the preparation of leaders ready to tackle district problems. In short, the partners accomplish mutual benefit.

To give readers a peek at the processes that lead to supportive mutual-benefit partnerships, we begin by highlighting this volume's major headlines. First, each institution confirmed mutuality as the end goal for their collective actions. Second, these districts, schools, and universities take up problems where the partners need each other to make progress. Lastly, the members of each partnership constantly work to create social glue (Churchill, 2009) that binds them together in the form of new social arrangements, routines, and tools that discipline their work together.

Readers will also note how place and unique local characteristics are essential to joint organizational work. While the partnerships presented here participate in a shared network, their respective geographic regions and historical contexts shape them in fundamental ways. Their experience underscores that, initially, their institutions were not well-equipped to take up the work of mutual-benefit collaborations. Undoubtedly, all organizational partnerships face a social learning challenge (Wenger & Snyder, 2000), and those in this book are no different. The organizations here had to realize, explicitly or implicitly, that their learning would be socially constituted; as such, each would need to build processes that facilitated learning together. For them, continuous improvement thinking was the facilitation mechanism for their learning journey.

Metaphorically, these partnerships needed a familiar and safe intellectual space to develop together. We refer to these spaces of joint work as "trading zones" and the tools that inhabit them as "boundary objects." We warmed to the notion of "trade" because it captures more than simple exchange. Trade historically has been a primary vehicle of the cultural diffusion of ideas. We elaborate the key issues, contexts, and considerations raised in this book in this chapter, and which characterize the efforts of these partnerships to create meaningful arrangements of mutual benefit where elements local organizational culture are traded and shared. These include the inter-organizational challenges when addressing equity-related problems of practice; partnerships as a social learning and cultural challenge; and the potential of continuous improvement as a shared language and method.

Navigating the Tangles of Inter-Organizational Work

Our field experiences over several decades tell us that when organizations like IHEs and LEAs work on grand issues, they encounter nettlesome concerns (Gomez et al., 2020). Dawes et al. (2009) refer to the landscape where organizations come together to address shared problems as "tangles," spaces that involve diverse actors who must figure out how to collaborate across organizational lines. There are three essential aspects to understanding inter-organizational tangles. First, they are not temporary. Since organizations are in constant evolution, cross-organizational actors are always, to one degree or another, figuring out how to work together. Second, the act of figuring it out involves a radical commitment to sharing, what Dawes and colleagues call "a need to share." Finally, this need to share is cultural work because it responds to developing interpersonal and inter-institutional needs to make work practices legible across organizational boundaries.

Mutual-benefit partnerships create an imperative to share across organizational boundaries. This imperative demands that actors develop spaces where they can create new patterns of feeling, thinking, and acting within a partnership rather than in silos. Muller et al. (2020) describe this intellectual space as an "in-between" region or a "third space," a fertile environment in which participants, via their interaction, combine diverse knowledge with new insights and plans for action that reform the needs of their organizations, institutions, products, and services.

The chapters in this volume describe how 11 school districts and local universities forged partnerships that allowed them to create an LEA–IHE trading zone rarely seen in education—a mutual-benefit partnership (Radinsky et al., 2001). The narratives are authored by those who waded into and negotiated the tangles of such alliances. They describe their learning journeys, highlighting key lessons others can leverage in their efforts to build more productive collaborations.

"It Takes a Village" to Redress Inequities

Schools cannot educate children alone. Likewise, universities alone cannot prepare the teachers, school leaders, and other staff required to effectively educate all students. It seems natural that schools and universities would rely on each other to educate not only the children but also the professionals charged with this task. Each takes a different role in providing practical learning experiences for the community of P-20 learners and professionals.

Consider, for example, the widely acknowledged challenge of improving the inequitable learning opportunities and outcomes in our schools. There is ample evidence from a number of mission and vision statements that universities, districts, and schools recognize the importance of resolving inequities in their communities. There is less evidence, however, that they work well together to deliver this recognition through collective and organized action. The authors in this volume argue that part of this disconnect between vision and shared action is common knowledge about how school and university partners should productively engage in these tangles of activity so that both LEAs and IHEs derive reciprocal organizational value through the joint work of improving children's learning and life chances. In essence, the cases herein are all studies in "learning by doing." They each, in ways disciplined by their local contexts, are telling a story of taking up an LEA–IHE inter-organizational tangle.

The Improvement Leadership Education and Development (iLEAD) Network

The context for the stories in this volume is the Improvement Leadership Education and Development (iLEAD) network. iLEAD is a collaborative of 11

Figure I.1 Locations of the 11 iLEAD Partnerships.

district-university partnerships from across the United States (see figure I.1). With funding support from the Carnegie Corporation of New York and coordination by the Carnegie Foundation for the Advancement of Teaching, these LEA–IHE partners aim to develop and support educational leaders capable of leading continuous improvement efforts that strengthen schools and school systems for all students and redress longstanding inequities in educational opportunities and outcomes (Velásquez et al., 2019). By engaging in local problem-solving and using educational improvement science as a shared method (Bryk et al., 2015; Hinnant-Crawford, 2021), iLEAD seeks to bridge IHEs and LEAs so they may reconsider their institutional practices and social relations for mutual benefit and progress. The partnerships

Figure I.2 iLEAD Group Photo (February 2020).

and institutions represented in this volume are as follows (see figure I.2 for a recent photo of the iLEAD network):

1. Avondale Elementary School District and Arizona State University
2. Bronx School District and Fordham University
3. Chesterfield County Public Schools and the University of Virginia
4. Chicago Public Schools and the University of Illinois, Chicago
5. Denver Public Schools and the University of Denver
6. Fairfax County Public Schools and George Mason University
7. Myrtle Creek School District (pseudonym) and the University of South Carolina
8. High Tech High's Graduate School of Education and the High Tech High Network
9. Oxford School District and the University of Mississippi
10. Portland Public Schools and Portland State University
11. Prince George's County Public Schools and the University of Maryland

Social Learning Theory and Culture

Among the things that bind the iLEAD partnerships into a network of common purpose is the belief that IHEs and LEAs need to do much more before their institutional partnerships, as a regular matter, serve children and adults in ways that meet the intellectual and practical demands of today's world. These cases are compelling illustrations of what "more" looks like in the mutual-benefit sense. As this book unfolds, it becomes apparent that there is substantial variability in the look and feel of these partnerships and how they have been built and sustained. The volume does not simply tell the tales of unqualified successes. It is also about repair. The chapters illustrate things going awry and what partners do to get things back on track. The stories are told as practice cases written by people living the work.

Readers will notice how each case is a social learning journey that illustrates how different institutions establish social arrangements that allow them to adopt the shared responsibility of educating children and preparing school leaders. These narratives fall within an organizationally-centered, social theory of learning (Gomez et al., 2021; Lave & Wenger, 1991; Wenger, 1998). This theory helps explain how people come together in communities of practice, where meaning is derived through practice, and learning is accomplished through joint activity. Learning is sustained by belonging to the community, and belonging produces learner identity within the community (Lave & Wenger, 1991; Wenger, 1998). It follows then that social learning, in the sense depicted here, is a cultural activity. Taking up cross-organizational tangles and traversing organizational boundaries is emblematic of culture, cultural negotiation, and cultural learning.

The chapters, in particular, illustrate four important aspects of cultural development in organizations' social learning (Gomez et al., 2021). First, culture unfolds at multiple levels. The cases demonstrate the prominent influence of "place." These stories also show how culture is accomplished at the meso level (Fine, 2012), a level that is made up of groups of various sizes, including place-based groupings like school districts and universities. Second, culture is agentive. Archer and Archer (1996) argue that culture is made and remade by people. Readers will note that the separate doings in organizations of IHEs and LEAs and their actions jointly lead to recognizable cultural cross-organization formations. Third, culture is malleable. Once shaped, culture is not fixed. These chapters underscore the activities of critical actors in LEAs and IHEs that shape and reshape the shared cultural environment. Finally, culture develops in activity systems (Engeström, 2009). We can use activity systems as a prism to examine how members working in districts, schools, and universities use material and conceptual tools to move toward achieving intra- or inter-organizational objectives. We understand that the same work can be different and similarly organized in different institutional settings. These stories provide a window to how iLEAD partnerships move from work that is individually motivated to work that is more community focused.

Moving Beyond Transactional Relationships

The history of the educational sector crafting partnerships between IHEs and LEAs that address deep and shared problems of practice is spotty at best. Collaborations between universities and school districts have been isolated and rarely known or shared beyond the local contexts in which they occur. As a result, the work seldom results in sustained and widespread partnerships. Highly transactional arrangements between LEAs and IHE are often the norm (Whipple et al., 2010). At their core, transactional relationships are exchange-based and serve a highly targeted, often short-term, objective. For example, today, the lion's share of district-university partnerships is driven by LEAs, providing opportunities for university students to complete clinical practicum experiences in the 2,000 separate institutions offering nationwide teacher certification programs. By contrast, mutual-benefit partnerships are more resource and time intensive and take up broader areas of concern.

Goodlad (1993) noted that even when LEA–IHE partnerships pursue more ambitious agendas, such as allying to ensure that all third graders in a region are proficient readers, they are often moved by individual relationship energy rather than institutional energy. Goodlad argued that when partnerships are primarily tied to individuals who hold conceptual sway, the partnerships are prevented from becoming genuinely ambitious and owned by the participating institutions. In a related concern, Gorman et al. (2000) argue that in a social arrangement where one or a few actors hold vital knowledge, learning tends not to travel, sustainability is unlikely, and distributed understanding is stymied. Such arrangements are not mutually beneficial and tend to crumble and not outlast the originating actors.

Trading Zones and Boundary Objects

The districts, schools, and universities that share their stories in this volume benefit from structured spaces that encourage "trading" ideas, tools, and language in the service of a shared mission. Galison (2010) and others (e.g., Collins et al., 2007; Gorman, 2002) refer to such intellectual spaces as "trading zones." Trading zones allow two or more perspectives or members of expert communities to combine to create new ideas, the tools to mobilize them, and a common language to jointly communicate about them. As described in this book, these trading zones help LEAs and IHEs to move beyond transactional relations and learn how to craft relationships that attend to deeper educational problems that both institutions care deeply about.

The work of the trading zone is institutionally centered and not driven by the intellectual tastes of one or a few actors. Trading zones are multi-layered in that they support collaboration when stakeholders are not exactly on the same page regarding things such as a mental model or technical approach to a particular problem. A trading zone allows partners to establish local means of coordination even when both face broader challenges. Gorman et al. (2000) see this as a common intercultural practice where partners create "contact languages and systems of discourse" geared to the problem of the moment.

Chapters in this volume contain several examples of partners negotiating the fits and starts of working together in trading zones. For instance, one partnership has taken up school improvement planning as a shared problem. In their early work, the LEA and IHE partners differed in their understanding of the notion of school improvement planning. Here, school improvement planning served as a boundary object in the trading zone (Star & Griesemer, 1989). As abstract or physical artifacts, boundary objects afford knowledge sharing, sensemaking, and shared meaning across the boundaries of different institutions such as IHEs and LEAs (Akkermann & Bakker, 2011; Star & Griesemer, 1989). Boundary objects are plastic enough to adapt and share meaning across local contexts while maintaining semantic integrity, allowing disparate groups to use them as a common language to communicate across sites while maintaining local group identity. As a boundary object, by definition, school improvement planning has some shared as well as local institutional meaning. The early going in partnership-formation trading zones is meant to contain objects and ideas like these that allow people to span boundaries across contexts.

Trading zones also accommodate collaboration when the partners are at more mature points in their partnership. Trading zones morph to accommodate those involved, evolving into a more harmonious relationship where members have a shared mental model of the problem to be solved and the work to be done (Gorman et al., 2000). At this state of partnership accomplishment, actors not only share the problem but also understand what needs to be done, at the routine level, to address the problem in a coordinated manner across the organization. This is a classic matrix organizational arrangement with two CEOs (e.g., superintendent and dean) and a jointly structured organization designed to address a specific problem.

Such arrangements are rare and difficult to get right (Worren, 2018). This rarity makes it all the more impressive that at least some of the partnerships described in this volume were able to accomplish a matrix state; for instance, some in iLEAD have engaged in the hiring of joint staff to enable the partnership's goals to be met. The partnership work described in this volume carries a heavy inter-organizational coordination burden. This is true whether partnerships in trading zones share boundary objects (while essentially keeping separate organizational identities and goals) or stretch their organization borders in ways that start to look like a matrix. At the core of their coordination activity is the exchange of expertise and tools needed to accomplish a common objective (McNamara, 2012).

Creating boundary objects and boundary-spanning opportunities is core to the work of iLEAD. Readers will note how each chapter portrays the roles boundary objects and boundary spanners play in helping members develop and attain shared goals. One example can be seen in the Fairfax County Public School and George Mason University partnership. Fairfax County staff introduced and workshopped improvement science ideas with the George Mason faculty, energizing that partnership. Here, the Fairfax staff served as informal boundary spanners whose effort laid the groundwork for expertise building, which, in turn, allowed the two organizations to cooperate on school improvement planning efforts. The efforts of this collaboration were subsequently supported by an official, formally hired, boundary-spanning employee tasked with identifying other expertise-sharing opportunities.

iLEAD's Developmental Progressions Framework as a Boundary Object

The Developmental Progressions framework is the most critical boundary-spanning resource created by the iLEAD partnerships. The Progressions serve as a common language tool that anchors and defines the work in which partnerships engage. Network members co-constructed this framework in January 2018 during a series of facilitated group discussions in its second network convening. Together, members identified 24 areas of work critical to meaningful district-university collaborations (see table I.1). These areas capture enabling activities not only within IHEs and LEAs but also within the partnership itself. They include institutional leadership commitment, professional development of staff, and strengthening inter-organizational relations. Rather than a precise plan to be implemented across sites with fidelity, the Progressions offer a common way to organize the work of the partnerships and the learning mechanisms at the boundaries.

To a greater or lesser extent, each partnership in this volume uses the Developmental Progressions framework. While some members are well along in the co-creation of new joint programs that meaningfully incorporate the ideas and aspirations of both the LEA and IHE (i.e., they are "institutionalizing and sustaining the work" as defined by the Progressions), others are at the early stages where they may be engaged in exploratory meetings to ascertain one another's aspirations and priorities (i.e., they are "exploring change ideas" as defined by the Progressions).

We note previously that some iLEAD partnerships, likely the majority, have formed trading zones, where they conduct partnership work relying on their local institutional integrity. These partnerships tend to use the Progressions as a backward-looking, stock-taking device; that is, they check their progress against the areas of work identified as essential in the Progressions. By comparison, other partnerships that have

Table I.1 The Developmental Progressions Framework

Domain	Area of Work	Description	"Exploring Change Ideas"	"Small Change Implementation"	"Integrating IS/NICs into the Core Work"	"Institutionalizing and Sustaining the Work"
Institutions of higher education (IHEs)	1. Commitment to the idea of improvement science (IS)/ networked improvement communities (NICs)	Active faculty engagement in IS/NICs and recognition of IS/NICs as departmental or divisional priority.	Discussions are occurring about embracing improvement science (IS) and networked improvement communities (NICs) as central to education leadership efforts. A small number of faculty attend the Improvement Summit and use it as an opportunity to explore ideas further.	A small number of faculty are bringing IS/NICs into their teaching and work with students.	IS/NICs are recognized as a departmental or divisional priority (versus just one to two interested faculty members).	Embrace of IS/NICs is spreading to other clinical and tenured faculty throughout the IHE.

(continued)

Table I.1 Continued

Domain	Area of Work	Description	"Exploring Change Ideas"	"Small Change Implementation"	"Integrating IS/NICs into the Core Work"	"Institutionalizing and Sustaining the Work"
	2. Curriculum/ program development	Integration of IS/NICs into the curriculum, ranging from the adaptation of discrete courses to the development of a coherent program of study.	Explorations are underway as to how IS/NIC ideas might be integrated into existing programs and/or how new programs could be developed.	IS/NICs: Courses/modules are being piloted. Some apprenticeship opportunities are emerging. Projects are possible as a capstone option.	A coherent program of study is being formulated from introductory courses to capstone projects.	A coherent program of study has been adopted. This is visible in program descriptions that link from introductory courses through to capstone projects. All aspects of these programs are now operational. These developments are impacting design conversations about other IHE program initiatives.
	3. Faculty development and promotion	Supports exist for developing faculty improvement capability, and there is recognition of IS/NIC work in promotion and tenure policies.	Discussions begin about the possible need for faculty development since IS/NICs will be new work for many. Faculty explore support options available through the Higher Education Network (HEN), as well as other resources that iLEAD may subsequently develop.	Professional development supports for faculty in teaching and coaching IS/ NICs have been identified, and discussions are underway as to how to strengthen IHE capabilities.	Opportunities for faculty development exist, and resources are in place to respond.	New promotion and tenure policies are in place, acknowledging IS/NICs contributions as a significant criterion in these processes. One or more junior faculty have successfully engaged with these new criteria.

4. Faculty engagement	Active, regular, and supported faculty engagement in IS/NICs.	iLEAD faculty are cultivating interest among their colleagues about the potential for integrating IS/NICs in their program work.	iLEAD faculty are introducing IS/NIC principles, tools, and methods into their teaching and research work with students.	Stable staffing has been secured within the IHE so that the program can be sustained and continued to develop over the years ahead (a base of faculty is assured beyond the initial adopters).	Both professional practice and tenure-line faculty are engaged in IS/NICs. Support for these efforts is recognized as a regular part of faculty workload.
5. Improvement science as a signature pedagogy	Recognition of improvement science as a signature pedagogy.	The concept of a signature pedagogy for educational leadership programs has been raised.	Discussions are now underway as to the possibility of IS becoming a signature pedagogy for the educational leadership program.	IS is now publicly recognized as a signature pedagogy for the educational leadership program.	IS is formally recognized as a signature pedagogy for the school's professional education initiatives more generally.

(continued)

Table I.1 Continued

Domain	Area of Work	Description	"Exploring Change Ideas"	"Small Change Implementation"	"Integrating IS/NICs into the Core Work"	"Institutionalizing and Sustaining the Work"
	6. Institutional leadership commitment	Active support from dean/dean's cabinet and public recognition of IS/NICs as a distinctive contribution.	Faculty members, program chair, and dean are engaged with the iLEAD program by applying in partnership with a local LEA.	Dean/program chair is aware of the initiative and is providing seed resources to get the initiative off the ground (e.g., professional development for faculty; release time for a course and program development; travel support to iLEAD community meetings).	Dean/dean's cabinet expresses support for this with faculty across the school and with senior university leaders.	Dean/dean's cabinet continues to actively express support. University communications recognize this as a distinctive and "innovative" contribution.
	7. Institutional and state approvals	Resolution of possible issues around institutional and state approvals on courses, programs, and accreditation.	Possible issues around institutional and state approval of courses, programs, and accreditation issues have been identified.	Processes are underway to help resolve these professional, institutional, and state issues.	Issues have been satisfactorily resolved, and new program designs are now moving forward.	These new program designs are impacting the conceptions of other IHE program initiatives.

8. Scholarship of improvement: an academic community is forming	Presentation of improvement research in scholarly venues and publications.	Some faculty members are exploring resources for improving their pedagogical practice in courses and programs.	Faculty attend the Improvement Summit (including the academic symposium) and use it as an opportunity to deepen their knowledge, practice, and research interests.	Faculty present their work at the Improvement Summit (including the academic symposium), and contributions to a scholarship of improvement are being initiated.	Faculty regularly present their improvement research at the Improvement Summit and in other scholarly venues and publications.
9. IHE as a support hub for improvement networks	Development of IHE capacity to serve as a network hub.	IHE is learning about the functions of NIC hubs.	IHE identifies and begins to assemble core capabilities needed to serve as a hub for a NIC.	One or more IHE-based networks are now active.	IHE has the capacity to support multiple networks, including the possibility of inter-district networks.
10. A new professional education narrative	Development of an institutionally recognized and broadly owned narrative.	Urgency and need for change are recognized by a core group of program faculty.	A narrative is developing among participating faculty for building our program that prepares our students to succeed.	The ownership of this narrative is now shared beyond the initiating faculty member/group.	An institutionally recognized (and broadly owned) narrative exists about what we do and why we do it. Successes are celebrated. Student struggles are something we "own."

(continued)

Table I.1 Continued

Domain	Area of Work	Description	"Exploring Change Ideas"	"Small Change Implementation"	"Integrating IS/NICs into the Core Work"	"Institutionalizing and Sustaining the Work"
Local education agencies (LEAs)	11. District leadership engagement	Active engagement of district leadership in (IS)/(NICs) and partnership work.	Senior district leaders have expressed interest in a possible iLEAD partnership and have supported the proposal to participate.	Senior district leaders are regular participants in iLEAD meetings, and a planning and development team is meeting regularly with their IHE partner.	The district designates a lead for the iLEAD partnership based on IS/NIC experience. This person holds a senior role on the district leadership team.	A broad base of expertise exists across the district's senior leadership team responsible for IS/NICs. Coordination with the IHE partner is viewed as an important senior staff responsibility.
	12. Professional development of district staff	IS/NICs training for teachers and leaders is a standard part of professional development offerings.	Select district participants are learning about IS principles, tools, and methods, as well as the work of NICs.	A district iLEAD group is deepening their learning about IS/NICs. Professional development offerings are appearing to introduce knowledge about IS/NICs to LEA staff.	IS/NICs training for teachers and leaders has become a regular part of the professional development offerings of the district.	IS/NICs training is also integrated into the onboarding process of new hires, including teachers and leaders.

13. Implementation of IS/NICs	IS/NICs are integrated into planning processes and utilized to make measurable improvements in local problems of practice.	Explorations are underway about possibly using IS and NICs to tackle problems of practice.	IS/NICs are taken up in a small number of K-12 schools and provide the initial practice context for iLEAD. One or more district-led efforts are now underway to try out improvement science and improvement networks.	IS/NICs are being utilized in a broader number of schools and adapted for use on district-wide problems and challenges. District embraces IS, and the use of NICs is expanding.	IS/NICs now anchor the district's current improvement efforts and planning for future work. Evidence is accumulating that working in this way has made measurable improvements for students, schools, and the district.
14. Improvement science and networks as district policy	IS/NICs are integral to strategy and policy conversations among district leadership	The LEA re-examines past approaches to school improvement, exploring a "better way."	A coherent plan is being formulated anchored around IS/NICs.	Executive leadership endorses and actively affirms the adoption of a networked improvement science strategy.	IS/NICs are now a regular part of strategy conversations among the superintendent, other senior system leaders, and board members.
15. Funding support	External funding stream(s) are secured, and internal resources are properly allocated to support partnership work and participation.	Local, state, regional, and national funding opportunities are being explored.	Plans for local, state, regional, and/or national support are being developed.	Internal resources have been reallocated, and, where needed, external sources of support have been secured, ensuring ongoing district participation.	Funding stream(s) have been secured on a continuing basis, going forward to regularize partnership participation. It is an integral part of the budget now.

(continued)

Table I.1 Continued

Domain	Area of Work	Description	"Exploring Change Ideas"	"Small Change Implementation"	"Integrating IS/NICs into the Core Work"	"Institutionalizing and Sustaining the Work"
	16. IS/NICs expertise integrated into promotion and hiring decisions	Recognition of IS/NICs expertise in hiring, development, and promotion strategies.		District is beginning to discuss how using IS/NICs might impact hiring, development, and promotion decisions as part of a human capital strategy.	District is moving to include evidence about success in coaching improvement efforts as part of hiring, development, and promotion criteria.	Demonstrated expertise in IS/NICs has now become a highly-valued criterion in hiring, development, and promotion as part of a human capital strategy.
	17. Broadening stakeholder engagement	Strategies exist to actively include students, parents, and community stakeholders in improvement efforts.	District is exploring ways to include student, parents, and community members in improvement efforts.	Efforts are underway to involve students, parents, and community members as appropriate to further improvement efforts.	District has identified three to five successful strategies for broadening stakeholder engagement.	LEA has adopted formalized mechanisms for broadening stakeholder involvement.

18. Partnership relationships	Cultivation of partnership relationships built around active joint work and characterized by positive attitudes and strong bonds of trust	Initial explorations and commitments make it possible to apply to become a member of the iLEAD community. A landscape analysis is initiated of past and existing partnership efforts between LEA and IHE as a basis for learning how to work productively together going forward.	Regular meetings and other possible activities are occurring and provide a basis for exploring working relationships. Success and shortcomings from past partnership efforts have been identified and now inform emerging new partnership commitments.	Active joint work is occurring between IHE and LEA staff, and positive attitudes characterize the work.	A strong bond of trust and respect has formed and provides the basis for even difficult conversations to happen.
19. Joint development of targeted problems of practice	Joint identification of one or more problems of practice that can focus on education doctorate (EdD) and/or master students' capstones	Conversations have been initiated between IHE and LEA about possible problems of practice as issues to solve.	One or more problems of practice have been jointly identified by the local IHE and LEA partners as options for students to pursue in their coursework.	Many LEA EdD and/or master students are engaged in capstones on problems of practice. A density of work on each targeted problem of practice is emerging.	A regular process exists for reviewing capstone learning. The IHE and LEA are jointly planning out topical priorities going forward.

(continued)

Table I.1 Continued

Domain	Area of Work	Description	"Exploring Change Ideas"	"Small Change Implementation"	"Integrating IS/NICs into the Core Work"	"Institutionalizing and Sustaining the Work"
	20. Learning to improve	Joint development of a continuous quality improvement system that captures, consolidates, and uses data and evidence for ongoing improvement	Partnership members are exploring how to work together using IS/NICs to improve their respective and joint efforts.	The LEA and IHE have initiated new structures to consolidate their learnings about the use of IS/NICs.	The partnership is developing a continuous quality improvement system that includes regular data feedback from program participants during and after the program.	The LEA and IHE are jointly reviewing evidence from a quality improvement system and using this to plan the next set of improvement cycles for the partnership. The partnership can document learnings from capstones that have advanced local improvements.
	21. Formalizing a Joint LEA-IHE "New Leaders Development Program"	LEA cohort participation in IHE programs as central to the development of place-based and problem-focused district leadership		Conversations are underway about enrolling cohorts of teacher-leaders/future principal candidates in the IHE.	An agreement has been reached to support the participation of annual cohorts of aspiring new leaders.	The local LEA–IHE partnership is now central to how the district is developing new leadership talent; it's not just "another project."

			A distinctive partnership narrative is emerging: "what this is; why are we doing it; why this really matters for our educators and their students."	A narrative is developing among IHE faculty and LEA senior leaders with ownership emerging for building OUR program that prepares OUR students to succeed.	Organizational norms now operate as a forcing function on the partnership (e.g., "We need to do 'x,' because we said we are about 'y'") and they operate as a form of a moral imperative.
22. A Shared partnership narrative	Development of a shared narrative and set of norms				
23. Public communications	Communication about partnership improvement work is part of both the IHE and LEA communications program		A plan is being developed (first steps taken) to communicate about the emergent partnership more broadly.	Communications are widely broadcasting the partnership and its initial work.	The partnership improvement work is now a regular part of both IHE and LEA communications programs.

The Developmental Progressions framework, which emerged from the iLEAD community, is a tool for LEAs and IHEs to assess their partnership from a shared vantage point. Each row highlights a high-leverage objective that partners have identified as key to the IHE, LEA, and their joint work. The framework provides participants with a common language for collective action. Unlike other efforts (e.g., King, 2014), the Progressions support the continuous improvement of partnerships. They encourage institutions to consider and represent local relational realities and aspirations. The framework does not aspire to be a detailed plan to be "implemented with fidelity." There is no assumption that there is one best route to follow. Rather, each partnership maps its own journey.

achieved more of a standard mental model, where they share conceptions and some administration (e.g., they leverage shared employees to accomplish joint aims), tend to use the Progressions more actively to guide their regular planning, activities, and strategies.

While the use of the Developmental Progressions framework varies in the following chapters, it provides a level of focus and specificity to the partnerships' work in each case. Similar to a set of professional standards, the Progressions introduce externally generated criteria that partners can agree to consider together. The framework brings clarity to the competencies necessary to vitalize and sustain partnership work at the individual, institutional, and joint organizational levels. The Progressions also help ensure that leaders keep in view the knowledge, skills, and dispositions necessary to orchestrate continuous improvement work that effectively redresses systemic inequities in educational outcomes and opportunities.

The Desiderata to Sustain Trading Zones

This book conveys the value of partnership to educational progress and describes how partnerships are brought to life at the boundaries between IHEs and LEAs. Establishing relationships and using boundary objects, while creating trading zones, is a recurrent theme in many of the stories in this book; they are vital to authentic and sustainable inter-organizational collaborative work. One might ask what foundational processes make them organizationally tenable. What are the desiderata—the desired processes that school districts and university departments of education have—to sustain a trading zone? In iLEAD, we observe four inter-related processes at play: continuous improvement, equity, coordination, and capacity building.

Continuous Improvement

Continuous improvement is the essential infrastructure that permeates every case in this volume; it is the process and attitudinal center of each partnership's work. As a values-centered epistemology and method, continuous improvement plays an enlivening process role in the partnerships and the trading zones where they work. Every story, in subtle and not-so-subtle ways, relies on continuous improvement to shape local attitudes and guide action. For these iLEAD partnerships, continuous improvement is foundational to the processes and agreements in trading zones.

Continuous improvement enables a shared sense of the non-negotiable aspects of organizational and inter-organizational life. For example, a shared understanding of evidence is one such non-negotiable. Left to their own devices, friction develops between organizations when agreeing on what counts as evidence. The trading zones in this volume link organization members, from local schools and districts with university staff members, in a way that allows them to coexist and work naturally. Improvement attitudes and methods are crucial in this development. These are the mechanisms that smooth some of the rough edges that frequently present themselves in the search for frictionless joint professional practice.

A commitment to continuous improvement harmonizes the endeavors of partnership members and allows them to accomplish some of the important aspects of inter-organizational partnerships. For illustration, we place in relief the essential goals of equity and continuous improvement as they are connected to systems thinking and capacity building in this volume's partnership stories.

EQUITY

Today, equity leads, or is very near the pole position of, the desiderata that motivate our engagement in policy, practice, and research efforts in education. Indeed, equity is the overarching aim of the iLEAD network (see iLEAD's Field Transformation Strategy in figure I.3). However, equity is a contested terrain. The professional literature and popular press tend to treat equity as a monolith. That is, either an organization has accomplished "equity," or it has not. Yet equity is not monolithic—it means different things to different people (Welton et al., 2018).

The contested nature of equity makes it a candidate to introduce friction in joint organizational work and goal setting. For instance, suppose equity is taken to be monolithic and fixed rather than processual. In this case, it opens the door to inter-organizational friction between actors who question whether "my sense of equity is the same as your sense of equity." This sameness assumption might lead one organization to believe that "I am free to measure equity for you," or to assume that "I am free to define equity for you." These iLEAD partnerships use continuous improvement to develop a more nuanced feedback-focused sense of what it means to have equity-centered goals. Readers will observe, for example, that the partnerships realize that coming to understand equity relies on developing symmetrical relationality (Digiacomo &

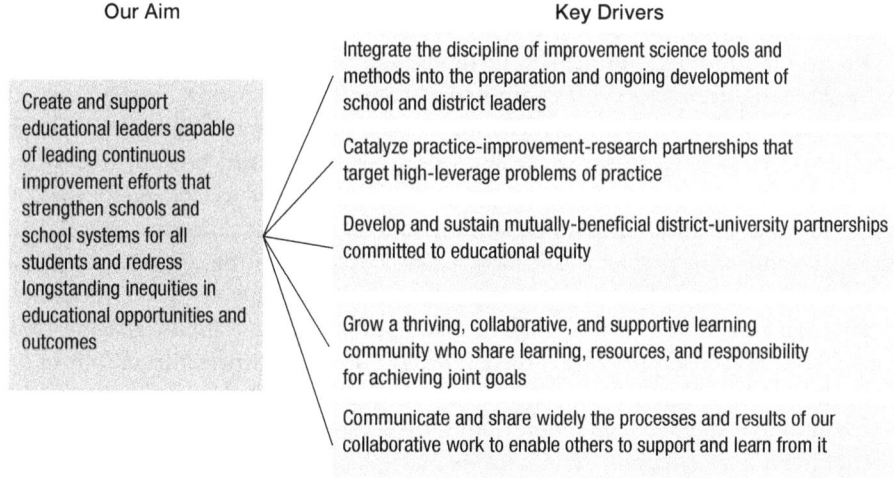

Figure I.3 iLEAD's Field Transformation Strategy.

Gutiérrez, 2016). Mutual understanding of complex notions such as equity requires purposefully shared processes, allowing the situated expertise resident in LEAs and IHEs to take intellectual prominence as necessary in collaborative activity.

iLEAD's field transformation strategy (figure I.3) places continuous improvement at the center of partnership action focused on equity and leadership. Continuous improvement practices require a specific focus on a person or group connected to a particular problem. Minimally, if the partnerships adhere to this aim, it would be necessary to probe how the specific organizations and individuals who are part of them understand equity. Thus, when contending with equity, these partnerships take on issues such as whether problems arise from race, ethnicity, class, or some intersectional combination. A continuous improvement perspective on equity demands that partnerships are specific about the question: "What specifically are we trying to accomplish?" Within the context of partnership trading zones, continuous improvement encourages specific processes to help harmonize collective action and mitigate friction.

Figure I.3 also suggests that to achieve relationality in developing equitable leaders, partnerships must operate in concert to (1) integrate improvement science tools into leadership preparation; (2) catalyze high-leverage problems in partnership work; (3) attend to the mutual benefit in partnerships; (4) grow communities with shared resources; and (5) document processes so others can learn. The partnerships in this book recognize that schools need mutual-benefit partnerships to educate children. As Goodlad (1993) noted, the energy for these partnerships ought to be community-centered to succeed. Thus, trading zones require processes that do more than knit individuals together. They need processes to incorporate systems together for a common purpose.

COORDINATION

Left unaided, when complex systems like LEAs and IHEs come together, it is often not a recipe for coordination or alignment. Rather, it is a recipe for being urged away from common action and into silos of activity (Bouckaert et al., 2010). With the help of continuous improvement principles, methods, and tools, the trading zones described in the chapters are focused on coordinating complex systems. Stories here are rife with examples of how iLEAD partnerships seek opportunities to coordinate plans and activities. For example, some partnerships use classroom instruction for leaders and aspiring leaders as a site to introduce and teach improvement science. As they engage in instructional practice, the partners work hard to ensure that university instructional examples come with problems of practice that are active in the school district. The partnership uses what Meadows (1997) calls "leverage points" or what continuous improvement practitioners call "high-leverage problems" in complex systems (Bryk et al., 2015). Meadows (1997) says these leverage points are "where a small shift in one thing can produce significant changes in everything" (p. 78). In the case of instruction, continuous improvement guides and spurs inter-organizational thinking forward by coordinating instructional examples in leadership in classrooms and problems of practice leaders can work on as part of their everyday professional work.

CAPACITY BUILDING

The role of capacity building to accomplish mutually beneficial actions is critical to iLEAD's efforts to transform the field (figure I.3). Capacity building is a learning enterprise that, at its most effective, is achieved through learning by doing. The partnership cases readers will encounter in this volume are full with examples of learning through action. One might ask why school districts and university departments of education need to learn to be in partnerships. After all, for most such organizations, working collaboratively in service to others is the raison d'être. Yet inter-organizational relationships among IHEs and LEAs tend to unfold as one-way enterprises. In the main, universities think of themselves as channeling resources and insights to school districts. Both universities and school districts are well-practiced in engaging in this dance. In mutual-benefit partnerships, the partners, as equals, mobilize and instantiate knowledge that will serve both well. Each partner has to appreciate the political, social, and cultural contexts. For most universities and school districts, working this way requires individual and institutional learning. Each has to respect the other's limitations on action disciplined by financial, technical, and other material resource limitations.

Readers will also note that in some cases, improvement science and continuous improvement helped the partners grow a thriving learning community. Some partnerships used experimental thinking, shaped by Plan Do Study Act (PDSA) cycles, to build capacity and understand the change in their organizations. Others used empathy interviews to reveal how university-partner thinking diverged from those of district partners. In all, continuous improvement is the throughline learning engine that defines iLEAD partnerships.

Conclusion

In closing, each case in this volume documents key issues as well as the learnings partnerships were able to accomplish. Readers should consider these lessons as starting points. The partnership stories told here are not meant to neatly tie a bow on the accomplishments of the LEA–IHE partnerships and, having done so, suggest that the partnerships should now be allowed to ride successfully off into the sunset. Instead, these stories are meant to be kick-starters to shared action. Each of our storytellers hopes that others will see something of themselves in the stories and that the stories will, in turn, offer an assist to others as they begin their own mutual-benefit partnership sagas.

References

Akkerman, S. F., & Bakker, A. (2011). Learning at the boundary: An introduction. *International Journal of Educational Research, 50*(1), 1–5. https://doi.org/10.1016/j.ijer.2011.04.002

Archer, M. S., & Archer, M. S. (1996). *Culture and agency: The place of culture in social theory.* Cambridge University Press.

Bouckaert, G., Peters, B. G., & Verhoest, K. (2010). Coordination: What is it and why should we have it? In B. Peters, G. Bouckaert, & K. Verhoest (Eds.), *The coordination of public sector organizations* (pp. 13–33). Palgrave Macmillan.

Bryk, A. S., Gomez, L. M., Grunow, A., & LeMahieu, P. G. (2015). *Learning to improve: How America's schools can get better at getting better.* Harvard Education Press.

Churchill, E. (2009). Introduction: Social glue. In K. S. Willis, G. Roussos, K. Chorianopoulous, & M. Struppek (Eds.), *Shared encounters: Content sharing as social glue in public places.* Springer-Verlag.

Collins, H., Evans, R., & Gorman, M. (2007). Trading zones and interactional expertise. *Studies in History and Philosophy of Science Part A, 38*(4), 657–666.

Dawes, S. S., Cresswell, A. M., & Pardo, T. A. (2009). From "need to know" to "need to share": Tangled problems, information boundaries, and the building of public sector knowledge networks. *Public Administration Review, 69*(3), 392–402.

DiGiacomo, D. K., & Gutiérrez, K. D. (2016). Relational equity as a design tool within making and tinkering activities. *Mind, Culture, and Activity, 23*(2), 141–153.

Engeström, Y. (2009). The future of activity theory: A rough draft. In A. Sannino, H. Daniels, & K. D. Gutierrez (Eds.), *Learning and expanding with activity theory* (pp. 303–328). Cambridge University Press.

Fine, G. A. (2012). *Tiny publics: A theory of group action and culture.* Russell Sage.

Galison, P. (2010). Trading with the enemy. In M. E. Gorman (Ed.), *Trading zones and interactional expertise: Creating new kinds of collaboration* (pp. 25–52). The MIT Press.

Gomez, L., Biag, M., & Imig, D. (2020). Learning at the boundaries: Reconsidering university-district partnerships for educational leadership. In N. Suad Nasir, C. Lee, & R. Pea (Eds.), *Handbook of the cultural foundations of learning* (pp. 365–384). Routledge.

Goodlad, J. I. (1993). School-university partnerships and partner schools. *Educational Policy, 7*(1), 24–39.

Gorman, M. E. (2002). Levels of expertise and trading zones: A framework for multidisciplinary collaboration. *Social Studies of Science, 32*(5–6), 933–938.

Gorman, M. E., Mehalik, M. M., & Werhane, P. H. (2000). *Ethical and environmental challenges to engineering.* Prentice Hall.

Hinnant-Crawford, B. N. (2020). *Improvement science in education: A primer.* Myers Education Press.

King, C. L. (2014). *Quality measures partnership effectiveness continuum.* Education Development Center, Inc.

Langley, G. J., Moen, R. D., Nolan, K. M., Nolan, T. W., Norman, C. L., & Provost, L. P. (2009). *The Improvement guide: A practical approach to enhancing organizational performance.* John Wiley & Sons.

Lave, J., & Wenger, E. (1991). *Situated learning: Legitimate peripheral participation.* Cambridge University Press.

McNamara, M. (2012). Starting to untangle the web of cooperation, coordination, and collaboration: A framework for public managers. *International Journal of Public Administration, 35*(6), 389–401.

Meadows, D. H. (1997, Winter). Places to intervene in a system. *Whole Earth.* http://www.wholeearthmag.com/ArticleBin/109.html

Muller, L., Froggett, L., & Bennett, J. (2020). Emergent knowledge in the third space of art-science. *Leonardo, 53*(3), 321–326.

Radinsky, J., Bouillon, L., Lento, E. M., & Gomez, L. M. (2001). Mutual benefit partnership: A curricular design for authenticity. *Journal of Curriculum Studies, 33*(4), 405–430.

Star, S. L., & Griesemer, J. R. (1989). Institutional ecology, "translations" and boundary objects: Amateurs and professionals in Berkeley's Museum of Vertebrate Zoology, 1907–39. *Social Studies of Science*, *19*(3), 387–420. https://images-insite.sgp1.digitaloceanspaces.com/dunia_buku/koleksi-buku-lainnya/institutional-ecology-translations-and-boundary-objects-amateurs-pdfdrivecom-42531582402862.pdf

Velásquez, C., Biag, M., Gomez, L., & Imig, D. (2019). Partnering for leadership development and continuous improvement: Carnegie's improvement leadership education and development network. *AERA Learning and Teaching in Educational Leadership Newsletter*.

Welton, A. D., Owens, D. R., & Zamani-Gallaher, E. M. (2018). Anti-racist change: A conceptual framework for educational institutions to take systemic action. *Teachers College Record*, *120*(14), 1–22.

Wenger, E. (1998). Communities of practice: Learning as a social system. *Systems Thinker*, *9*(5), 2–3.

Wenger, E. C., & Snyder, W. M. (2000). Communities of practice: The organizational frontier. *Harvard Business Review*, *78*(1), 139–146.

Whipple, J. M., Lynch, D. F., & Nyaga, G. N. (2010). A buyer's perspective on collaborative versus transactional relationships. *Industrial Marketing Management*, *39*(3), 507–518. https://doi.org/10.1016/j.indmarman.2008.11.008

Worren, N. (2018). *Organization design: Simplifying complex systems*. Routledge.

SECTION I

Improvement Methods, Equity, and Problems of Practice in Local Context

Steve Tozer

Section I presents the efforts of four different school district–higher education partnerships to address educational inequities using improvement science methods. The school districts portrayed here vary greatly, from the Bronx to two very different districts in Virginia, to an innovative network of schools in San Diego. We also see a variation in the higher education partners: large universities, public and private, and a small, independent graduate school of education. Across these differences, the cases demonstrate how the intentional application of improvement methods has led to the building of new systems, structures, and routines in all four districts and their higher education partners—in all cases collaboratively designed to respond to local problems of practice that affect equity in student learning outcomes.

In the first case, for example, we see a partnership for improvement involving Chesterfield County Public Schools, a sizable district with 65 schools, and the nearby University of Virginia, a large research-intensive university. The Chesterfield/UVA partnership sought to confront persistent inequities in local schools by collaboratively redesigning the UVA leadership development program to improve school leadership in the district. The UVA/Chesterfield chapter documents the evolution of a complex "braiding" of partnership work that is explicitly anchored in the four priorities of iLEAD's Developmental Progressions: Professional Development, Curriculum, Programmatic Improvement, and Systems Partnership, leading to growth in individual and organizational capacity that has already had a documented impact on both the district and the university. The initial emphasis on pre-service preparation of leaders grew to "braid" the use of improvement science in the university with improvement science in the district development of leaders at multiple levels—regional, central office, and schools.

A similar problem identified in Bronx public schools was the inadequate development of leadership knowledge and skills to address persistent inequities in student outcomes. Fordham University, a large private institution, thoroughly redesigned its EdD program to improve the preparation of advanced educational leaders who could transform schools and student learning. The redesign incorporated collaboration with Bronx leaders, some of whom enrolled in and completed the program. This later led to developing two cohorts of school and district leaders as a borough-wide strategy. These collaborative routines were explicitly guided by improvement science principles and, again, by iLEAD's Developmental Progressions framework. These successful leadership development initiatives were accompanied by other joint improvement initiatives and methods, including the use of Networked Improvement Communities (NICs) to develop the leadership capacity of Bronx assistant principals, three principal NICs in one Bronx district, and targeted school improvement in 37 Bronx schools.

The second of the two Virginia districts in this section is Fairfax County Public Schools, one of the nation's larger districts, with over 200 schools, partnering with Virginia's largest public university, George Mason. For the Fairfax County/George Mason partnership, a long-standing, collaborative IHE–LEA relationship coalesced around the systematic infusion of improvement science principles into both pre-service and in-service leader development, via district professional development as well as the redesigned MEd Program at GMU. This approach provides aspiring and practicing leaders with new tools and methods for collaborative problem identification and improvement planning in multiple settings, resulting in a remarkable reach of improvement practices throughout the district.

The problem of practice identified in the network of High Tech High (HTH) Schools was that high teacher turnover is especially damaging for low-income student populations. The HTH Graduate School of Education is using improvement principles to work closely with teachers and leaders in the HTH network of 16 schools—elementary, middle, and high—to improve teacher retention and accelerate their learning, with promising early results. The graduate school and the K–12 schools alike have had to learn new approaches to problem identification and data-based problem-solving to work together using improvement methods. This chapter demonstrates in detail the challenges and successes of applying the Carnegie Foundation for Advancement of Teaching Core Principles of Improvement to the complex problem of novice teacher support and development, with a particular emphasis on the need to develop systems to support effective coaching and mentoring. The HTH authors have also included links to an Appendix on the Rowman & Littlefield website that provides illustrations of how these systems are supported.

Readers are encouraged to look for a number of resonances to their own challenges and prospects for improving equitable outcomes in schools. District leaders and higher education leaders alike may find value in how specific problems of practice required resources greater than districts or higher education *alone* could adequately address, and how partnerships provided greater leverage for changing institutional practices and norms to achieve more equitable outcomes in schools. Higher education leaders may find it instructive to see how the tailoring of professional programs around *district* needs can lead to increased individual and organizational capacity in graduate schools. Conversely, districts may find value in seeing how methods of disciplined collaboration with higher education can build the capacity of district personnel. Leaders from higher education and school districts alike can look for ways in which improvement principles and the Developmental Progressions provide measures against which their collaborative work can be assessed: is the organizational capacity for equity really being built, or is "business as usual" pushing back against much-needed change?

CHAPTER 1

Braiding Improvement into the Fabric of District Leadership Preparation and Practice
UNIVERSITY OF VIRGINIA AND CHESTERFIELD COUNTY PUBLIC SCHOOLS

David Eddy-Spicer, Tinkhani Ushe White, and Michelle M. Beavers

This chapter charts the evolution of a partnership between the University of Virginia (UVA), a large, public, research-intensive university, and Chesterfield County Public Schools (CCPS), a peri-urban district of more than 61,000 students and 65 elementary, middle, and high schools that are diverse in enrollment and in levels of academic success. The university and district transformed pre-existing working relationships into a more focused, more disciplined, and more collaborative partnership built around strategies to improve equity in opportunity for all students throughout CCPS. The partnership accomplished this by leveraging its participation in the Carnegie Foundation for Advancement of Teaching's iLEAD initiative to support the use of improvement science as a set of principles and methods for evolving from older to newer modes of collaborating around equity challenges. The partnership evolved from coordinated, parallel efforts to embed improvement science in leadership development and school improvement to a braided, more coherent approach that required new individual and organizational capacities both to prepare future school leaders and to develop current school leaders to lead local continuous improvement efforts. The process of braiding district and university activities required learning at multiple levels on both sides by university faculty, aspiring leaders in the university program, district leaders, and currently serving school leaders. The district engaged central-office, regional, and school-level leaders in intensive professional learning focused on improvement science supported by the university while the university simultaneously redesigned its curriculum and internship experiences in leadership preparation around improvement science supported by the district.

The braiding process touched on many different facets of the 24 key objectives delineated in iLEAD's Developmental Progressions (Gomez et al., 2020). Several stand out as most prominent. For CCPS as the local education agency, Professional Development of district staff (#12) proved crucial; for UVA as the institution of higher education, Curriculum/Program Development (#2) coupled with Improvement Science as a Signature Pedagogy (#5) proved foundational; and for the partnership as a whole, Formalizing a Joint LEA/IHE Leadership Development Program (#22) anchored our relationship. The story we tell below relates how we moved from the initial stages of exploring ideas together to sustaining the work through our mutually constituted improvement braid.

Partnership Context

The initial vision of the partnership was straightforward, albeit ambitious—collaborating together on developing leaders capable of accomplishing meaningful work on ensuring that all children had robust and equitable opportunities to learn. At the start of our partnership, essential components that would lead to enacting that vision were in place. Under the leadership of former Superintendent Dr. James Lane, CCPS focused in 2017 on redressing growing disparities within and across its schools through an equity initiative, committing to making a focus on equity central to its approach to school improvement. Dr. Lane and other district leaders at the time were eager to prepare a new cadre of leaders to take on the challenge presented by the demands of a district under rapid change. University of Virginia faculty in the School of Education and Human Development was in the midst of an overhaul of the initial principal preparation program with equity at its core. Faculty teaching in this program, the Administration and Supervision M.Ed. with administrative endorsement (A&S M.Ed.), had committed to using improvement science approaches and principles as the basis for field-based experiences that wove together learning *about* leadership with learning *through* leading, supporting aspiring leaders to take on increasing responsibilities for improvement initiatives in their schools. A belief shared between CCPS and UVA was that improvement science could serve as an essential fulcrum for systemic change.

UNIVERSITY OF VIRGINIA

The University of Virginia's School of Education and Human Development (EHD) worked in partnership with the Chesterfield County Public Schools as one of the original 11 leadership preparation partnerships connected through the Carnegie Foundation's iLEAD initiative. In EHD, the partnership was led by faculty in the Administration and Supervision (A&S) Program Area, a nationally recognized program that was ranked ninth nationwide in 2022 by US News and World Report among graduate programs in educational administration. At EHD, the partnership has also drawn on the expertise of colleagues in the school's Motivate Lab, which conducts research into student, teacher, and leader learning mindsets as well as the Center for Race and Public Education in the South, which studies issues that lie at the intersection of race, education, and schooling in the southern United States.

CHESTERFIELD COUNTY PUBLIC SCHOOLS

Chesterfield County Public Schools serves 61,119 students in grades preK–12 in 65 schools. Of these students, 30% receive free or reduced lunch. About half of the students are white, one-quarter African American, and one-seventh Latino. Chesterfield reflects characteristics of other peri-urban counties surrounding rapidly growing Richmond, Virginia, in holding a diverse range of communities from urban-ring to rural. Moreover, Chesterfield's communities tend to be stratified by socioeconomic status, with high concentrations of wealth at one end of the county and less affluent communities at the opposite end. Additionally, Richmond's rapid growth has led to ongoing demographic change within Chesterfield, including a rapidly growing school-age population spurred in part by growing numbers of families, including new immigrants and those moving out of Richmond City in search of economic opportunity and lower costs. These characteristics identify Chesterfield as an "in-between" district (Eddy-Spicer et al., 2017) that needed to adapt rapidly to an increasingly diverse student population with a teacher and leader workforce that was predominantly white.

An Educational Leadership Preparation Partnership Emerges

Leadership preparation research over the past two decades has highlighted the ways in which educational leadership preparation programs can serve as a solid foundation for developing specific leadership practices that contribute to improved student learning. District partnerships with higher education are among the chief attributes of highly effective programs identified in research (Cosner, 2019, 2020; Darling-Hammond et al., 2009, 2022; Orr & Barber, 2006). Emerging research literature highlights the importance of cohort-based programs and district-university partnerships in promoting leadership preparation that embeds emphases on cultural competency and social justice leadership (Barakat et al., 2019; Byrne-Jimenez & Orr, 2013; McKenzie et al., 2007; Orr, 2020).

The vision of the iLEAD partnership between CCPS and UVA was of a district-university pairing that would engage emerging and current leaders in active learning and action to address the complex issues that systemic inequities entailed. A particular focus throughout our story concerns the roles of middle-level leaders in spanning boundaries across organizations and creating spaces for developing "boundary infrastructures" (Bowker & Star, 1999), the structures, routines, and artifacts that enable practice to cross organizational boundaries—or in the absence of functional boundary infrastructure, lead to breakdowns. By "middle-level leaders," we mean middle-level central-office leaders on the CCPS side and program faculty on the UVA side. The partnership of CCPS and UVA demonstrated the importance of the role that middle-level leaders played in building the boundary infrastructure in ways that bridged each organization's separate interests to define a territory of shared, mutual interest.

To chart the evolution of the partnership towards these ends, we turn to two frameworks explicitly focused on partnership evolution, one drawn from the literature on inter-organizational collaborative alliances (Gulati et al., 2012) and the other from the literature on educational partnerships (Barnett et al., 2010). Gulati et al. articulate a crucial step in partnership development from *cooperation* to *coordination*. Cooperation concerns each partner's commitment to the alliance and the alignment of interests; coordination emphasizes the *enactment* of alignment across organizations and explores the mutual adjustment of partners' actions as a consequence of carrying the partnership forward (Gulatti et al., 2012). Barnett et al. (2010) offer an elaboration beyond coordination, suggesting the further developmental stage of *collaboration*, which entails high levels of interpersonal trust and an ongoing dialogic exchange that is "intensive and sustained mutual exchange and benefit" (Barnett et al., 2010, p. 25). The story that follows concerns the evolution of the partnership in two stages, initially from cooperation to coordination, which we label the "improvement sandwich" stage, and then from coordination to collaboration, the "improvement braid," in the development of improvement science as a signature pedagogy of the leadership preparation program as well as a signature approach to professional and organizational learning in the strategic planning processes of the district.

The "Improvement Sandwich": Cooperation into Coordination

The initial phase of our work together stands out as a time when we were each setting the strands that would become the braid. Well before the advent of our partnership, both the University of Virginia's A&S Program and CCPS separately arrived at anchoring school improvement in leadership that expanded opportunities for every student to learn and to succeed. The initial steps of our partnership occurred before the advent of iLEAD and around the launch of an inaugural cohort of 15 aspiring leaders from CCPS in the summer of 2017. The planning and design of learning that went into the launch of the cohort provided the partnership's first forum for the alignment of our interests. Dr. James Lane, Superintendent of CCPS in 2017, and Dr. Thomas Taylor, Chief Academic Officer at the time, had been advancing a major focus on four core values of integrity, equity, teamwork, and ingenuity through the development of the CCPS strategic plan, *Imagine Tomorrow* (Chesterfield County Public Schools, 2019). In 2017, an aspect of the development of that plan was the crafting of an equity report that, as anticipated, revealed inequitable outcomes and opportunities for students across the system (Chesterfield County Public Schools, 2017). These inequities were especially apparent in opportunities and access for Black and Latinx students, as well as students with disabilities and English learners. *Imagine Tomorrow*, the CCPS strategic plan, built on the findings from the equity report and spotlighted equity as a core value with a focus on promoting a "culture of high performance, continuous improvement, and evidence of impact" as a priority area (Chesterfield County Public Schools, 2019, p. 8).

At the same time, UVA faculty were in the midst of the redesign of the Master's program, which aimed for a fundamental shift in the program's "signature pedagogy" (Shulman, 2005; Black & Murtadha, 2007). In Shulman's (2005) terms, a signature pedagogy in any professional field consists of "the types of teaching that organize the fundamental ways in which future practitioners are educated for their professions" (p. 52). Shulman highlights three dimensions that such a signature pedagogy must address: the *intellectual*, comprising the foundational "know what" that defines a professional field; the *technical*, the "know how"—tools and tradecraft—that characterizes the work of experienced practitioners of a given field; and the *moral*, the "know why" of ethical dimensions and values basis for the kinds of complex decision making and trade-offs professionals must make daily as an inherent part of their practice. In the UVA redesign, four domains served as anchors for these intellectual, technical, and moral dimensions: continuous improvement, equity, adult learning and development, and leadership. For the domain of continuous improvement, the redesign of the program aimed to leverage the principles and approaches of improvement science to scaffold self-reflective inquiry at the individual level and systemic change within and across schools at the organizational level (Black & Murtadha, 2007).

At the launch of the partnership, each of the two partners recognized that they held in common complementary visions for the kinds of leaders and the characteristics of leadership that defined our aspirations. The launch of the cohort and the advent of the iLEAD partnership overall served as a laboratory for coordination through the closer alignment of these aspirations. The first strands of the braid came clearly into view in our joint proposal to join Carnegie's iLEAD initiative—the strand of equity-oriented leadership preparation on the UVA side, with support from Chesterfield through its investment in aspiring leaders who would comprise the inaugural cohort, and the emphasis on a strategic overhaul of the school improvement planning process to address fundamental concerns around students' opportunities to learn on the CCPS side, with support from UVA on the learning and doing of improvement science. Carnegie accepted our application, and White, who held the position of School Improvement Specialist at that time, became the coordinator for CCPS, while UVA faculty member Eddy-Spicer led the initiative from the UVA side.

Eddy-Spicer was an active and early participant in Carnegie's Higher Education Network, which allowed him to leverage engagement with other faculty from around the country to develop a series of research courses for the education doctorate that used improvement science principles and approaches to develop powerful learning experiences that focused on central concerns around the leadership of equity-oriented teaching and learning. He had begun to offer professional development workshops that focused on improvement science to professional groups around the state and nationally. White and Eddy-Spicer had originally met when White participated in a 2017 workshop facilitated by Eddy-Spicer that emphasized improvement science approaches. White recognized improvement science as a possible framework for school improvement that offered the "pull" of continuous learning rather than the "push" of compliance. When Eddy-Spicer contacted her about collaborating on a proposal to be part of the nascent iLEAD network, she recognized the opportunity it presented to her district.

In this initial period, two parallel sets of activities defined the shared space for aligning interests across the partnership, with each partner taking the lead in separate areas. University faculty focused on the initial principal preparation program and the preparation of the cohort of aspiring leaders for the leadership roles they were to take on in Chesterfield. Central-office CCPS staff focused on re-envisioning the district's school-level strategic planning processes in ways that supported continuous improvement. These two parallel streams of activity comprised what together those in the partnership called the "improvement sandwich," with aspiring leaders in the UVA program forming the bottom layer of the sandwich and the top layer comprised of central-office leaders promulgating more flexible and adaptive strategic planning processes, meant to cultivate relationships with schools that prioritized developmental support rather than accountability and consequences. The middle layer, as we saw it then, had to do with existing school leaders and senior leadership teams that were carrying forward the daily work of schools. At the time in these early days, both partners assumed that coordination of the work between the bottom and the top layer of the sandwich would be enough to bring along the important middle—the senior- and middle-level leaders and other teachers. In retrospect, we had much to learn.

CCPS STRAND: FOCUS ON PROGRAMMATIC EQUITY AND SCHOOL IMPROVEMENT PLANNING

For CCPS, the top layer of the "improvement sandwich" focused on shifting the district's strategic planning process for schools from a compliance exercise to a tool for supporting continuous learning and improvement through the district's 65 schools. Of particular concern at the start of the partnership in 2017 was the fact that CCPS had several schools that had not met the accreditation benchmarks for state and federal accountability, including two that were denied accreditation and were under a state memorandum of understanding to improve. There was a need to change the school improvement process from one solely focused on completing an annual plan to demonstrate compliance to one that leveraged continuous improvement to support all leaders, teachers, and school staff to learn their way into better serving the particular needs of each school and its community.

In these early days, White visited the Menomonee Falls School District in Wisconsin, seeing improvement work in action and observing how Plan-Do-Study-Act

(PDSA) cycles (Langley et al., 2014) enabled staff throughout the district to make meaningful and measurable progress towards improving learning and the environment for learning for students of all backgrounds (Bryk, 2020). White's experience learning about improvement science and seeing it in action in Menomonee Falls enabled her to convince other central-office leaders that the approach held the potential for putting in place processes that would provide not only the impetus for every school to serve all students better but also a specific method for doing so. However, she and other CCPS leaders also recognized that doing so would require deep system learning about the processes of continuous improvement.

CCPS leaders realized that it was especially important to be intentional in building leadership capacity for this work throughout the district, not only for the aspiring leaders in the UVA cohort. Leadership students were working in isolated pockets across the district on small-scale changes that might have the potential for transforming practice in more than one classroom or grade level, but no means to expand these efforts existed absent a robust improvement infrastructure within their buildings and across the district. The sitting building leaders were not as well-versed in improvement science as the leadership students they might need to support. As a result, cohort students had begun to run into barriers of lack of understanding as they launched efforts informed by improvement science in their new schools.

CCPS central-office staff undertook several initiatives with an improvement science focus and with varying levels of support from UVA faculty. The first of these was revamping the School Innovation and Improvement Planning (SIIP) process from its current model of accountability-driven initiative implementation. For example, a common directive from the central office preceding this shift might have been, "we need everyone to do one project-based lesson," without support around the "how" and the "why" of doing so, nor the means to know whether any change would result in improvement. School and central leaders realized that there was an opportunity to leverage the required SIIP planning process to engage school staff and district leadership in establishing the "how" and "why" for themselves—to get better at understanding the problems they were seeking to solve and creating local systems that integrated innovations adaptively and allowed for continuous learning from those efforts to adapt. This emphasis on continuous learning led to the first iteration of the current SIIP planning process.

The school improvement team along with specialists from the curriculum, Title I, special education, and English as a Second Language (ESL) offices started to use what they were learning in relation to improvement science to support schools that were close to the accreditation line by supporting their engagement in monthly improvement cycles. These cycles focused on exploring specific change ideas as a means of learning how to better meet the needs of students. These cycles resulted in marked growth in student outcomes as well as teacher and administrator efficacy in doing the work. Throughout these encounters with school leaders and schools, a theory of action around the strategic planning process and the role it could play began to emerge. The theory was that the district-wide SIIP template might serve as one means of developing building leaders' skills and knowledge around continuous improvement if the principles and approaches of improvement science were "baked in" to the process itself. Consequently, the district leadership changed expectations around data analysis, interpretation, and reporting from "using data as a hammer to using it as a flashlight" (Data Quality Campaign, 2017). The SIIP template came to serve as an important component of the boundary infrastructure that enabled the translation of improvement science principles and tools into the daily work of leaders and teachers in schools.

The process was not just concerned with redesigning the district-wide school planning template, the latest version of which included prompts for conducting causal analyses, identifying improvement aims, and elaborating a working theory of improvement—all essential tools in the improvement science toolkit. The overall approach also entailed more direct support through coaching and consultation. For example, one Chesterfield school experienced a spike in chronic absenteeism. Previously, leaders in this school would have been asked to adopt a common district strategy to address the issue. However, White and other central-office staff coached senior leaders and teachers to work together to understand the particular dynamics of the issue in their building. Coaching and central-office support enabled school leaders and teachers to engage in a more thorough analysis of available data, including conducting empathy interviews with students and their families. Their exploration of the issue led to the discovery that many of the assumptions they had about why students were not coming to school simply did not hold. The insights these teachers and leaders in one school had gleaned subsequently led the district office that supports attendance to examine the guidance they gave to schools about how to support students, a vital step towards building capacity system-wide to address the actual issues that students and their families were experiencing (e.g., Tozer & Walker, 2021).

UVA STRAND: REDESIGNING THE M.ED. PROGRAM

The development of the redesigned UVA initial principal preparation program, the A&S M.Ed. with administrative endorsement, was a collective effort of the A&S area faculty, led by Pamela Tucker, program area coordinator at that time, and developed in collaboration with program faculty Sara Dexter, David Eddy-Spicer, and Michelle Young. Sandra Mitchell joined the faculty in 2017, and Michelle Beavers in 2018. As mentioned earlier, the three themes of continuous improvement, adult development, and equity animated the primary focus on leadership. The redesign had, at its core, the four domains of the Ontario Leadership Framework (OLF)—setting direction, developing people, redesigning the organization, and managing the instructional program (Leithwood, 2017). Moreover, these dimensions were mapped to two sets of leadership standards, the National Educational Leadership Preparation standards (NELP) (NPBEA, 2018) and the Virginia Competencies for the Preparation of School Leaders (Code of Virginia, n.d.). The emphasis on core themes, OLF domains, and state and national standards grounded the redesign of individual courses and the coherence of curricular content and instructional approaches across the course sequence overall. The signature pedagogy of the redesigned program aimed to animate learning at the intersection of these domains and the standards through two key pedagogical innovations adapted from best practices in contemporary approaches to school leadership preparation (Young & Eddy-Spicer, 2021). These included the processes of powerful learning experiences and the structure of collaborative partnerships with districts (Cosner et al., 2018; Cunningham et al., 2019). These elements, operating together, served as the foundation of the boundary infrastructure that UVA faculty assembled in support of the partnership. The central focus of this boundary infrastructure was a bias toward action evident in leadership students' application of their learning in their work settings, whether in school classrooms or central-office departments (Dexter et al., 2020).

UVA A&S faculty had a wide range of inter-organizational resources on which to draw to support the program redesign and partnership with Chesterfield. In addition to the connection with iLEAD and the quarterly convenings sponsored by Carnegie, faculty also took part in an initiative under the aegis of the University Council for Educational Administration (UCEA) that involved monthly meetings with educational leadership program faculty from four other universities. The UCEA Program Design Network was a national initiative created by the then Executive Director of UCEA, Michelle Young, who also served on the UVA A&S faculty. Eddy-Spicer helped with the design of the overall program and facilitated the network in which UVA participated, the Curriculum, Instruction and Coherence Networked Improvement Community (CIC-NIC). CIC-NIC enabled faculty teams from each of the participating universities to explore improvement science as they learned about each other's approaches to program redesign and workshopped planned revisions together. The initiative also involved annual field visits to exemplary programs (Stone-Johnson & Hayes, 2021). The field visit that UVA faculty made as part of CIC-NIC to the University of Illinois, Chicago program (see Chapter 11 of this volume) in the fall of 2019 proved to be a critical turning point in faculty conceptions of partnership and the alignment of field-based and course-based learning.

Field-Based Learning as Boundary Infrastructure

Unpacking the infrastructure that enabled field-based learning requires a closer understanding of how UVA faculty sequenced leadership learning across the program. The program consisted of a sequence of 11 courses overall. In each semester of this part-time, two-year degree, students took two paired courses, one of which was a designated course on a focal area of leadership such as *Family and Community Engagement* (EDLF 7806) paired with what we labeled a "Field-Based Learning Application" (FBLA) course, *Leadership for Continuous Improvement* (LCI, EDLF 7812), which aimed to integrate knowledge of continuous improvement with scaffolded leadership practice cued to leadership standards in students' work settings. Repeated pairings such as this occurred over the subsequent two semesters, with *Leadership Experiences, Applications, and Development (LEAD) I & II* (EDLF 7807 & 7140). For the first CCPS cohort, district-level leaders with doctoral degrees, including several graduates of UVA, served as adjunct instructors in the content courses (e.g., EDLF 7806, 7811, 7810, etc.).

The infrastructure of pairing focal courses with field-based courses aimed to bridge the idea-action gap (Perkins, 2009) by serving as a concerted means of activating students' learning through practical action. Such inquiry learning approaches that are assigned in class and enacted in the field are well-supported by a growing research base and recognized as among the best pedagogical practices of exemplary leadership preparation programs (Cosner, 2020; Darling-Hammond et al., 2022; Dexter et al., 2020; Ni et al., 2016). We set ourselves the additional challenge of not only nurturing individual learning through such inquiry learning approaches but also attempting to leverage the applied learning of graduate students to initiate and sustain organizational learning across the district in alignment with the aims of the partnership. The overall goal was to sensitize the leadership students to the need to develop organizational infrastructure and a culture of improvement through iterative, short-cycle inquiry that enabled a specific and action-oriented focus on systemic and structural determinants of inequity (Bryk, 2015, 2020; Grunow et al., 2018).

Leadership students took three field-based courses in sequence, Leadership for Continuous Improvement (LCI); Leadership Experiences, Application, and Development (LEAD) I; and LEAD II, all of which had the same overall structure, inspired by a 90-day improvement cycle (Park & Takahashi, 2013) and using iterative PDSA cycles as core units of learning. The three-course sequence plus internship scaffolded students' exploration of change ideas, drawing on improvement science principles and approaches to integrate students' learning with the core work of their schools. Students engaged in partnerships with their schools to identify equity-oriented problems of practice and develop improvement initiatives that evolved from semester to semester. This field-based sequence culminates with an administrative internship, which also involves orchestrating cycles of inquiry with an improvement team. Cohort members could fulfill the requirements of the internship in a current leadership role if they already held such a role, or they had the unique opportunity to apply for a two-year internship funded by CCPS as Dean of Students, an assistant principal on a teacher contract. The signature pedagogy represented in this course design was initially adapted from a series of other courses drawing on improvement science that had been developed for the education doctorate by Eddy-Spicer. Beavers, who took a faculty position at UVA in 2018 after working as Director of Professional Development in CCPS for four years, applied her experience with a quality improvement approach that was complementary to improvement science, Agile, to enrich the LEAD courses and the internship.

To illustrate this journey, we highlight the path followed by one member of the first cohort, Blair Jonas, whose group's focus was students with disabilities. Her improvement work in the first semester of LCI highlighted the need to cultivate student engagement in independent reading. However, Jonas was promoted to a Behavioral Intervention Specialist at the district level in this first semester and decided to shift her focus in the subsequent LEAD courses to address racial disparities in disciplinary referrals in the K–2 setting. The program requires graduate students working in a central office to establish a relationship with one school as a site for their improvement initiative. For Jonas, this was the school in which she had most recently worked. Using school and district data to inform her understanding of the problem of disciplinary referrals at that school, she crafted a change idea that emphasized strategies for teachers to address behavioral concerns in the classroom of the youngest learners through the development of positive interpersonal relationships. The change idea aligned with efforts to integrate multi-tiered systems of support in schools across the district. Moving into LEAD II, the goal of Jonas' improvement initiative was to provide the kindergarten team with lessons they could use to develop self-regulation skills for their students. Jonas's testing of these lessons in kindergarten classrooms showed that the development of self-regulation skills resulted in a marked decrease in discipline issues, limited use of exclusionary practices, and increased instructional time.

Jonas reports that an important insight from this experience had to do with understanding each participating teacher's readiness to change. She notes that the improvement team used knowledge of people's capacities to engage with change to guide the coaching that accompanied testing the use of the lesson plans. Jonas continued to draw on these lessons in the final phase of the program, the internship. The majority of students in her cohort successfully applied for fully-funded Dean of Students positions to fulfill their internship requirements. Jonas continued in her role as Behavioral Intervention Support Specialist for Elementary Schools in the district office for one year after completing her administrative endorsement and then moved to become Assistant Principal of a CCPS elementary school in 2022.

For Jonas and other graduate students, the iterative work on improvement initiatives across field-based courses created a bridge that supported the integration of learning into the core work of the school as students moved through the program. The improvement work offered a scaffold for leadership learning, enabling students to gain valuable experiences in a wide range of areas, from discrete improvement initiatives associated with particular courses to multifaceted professional learning in their internship roles as Dean of Students or as a central-office leader. Graduate students report that these experiences are foundational in their abilities to step into higher-level administrative positions with both confidence and humility.

Securing the Braid: Coordination into Collaboration

DEEPENING COORDINATION ACROSS SCHOOL LEVELS AND WITH CENTRAL OFFICE IN CCPS

CCPS and UVA launched their second cohort in the fall of 2019 with an emphasis on collaborative instruction and embedded practice through broader integration of the School Improvement and Innovation Plan in the ongoing improvement work underway in schools. Experience had taught us that systemic continuous improvement demands attention not only to the layers of the sandwich but to the processes of relating among those layers, what we came to characterize as "the braid" of more closely knit collaboration.

By that time in the partnership, the iLEAD Coordinators White and Eddy-Spicer had put in place several routines that allowed for regular communication and coordination across the two partners. In addition to bi-weekly coordinator check-ins, iLEAD coordinators also held quarterly meetings of a steering committee for the iLEAD partnership that included all program area faculty on the UVA side and the Deputy Superintendent and Chief School Officer on the CCPS side. Attendance at these meetings varied with the rhythm of the school year. Below we describe the emergence of increasingly collaborative activities as coordination and communication became more structured and routine. Important to note, especially in this period, were the contributions of Albert Bertani, a Senior Fellow of the Carnegie Foundation who served as a coach/mentor to the coordinators as part of the iLEAD initiative. Bertani brought his extensive experience with orchestrating educational collaborations at various levels and offered proactive insight into the political and social challenges of coordination and communication that are often apparent only in retrospect.

Collaborating across School Levels in CCPS

CCPS had been striving to make an aligned process for elementary, middle, and high schools so that each school level held the overarching goal of ensuring that every student was ready for the next level. The Carnegie Foundation's Improvement Summit in 2020 and 2021 played important roles in providing opportunities for CCPS staff to see improvement in action. In 2020, ten people including a mix of school- and central-office leaders and teacher leaders attended the Summit; that number doubled in 2021 with 18 attendees, enabled with support from Carnegie partially sponsoring the fees and the Summit being offered in a virtual format. Participation in the Summits enabled CCPS to build capacity, but perhaps most important, the Summit and follow-on activities facilitated the integration of diverse stakeholders' perspectives and ideas. Outcomes included a clearer focus on the adaptation of multi-tiered systems of support (MTSS) and also the creation of an ad hoc "think tank" run by school improvement specialist LaShel Bradley to support the cultivation of an improvement mindset and a problem-solving, user-centered focus on school improvement among a growing "coalition of the willing." The members of the think tank included a school-level instructional designer, two principals, and two assistant principals, as well as central-office content specialists and coordinators from the Title I office, research and evaluation office, MTSS office, and school improvement office. The "think tank" continued learning together by identifying sessions from the Summit for reflection, and then reflecting on the Summit in each monthly meeting while directly applying the learning to current practice between monthly meetings.

An example of this is Principal Kristin Saady who first came to the improvement work CCPS was doing when she was an associate principal at a school receiving mandated support from the Department of School Improvement due to not meeting state benchmarks. In March 2020, when the Summit pivoted to being virtual due to the pandemic, Saady, along with the district's school improvement team and other school-based leaders, attended the Summit virtually. Saady's team took this as an opportunity to "learn by doing," implementing improvement science as they were learning to carry improvement forward.

In 2021, when she became principal at her own school, she decided that improvement science was going to be the approach she and her team would use for addressing declining reading performance. In working with her reading team, they were met with resistance from teachers when they sought to test out a new reading program that was more aligned with current research in literacy development. Saady and her team took the dilemma to a "think tank" meeting, which helped them realize that they had neglected to involve those closest to the work in the construction and the learning of the work. Saady and her team revised the next two professional learning community (PLC) meeting agendas to provide time for deeper learning and engagement. Teachers responded surprisingly positively, agreeing to try it in their classrooms. Instead of planning weeks in advance, teachers started really looking at what was happening in the classrooms and making adjustments based on current circumstances. When teachers began to see student progress after just a short two months, they wanted to learn more. Saady noted, "I am so proud of the improvement work being done at [the school she led]! Our teachers are invested in the work and students are growing in their reading! Win-win for all!"

At the 2022 annual summer gathering of school leadership, the CCPS Leadership Academy, the "think tank" was announced as a district-wide opportunity to explore learning and test out ideas that are not fully formed with support from colleagues, an indication of its institutionalization in terms of the Developmental Progressions dimension of LEA professional learning. These activities led to a wholesale reappraisal of the School Improvement and Innovation Planning process, ranging from school leadership engaging in geographical feeder-pattern meetings to analyze systemic problems to aligning initiatives put into place to meet common challenges.

Collaboration in Teaching and Learning at UVA

We had learned from the first cohort that the "improvement sandwich" did not assemble itself. As we noted earlier, our initial theory of action held that if UVA worked to support central-office staff while also preparing aspiring leaders, these efforts would be adequate to support and motivate school leadership to approach school improvement planning and practice differently. We realized that the system of support and incentives had to be more explicitly articulated to bring school leadership along on the improvement journey. Part of this entailed the activities CCPS undertook described above that related to the school improvement planning process. On the UVA side, promoting more explicit articulation of connections entailed shifting from parallel teaching to a collaborative journey in which the CCPS Director of School Improvement (White) and other central-office leaders partnered with university professors to co-create and instruct the field-based course sequence. Before the beginning of a particular course, UVA and CCPS co-instructors met weekly to ensure the content was presented as a blend of theory and practice. Weekly meetings of UVA faculty with CCPS co-instructors continued throughout the semester, enabling formative iterations on course design, taking into consideration the needs of the graduate students and the evolving demands of their plans as they enacted these in particular schools and across the district.

The partnership also afforded a unique coaching model throughout each semester. As the semester launched, graduate students in LCI, LEAD I, and LEAD II reviewed the most current data available on school performance and then held initial meetings with their school leadership to identify an equity-grounded problem of practice, identify a team, and develop a proposal aligned both with the needs and goals of the school and the district and with the school leadership competencies targeted for a particular course. This provided organic conversations about continuous improvement and leadership practices, as well as offered opportunities for students in the program to participate in their school's improvement efforts as they enacted their improvement initiatives. The design of each of the field-based courses included at least three key moments during the semester when students consulted one-to-one with instructors, receiving coaching around their improvement initiatives. This close connection proved to be another key feature of the program's signature pedagogy, a moment at which the intellectual, technical, and moral aspects of learning came together as instructors and students worked to make explicit the tacit learning students gained through the experience of enacting their improvement initiatives. In a more instrumental way, these coaching conversations also ensured the alignment of course objectives with school and district goals throughout the semester.

Results: Organizational Practice and Partnership

By the end of 2021, the confluence of improvement practices within the district, coupled with the leadership program emphasis on direct connections with equity-oriented professional practice, shifted the partnership towards "institutionalizing and sustaining the work" in the language of iLEAD's Developmental Progressions (Gomez et al., 2020). Our first two cohorts of 37 aspiring and emerging leaders carried out over 60 ninety-day cycles of improvement initiatives in areas ranging from addressing racial disparities in discipline to modeling identification and differentiation strategies for English learners who are also students with disabilities. The third cohort of 20 aspiring leaders launched in spring 2022; these leadership students have already begun working on similar initiatives throughout the district. Nine out of fourteen of the members of the initial cohort are currently assistant principals (APs), principals, or central-office leaders in the system; 14 of 16 in the second cohort are currently deans, APs, principals, or central-office leaders. These early-career leaders are spearheading a renovated School Improvement and Innovation Planning process that integrates iterative cycles of improvement into the everyday work of learning and teaching and proactively addresses disproportionate discipline through multi-tiered systems of support. All of Chesterfield's 65 schools are now working with this process, too. In terms of early indicators of student outcomes related to the partnership's original improvement aim, 2021 saw the most racially diverse class accepted to CCPS selective magnet schools and programs. While this does not provide direct evidence of the impact of continuous improvement initiatives within the district, these initiatives are among the primary efforts in the district to provide all students with equitable opportunities for learning and growth.

Through this partnership, we have trained over 500 CCPS staff members at all levels from the deputy superintendent to classroom teachers to understand and apply the principles and tools of improvement science woven into the school improvement planning process. Because of this partnership and the research behind this work, Chesterfield shifted the SIIP process to focus on problem identification and understanding before the implementation of strategies. School leaders and teachers currently draw on both formative as well as summative measurements of student outcomes as well as active monitoring not only of the outcomes of efforts to improve student learning but also the processes of implementing change in instructional and organizational approaches to ensure that we are addressing barriers associated with implementation and continuously learning to improve along the way.

Conclusions and Lessons Learned

The previous sections have highlighted the ways that our partnership has evolved from our original vision of an "improvement sandwich" into a braid with multiple overlapping strands. In this section, we synthesize key findings that offer the greatest insight into the dimensions of the Developmental Progressions that we found to be most consequential to our efforts to form a braid. Professional learning features as a throughline across the highlights that follow, offering a foundation for curricular and programmatic improvement that, in turn, led to the elaboration of boundary infrastructure within each organization and across the partnership. We treat the two organizations in turn followed by a concluding spotlight on the partnership.

CCPS LESSONS LEARNED

From Professional Development to Intrapreneurial Collective Learning

Among the lessons we learned from our initial efforts to build an "improvement sandwich" through multi-tiered support for professional learning was the importance of cultivating a cadre of middle leaders who can serve as boundary spanners between school leadership teams and senior district leadership. These *intrapreneurs*, or in-house entrepreneurs (Pinchot, 1985), can be extraordinarily agile and adaptive in crafting coherence between the day-to-day work of school leaders and the broader vision that a district may hold of continuous improvement and vice versa. The nominal roles these leaders might hold include such titles as principal supervisors, curriculum directors, improvement leads, accountability leads, research and evaluation leads, intervention specialists, and student support central-office leaders. When given the space, skills, and resources, these middle leaders in the central office develop the capacity to interact on equal terms with both school-level teams and executive leadership. Such leaders are uniquely positioned because they connect with teachers and school leaders and have the regular ear of upper leadership. Such middle leaders are crucial to bridging the "street level" work of improvement in school improvement and leadership teams with policy-level decisions of senior management. Depending on the roles they occupy, these middle leaders inevitably have varying orientations to improvement work, from the technical (e.g., instructional coach) to a policy focus (e.g., curriculum director). However, our experience shows us that diverse orientations to the work are a benefit, not a drawback, offering multiple channels for supporting improvement in schools.

Enhancing the agency of middle leaders was one aspect of a broader recognition that improvement work entailed becoming different kinds of learners—co-learners. Conventional policy approaches to accountability place the onus on the district to move in when schools fail to meet a state or federal benchmark of student achievement or performance. In CCPS, the initial impetus for schools to engage with the central-office improvement team was a failure to meet benchmarks; however, the improvement team used this to reset the conventional relationship by becoming co-learners and co-creators of the learning necessary to make change within schools that fell under state scrutiny. The improvement team worked with school leaders to create systems that offered essential time and support to probe the root causes of the issues that they were experiencing, a required step in the accountability process; use robust data systems to identify parts of the system that needed to change; and then put in place processes to make changes and monitor those changes over time. In the accountability-driven past, this would have been done as an exercise in compliance—a box to check for the next time state officials came to visit. The improvement-focused present shifts the emphasis from compliance to a focus on developing internal capacity and corresponding systems, including technical as well as social systems, for enabling professionals in schools to take agency in enacting improvement. Accountability requirements can still be met but with a broader sense of engagement and co-construction of improvement from the whole school community.

Collective learning is about resetting the relationship between a central office and schools through the development of adaptive systems within and across levels (Honig, 2012). On the technical side, a robust data infrastructure that enables school-level professionals to access the data they need in an accessible format is essential to provide those in schools with the information they need to take action and learn from the outcomes of that action. However, most important are the social systems that empower those in schools to make explicit what they are learning while creating the space for pivots that do not risk punishment as a result of that learning. With robust technical and social systems, the district office can serve as a support while the ownership of change is securely held in schools.

UVA LESSONS LEARNED

A&S Faculty Collective Learning

Learning while carrying change forward was also central to developing the capacities of UVA's A&S Program Area to integrate improvement science effectively as a core element of its program redesign. The coherence of the revised UVA M.Ed. program in A&S hinged on the collective learning of the program faculty around how to develop the new program. This required moving from a model in which particular faculty "owned" specific courses to one in which faculty took the lead on designing, updating, and ensuring the integrity of specific courses while sharing responsibility for the connection of the course to the overall program with other program faculty. Faculty met weekly for 90 minutes to discuss programmatic business in a faculty PLC, with the program coordinator (initially Tucker and then Dexter followed by Beavers) taking responsibility for setting an agenda in advance and facilitating discussion. These conversations were where we learned collectively how to bring together the intellectual, technical, and moral aspects of our separate curricula into a coherent and cohesive program with a signature pedagogy that centered on translating theory into practice and reflecting practice back into theory through field-based learning.

The regular PLC meetings were concerned with all program business, including matters concerning the Ed.D. program and preparing for accreditation visits. Among the gamut of topics, the redesign and running of the M.Ed. program was always the most prominent and took up the greatest amount of time. Initial emphasis went towards deconstructing existing courses and determining the overarching course sequence; subsequently, attention turned to course revisions and approvals in alignment with the anchoring principles of equity, adult development, continuous improvement, and leadership discussed earlier. Recent focus has turned to integrating central-office leaders from the Chesterfield partnership and other partnerships as co-instructors, as well as taking time to go through each of the program anchors separately to align the learning activities and assignments related to that program dimension across courses.

PARTNERSHIP LESSONS LEARNED: CO-DEVELOPMENT OF LEADERSHIP PEDAGOGIES

The formalization of the leadership preparation partnership of CCPS with UVA has happened through the elaboration of boundary infrastructure and not through the contractual instruments that typically constitute formalization, such as the drafting of a memorandum of agreement. The boundary infrastructure consists of well-developed procedures for collaboratively conducting the initial assessment of program applicants, the co-instructor arrangements between UVA faculty and CCPS central-office leadership, the articulation of protocols for graduate students' connections with their school leadership, the development of workshops and other professional learning opportunities for school leadership teams, and the creation of scaffolded opportunities for exploring system improvement for program interns taking on the role of Dean of Students during their paid internship year.

One other area of "formalization" is crucial to highlight and that is the co-development of approaches to leadership learning that span the initial preparation program itself and include the preparation of existing school and central-office leadership to take on the mantle of "improvers." As we noted at the start of our chapter, a signature pedagogy consists of the intellectual "know what," the technical "know how," and the moral "know why." The development of a signature pedagogy for the preparation program has been an explicit focus of our efforts and of our documentation of those efforts throughout this chapter. The process of elaborating that signature pedagogy has raised our awareness about the approach to professional and organizational learning that has developed around the reorientation of the school improvement planning process from an emphasis on compliance to a focus on co-construction. Such structured attention to learning as integral to ongoing work cannot be considered a "signature pedagogy" in Shulman's (2005) terms because of its organizational emphasis. Nonetheless, what might be called a "school improvement pedagogy" shares similar characteristics in its attention to the three defining elements of a signature pedagogy—the intellectual "know what" of school leadership and organizational change, the technical "know how" of improvement science, and the moral "know why" of a grounding in concerns around equity and social justice. This school improvement pedagogy is formalized through structures such as the planning document itself as well as the accompanying opportunities for collective and individual learning through workshops and coaching. It includes formal as well as informal opportunities for learning—the annual district-wide Leadership Academy and the voluntary "think tank" of those interested in digging deeper. These structures and opportunities are what enable leaders and teachers throughout Chesterfield to embrace the know what, know how, and know why of equity-oriented improvement. The marriage of these three elements is the fundamental fiber of the braid for both the preparation program as well as the district improvement work.

ESSENTIAL LESSONS OF PARTNERSHIP WORK

The robust, collective learning that has occurred at the middle levels of both organizations demonstrates the power and agency that middle leaders brought to the creation of boundary infrastructure that strengthened the partnership while meeting the separate needs of each of the partners. The second Chesterfield cohort graduated in 2021, and in 2022, we launched the third cohort of aspiring leaders from Chesterfield. Central-office staff in Chesterfield continue to work closely with UVA faculty on the co-instruction of field-based courses, and the spread of improvement science in relation to school improvement planning has clearly taken hold in Chesterfield. The 2022 Leadership Academy, drawing together leadership teams from all of Chesterfield's 65 schools, emphasized the integration of improvement science principles and tools and iterative experimentation with school strategic planning processes. In addition, several members of the first and second Chesterfield cohorts are now supporting the improvement initiatives of students in the third cohort, providing the level of sustained and systemic learning that we had initially envisioned in describing the "improvement sandwich." For its part, the UVA A&S Program Area has forged similar preparation partnerships with four other school districts around Virginia. The initial model appears robust and resilient.

The early stage of our partnership was defined by an increasingly intensive alignment of interests, what Gulati et al. (2012) characterize as cooperation. In this initial phase, middle-level leaders worked within their own organizations to integrate the work of continuous improvement, taking advantage of the convening opportunities offered by the iLEAD initiative to learn together and contribute to the development of each partner's understanding of the continuous improvement process. The more recent phase, from 2019 to 2022, provides evidence of the enactment of those shared interests through mutually developed boundary infrastructures (Bowker & Star, 1999) that enabled deeper levels of coordination and, ultimately, collaboration based on increasingly explicit and mutually shared outcomes for aspiring and existing leaders in relation to enacting continuous improvement both through coursework in the program and school improvement work throughout the district. The braid that we use to characterize the partnership requires building relationships, ongoing commitment, and shared goals. These essential dimensions of partnership work enable the development of boundary infrastructure capable of sustaining intensive and generative collaborative exchange.

Questions for Discussion

1. The Chesterfield County Public Schools/University of Virginia partnership clearly leveraged participation in a national network, iLEAD, to bring about significant changes in partnership and partner outcomes. Would such organizational outcomes/changes likely be achievable for districts *not* involved in such networks, or is such network participation essential for partners if they are to use improvement science "as a set of principles and methods for evolving from older to newer modes of collaborating around equity challenges"? Explain your perspective on this.
2. The authors make a prominent distinction between "coordinated, parallel effort to embed improvement science in leadership development and school improvement" vs. a "braided, more coherent approach that required new individual and organizational capacities." What evidence do you see that such a distinction holds up in the narrative, and how are we meant to understand what "braided" means in this case?
3. The authors of this case emphasize the importance of how "signature pedagogies" were instrumental to learning and change for the university and the district. What do they appear to mean by this term, and why do they attach so much importance to it?

References

Barakat, M., Reames, E., & Kensler, L. A. W. (2019). Leadership preparation programs: Preparing culturally competent educational leaders. *Journal of Research on Leadership Education*, *14*(3), 212–235. https://doi.org/10.1177/1942775118759070

Barnett, B. G., Hall, G. E., Berg, J. H., & Camarena, M. M. (2010). A typology of partnerships for promoting innovation. *Journal of School Leadership*, *20*(1), 10–36. https://doi.org/10.1177/105268469900900602

Black, W. R., & Murtadha, K. (2007). Toward a signature pedagogy in educational leadership preparation and program assessment. *Journal of Research on Leadership Education*, *2*(1), 1–29. https://doi.org/10.1177/194277510700200101

Bowker, G. C., & Star, S. L. (1999). *Sorting things out: Classification and its consequences*. The MIT Press.

Bryk, A. S. (2020). *Improvement in action: Advancing quality in America's schools*. Harvard Education Press.

Bryk, A. S., Gomez, L. M., Grunow, A., & LeMahieu, P. G. (2015). *Learning to improve: How America's schools can get better at getting better*. Harvard Education Press.

Byrne-Jimenez, M., & Orr, M. T. (2013). Evaluating social justice leadership preparation. In L. Tillman & J. J. Scherich (Eds.), *Handbook of research on educational leadership for equity and diversity* (pp. 688–720). Routledge.

Chesterfield County Public Schools. (2017). *2017 equity report*. https://mychesterfieldschools.com/download/195/school-board/14749/equity-report-2017.pdf

Chesterfield County Public Schools. (2019). *Imagine tomorrow: Creating a better tomorrow*. https://mychesterfieldschools.com/download/166/academics/16468/strategicplan_it_04082019.pdf

Code of Virginia, Administrative Code. § 8VAC20-543-570. *State board of education-regulations governing the review and approval of education programs in Virginia-competencies for endorsement areas-administration and supervision pre K-12*. https://law.lis.virginia.gov/admincode/title8/agency20/chapter543/section570/

Cosner, S. (2019). What makes a leadership preparation program exemplary? *Journal of Research on Leadership Education*, *14*(1), 98–115. https://doi.org/10.1177/1942775118819661

Cosner, S. (2020). A deeper look into next generation active learning designs for educational leader preparation. *Journal of Research on Leadership Education*, *15*(3), 167–172. https://doi.org/10.1177/1942775120936301

Cosner, S., De Voto, C., & Rah'man, A. (2018). Drawing in the school context as a learning resource in school leader development: Application-oriented projects in active learning designs. *Journal of Research on Leadership Education*, *13*(3), 238–255. https://doi.org/10.1177/1942775118763872

Cunningham, K. M. W., Vangronigen, B. A., Tucker, P. D., & Young, M. D. (2019). Using powerful learning experiences to prepare school leaders. *Journal of Research on Leadership Education*, *14*(1), 74–97. https://doi.org/10.1177/1942775118819672

Darling-Hammond, L., Wechsler, M. E., Levin, S., Leung-Gagné, M., & Tozer, S. (2022). *Developing effective principals: What kind of learning matters?* Learning Policy Institute. https://doi.org/10.54300/641.201

Darling-Hammond, L., Wei, R. C., Andree, A., Richardson, N., & Orphanos, S. (2009). *Professional learning in the learning profession: A status report on teacher development in the United States and abroad*. National Staff Development Council. https://learningforward.org/docs/default-source/pdf/nsdcstudy2009.pdf

Data Quality Campaign. (2017). *From hammer to flashlight: A decade of data in education.* https://dataqualitycampaign.org/resource/from-hammer-to-flashlight-a-decade-of-data-in-education/

Dexter, S., Clement, D., Moraguez, D., & Watson, G. S. (2020). (Inter)active learning tools and pedagogical strategies in educational leadership preparation. *Journal of Research on Leadership Education, 15*(3), 173–191. https://doi.org/10.1177/1942775120936299

Eddy-Spicer, D. H., Anderson, E., & Perrone, F. (2017). Neither urban core nor rural fringe: "In-between" districts and the shifting landscape of school performance in the United States. In C. V. Meyers & M. Darwin (Eds.), *Enduring myths that inhibit school turnaround* (pp. 49–69). Information Age Publishing.

Gomez, L. M., Biag, M., & Imig, D. G. (2020). Learning at the boundaries: Reconsidering university-district partnerships for educational change. In N. S. Nasir, C. D. Lee, R. Pea, & M. McKinney de Royston (Eds.), *Handbook of the cultural foundations of learning* (pp. 365–384). Routledge.

Grunow, A., Hough, H., Park, S., Willis, J., & Krausen, K. (2018). *Towards a common vision of continuous improvement for California.* Stanford University Policy Analysis for California Education (PACE). https://www.edpolicyinca.org/publications/towards-common-vision-continuous-improvement-california

Gulati, R., Wohlgezogen, F., & Zhelyazkov, P. (2012). The two facets of collaboration: Cooperation and coordination in strategic alliances. *The Academy of Management Annals, 6*(1), 531–583. https://doi.org/10.1080/19416520.2012.691646

Honig, M. I. (2012). District central office leadership as teaching: How central office administrators support principals' development as instructional leaders. *Educational Administration Quarterly, 48*(4), 733–774. https://doi.org/10.1177/0013161x12443258

Langley, G. J., Moen, R. D., Nolan, K. M., Nolan, T. W., Norman, C. L., & Provost, L. P. (2014). *The improvement guide: A practical approach to enhancing organizational performance* (3rd ed.). Jossey-Bass.

Leithwood, K. (2017). The Ontario leadership framework: Successful school leadership practices and personal leadership resources. In K. Leithwood, J. Sun, & K. Pollock (Eds.), *How school leaders contribute to student success: The four paths framework* (pp. 31–43). Springer International Publishing.

McKenzie, K. B., Christman, D. E., Hernandez, F., Fierro, E., Capper, C. A., Dantley, M., González, M. L., Cambron-McCabe, N., & Scheurich, J. J. (2007). From the field: A proposal for educating leaders for social justice. *Educational Administration Quarterly, 44*(1), 111–138. https://doi.org/10.1177/0013161X07309470

Ni, Y., Hollingworth, L., Rorrer, A., & Pounder, D. (2016). The evaluation of educational leadership preparation programs. In M. D. Young & G. M. Crow (Eds.), *Handbook of research on the education of school leaders* (pp. 173–201). Routledge.

NPBEA. (2018). *National educational leadership preparation (NELP) program standards - Building level.* http://www.npbea.org.

Orr, M. T. (2020). Reflections on active learning in leadership development. *Journal of Research on Leadership Education, 15*(3), 227–234. https://doi.org/10.1177/1942775120936305

Orr, M. T., & Barber, M. E. (2006). Collaborative leadership preparation: A comparative study of partnership and conventional programs and practices. *Journal of School Leadership, 16*(6), 709–739. https://doi.org/10.1177/105268460601600603

Park, S., & Takahashi, S. (2013). *90-Day cycle handbook.* Carnegie Foundation for the Advancement of Teaching. https://www.carnegiefoundation.org/resources/publications/90-day-cycle-handbook/

Perkins, D. N. (2009). *Making learning whole: How seven principles of teaching can transform education.* Jossey-Bass.

Pinchot, G., III. (1985). *Intrapreneuring: Why you don't have to leave the corporation to become an entrepreneur.* Harper & Row.

Shulman, L. S. (2005). Signature pedagogies in the professions. *Daedalus, 134*(3), 52–59. https://doi.org/10.2307/20027998

Stone-Johnson, C., & Hayes, S. (2021). Using improvement science to (re)design leadership preparation: Exploring curriculum change across five university programs. *Journal of Research on Leadership Education, 16*(4), 339–359. http://doi.org/10.1177/1942775120933935

Tozer, S., & Walker, L. (2021). *Reducing chronic absence: Making equity strategies specific, adaptive, and evidence-based.* The Center for Urban Education Leadership (CUEL). https://urbanedleadership.org/

Young, M. D., & Eddy-Spicer, D. H. (2019). Bridging, brokering, bricolage: Building exemplary leadership programs from the inside out. *Journal of Research on Leadership Education, 14*(1), 3–10. https://doi.org/10.1177/1942775118820129

CHAPTER 2

A University–School District Collaboration to Improve Equity- and Inquiry-Driven School Leadership

FORDHAM UNIVERSITY AND BRONX SCHOOL DISTRICTS 9 AND 11

Margaret Terry Orr, Kris DeFilippis, Meisha Porter, and Elizabeth Leisy Stosich

This chapter describes how one university and its district partners reformed their approaches to leadership preparation and development by jointly learning about improvement science and its potential to promote continuous school improvement. Working together, the partnership supported Fordham University's redesign of its doctoral program, while the Bronx district partners launched a series of leadership development and school improvement approaches, some with university faculty involvement, leading to improved leadership capacity, adoption of improvement science principles as core practices, and progress on persistent problems of practice.

Context

This collaboration takes place in the Bronx in New York City—between two Bronx community school districts (CSDs) and Fordham University, made possible by the Carnegie Foundation for Advancement of Teaching (CFAT) new Improvement Leadership Education and Development (iLEAD) initiative. The Bronx is one of five NYC boroughs and is its poorest and most densely populated. As figure 2.1 shows, the Bronx is in the northern part of New York City, and Fordham's main campus is centrally located there. Six large K–8 public school districts and two high school districts serve the Bronx.

The Fordham–Bronx partnership began with Fordham University and two Bronx districts (9 and 11), which combined served 67,989 students and 112 schools. Both

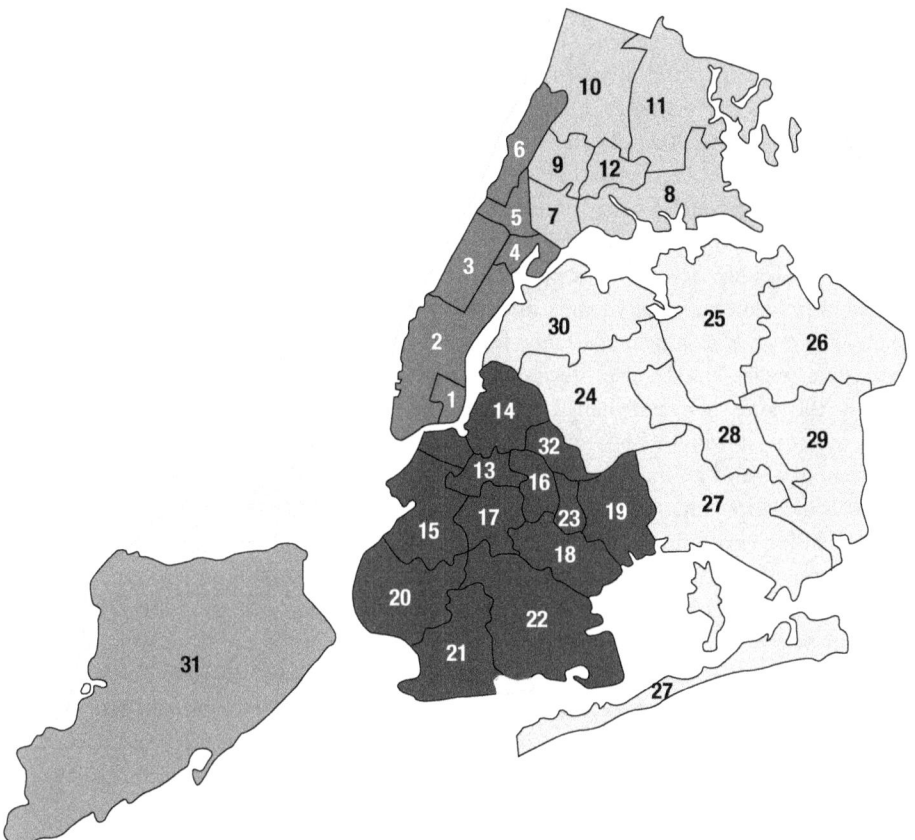

Figure 2.1 NYC school districts by borough. *Note:* The Bronx consists of districts 7–12.

districts had several schools that had been identified as under-performing and under state review. These districts were led by Black/Latina women who became superintendents following a series of prior teaching and leadership roles. Both were fairly new to their role at the time the collaboration was launched but had deep ties to their districts and communities.

These districts serve primarily Hispanic and Black students (97% and 81% respectively) who are also primarily economically disadvantaged (79% and 93% respectively). They struggled with teacher turnover (17%), particularly among novice teachers (22%), and had persistently low student achievement (e.g., from 2015 to 2019, the percentage of students scoring at grade level in math remained low, increasing slightly from 19% to 29% in CSD #9 and from 25% to 33% in CSD #11).

This district context and its leadership shifted several times early in and throughout the partnership, which presented both challenges and opportunities for growing the partnership. During AY 2017–18, then NYC Chancellor Carranza reorganized district governance, creating borough-based superintendencies to support districts. The Bronx K–8 and high school districts were consolidated under the Bronx Borough office, with Meisha Porter, then CSD #11 superintendent, selected as the borough's first executive superintendent. Cris Vaughan, a CSD #11 principal replaced her as the CSD #11 superintendent. In AY 2019–20, our CSD #9 partner superintendent, Leticia Rodriquez retired and was replaced by Harry Sherman, a former CSD #11 principal. In spring 2021, Porter became interim chancellor for the entire New York City school system. Dr. Erika Tobia, former CSD #10 superintendent, replaced her as the borough's executive superintendent.

At the time the collaboration was formed in the fall of 2017, the two districts had separate leadership development or school improvement initiatives: focusing on instructional improvement, inquiry teams, and equity training. Both districts had access to Fordham University's technical assistance for individual schools or teacher training, so they had prior, service-based and professional relationships with one or more Fordham faculty.

At the same time, Fordham University was undergoing its own educational leadership renewal. Fordham University has three campuses—Bronx, Lincoln Center, and Westchester—and a Graduate School of Education (GSE) with both public and faith-based leadership preparation master and doctoral programs. Many of these programs had declining enrollments in recent years. In 2017, the then new dean, Virginia Roach, was charged with increasing these enrollments. To do so, she developed a contract for an online EdD program, took steps to rethink its doctoral program approach for both in-person and online based on its Carnegie Project for the Education Doctorate (CPED) affiliation, and recruited two new faculty. One was Margaret Terry Orr, who brought over 30 years of local and national research and development experience in leadership preparation and partnerships (Darling-Hammond et al., 2010; Orphanos & Orr, 2014; Orr, 2012; Orr & Pounder, 2010). The other was Elizabeth Stosich, who had recently published research on instructional coherence (Forman et al., 2017). Dean Roach tasked these two faculty, and a third, Tiedan Huang (a fairly new assistant professor with quantitative expertise), with revamping the EdD program to be ready for the in-person and online program launch in 2018. A number of senior faculty had recently retired, and the new faculty members were open to significant programmatic change.

A fortuitous invitation in the fall of 2017 from the Carnegie Foundation for Advancement of Teaching (CFAT) to join its new Improvement Leadership Education and Development (iLEAD) initiative enabled Fordham faculty to work with local districts on developing new and experienced leaders for continuous educational improvement. The periodic convenings since the fall of 2017 enabled the partners to tackle their shared problem of practice, applying the principles of improvement science and working iteratively on testing new solutions. The iLEAD developmental progressions framed expectations for the shared work. When reflecting on why she decided to engage in the partnership when she had been CSD #11 superintendent, Meisha Porter pointed to her relationship with one Fordham clinical faculty member who recruited her to this partnership and her discovery that leading her district was so complex. She was open to engaging with different types of partnerships to see how the iLEAD approach might benefit her efforts to improve schools. What stood out for her from the beginning in both the iLEAD initiative and Fordham's redesigned EdD program was the orientation to seeing problems differently and as solvable. While she believed that it was possible to improve performance, she found that so many people saw this sad situation as just the nature of the Bronx, and thus she would never be able "to move the needle." Still, while recognizing the significant poverty of the Bronx as destabilizing, she strongly believed that the conditions and outcomes for students could change by just seeing the problems differently and thereby finding new solutions.

The collaboration faced several organizational challenges: competing priorities, insufficient resources, and leadership turnover, as are typical in developing and sustaining district-university partnerships (Orr et al., 2010). The CSD #9 superintendent bowed out after the first year, despite active and thoughtful participation, because of district demands and then retirement. Porter was promoted twice, each time causing shifts in relationship building at the borough and district levels.

On the Fordham side, there was less turnover, but significant role change. Orr was tenured after the third year (spring 2020), promoted to full, and became division chair, while remaining the EdD program director. By the fourth year (2020–21), Stosich, an assistant professor, became associate chair and master's program director. A new assistant professor, Elizabeth Gil, was hired in the initiative's fourth year, adding a focus on family and community engagement and expertise in practitioner research. Moreover, Fordham's leadership division continued to struggle with enrollments while its programs were being redesigned, creating significant pressure for recruitment and program marketing. Then, in the spring of 2020, Dean Roach resigned and was replaced with an interim dean, followed by a new dean the following year.

A related challenge was relationship building, both among the Fordham faculty and with the Bronx partners. At the launch of this work, the Fordham faculty were new to each other, lacking norms and shared experience in program design and partnership work, while facing their individual pressure to achieve tenure and promotion (including conducting and publishing research and developing and teaching new courses). Similarly, the two superintendents, while friends, did not have an existing relationship with the Fordham faculty and were under intense accountability pressure to improve student learning in their schools. Even with these competing pressures and personal demands, all five core partnership members quickly adopted an openness and respect for each other and a willingness to explore the potential of improvement science for leaders to learn for school improvement. Despite respective shifting leadership and faculty context, the Fordham–Bronx districts made considerable headway in addressing their shared problem of practice and solution testing over time. In reflecting back on why this occurred, we concluded it was because we approached our work together as co-inquirers around a shared problem of practice, rather than an expectation of resource exchange (such as recruiting students for a program or charging for particular services). We also shared a respect for learning from each other and exploring what opportunities such shared effort could bring.

The periodic iLEAD convenings and guidance of the iLEAD developmental progressions created time, space, and focus for the partnership work. When Fordham faculty and Bronx superintendents tried to meet together locally they were often disrupted by competing district or university demands. In contrast, when attending iLEAD convenings, they were more able to actively engage in the shared work. The informal time together traveling, eating, and talking greatly strengthened the partnership members' relationships, enabling informality and openness for input, criticism, and feedback. Further, the partners' shared work created opportunities for Fordham faculty and Bronx superintendents to be both learners and designers about how improvement science principles could be used by leaders in pursuing continuous school improvement. This shared work was stretched by using the iLEAD developmental progressions as benchmarks with which to question our objectives and measure our progress within our institutions and our partnership.

Beginning in the spring of 2020, the unfolding COVID pandemic disrupted the partnership work. This created intense challenges for school and district leaders to improve teaching and learning in their schools and threatened the continuation of new program efforts. As they reorganized their operations online, so did the university and the iLEAD conveners. In some ways, switching to an online forum for meetings, coursework, and professional development enabled us to convene more easily and make our work more transparent. The use of tools like Jamboard and Google docs allowed NICs and student groups to collaborate on their learning and create records of their work. The uncertainty and challenges of continuing school under these pandemic conditions strained everyone and shifted the problem foci to pandemic-related issues (such as attendance, engagement, and resources to support online learning). The partnership structures, NICs, and graduate programs enabled speedy knowledge sharing and problem-solving.

Problem

In 2017, Bronx public school students had made little progress in their academic performance despite districts' efforts to improve curriculum, teaching, organizational structure, and state expectations. Racial/ethnic disparities in student learning were worsening, complicating improvement efforts and pushing districts to consider new approaches. Fordham's leadership preparation programs had been disconnected from these field conditions and solutions. Few models existed about how school and district leaders and their teachers should and could work in new ways, and even fewer models were available to inform how to develop this capacity.

The problem of practice that Fordham and iLEAD partner districts defined together was that school and district leaders varied widely in their capacity to foster continuous school improvement that serves all children well. On the university side, faculty recognized that graduates varied widely in how well they were prepared for leading continuous school improvement, based on the nature of their dissertation research (little of which addressed this priority) and school leader assessment results[1] (with doctoral students scoring more poorly on items related to this leadership area in contrast to other leadership practices). Much of the district leaders' evidence came from their work with school leaders and the lack of significant performance improvement progress within and among schools. Porter believed that her district and others were not solving its problems effectively and that the solutions lay in addressing what she called the "adult moves and behaviors." This means learning to identify a problem, break down the root causes, and uncover the aspects of the system that "actually

---

[1] We developed an Improvement Leadership Practices survey to measure problem solving practices.

perpetuates the problem." As the Bronx executive superintendent, she addressed racial/ethnic disproportionality in discipline and special education. In training all school and district leaders in equity principles, she saw that they were unprepared for the leadership work to reduce inequities and strengthen continuous improvement.

With the first iLEAD convening of 11 district-university partners in 2017, Fordham faculty and partner districts' representatives[2] had an opportunity to begin clarifying the problem and analyzing the system that produced it. We integrated the causes and factors contributing to leaders' varied capacity to foster continuous school improvement. We brainstormed possible factors and then organized them thematically as illustrated in the fishbone diagram in figure 2.2.

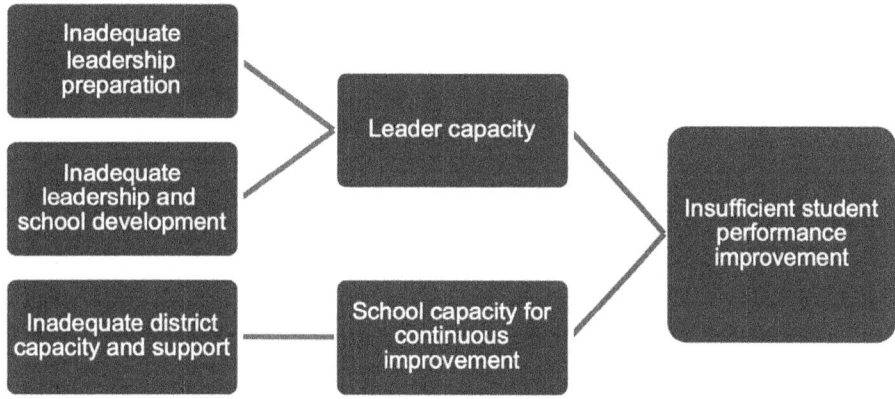

Figure 2.2 System that contributes to the problem.

We split the school leader capacity problem into two contributing factors. Leaders appeared to have insufficient capacity to plan for and support their schools in engaging in collective improvement work for stubborn student learning gaps. Second, school leaders and staff appeared to have insufficient ability to engage in continuous improvement work—particularly to unpack student learning problems, pinpoint contributing factors, and try out solutions collaboratively. Together we concluded that there were three insufficient conditions that contributed to these three primary factors—(1) leadership preparation, (2) leadership development, and (3) district support—all of which became areas to focus our theory of action and try out new solutions.

Challenges, Solutions, and Evidence

Following the analysis of our problem, the Fordham–Bronx partners were able to frame our work succinctly as one overarching theory of action:

---

[2] Our partnership began with two suburban districts that did not sustain participation or adopt the improvement science principles.

IF we develop and improve practices in the preparation and support of school and district leaders in using improvement science for continuous school improvement,

THEN school and district leaders will be able to promote and engage others in inquiry-based continuous school improvement and improve learning for all students, particularly those most underserved.

DEVELOPMENT

Pursuing our theory of action represented two significant design challenges for Fordham University's leadership faculty and our partner district superintendents: how best to develop leaders' capacity to promote continuous school improvement and what skills and practices they would need to develop and use to be effective. On the university side, the challenge was how to identify what is essential for leaders to learn and then how to organize this learning into a sequence of courses and learning experiences that would culminate in a doctoral degree. On the district side, the primary challenges were similar, identifying what leaders need to know and be able to do and how to enable them to learn and use continuous school improvement strategies. However, unlike the university faculty, districts lacked the resources to design and lead such leadership development. They also lacked the time and capacity to try out new approaches on a large scale, while simultaneously implementing other system-wide directives and reforms to promote school improvement. Moreover, unlike the university where students select the program's approach voluntarily, the district superintendents would have to convince local principals about the promise of any new approach, which was made more challenging by the lack of evidence of the success of improvement science as a school improvement approach.

We worked on the two sides of this design challenge simultaneously, testing out new approaches while comparing and contrasting what we were learning during the periodic iLEAD convenings of all the partnerships and occasional local partnership meetings. Adopting improvement science principles represented a fundamental shift in how we approached leadership work, shifting how we defined problems and solutions and the data used to understand problems and monitor improvement progress.

The iLEAD convenings provided us with opportunities to raise design considerations and challenges and learn how others approached the work, what design choices they made and why, and the consequences of their decisions. We shared our efforts with other partnerships in the iLEAD initiative, comparing our efforts with others. The iLEAD developmental progressions provided further guidance about how to advance the work, by reflecting on the next steps for each side of our partnership.

Taken together, we decided to operationalize our two secondary drivers of leadership preparation and leadership capacity building by testing out five change ideas, each of which had multiple components and varied approaches to training on improvement science and solving problems of practice. Each design questions by organizing differently around improvement science skill development, applying an equity lens,

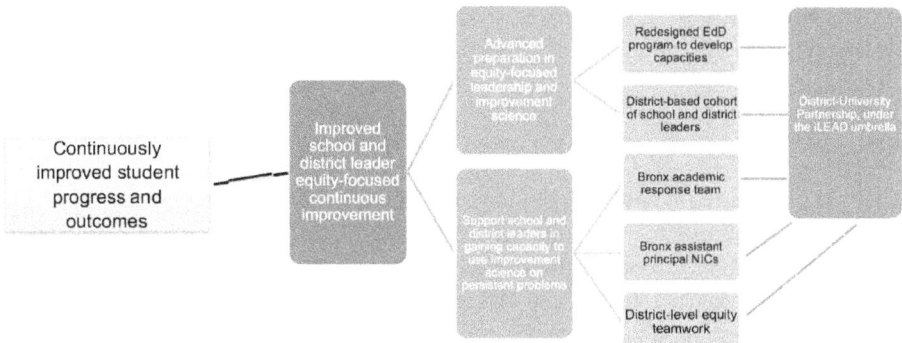

Figure 2.3 Theory of action, drivers, and change ideas.

tackling a problem of practice and trying out solutions, and learning collaboratively with others.

Figure 2.3 presents the driver diagram that situates the five change ideas in relation to the aim of improving student outcomes. Each change idea, related design consideration, component parts, and early lessons are described below. The box on the far right shows the role of the partnership in operationalizing the change ideas and supporting the work; it does not follow from the change ideas, but rather is the context for enacting them. Table 2.1 summarizes the change strategies and the number of school

Table 2.1 Number of school and district leaders in the Fordham-Bronx district iLEAD efforts

	Change Strategy	iLEAD Year 2 AY 2018–19	Year 3 AY 2019–20	Year 4 AY 2020–21	Year 5 AY 2021–22
Advanced leadership preparation	Redesigned EdD program in advanced leadership	15	27	45	50
	Bronx EdD cohort at Fordham			19	34
Leadership development	Assistant principals Networked improvement Community		5	15	
	Academic response team Initiative		6	37	
	Equity-networked Improvement community			51	53

and district leaders who participated in these efforts over time. In the sections below we describe the development of each of these change ideas in detail.

ADVANCED LEADERSHIP PREPARATION

The first testable change idea was to redesign Fordham's EdD program model to prepare advanced leaders to engage in equity-focused improvement science. We view the EdD program as a form of advanced leadership preparation to transform schools, districts, and communities and thus took steps to operationalize this driver. The second testable change idea was to extend this program model to develop a cadre of school and district leaders who would tackle key problems of practice in the Bronx (at the executive superintendent's request) and foster a leadership network using a shared inquiry approach while earning their EdD degree.

Redesigning Fordham's EdD Program

Faculty efforts to redesign Fordham's EdD program began the summer before the iLEAD launch. In 2017, newly hired faculty and the dean attended a CPED convening in Pittsburgh, joining discussions about advancing the EdD project. The dean had committed the faculty to using some design features—a 50-credit advanced degree that would be finished in three years, with two one-credit immersive summer courses—as a result of the university's contract with an online degree program vendor. The CPED model offered additional design principles: a focus on preparing scholarly practitioners; creation of a signature pedagogy; a view of inquiry as practice; incorporation of laboratories of practice to integrate theory, research, and practice; support for a dissertation in practice; and a focus on problems of practice (CPED, 2021). These principles match well with improvement science in focusing on preparing advanced leaders who could draw on research, theory, local data, and practical wisdom to understand and address complex problems of practice.

Because of Fordham's online degree program contract, the dean committed the faculty to an aggressive planning schedule: to draft a program plan for GSE approval by early winter 2017–18, to then be submitted for state approval for launching the following fall (2018). Thus, the new faculty began their first academic year in late August 2017 questioning how to operationalize these design features and principles, what core theoretical and applied leadership domains to privilege, how to shift methodological preparation content and pacing around applied research to be completed in three years, and how to structure laboratories of practice and dissertation in practice experiences. The iLEAD initiative gave us the means of exploring design questions with school district leaders, other district-university partners from around the country, and CFAT specialists. Through initial collaborative work, the faculty quickly agreed that improvement science and social justice would be the two pillars around which the program would be designed.

At iLEAD convenings, the Fordham faculty and Bronx superintendents developed a series of agreements about critical leadership skills and capacities for equity-focused continuous school improvement. They agreed that advanced leadership development, for an EdD program, should focus on both problem-solving and innovation, aim for transformation, not just improvement, and attend to all children, through an equity lens. From this work, the faculty articulated the following goal for the leadership preparation program:

> The Doctorate in Educational Leadership, Administration and Policy (ELAP) is designed to prepare transformative leaders who are equity-minded problem solvers and designers of innovative solutions, using scholarly inquiry to improve schools, districts, and communities for all children.

Next, the faculty drafted a 50-credit, three-year EdD program model, organized around four domains of theory and practice with related laboratories of practices, and a series of applied research methods and design courses supporting dissertation in practice research in solving equity-focused problems of practice.

While their redesign proposal was reviewed by other division faculty and GSE faculty, the core faculty met bi-monthly with their iLEAD district superintendents to flesh out the program further, starting with the first-year curriculum and initial laboratory of practice, to ensure that the coursework would meet our shared agreements about leadership knowledge and skills. Early feedback from the superintendents sharpened the course content and expectations for the laboratories of practice, providing a template for further course development work. The faculty also established the norm of sharing course syllabi to ensure coherence and course alignment with the program principles. They recruited other experienced school and district leaders to co-design and teach several courses, as adjunct faculty.

By the spring of iLEAD Year 1 (2018), the Fordham faculty began recruiting students for two EdD cohorts—one at Lincoln Center (focused on NYC school and district leaders) and the other in West Harrison, NY (for school and district leaders from the greater metropolitan area)—while waiting for state approval of its program redesign. Among the 15 new recruits was one of our partners—CSD #11 superintendent, Meisha Porter—who was so intrigued by the new program approach that she joined.

During Years 2 and 3 of iLEAD, the Fordham faculty continued to develop new or redesign existing courses, fleshed out guidelines for a dissertation in practice, and developed an EdD handbook that clarified the program's design and elements and provided guidance. By summer of Year 2 (2019), we successfully recruited 10 new students for our West Harrison campus and 17 students for the new online version of our program. The following year (Year 4 of iLEAD), we recruited two cohorts of 20 students each (one online) and retained almost all students from the existing four cohorts.

The first cohorts of students completed their coursework during iLEAD Year 4 and three of the 13 completed their dissertations in practice on time (with most of the rest completing within a year) despite COVID-related challenges. The initially completed dissertations exemplified the program's aim by addressing significant problems of practice (related to reading, math, and social-emotional engagement) and testing out successful solutions that actively engaged teachers in communities of practice, creating conditions for continuous school improvement. One dissertation won the CPED Dissertation of the Year Award, which served as evidence of the redesigned EdD program's success in developing leaders as scholarly practitioners, in alignment with CPED principles, and leaders of equity-focused improvement.

TEXTBOX 2.1 DISSERTATION IN PRACTICE EXAMPLE

This dissertation in practice focused on improving the reading performance of middle school African American boys. The principal worked with her staff to learn and apply culturally responsive teaching practices, using the Japanese lesson study approach and three cycles of inquiry. As a result, the teachers developed strong inquiry-on-practice skills, strengthened instruction aligned with culturally responsive teaching practices, and saw strong improvement in African American boys' engagement, participation, and work completion. The teachers continued their small group collaboration after the study was completed to share lesson plans and support instruction (Barnes, 2021).

In reviewing the first two cohorts' completed dissertations, as shown in table 2.2, we found that it was feasible for most students to enact improvements in science–framed dissertations using a strong equity focus. Typically, their change strategies combined both a focus on an aspect of teaching practice as well as new ways of working together, yielding positive student outcomes. Occasionally, district policy thwarted candidates in using improvement science over conflict of interest issues.

Through iterative implementation of the EdD program model (both online and in person), Fordham faculty found that the model as a whole was effective and met our intended goals. We refined the organization and pacing of how we engaged students in addressing their own problem of practice for their dissertation research and continuously updated readings and discussions to be even more relevant and engaging. Increasingly, we grappled with how to more strongly incorporate an equity perspective and connect foundational theory and research to better address systemic and complex problems of practice.

Creating a Bronx EdD Cohort in Equity-Focused Improvement Science

While the newly redesigned EdD program included the Fordham iLEAD partners' priorities for advanced leadership development, there had been no initial plans for districts to sponsor their own cohorts. As a private higher education institution, Fordham's tuition is expensive, compared with nearby public and less selective private institutions. None of the district partners could offer tuition support for its leaders to enroll.

At the start of iLEAD Year 2 (2018)—the first year of the new Fordham program—Porter, now the Bronx executive superintendent, was enrolled in the EdD

Table 2.2 Initial completed dissertations in practice, 2021-2022

No.	Approach	Equity-focused	Changes in practice tested	Student outcomes
1	Improvement science	Equity-focused	Changed teacher practice to use CRT to engage African American boys in reading	Improved student ELA and reading proficiency
2	Improvement science	Equity-focused	Changed math teaching and collaborative practice	Improved student math achievement
3	Evaluation of improvement science PD	Support equity focus in participant problem-solving	Changed AP practice in improving math instruction	
4	Autoethnography and multi-district comparison	Equity-focused	Reflection on system change to address implicit bias and racism	
5	Comparison of exemplary CTE programs	Considered equity as an exemplary measure	Highlights effective practices	
6	Improvement science	Equity-focused	Change school and district approach to use improvement science practices	Supported improved student outcomes
7	Improvement science	Support equity focus in participant problem-solving	Change system approach to improving math instruction, developed collaborative capacity K-12	
8	Improvement science	Support equity focus in participant problem-solving	Changed teacher practice	Improved outcomes for SWD
9	Improvement science	Engaged all teachers	Changed Pre-K-K teacher SEL practice	Improved student sense of belonging
10	Improvement science	Engaged all teachers	Changed teacher practice in SEL	
11	Improvement science	Engaged all teachers	Changed teacher practice in nature-based practice	

program. At the end of her first year in the program, she was very enthusiastic about the program's equity-focused improvement science approach and wanted a cadre of similarly prepared Bronx school and district leaders. She proposed that Fordham and the Bronx Borough Office sponsor a Fordham–Bronx EdD cohort that would prepare Bronx school and district leaders to address Bronx goals and priorities. Fordham agreed to offer a 20% tuition discount and the Borough Office agreed to pay for course books. Together, the Bronx executive superintendent (Porter) and a Fordham faculty member (Orr) organized a series of recruitment sessions, with almost 100 interested school and district leaders attending. Despite the strong interest, the tuition cost remained an obstacle for many. But by the fall, 20 Bronx school and district leaders (including one district's three-person leadership team) had enrolled. Porter and Orr began planning how to foster synergy between the students' individual problems of practice and the region's improvement efforts.

Subsequent COVID problems hindered these plans, as much of the borough and districts' efforts were focused on ever-changing COVID-related policies and responses, particularly for opening (and closing) schools. Meanwhile, the cohort members were enthusiastic about their ability to collaborate and the importance of their work for the Bronx. Several reiterated this when helping to recruit colleagues to participate in the program and sharing with individual faculty how they were using what they were learning in courses to tackle current problems and priorities.

In the fall of 2019, Porter and Orr took steps to recruit a second Bronx cohort, further advancing the vision of developing a large cadre of similarly prepared advanced leaders. Recruitment for the second round was more challenging, due to COVID and remote meetings, but an initial information session was well attended. Then, in the spring, Porter became the NYC Chancellor of schools, and Erika Tobia became the Bronx executive superintendent. She readily welcomed her partnership role in supporting the existing cohort of students and in helping to recruit a new group of 15 school and district leaders for the coming academic year. By the end of the first year in the program, the first Bronx cohort retained almost all participants (only one student dropped out). They began the summer session framing their problems of practice for their dissertations in practice, focusing on challenges primarily in the following areas:

- Lack of school leader skills in building community and forming strategic collaborations in service to a school-wide culture of improvement.
- Insufficient student career readiness.
- Highly mobile students who were making poor academic progress.
- Poor academic progress for ELL students with disabilities in grades 3–5.
- High rates of teacher and principal turnover.

Attention to such problems aligned with the borough's priorities for improvement. Threaded throughout the problem framing were attention to the role and use of an equity perspective. The adoption of an EdD cohort as a systems change strategy presented a powerful, but challenging, opportunity. We are still exploring how to realize its potential beyond the advanced development of individual school and district leaders.

LEADERSHIP DEVELOPMENT

In iLEAD Year 2 (2018–19), Fordham University–Bronx district partners began exploring how districts could train current leaders in learning and using equity-focused improvement science for continuous school improvement. During the fall 2018 iLEAD convening, partnership members identified factors contributing to the problem of insufficient leadership capacity to engage in continuous school improvement and considered possible solutions. Several questions emerged regarding content, structure, and support at the district level, as well as the logistics of engaging in this work.

The partnership members used Fordham's new improvement science course to structure instructional experiences around specific improvement science principles and tools, and explored ways to test out various means of training and supporting school leaders to apply improvement science to persistent problems of practice. But other questions about how to support leadership development and school improvement remained. In the fall of 2018, the new CSD #11 superintendent (Cris Vaughan) was open to letting Orr try out a NIC-based approach to training assistant principals (APs) in improvement science, focusing on the district's lack of progress in improving math scores. Porter, as executive superintendent, hired Fordham graduate student, Kris DeFilippis, to direct the Bronx part of a city-wide initiative—Academic Response Team (ART)—to support under-performing schools in making progress in addressing equity-framed problems of practice, using short inquiry cycles based on improvement science. In the fall of 2019, superintendent Vaughan worked with ART director DeFilippis to design and facilitate three principal NICs; Fordham faculty Stosich volunteered to study the NICs to learn how they engaged in collaborative problem-solving.

Assistant Principal Math Networked Improvement Community

Through an introduction from the executive superintendent, Porter, Orr met with the new CSD #11 superintendent, Vaughan, to explore creating a school leader NIC focused on a shared problem of practice. Having already been part of a leadership development effort through the University of Washington, Vaughan proposed a hybrid model: hosting some sessions virtually and others in person. As superintendent she identified five promising APs and provided release time for morning in-person sessions; virtual sessions were scheduled for after school. She asked that the focus be on the lack of progress in math performance, despite district investments in curriculum, instruction, and assessments. In early fall 2019, Orr led this work with two graduate students: DeFillppis (as Academic Response Team director) and Ainsley Rudolfo (who used this work for his dissertation research). Five APs (four elementary and one middle school), the superintendent, Vaughan and the director of continuous improvement, Heather Morabito, participated.

In the first session, the participants, district leaders, and Fordham faculty and students jumped into analyzing the problem of students' lack of math performance improvement, demonstrating how to brainstorm contributing factors as a means of explaining the first three improvement science principles[3] (Bryk et al., 2015). Using the superintendent's proposed solution—having students grapple with a challenging problem each week—the group simultaneously explored how the teachers were doing this and the related challenges. In meetings every three weeks, we worked with the APs to document the wide variation in how teachers were using this problem-of-the-week approach with their students. Over time, they uncovered issues about where teachers were having difficulty and tested out solutions: guiding teachers to limit time spent on these problems so they did not supplant math instruction; providing teachers with challenging problems that were grade- and standard-aligned; and guiding teachers to facilitate students in productive struggle, rather than jumping to provide the answers.

In February 2020, several assistant principals and the director of continuous improvement from this NIC participated in the NYC iLEAD convening, sharing their work with other iLEAD partners as part of a consultancy protocol process. Further work was derailed by the COVID shutdown in March. After a brief hiatus, the NIC met again online to share what the APs were experiencing and how learning was shifting online. Without spring assessment testing, the NIC members could not evaluate the impact of their work on students' math performance. Despite the challenges, the group asked to continue meeting for another year, with more intensive training in improvement science. During our year-end reflection, we concluded that we focused too much on process and gave too little attention to gathering and comparing documented evidence (the APs would report on their observations in summary). We also struggled with how to actualize the group as a NIC—getting beyond simply sharing experiences and strategies to become more self-sustaining as a learning group. Superintendent Vaughan and director Morabito told us that they were thrilled with the leadership development work and leadership learning that APs gained through this process. They asked that we expand this work to two more AP NICs (of five APs and one improvement director each) for the next academic year (AY 2020–21), while continuing with the original NIC, focusing on improving math performance.

Orr and Rudolfo used this as an opportunity to test how to support multiple NICs that investigated a shared problem of practice. Each led one group alone and together they continued to support the original AP NIC through monthly virtual morning meetings. Given concerns regarding COVID, all sessions were online and focused on student engagement in math (as the only measurable outcome available). Based on our first-year experience, we refined our process to set the first five sessions to address one improvement science principle, drawing the assistant principals into unpacking their problems and proposing and testing solutions, incorporating focused readings for each session. The latter sessions were used to support two to three cycles of inquiry to test and improve solutions to their problems of practice.

To support this work, Orr and Rudolfo met regularly to plan out each session, sharing presentation slides and readings to use with the three NICs. They used a standard feedback survey that collected APs' reactions and documented each NIC session and shared meeting minutes with the AP groups, summarizing what was discussed,

---

[3] Identifying the problem as user-centered and problem specific; exploring variation; and seeing the system that produces the problem.

evidence shared, and proposed next steps. To facilitate learning, they created Google slides and Jamboards for group work and documentation.

Despite the constant demands of supporting their schools (and changing schedules) during COVID, most APs were able to participate in their NICs throughout the year, through ten sessions hosted every three to four weeks. Working iteratively, they addressed a series of issues related to the larger problem of practice (too much direct instruction and teacher talk, need for rich math problems, lack of skill in using online tools and platforms, and insufficient skill in facilitating student group work). One group developed a teacher observation and reporting guide that the others adopted, enabling better data collection and analysis as solutions were tried. By the end of the spring, there was a combined celebration and presentation by the three NICs with each other, the superintendent, and the director of continuous improvement. While sharing what they had learned about the problem and the solutions developed (including planning for the next steps in the fall), the APs also stressed the value of using improvement science practices and meeting together regularly to dive deeply into one problem of practice. They valued the professional camaraderie and group-directed learning, so they asked the superintendent to adopt this practice for the fall, instead of the existing AP meeting format with brief small group discussions. In this way, the focus on improvement science is becoming more deeply embedded in the design of district support from school leaders.

Creating Positive Change through the Bronx Academic Response Team Initiative

In the fall of 2019, the NYC Department of Education Office of the First Deputy Chancellor created the Academic Response Team (ART) as a school support initiative for schools designated by New York State as being in "good standing," but at risk of falling below, to enable better student performance growth and school improvement. Each executive superintendent (ES) and ART director could decide how best to enact the initiative, and Porter and DeFilippis decided to use it to integrate improvement science into how targeted schools improve student learning. The Bronx ART initiative also built on Porter's strong focus on advancing equity, including her efforts to address implicit bias and racial disproportionality with school and district leaders borough-wide.

The Bronx ART team consisted of ten educational administrators (known as ART specialists) and one ART director, all selected as new for the ART initiative in 2018–19. The Bronx ART director and staff created a strong team approach to standardizing how they worked with schools, defining a shared set of intentions, developing a guidebook for support protocols, and establishing a team culture where critical feedback was expected and encouraged, failure was celebrated as much as successes, and team roles were more flat than hierarchical.

Initially, the Bronx ART services targeted vulnerable schools with elevated levels of racial/ethnic disproportionality regarding attendance, suspensions, or special education referrals, using Fergus' (2016) framing of Relative Risk Ratio and subgroup likelihood comparisons. This strategy provided an equity-based approach to examining variations in the schools' problems and developing solutions. Through discussions with each of the eight Bronx CSD superintendents, six schools were selected based on elevated levels of disproportionality, principal readiness/willingness, contextual uniqueness, and community need. Through these conversations, one school from six of the eight districts was selected for the first cycle of ART support.

A team of two ART specialists worked with school leaders and teachers through short cycles of inquiry, lasting six to eight weeks, analyzing contextually unique problems of practice using improvement science. Over two pandemic-interrupted years, the Bronx ART initiative completed four inquiry cycles with 37 schools. Each six- to eight-week inquiry cycle included completing an intensive quantitative data dive (e.g., student achievement on state assessments, suspensions, family surveys, quality reviews) and analysis over two days. Following quantitative analysis, ART specialists and the ART director met with the building principal to provide an overview of collaborative support, establish expectations, and offer insights regarding the quantitative data. The support included approximately two weeks of continued qualitative data gathering in the form of empathy interviews, observations, community member interviews, and historical analysis, to understand the unique context in which the quantitative data was situated. Next, ART specialists met again with the principal and his or her designees to discuss the evidence, define the problem of practice, and move through a fishbone diagram analysis (identifying the contributing factors), develop an aim, theory of action, and a driver diagram. Together they would then settle on a change idea.

The change idea was enacted through a Plan-Do-Study-Act (PDSA) cycle that took place over the next four to five weeks. Throughout the process, the Bronx ART built in strategic "equity pauses" to diminish the potential of centering solutions not grounded in the needs and strengths of the communities served. In each school supported by Bronx ART, problems of practice (PoP) centered on promoting equitable outcomes within the context of each school community. Problems of practice were grounded in either teacher practice, student achievement, systems and structures within the school, or directly on disproportionality experienced by one group of students in the school regarding attendance, referrals to special education, or suspensions.

The Bronx ART initiative successfully supported 90 percent of its targeted schools in identifying a meaningful change idea, increasing equitable student experiences, and

TEXTBOX 2.2 ART TEAM EXAMPLE OF SCHOOL IMPROVEMENT

One example of an early problem of practice was a focus on disproportionate suspensions of Black males in a high school. Bronx ART supported school leadership to create an afternoon huddle comprised of teachers, deans, administrators, teacher's aides, and students, which eventually identified what they termed "vulnerable decision points" throughout the day that led to an increase in student suspensions. Over the course of eight weeks, suspensions of Black males decreased by 24 percent. As Bronx ART was designed to build the capacity of school leadership to conduct equity-based inquiry cycles through improvement science, school leaders were able to iterate on the initial change idea and continued to experience significant decreases in suspension disproportionality.

building leadership capacity to engage in quick adaptive improvement science based cycles of inquiry. Almost universally, participating school leaders and teachers reported that they found the improved science-focused ART process helpful in organizing and prioritizing competing demands. They noted that the process enabled them to think through disproportionality in student experiences by isolating root causes and identifying appropriate change ideas related to their desired outcomes. Following their experience with Bronx ART, most participating school leaders continued a form of inquiry cycles to process through and address additional contextually unique problems of practice.

Principal Equity Improvement Networked Improvement Communities

CSD #11, through experience with the AP NICs and the ART work in individual schools, adopted the NIC approach for principal development and equity improvement in Year Four (2020–2021) of the iLEAD work. The district had established an equity team at the district level composed of diverse stakeholders, and the superintendent sought to expand this work to involve all principals in working towards the district's equity goals. The district started by forming an equity team of about 20 school and district leaders who would plan and lead this work and engaged ART to promote equity work with all school principals through three separate NICs related to Social-Emotional Learning (SEL), Culturally Responsive Sustaining Education (CRSE), and Attendance/Engagement (A/E). Initially, an ART specialist met weekly with leaders of each of the three NICs to plan how to use the improvement science process and NIC team building. Every principal (n=45) in the district self-selected into one of the NICs. The three NICs met every one to two weeks, starting with training on the improvement science process and identifying a problem of practice. The ART facilitators then led their NICs through fishbone diagramming to isolate root causes for the problems of practice, generate a theory of action, map out driver diagrams, and finally adopt Plan-Do-Study-Act cycles. Principals interviewed and/or surveyed students as part of their change ideas and adopted a shifted classroom practice or school policy as a result. While each NIC moved through one or two PDSA cycles, each school also conducted its own PDSA cycle based on the change idea proposed through their NICs.

Stosich partnered with the district to study and support their efforts. Evidence from interviews with district and school leaders, surveys, and NIC meeting observations suggests that the design of the NIC helped to sustain attention to and support improvements related to critical equity concerns, which was greatly valued by many of the school leaders given the turbulent environment created by the pandemic. As a result, leaders in each NIC took action to address their PoPs. However, the NIC that was focused on increasing attendance and reducing absenteeism found it easier to measure their progress than the groups focused on CRSE and SEL. The A/E group saw a decrease in chronic absenteeism of 9% over two months and a 7% increase in overall attendance to over 93% district-wide. Notably, measures for tracking changes in attendance and chronic absenteeism were more readily available to leaders. By contrast, the SEL and CRSE groups invested more time and attention in surveying students and auditing the curriculum to understand these problems and monitor their progress in addressing them. The SEL NIC created student surveys that were administered in each school to identify the climate and SEL experience of every student in their schools and used the results to form student advisory groups, mentoring relationships, and deeper family engagement. The CRSE NIC created teams of teachers in many participating schools to develop and conduct culturally responsive lessons. While the SEL and CRSE groups took action in these areas, questions remained about the extent to which students experienced their school environment as more affirming and inclusive and the curriculum as more culturally responsive–sustaining, the aim of each group respectively. Nevertheless, the learning process in each NIC was designed to be educative for each school leader just as much as it was meant to identify specific actionable change ideas. Following its experience, CSD #11 district leaders adopted improvement science in their equity team process and continued to use inquiry cycles for improvement.

Conclusions and Lessons Learned

The most significant lesson gained through this partnership was to learn what is feasible—that we could create meaningful change for students and communities by integrating equity-focused improvement science in advanced leadership preparation (e.g., Fordham's EdD program) and ongoing leadership development in districts. Through our varied programs and initiatives, we as university faculty and district leaders experienced firsthand the benefit of preparing and supporting school and district leaders in improvement science by helping them to focus narrowly on a problem of practice and test out solutions. This approach was shown to be applicable to a range of school performance problems and innovative solutions. Through a comparison of these leadership preparation and development approaches (doctoral coursework, professional development seminars, NIC-based seminars, and one-to-one coaching) we learned how to adapt leadership development on equity-focused improvement science for different audiences, needs, and contexts. We also gained insight into the focus and pace of learning, engaging learners in applying the knowledge and tools to their own problem of practice, and supporting networked improvement communities. We also learned about the importance of documenting and reporting on the learning to accelerate learning and idea sharing.

The synergy among these leadership preparation and development efforts strengthened their application and use. Each primary iLEAD partner had both leadership preparation (as a student or faculty) and development (as facilitators and designers) experiences. Further, iLEAD convening experiences enriched this insight and learning. As DeFilippis explained, the partnership between Fordham and the Bronx and their experience in the redesigned EdD program informed the superintendent's and his approach to leading improvement; together they developed the Equity and improvement science framework, which was central to the ART initiative and Principal Equity NIC. The iLEAD convenings accelerated their work. As DeFilippis elaborated, "The convenings helped in letting me know we were not alone. When functioning in a new way [as they were doing in their ART initiative approach], it can feel alienating. So it was good to be with others who were working similarly and better." Otherwise, he would find himself questioning himself, and others questioning the way he was approaching the improvement work.

Following the Fordham–Bronx partnership's theory of action and driver diagram, we find that we have successfully tested our change idea strategies, in operationalizing, improving, and sustaining Fordham University's EdD program and embedding the NIC approach more systemically into one district's ongoing approach to school improvement. We have learned that these change strategies yielded our intended improvements—the creation of successful means of developing and supporting leaders through advanced graduate preparation and district structures. These approaches are yielding improvements in leadership work in schools that have, in the near term, led to changes in practices and some improved student outcomes (as noted above). The larger implications for Fordham University are reflected in the continuous improvement of its EdD program for K–12 educational leaders through refining what is taught and how, deepening attention to equity, and promoting NIC-like structures to support students throughout their program of study. The shared work—between faculty and district leaders—in both leadership preparation and development provides new tools, modalities for training in improvement science, and examples of its application to local problems of practice. Fordham's educational leadership division is now looking into expanding the approach to our master's program, as part of initial leadership preparation.

Fordham faculty draw on these experiences for their research on leadership problem-solving and school improvement, through the development of case studies, follow-up research, and refinement of an Improvement Science Leadership Proficiency survey developed to evaluate our progress. The faculty also gained experience in collaborating with local districts for strategic leadership preparation and development, which we anticipate would be sustainable. We have found it essential to work collaboratively with local district leaders, as we expand our work, particularly to continue program refinement and serving local districts' improvement needs.

For the Bronx, its executive superintendent (for its borough-wide office) and the district's leaders have gained tremendous insight and benefit from the various iLEAD-related initiatives—including potential advanced doctoral preparation of 40 school and district leaders, improvement in various problems of practice throughout the borough and most intensively in District 11. The challenge for the LEAs is how to sustain and expand this work. Our formal Bronx partnership will conclude at the end of iLEAD but will evolve into a series of collaborative projects with individual districts. Most of the lead district representatives have retired or transitioned into new positions, ending pilot and demonstration efforts, but making new ones possible. With these transitions come new opportunities to engage in this work in other settings and to deepen the work with individual districts, rather than working borough-wide. The evidence for the work completed thus far helps to demonstrate the validity of this approach for school improvement.

Throughout this partnership experience, several developments offered teachable moments that we came to recognize as both opportunities and challenges. For example, while becoming executive superintendent while starting a doctoral program was overwhelming at the time, Porter found significant synergy between her coursework and her borough-wide improvement efforts leading to new efforts, such as the Academic Response Team and other NIC work. We have since encouraged other students to strive for similar synergy in their work.

The demands and challenges of working during the COVID pandemic taught us all to be flexible and adaptable, creating new opportunities to work together and learning to work differently. We maintained a strong focus on our problem and our aim, enabling us to take advantage of new opportunities or propose new approaches as needed.

The iLEAD developmental progressions help to center goals and expectations, create a common language and foster a shared understanding of what we were aiming to accomplish and how. It enabled us to add in new partner members as participation shifted over time. It also reminded us to look for evidence of what we were accomplishing in meeting our benchmarks, an important practice to incorporate.

Questions for Discussion

1. The Bronx/Fordham case is intended in part to demonstrate how joint learning about improvement science enabled equity-focused change and capacity building in both the university and the school district. In your reading of the case, what are some compelling examples and evidence that this actually happened? Put differently, what is the evidence that both the district and the university substantially benefited from learning about improvement science?
2. The theme of "problems of practice" as a focus of change begins on the first page of this case and is sustained throughout. Judging from this account, why does a focus on problems of practice provide high leverage for institutional partnerships and equity-focused school improvement?
3. In the concluding pages, the authors write, "The challenge for the LEAs is how to sustain and expand this work." Does the case suggest that this challenge will likely be met going forward? Why or why not?

References

Bryk, A. S., Gomez, L., Grunow, A., & LeMahieu, P. (2015). *Learning to improve: How America's schools can get better at getting better.* Harvard Education Press.

Carnegie Project on the Education Doctorate. (2021). *The CPED framework.* https://www.cpedinitiative.org/the-framework

Darling-Hammond, L., Meyerson, D., La Pointe, M. M., & Orr, M. T. (2010). *Preparing principals for a changing world.* Jossey-Bass.

Fergus, E. (2016). *Solving disproportionality and achieving equity: A leader's guide to using data to change hearts and minds.* Corwin Press, SAGE Publications, Inc.

Forman, M. L., Stosich, E. L., & Bocala, C. (2017). *The internal coherence framework: Creating the conditions for continuous improvement in schools.* Harvard Education Press.

Mintrop, R. (2016). *Design-based school improvement.* Harvard Education Press.

Orphanos, S., & Orr, M. T. (2014). Learning leadership matters: The influence of innovative school leadership preparation on teachers' experiences and outcomes. *Educational Management, Administration & Leadership, 42*(5), 680–700.

Orr, M. T. (2012). *Creating high quality internships in suburban and small city districts.* University Council for Educational Administration.

Orr, M. T., King, C., & La Pointe, M. M. (2010). *Districts developing leaders: Eight districts' lessons on strategy, program approach and organization to improve the quality of leaders for local schools.* Report prepared for The Wallace Foundation. Educational Development Center, Inc.

Orr, M. T., & Pounder, D. G. (2010). Teaching and preparing school leaders. In S. Conley & B. S. Cooper (Eds.), *Finding, preparing, and supporting school leaders: Critical issues, useful solutions.* Rowman Littlefield.

CHAPTER 3

Moving a Partnership from Itinerant to Integral: Using Improvement Science as a Catalyst for Change in Leadership Preparation and Induction
GEORGE MASON UNIVERSITY AND FAIRFAX COUNTY PUBLIC SCHOOLS

Samantha Viano, Farnoosh Shahrokhi, Regina Biggs, Natasha Saunders, Claire Silva, and Paige Whitlock

This is the story of a partnership located outside of the nation's capital that leveraged long-standing ties to build a community of continuous improvement. Although historically, these institutions had a mutually beneficial relationship, iLEAD was the first time they coordinated closely on building a shared language and processes around continuous improvement. Empowered by a countywide racial and equity policy and driven by the goal to increase educational equity in the school system, the team launched independent and joint initiatives to advance the use of improvement science in university coursework, leadership development, and the school improvement process. This story discusses the details of these initiatives and how improvement science catalyzed this successful partnership. Additionally, this narrative illustrates how the team was able to draw on their knowledge of improvement to respond to COVID-19 and the natural arc of partnership work.

Arriving at the Fairfax County Public Schools (FCPS) conference space that day in October 2018, Educational Leadership (EDLE) faculty from George Mason University (GMU) did not know what to expect. Glancing around the crowded room, they found the table with a "GMU" placard half-filled with people who most EDLE faculty were meeting for the first time. The representatives from the FCPS Instructional Services team were excited to be there and knew many others in the room who hailed from universities and school districts across the country. As the EDLE faculty settled in, Sloan Presidio, FCPS Assistant Superintendent at the time, spoke to the room about how honored FCPS was to be hosting this convening for the Carnegie Foundation for the Advancement of Teaching's iLEAD initiative. He spoke about how passionate FCPS was about the work of iLEAD because of the potentially transformative nature of improvement science (IS). Meanwhile, several EDLE faculty members whispered to each other, "What is iLEAD?"

This case study tracks the development of the FCPS/GMU relationship from one with parallel, complementary strengths in leadership development to a partnership with co-constructed, IS-driven programming designed to advance equity in FCPS. What this means is that, at GMU, the core principles of IS are infused into our coursework and disciplined inquiry, through Plan-Do-Study-Act (PDSA) cycles, into the clinical leadership internship. In FCPS, IS is taught as part of the district's professional learning as well as being foundational to the comprehensive needs assessment and leadership induction programs. Our partnership supports all of these efforts through co-facilitation and joint planning. This chapter presents a review of how our partnership came to be, how we structure our work, and how our work has progressed and been guided by the Developmental Progressions framework over our first few years as part of iLEAD. The Progressions have served as a valuable tool for providing milestones for our progress on making IS core to our work as an LEA, IHE, and as a partnership.

We offer three lessons learned for others who wish to build a successful IHE–LEA partnership. To integrate IS into a leadership development partnership we (1) started with the historical foundation between the two organizations, (2) had willing participation where leadership and staff at both organizations have an interest in improvement science, and (3) leveraged this capacity and eagerness to make time for collaboration. We reflect on several times during our partnership when we were able to pivot to be user-centered while still remaining true to the goals of IS. Overall, this case describes how improvement science has served as the conduit to help our partnership flourish in new, transformative ways to advance educational equity in schools.

Context

Even though the EDLE faculty was meeting many members of the FCPS iLEAD team for the first time, these organizations have had a history of partnering on leadership development. FCPS and GMU are public educational institutions that serve the local community in and around Fairfax, VA, leading us to often collaborate on specific initiatives like leadership training cohorts. However, our partnership work had not been fully realized prior to iLEAD with no coordinated efforts related to training, induction, or curriculum. Below, we describe each organization and the history of our relationship (see figure 3.1 for a timeline).

EDLE PROGRAM AT GMU

GMU is the largest Carnegie Research 1 university (doctoral universities: highly intensive research activity) and the most ethnically diverse public institution in Virginia (Indiana University Center for Postsecondary Research, 2021; "Education Leadership

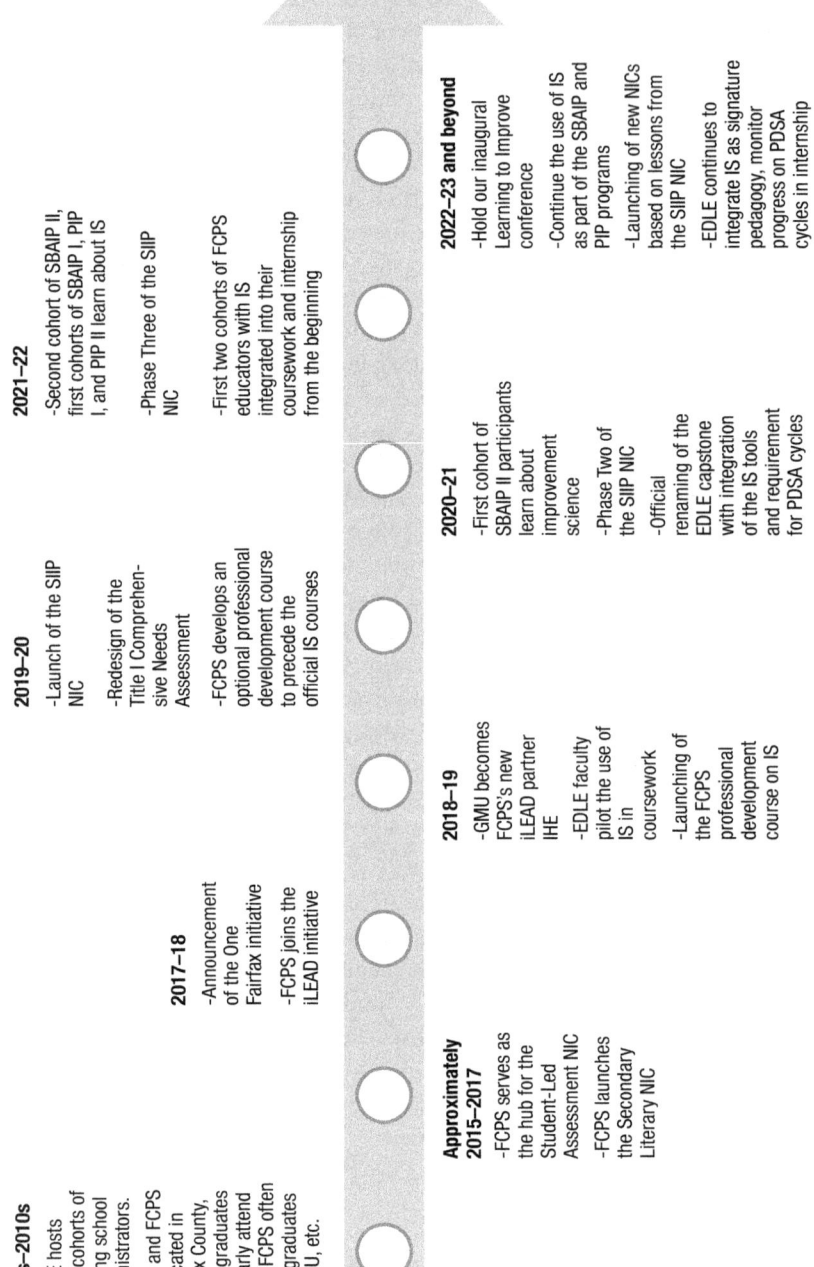

Figure 3.1 Timeline of the FCPS-EDLE Partnership.

Program," 2022). Serving in-person and online cohorts of students, the EDLE program graduates over 100 students a year. FCPS is the largest employer of GMU graduates. About 50% of the administrators serving in Northern Virginia schools are alumni of GMU ("Education Leadership Program," 2022).

FCPS

FCPS is one of the largest school districts in the United States, serving over 180,000 students across almost 198 schools/centers. Prior to FCPS joining iLEAD, the Instructional Services Department began integrating the use of IS tools to facilitate strategic planning, program and project development, and FCPS launched or joined several Networked Improvement Communities (NICs). FCPS served as the hub of a student-led assessment NIC which included 11 school districts across Virginia. The Secondary Language Arts team established a NIC with six schools within FCPS to study the integration of disciplinary literacy into core instruction.

FCPS AND GMU PARTNERING PRIOR TO ILEAD

FCPS and GMU have a long-standing partnership. Farnoosh Shahrokhi, division director and co-academic program coordinator of EDLE, recounts collaborating with FCPS since the early 2000s with official cohorts of FCPS educators seeking administrative licensure through coursework taking place in FCPS facilities. As both institutions are located in Fairfax County, Virginia, FCPS and GMU have a history of working together to support teacher preparation, school leadership and policy, technology education and infrastructure, curriculum, and instruction, and facilities use.

JOINING TOGETHER AS ILEAD PARTNERS

Although FCPS and EDLE had a history of partnering on leadership development, GMU was not FCPS's original iLEAD partner. A year into the iLEAD initiative, Sloan Presidio, the FCPS IS champion, was concerned that the work with the first IHE partner had stalled and that FCPS was not maximizing its participation in iLEAD. To jumpstart progress, Sloan approached Mark Ginsberg, GMU's College of Education and Human Development (CEHD) Dean at the time, about partnering with FCPS as a part of the iLEAD Network. CEHD and FCPS were well positioned to partner for iLEAD, as FCPS had hired a Project Liaison in 2013 to facilitate collaborations on professional development, research, and policy with GMU. To initiate the iLEAD partnership with EDLE, Sloan asked the Project Liaison to serve as our boundary spanner. Specifically, the Project Liaison helps with scheduling meetings and retreats while also monitoring agendas and deliverables to the iLEAD network, providing vital routines of collaboration that allow our partnership to thrive.

As luck would have it, around the time Sloan approached Mark, FCPS was set to host an iLEAD convening of the iLEAD teams, the event described at the beginning of this chapter. Sloan invited Mark to attend the convening and asked if he would also bring EDLE faculty members to assess the potential for creating a productive partnership. After two intensive days, the EDLE faculty could not help but be swept up in the excitement of the room about IS. EDLE faculty immediately recognized the potential for using IS in partnership with FCPS to grow leaders.

Our iLEAD team is composed of EDLE faculty and members of the FCPS Instructional Services, and Office of Professional Learning and Equity. All EDLE faculty participate in some way in the iLEAD initiative with a core group of three to four faculty members who are particularly involved, including the authors of this chapter. The FCPS iLEAD team members include the Project Liaison, the FCPS authors of this chapter, and members of Instructional Services and Leadership Development who lead programs aligned with improvement science, particularly those who manage school-based administrator induction, Title I, equity and cultural responsiveness initiatives, secondary language arts, global classroom, and project management. Our full iLEAD team meets on a monthly basis with working groups focused on specific projects, meeting as needed with biannual iLEAD team retreats to encourage team building and a broader vision for our partnership.

Problems

Our partnership began with the shared recognition that each of our organizations had specific problems of practice that could be addressed through both IS and a partnership between our organizations: chronic problems of practice in FCPS and alignment between coursework and practice for EDLE. Maximizing our partnership with IS as the catalyzing agent of our work is successfully addressing these challenges.

STAGNANT PROGRESS ON SCHOOL IMPROVEMENT

FCPS already engaged in annual, state-mandated school improvement through the school improvement and innovation process which intended to redress inequities within FCPS, but our iLEAD team realized that this process was systemically static. The school improvement and innovation plans (SIIPs) were often written by the school's administration and solution-oriented by centering on a programmatic approach. Schools wrote their plans in a single document to be saved in a secure network folder, so schools could not view other schools' plans. Schools sometimes had opportunities to assess mid-year progress and end-of-year achievements, but this was done based on the preferences of regional principal supervisors.

The iLEAD partners realized we had a unique opportunity to enhance the school improvement process by shifting it to a dynamic, problem-based process. The SIIP itself was conceived as the problem of practice upon which we sought to improve. We theorized that if we introduced the use of IS, specifically Networked Improvement Communities, strategic planning tools, and cycles of disciplined inquiry we could expand school leaders' abilities to facilitate continuous improvement. By making the SIIP problem-specific and user-centered, school improvement became a team sport.

Specifically, we recognized that building leadership capacity for continuous improvement must involve a guiding coalition of teachers and other school staff to make improvement work actionable outside of the SIIP NIC.

These efforts were driven by our joint problem of practice that states, "There are inconsistencies in the capacity of school-based and central office leaders to use continuous improvement principles, tools, and routines in school improvement." While the SIIP NIC was concentrated in FCPS, EDLE faculty fully invested in co-planning, co-facilitating, and co-coaching this initiative. The system (FCPS) would be able to learn from itself to directly impact disparate student outcomes with the support of GMU. While we could not predict the impending success of our efforts, our partnership was dedicated to the work.

MISMATCH BETWEEN EDLE LEADERSHIP PREPARATION AND FCPS PRACTICE

The EDLE Program of Study has always incorporated research-based school improvement methods to facilitate the development of school leaders with the knowledge, skills, and dispositions to move schools to an inquiry footing. However, we noted a lack of cohesion in what EDLE students learned through their graduate work and the school improvement processes used by leaders in the school district. For instance, candidates are asked to identify a problem of practice in their school to address in their internship projects, but, as noted previously, students' schools often did not have problem-focused SIIPs. As a result, the methodology EDLE students learned was not necessarily useful or valued in the implementation process in schools.

As EDLE faculty collaborated to generate a theory of action, we began by identifying a change idea that we theorized could begin to make a positive shift in the mismatch—creating a shared language for improvement. While teaching the course *Using Research to Lead School Improvement*, Samantha Viano, an EDLE faculty member, recognized the lack of a common vernacular about change, as candidates discussed school improvement related to the design of their internship improvement projects. Bringing this revelation to the faculty as a result of the iLEAD engagement prompted a wondering: If we changed the program of study to embed the language of IS, would EDLE candidates become more significant assets on FCPS school improvement teams? To test this idea, we decided to initiate changes in the program of study and the internship to build a shared language across our candidates and their schools' SIIP work.

Challenges, Solutions, and Evidence

If Lance Fogelman had entered the EDLE program one year earlier, his experience would have been entirely different. Enrolled in Samantha's *Using Research to Lead School Improvement* course in the spring of 2019, Lance was part of the first class whose internship improvement planning fully integrated IS. Whereas students in the previous semester balked at using improvement science tools because its utility in the existing SIIP structure was unclear, FCPS guest speakers in Samantha's course provided a consistent message about FCPS support for IS. What took place in this course was a harbinger of our future partnership work.

This section begins with how our partnership initiated our iLEAD partnership work. We then review how each organization independently furthered the use of IS in our respective core activities. In closing, we will reflect on our most collaborative initiative, which brings us back to how Lance's experience as an EDLE graduate and FCPS teacher leader represents the full circle of how improvement science has guided our partnership work.

IMPROVEMENT SCIENCE AS OUR CATALYZING AGENT TO COME TOGETHER

In the fall of 2018, the GMU/FCPS iLEAD team was beginning to build the foundation of our partnership. The iLEAD network encourages reflection on our progress using the Developmental Progressions which we have found to be a helpful framework for establishing where we are and how we can build our partnership. When we reflected on where we were in the fall of 2018 based on the Progressions, we identified that our partnership relationship became formalized as part of iLEAD (Exploring Change Ideas stage of (18) Partnership Relationships through the convening and initial meeting with FCPS and Exploring Change Ideas stage of (6) Institutional Leader Commitment). We had meetings attended by senior FCPS leadership like Sloan (Small Change Implementation stage of (11) District Leadership Engagement). That is, we used the Progressions to understand how we began the year with the requisite commitment to commence our work together.

Improvement science was integral to catalyzing our partnership from the moment we joined the iLEAD partnership together. Our partnership was intentional about establishing a "meeting of the minds" by collaborating on the development of our aim statement, a vital IS tool. We met regularly, and our meetings were always in person pre–COVID-19. We had standing agenda items to provide updates on each of our activities, so everyone on the iLEAD team is up to date with each other's work. This enabled us to share lessons learned so as to benefit others on the iLEAD team. We were able to share the improvement knowledge we were gaining in our joint and independent work on a regular basis.

Through our discussions in team meetings, several members recognized the importance of establishing a shared and intentional stance about our purpose. While we were a like-minded collaborative, we thought it essential to start with an explicit shared understanding. The Project Liaison and Regina Biggs, co-academic program coordinator of EDLE, collaborated on developing a survey to collect each iLEAD team member's thoughts. Each partnership member anonymously answered five questions using a template that was collected, cut, and color-coded. Claire Silva, iLEAD team member and project support coach for Instructional Services, Beth Blankenship, innovation specialist from FCPS, and Roberto Pamas, from GMU, joined the Project Liaison and Regina to identify themes from each color-coded set of answers and synthesize the thinking represented to write a draft statement for review by the partnership team. With slight modifications by the larger team, our aim statement was complete. This activity grounded our partnership and facilitated our collective perspective on how our collaboration would enable us to improve our programs and practices in mutually beneficial ways. This led us to progress to the Small Change Implementation stage of Developmental Progressions (23) A Shared Partnership Narrative.

The aim development activity presents one example of the flexibility and autonomy the partnership team had to organize our work to grow on the iLEAD Development Progressions. As a part of the Project Liaison's boundary-spanning professional responsibilities, Sloan provided them with the flexibility to organize our partnership work (e.g., meetings, retreats, deliverables) while Mark verbally encouraged EDLE faculty to be active partners in the iLEAD work. As a result of the investment of high-level leadership, EDLE and FCPS matured on the Development Progressions (Institutionalizing and Sustaining the Work stage of (11) District Leadership Engagement and Small Change Implementation stage of (6) Institutional Leadership Commitment) and, in doing so, made progress to reach our equity-driven goals. The collective aim statement we wrote is, "The GMU/FCPS iLEAD partnership is committed to the use of IS to develop leaders, redress local problems of practice, and promote equitable educational opportunities and outcomes for all students." Establishing this aim and working theory provided clarity for identifying entry points within each organization and for our partnership.

Making Improvement Science EDLE's Signature Pedagogy

EDLE FACULTY'S INTRODUCTION TO IMPROVEMENT SCIENCE

The EDLE faculty had a history of commitment to continuous improvement. We focused bi-monthly faculty meetings on curriculum development informed by reviewing and analyzing key assessment data. For faculty, reflection through a lens of continuous improvement offered the optimal perspective of the shared norms that drive the annual lifecycle. As a result, we created detailed Data Yearbooks, SWOT (Strengths -Weaknesses-Opportunities-Threats) analyses, and calendar year reports as evidence of candidate proficiency to inform program and curriculum decisions. The reflective and continuous improvement practices were a stepping stone to the improvement work core to the iLEAD partnership. Hence, faculty were receptive and engaged with the work that ensued. Upon reflecting on the Developmental Progressions, we identified as being at the Exploring Change Ideas stage of (1) Commitment to the Idea of Improvement from the beginning of our work with iLEAD.

Early on, the faculty started reading about the principles of improvement science in *Learning to Improve* (Bryk, Gomez, Grunow, & LeMahieu, 2015) and dedicated program meeting time for discussions. Samantha, who had prior experience with IS, led program discussions. Through our discussions, it became clear that EDLE faculty were on board and excited about the opportunity to partner with FCPS through the iLEAD initiative. EDLE faculty agreed that embedding IS principles in the curriculum would elevate the program. Even though EDLE trains future school administrators from school districts across Northern Virginia, the EDLE faculty agreed IS would benefit all of our students regardless of their connection to FCPS. When we reflect on the Developmental Progressions, we can see how we soon transitioned to the Small Change Implementation of objective (1) Commitment to the Idea of Improvement. Members of the faculty team worked closely with FCPS to learn how they were using improvement science principles and tools for building capacity in leadership and tackling local problems within their large system by attending the FCPS-led professional development workshops on IS. Through the regular expectation from iLEAD that partnerships would track progress using the Developmental Progressions, we purposefully sought ways to develop several objectives including the EDLE program moving to the Exploring Change Ideas stage of (10) A New Professional Education Narrative. We also found common ideas that align the partners and ways to work on common problems of practice with our development tracking with Exploring Change Ideas of (19) Joint Development of Targeted Problems of Practice and Small Change Implementation of (18) Partnership Relationships. At the same time, EDLE faculty immediately recognized that our core work in EDLE as a higher education program was related to our coursework, so we needed to keep attention on Developmental Progressions principle (2) Curriculum/Program Development to shift towards a "coherent program of study" geared towards IS.

COMMITMENT TO IMPROVEMENT SCIENCE THROUGH CURRICULUM DEVELOPMENT

Our joint commitment to developing equity-minded leaders, who can use improvement science principles to tackle problems of practice, steered us to think about how we can better prepare such leadership candidates. Faculty engaged in deep discussions as we asked, "how can we actualize teaching graduate students about IS and show tangible performance outcomes for students?" As mentioned, the *Using Research to Lead School Improvement* course was well suited to embed IS tools and pedagogy. The course develops skills, insights, and understanding of how leaders use research to improve schools, emphasizing the use of assessment and research data to identify school improvement needs and design school improvement projects. Students in this course identify an objective in their school improvement plan (the SIIP in FCPS) to guide their data and research exploration. Students then propose an improvement project implemented and evaluated over six to twelve months during their internship. The internship improvement project is a program requirement. We agreed the infusion of IS principles and tools in this course and the internship would be a natural fit because this project was already well-aligned in many ways with IS in that it had a problem focus and involved designing a project integrating data and research to lead improvement. At the outset of our partnership, Samantha immediately began piloting ways to integrate improvement science into this course, upon reflection beginning with Small Change Implementation of (2) Curriculum/Program Development of the Developmental Progressions in the fall of 2018.

The faculty decided to scale these curriculum changes across the entire program, including our online, cohort, and hybrid courses. Beginning in 2021, EDLE faculty renamed the school administrator licensure capstone the *Internship Improvement Project*. The major changes to this capstone were requiring all students to engage in at least two PDSA cycles to inform the implementation of their project and building a driver diagram to organize efforts. While all full and part-time EDLE faculty are engaged in the iLEAD work, we held training for our adjunct faculty (composed of practicing or retired educational leaders in Northern Virginia) on IS to facilitate this change. This decision illustrates our growth in several objectives in the Developmental Progressions including Institutionalizing and Sustaining for (1) Commitment to the Idea of Improvement, Integrating IS/NIC Into the Core Work for (2) Curriculum/Program Development, and (5) IS as a Signature Pedagogy, and Small Change Implementation for (4) Faculty Engagement. Moreover, these shifts demonstrated a commitment to equip future FCPS leaders with the knowledge and skills to be successful school leaders.

Curriculum modifications and enhancements were in place for the new cohort of 25 FCPS educators that began in the summer of 2021. As a result of our partnership with iLEAD, we enhanced the application and selection process. The applicants underwent a screening process that included a joint interview with FCPS leaders and EDLE faculty. We modified interview questions to include equity and problems of practice questions. FCPS leaders made recommendations for who to select for the cohort, and EDLE faculty made final decisions on admission. The overwhelming success of the process prompted discussions on modifying the EDLE interview questions for all candidates. These are examples of the partnership work informing practice and program improvement.

The new cohort of FCPS students will be closely monitored as they progress through the program to provide feedback on the curriculum changes. Samantha guided this FCPS cohort in the fall of 2021, as they learned about IS principles and planned their PDSA cycles. We are interested in the progress of their PDSA cycles during their internships including how well these informed the implementation and outcomes of their improvement projects. In addition, a new EDLE school administrator licensure cohort of 16 FCPS teachers began in the fall of 2021. As part of the program, EDLE students submit PDSA forms detailing each step of their inquiry cycles to their internship supervisors. Both groups will provide ample opportunity to evaluate how graduate students embed PDSA cycles in their project implementation. EDLE faculty will examine how their findings informed their decision to adopt or abandon part of their plan and how they use the results to inform implementation.

To provide a platform for these future leaders to demonstrate their learning from their experiences, we are organizing our first Learning to Improve conference in spring 2023, an event we hope to hold annually. The conference will provide an opportunity to demonstrate improvement science in action, share the complexity of change, and disseminate information while highlighting the IS work within FCPS of those either enrolled in the EDLE program or in one of the FCPS iLEAD initiatives. This platform will provide the opportunity for intentional and authentic connections to the SIIP process with equity at the forefront. There is no question that such an annual conference speaks to the strength of our partnership and institutionalizing IS in both organizations. Through these curriculum-related initiatives, FCPS partners developed a better sense of the leadership program and the performance-based assessment embedded in the curriculum. These curriculum threads are both natural extensions of the work of the EDLE program and enhanced the partnership and made the leadership preparation of current and future leaders more cohesive.

The iLEAD work of the EDLE faculty has not extended outside of EDLE at GMU. One of the considerations over the coming years is the possibility of scaling our work to others within CEHD who focus on similar areas of instructional improvement like teacher preparation. The Learning to Improve conference might serve as a natural venue to share our IS work with GMU faculty, and organize future conversations with CEHD leadership to explore whether expanding our iLEAD partnership outside of EDLE within GMU is work worth pursuing. These kinds of efforts will be essential as we seek to advance on the Developmental Progressions (1) Commitment to the Idea of Improvement where we are currently at the Small Change Implementation stage and (5) Improvement Science as a Signature Pedagogy where we are currently at the Integrating IS/NICs into the Core Work stage.

Diverse Approaches to Supporting the Use of Improvement Science in FCPS

While EDLE had the autonomy to make these shifts in language, culture, and pedagogy, with IS already being in the spirit of their prior practices, FCPS's iLEAD team has the difficult task of facilitating significant cultural changes to how the district, schools, and teachers approach improvement. The approaches the FCPS iLEAD team have taken are a combination of grassroots education and leadership-driven changes including facilitating flexible, expansive professional development opportunities for district-level and building leadership and administrator induction programming for new assistant principals and principals. Most of the activities of the FCPS iLEAD team were chosen not only because they were geared toward building capacity for the use of IS by school and central office leaders but also because they were within the scope of responsibilities of the FCPS iLEAD team members. But we also describe the strategic efforts over what we might call our signature joint initiative, the SIIP NIC.

PROFESSIONAL DEVELOPMENT OPPORTUNITIES

Drawing upon the partnership's working theory, the FCPS iLEAD team members focused their initial efforts on building capacity with district staff (the GMU iLEAD team members were not involved in any of the professional development opportunities in FCPS described in this section) to advance to the Integrating IS/NICs into the Core Work phase of the Developmental Progressions (12) Professional Development of District Staff. In the fall of 2018, the FCPS iLEAD team members developed and launched a five-session course on IS called *Translating Equity into Practice using Improvement Science*. This course is offered three times per year for teams of central office administrators to build the capacities of district leadership in the tools and methodologies of IS for identifying and redressing long-standing inequities in district-wide programs and initiatives. The iLEAD team started small and engaged leaders in Instructional Services who were willing to learn more about IS. Enrollment in the course has expanded to include central office teams from the Department of Special Services, Department of School Improvement and Support, Department of Human Resources, Transportation, and Warehouse facilities. It has also expanded to include school-based teams of administrators and resource teachers. These courses had 40 participants complete the course during the 2018–19 school year; 55 during the 2019–20 school year; and 61 during the 2020–21 school year for a total of 156 participants.

Additionally, in early 2020, the FCPS Equity & Cultural Responsiveness team developed an optional course, *Equity & Innovation: Keeping Equity at the Center*, to precede the IS course. This course, taught by FCPS iLEAD team members, develops capacity for equity leadership to intentionally focus on equity at the center of planning and decision-making when considering changes to programs and projects. By engaging in deeper professional learning on identity, bias, power, and privilege as a foundation for transforming teams' equity actions, leaders develop awareness that translates to practice. For example, participants conducted an equity audit and considered their spheres of influence and loci of control to hone in on an area for improvement within their programs and projects. This course prompts participants to continue acting on their focus for improvement by taking the *Translating Equity into Practice using Improvement Science* course.

In addition to a multi-session offering, the FCPS iLEAD team also provided mini-workshops on *Identifying a Problem of Practice* and performing root cause analysis to instructional and assessment coaches, Title I resources and Advanced Academic resource teachers, AP/IB Coordinators, and other instructional staff. In the summer of 2021, the FCPS iLEAD team expanded the improvement science work by designing and implementing a workshop on *Framing the SIIP from a Problem of Practice* to support schools with planning for school improvement and Elementary and Secondary School Emergency Relief 3 (ESSER) budgeting. One hundred and seventeen participants across fifty-five schools attended. This accounted for a little more than a quarter of all FCPS schools.

While the pandemic presented difficulties it also created opportunities for growth, specifically in the Developmental Progressions. The team led the way to Integrate IS/NIC into the Core Work of objective (13) Implementation of IS/NICs by organizing NICs across literacy, school improvement, and innovation in English Language Learner programming. We are on the path toward the Institutionalizing and Sustaining stage of this objective, as PDSA cycles are operationalized as a core practice. The Instructional Services Department, instructional technology integration, leadership development, and college success programs within the central office now use and teach others to use PDSA cycles.

SCHOOL-BASED LEADERSHIP INDUCTION

Our iLEAD team approaches leadership development as a pipeline process beginning in the EDLE program followed by a select number of graduates who are interested and internally motivated then joining school-based administration as an assistant principal and, later, principal. While we do not have data on what proportion of EDLE graduates become principals, about half of FCPS school leaders are GMU graduates (as previously stated). To support the infusion of improvement science into this pipeline, the FCPS iLEAD recognized the need to embed IS into its leadership induction programs. Beginning in the summer of 2020, FCPS shifted leadership development to build leadership skills, knowledge, and actions by taking steps to redress inequity at the school level. Specifically, we embedded IS tools and methodologies into the induction curriculum. The School-Based Administrator Induction Programs (SBAIP) I & II and Principal Induction Programs (PIP) I & II require leaders to identify, plan, design, implement, and manage continuous improvement for an equity problem of practice. These professional learning programs are geared towards assistant principals (SBAIP) and principals (PIP) in their first two years in each role. The intent of these programs is to shift from training on how to manage school operations to developing the skills of school-based leaders for leading change for improved access and opportunities for students and staff. See textbox 3.1 for a list of goals of the SBAIP and PIP programs.

Amid the pandemic, 48 second-year assistant principals across 44 schools (of which 13 were Title I schools) participated in the 2020–21 SBAIP II program. In the 2021–22 school year, 16 first-year principals participated in PIP I, 22 second-year principals participated in PIP II, 55 first-year assistant principals participated in SBAIP I, and 52 second-year assistant principals participated in SBAIP II. Of these participants, at least 30% earned their administrative licensure through the EDLE program. At least three-quarters of first and second-year assistant principals and principals regularly participate in the SBAIP and PIP programs. While all first- and second-year

TEXTBOX 3.1 LEARNING GOALS FOR THE SBAIP AND PIP PROGRAMS

Learners in the School-Based Administrator Induction Program (SBAIP) I & II and Principal Induction Program (PIP) I & II:

- Used data to identify an equity problem of practice impacting their school.
- Established a guiding coalition of diverse stakeholders to engage in the improvement effort.
- Performed a needs assessment to understand the root causes and identify high-impact systems drivers.
- Aligned their school's improvement and innovation plan (SIIP) goals/strategies/actions to the systems drivers.
- Developed a working theory of improvement using a driver diagram.
- Planned cycles of disciplined inquiry called PDSA cycles for iterative improvement.
- Performed PDSA cycles, and collected data and shared the results of the PDSA cycles.
- Prepared a presentation of their project to share what worked with regional and school leaders.
- Reflected on the shifts in leadership dispositions as a result of this project.

principals and assistant principals are encouraged to attend induction programming, it is often difficult for them to sustain their attendance due to competing demands at their schools. Induction program participants engaged in learning using IS to plan and implement an equity improvement project, framed by a problem of practice and aligned with schools' SIIP plans. While the FCPS iLEAD team has offered IS professional development for years, embedding IS into leadership induction helps the team to transition to the Institutionalizing and Sustaining the Work phase of the Development Progressions (12) Professional Development of District Staff.

TITLE I COMPREHENSIVE NEEDS ASSESSMENT

The efforts from GMU and FCPS were expanding knowledge of improvement science tools and methodologies at a fast pace. Still, knowledge development on how to use IS for school improvement alone would not redress education inequities. We needed to combine our skills on IS-driven leadership development to help leadership teams use IS as an embedded and integral part of their regular school improvement process. An opportunity to embed IS into an existing component of the school improvement process for Title I schools in FCPS presented itself beginning in the spring of 2020, when Claire Silva and Evonne DeNome, Program Manager for Title I, re-designed the Title I Comprehensive Needs Assessment (CNA) process. Title I schools asked the Title I office to create a more efficient and streamlined process. This new process was developed to create greater efficiencies to ensure Title I schools had one plan that combined three processes: Title I Schoolwide Plan (federal requirement), the Virginia Continuous School Improvement Process (state requirement), and the FCPS SIIP process (federal/district requirement). Title I schools are required to conduct a CNA to identify areas of strength and growth for continuous school improvement. It ensures systematic alignment to the FCPS Strategic Plan goals and metrics and meets Federal Title I grant compliance. This synthesized process was developed to ensure Title I schools have a plan that meets federal and state program requirements.

The redesign of the needs assessment process embedded the use of IS methods and tools. The new FCPS Title I CNA was a shift from the previous process. Past CNA processes were program-focused, for example, schools were asked to identify what programs are working well, and what were areas for growth. The new FCPS Title I CNA process is problem-focused. It is a more equitable approach to school improvement. Problem-focused CNAs are learner-centered and consider problems of practice impacting student success and caring culture. Problems in education are complex and multifaceted. This process enabled schools to perform root cause analysis and identify systems drivers for continuous improvement. The use of IS within the CNA process can be attributed to the work of the FCPS iLEAD team within the Title I office where two members serve. As district leaders become more aware of the benefits of IS in redressing inequities there are more concerted efforts toward its use.

Now, Title I schools are required to identify a problem of practice aligned to the FCPS Strategic Plan goals. School teams then perform root cause analyses and identify high-impact systems drivers using affinity mapping, fishbone, and inter-relational diagrams. Title I schools aligned their SIIPs to the system drivers, which informed the FCPS SIIP process and Title I Budgeting and Resource Allocations. Gina Toler and Courtney White, FCPS iLEAD team members and Education Specialists for Title I, supported its implementation across 41 Title I schools (out of 198 schools in FCPS). The Virginia Department of Education named the re-designed FCPS CNA as exemplary. This effort exemplifies how FCPS is transitioning to the Institutionalizing and Sustaining the Work phase of Developmental Progressions (13) Implementation of IS/NICs.

Our Partnership-Driven Initiative: Piloting an Improvement Science Approach to School Improvement

IS helped our FCPS/GMU iLEAD team see that we would not accomplish our goals based on building knowledge alone; we had to purposefully network schools' learning as they engage in IS and disciplined inquiry. To further integrate IS into existing systems processes, the partnership decided to pilot the SIIP NIC. We believed the SIIP NIC could socialize a culture of continuous improvement, and we sought to understand what happens when the SIIP shifts from a traditionally static plan crafted by leadership to an iterative process including teacher leadership. We designed the SIIP NIC to enhance school improvement practices by tackling problems of practice related to access, opportunity, and achievement.

Unlike other FCPS-led iLEAD initiatives, selection into the SIIP NIC was not primarily based on access and scope of individual team members' professional responsibilities, instead, the selection of schools and design was very strategic to maximize the probability of a successful pilot. To seed the SIIP NIC, the partnership reached out to the leaders of FCPS Region 1. FCPS comprises five regions, each with approximately 40 schools. Region 1 leadership was uniquely positioned to support the SIIP NIC as one Region leader at the time was an adjunct professor for the EDLE program. Two criteria were used to identify possible candidates through an intentional selection process. First, we considered only elementary schools because all FCPS middle and high schools were involved in other initiatives at the time. Second, the elementary school list was whittled down to include only schools where students ultimately would attend two high schools identified as priority schools for being at risk of failing to meet state accountability targets. We also selected schools near the threshold for Title I funding (i.e., just above or just below). These criteria narrowed the field to six elementary schools, three of which were Title I schools at the time. Next, the Region 1 leader, the Director of Curriculum and Instruction from Instructional Services, and Claire Silva went together to visit each potential SIIP NIC school to invite them to join the pilot. We were happily surprised when each school's leaders elected to join the network.

TEXTBOX 3.2 THE LIST OF BENEFITS FOR PARTICIPATING IN THE SIIP NIC

Benefits of participation for SIIP NIC schools include:

- A structured network with schools that feed into two local high schools.
- Learning from one another around "what works" in school improvement.
- A suite of continuous improvement tools and methodologies for immediate use with staff.
- Dedicated time for strategic planning and reflection on your SIIP.
- Structured feedback opportunities for the NIC participants.
- Increased collective efficacy for attaining SIIP goals.
- Collaboratively reflecting during the mid-year and end-of-year SIIP review.

The SIIP NIC is a network of six school teams composed of the principal, at least one assistant principal and resource teacher/instructional coach, and two classroom teachers. While this initiative was limited in scope with only six schools out of 198 in the district, it was our most intensive effort, potentially maximizing the impact of this work. Each school is paired with an FCPS iLEAD team member and an EDLE iLEAD team member serving as SIIP NIC coaches. The SIIP NIC convenings were co-planned and co-facilitated by EDLE and FCPS iLEAD team members. While this initiative does not obviously connect with EDLE's curricular-driven work, it shows how we were able to make time to work together on each other's initiatives that supported our joint aim and were essential to making progress on (18) Partnership Relationships of the Developmental Progressions into Integrating IS/NIC Into the Core Work.

SIIP NIC schools were expected to attend quarterly network convenings where they were introduced to IS tools to advance their SIIP plans. Between convenings, SIIP NIC schools were expected to conduct PDSA cycles to test the SIIP actions named in their plans. Schools presented the results of their PDSA cycles at the subsequent network convening using a structure called PDSA slams. For a list of benefits of participating in the SIIP NIC that was communicated to participants, see textbox 3.2. The SIIP NIC progressed through three phases. Each of the phases illustrated below was critical in developing school leaders' capacity to lead continuous improvement while allowing the partnership to attend to its growth and development.

PHASE 1: CULTIVATING CULTURES OF CONTINUOUS IMPROVEMENT, 2019–20 SCHOOL YEAR

The first phase centered on developing empathy around and understanding of schools' attitudes toward continuous improvement, using data to shift from a program-centered to problem-focused approach to improvement, and using PDSA cycles to test small, but potentially mighty changes. During SIIP NIC convenings, time was divided into thirds. The first third of their time was spent learning about IS and how

TEXTBOX 3.3 THE ACTIVITIES OF EACH OF THE THREE SIIP NIC PHASES

In Phase 1, SIIP NIC schools:

- Partnered with one FCPS and one GMU iLEAD team member to provide guidance, thought partnership, and coaching support.
- Participated in empathy interviews conducted by their FCPS/EDLE partners to learn about their previous lived experiences with the school improvement process.
- Were introduced to PDSA cycles as the engine of continuous improvement, practical measures, and other essential tools from IS.
- Examined their SIIP plans to determine the organizational capacity for change using SWOT.
- Performed a comprehensive needs assessment that included the identification of a problem of practice related to students' success and/or caring culture.
- Conducted root causes analysis around the identified problem of practice impacting student success or caring culture using affinity mapping, fishbone diagrams.
- Identified high-impact drivers for improvement using inter-relational diagrams.
- Iterated PDSA cycles to implement SIIP actions.
- Spread what worked at quarterly convenings using PDSA slams.

In Phase 2, SIIP NIC schools further developed their use of methods and tools from IS to:

- Developed a working theory of practice improvement.
- Learn how to visualize improvement efforts for decision-making using driver diagrams.
- Continue to test SIIP actions using PDSA cycles to learn what works across different contexts.
- Share their improvement journey through storyboarding.

In Phase 3, SIIP NIC schools:

- Aligned the school improvement efforts to the ESSER 3/SIIP planning and budgeting.
- Continued learning about and constructing driver diagrams.
- Conducted PDSA cycles to test ESSER/SIIP actions.
- Participated in and considered the application of empathy interviews to understand the lived experiences of stakeholders.
- Given the challenges schools faced with interruptions to instructional time, selected levels of engagement with the network, called SIIP NIC snacks.

Examined opportunities for intentionally scaling SIIP strategies using processes that work between collaborative-level teams.

this knowledge can redress long-standing inequities at their schools. The second third was spent networking and sharing lessons learned. Finally, teams spent the last third of their time with their team and iLEAD coaches planning for the next action period and providing feedback to the iLEAD team about their experiences thus far. See textbox 3.3 for a list of Phase 1 activities.

Substantial learning occurred during the first phase. The feedback we received highlighted concrete gains after only the second convening. One school team shared that they were, "looking at our SIIP through a different lens. Finally, working [on] answering the question is 'what we are doing really working?'" while another team highlighted the importance of a shared process: "We have a process that will allow us to dig through complex problems. The discussions [allow] everyone to get on the same page." This feedback led the iLEAD team to believe that we had begun to crack the code to infuse IS in the school improvement process within FCPS. Nevertheless, we struggled to create a balance between learning time and processing time. When asked how we could have improved their learning teams shared, "More time to process things. I felt like there was a lot of great coaching happening, but not a lot of time to think and process." By the end of phase one, the team could infer that more processing and thinking time had resulted in increased capacity for continuous improvement even through the uncertainties at the beginning of the COVID-19 pandemic.

PHASE 2: REDRESSING INEQUITIES, 2020–21 SCHOOL YEAR

In Phase 2 during the 2020–21 school year, the SIIP NIC continued to draw upon the strength of the NIC's culture of continuous improvement for advancing school improvement goals to redress inequalities caused by the closure of school buildings due to the COVID-19 pandemic (schools began to phase in in-person instruction in late spring 2021). Coincidentally, one of the SIIP NIC principals, an EDLE alumnus, was promoted to Executive Principal on the Region 1 leadership team. As an Executive Principal, Ray Lonnett oversaw SIIPs for the Region and continued to serve as a significant champion for the SIIP NIC among the FCPS leadership team. For a list of Phase 2 activities, see textbox 3.3.

In hindsight, Phase 2 was likely the smoothest year of our pilot since schools were either partially or 100% remote for most of the school year. Only in April, after FCPS faculty/staff were able to be fully vaccinated, did schools phase in consistent in-person instruction. From the perspective of the SIIP NIC, this meant consistent virtual convenings of the NIC during weekly asynchronous learning days for students.

PHASE 3: SPREADING WHAT WORKS, 2021–22 SCHOOL YEAR

Despite many challenges (see Lessons Learned below), SIIP NIC schools elevated their profiles as improvement leaders and acted as lighthouses of school improvement in this final phase of the pilot. SIIP NIC school leaders who participated in Phase 3 activities reported that they were able to approach school improvement planning including budgeting ESSER funds more strategically thereby creating better alignment between needs assessment data and planned improvement in the areas of reading, math, and student wellness. As a result of these activities, SIIP NIC schools could plan more strategically for their SIIP and ESSER budgeting aligned to reading, math, and student wellness.

SHOWCASING OUR JOINT EFFORTS

We look forward to future opportunities for spreading what works in regards to shifting school improvement towards a more dynamic process by facilitating our joint Learning to Improve conference where EDLE students, SIIP NIC teams, SBAIP II participants, and PIP II school-based leaders present their findings for what school improvement strategies and actions improved teachers and learning. EDLE eagerly volunteered to co-host and organize with the FCPS iLEAD members the first conference on GMU's campus. This effort helps advance our progress to the Small Change Implementation stage of (24) Public Communications in the Development Progressions.

Synergy between Leadership Preparation and School Improvement

Discussing the SIIP NIC allows us to return to Lance, the student engaged in EDLE coursework in spring 2019. When the SIIP NIC launched in the fall of 2019, Lance was implementing his internship project at Dranesville Elementary. When his principal agreed to be part of the SIIP NIC, she might not have known about Lance's familiarity with IS, but he immediately became an asset to his SIIP's team when they joined the SIIP NIC pilot. One example of the partnership's synergy emerged at the second convening. That day, the SIIP NIC schools participated in a fishbone diagram exercise. The other schools in attendance slowly compiled root causes with coaching to help them with the task. Lance's school took off running with Lance's expertise guiding the team. Throughout the SIIP NIC pilot, Lance's school has been one of the most committed sites, consistently attending convenings (virtual and in person), including through a principal transition. When a new principal took the helm at Lance's school, this transition came with no guarantee that they would continue to be part of the optional SIIP NIC pilot. The principal had no experience with IS and was taking leadership over the school in the midst of the COVID-19 pandemic. Despite these potential obstacles, Lance's school remains part of the SIIP NIC, and he remains on the team. This experience has provided an initial glimpse of the vast potential of the GMU/FCPS iLEAD partnership.

Conclusions and Lessons Learned

When considering the journey from the FCPS conference facility with a continental breakfast to the coordinated integration of IS across the EDLE curriculum and FCPS leadership training, we suggest three essential components to this transition. Some of these components were present from the beginning due to the nature of GMU being a large, public university located within FCPS's boundaries, while others show how IS catalyzed our work. Specifically, these components are (1) building on historical partnership relations between the two organizations, (2) garnering immediate excitement about IS, and (3) leveraging this eagerness and capacity to make time for collaboration.

STARTING WITH A FOUNDATIONAL RELATIONSHIP TO BUILD UPON

It is important to reiterate that our organizations have a long history of collaborating on leadership development, and a large segment of FCPS employees are alumni of GMU. FCPS and GMU had developed a mutually beneficial relationship over many years before partnering to support the iLEAD network of school services. FCPS, due to its large size, requires a robust school leadership pipeline, and EDLE has helped meet this need by expanding cohorts when demand is higher. This relationship led to consistently strong enrollment in EDLE programs, and an ever-expanding pool of certified school administrators from FCPS to draw upon. When GMU joined the iLEAD network with FCPS, the relationship between FCPS and EDLE became more formalized, and adopted an integrative approach to embed IS into our core work to promote equity in student outcomes. To this day, both Sloan and Mark remain ardent supporters of the iLEAD initiative, as both have been promoted within their respective institutions. Our work together is consistently reinforced through the large cadre of teachers and leaders in FCPS with a GMU degree, many with training from the EDLE program specifically. In a recent survey of EDLE alumni (60% response rate), over half had entered a school-based administrator position within three years of graduation.

GARNER IMMEDIATE EXCITEMENT ABOUT IMPROVEMENT SCIENCE

As described earlier, prior to iLEAD, FCPS's Instructional Services team, particularly the Secondary Literacy staff, had already participated in several IS-driven initiatives and was taking steps to make IS the signature tool for improving instruction in FCPS. FCPS was searching for ways to accelerate efforts to advance equity in the school system beyond the specific programs schools were adopting at the time, and the equity orientation of IS was well suited for this goal. Instead of being a program, IS is an approach and set of guiding tools that the FCPS team immediately believed could help to increase equity in FCPS.

While EDLE faculty had not specifically used IS tools, the curriculum already had significant overlap with IS, focusing on identifying a problem of practice, engaging in root cause analysis, and a commitment to continuous improvement. After EDLE faculty were exposed to the excitement of FCPS's staff, saw the overlap with the curriculum, and read *Learning to Improve* (Bryk et al., 2015), they were quickly just as committed to making IS their signature pedagogical approach. All of this to say, we saw very little resistance to change, which is often a significant barrier to improvement efforts. All relevant parties quickly saw the potential of IS. Not only did this create a smoother partnership initiation, but also it helped to sustain our partnership.

This excitement continues to spread as EDLE has hired new faculty and FCPS has grown its team of central office leaders. These new additions continue to onboard with this same high level of interest, creating a deeper bench of people who contribute to this work and amplify our impact over time.

LEVERAGE EAGERNESS AND CAPACITY TO MAKE TIME FOR COLLABORATION

As described earlier, the FCPS iLEAD team and EDLE faculty meet regularly as a large group to maintain communication and monitor our growth on the Developmental Progressions. We have established working groups on various efforts to further our work. These meetings and working groups keep us connected. We met in person before March 2020, but we seamlessly pivoted to virtual meetings to maintain this meeting schedule throughout the pandemic. Our continuity is undoubtedly attributable to the Project Liaison, our boundary spanner, although we do not contend that we rely on any one person to stay connected. Other team members often organize these regular meetings, and we have established routines to prioritize iLEAD. In addition, multiple members of FCPS and EDLE attend iLEAD Convenings, Steering Committee meetings, and Carnegie Summits as engaged partners and presenters. These choices illustrate our strength on (18) Partnership Relationships. While the description of the first key component noted that we started strongly on (18), this component also affirms how we have quickly institutionalized and sustained our work in this area. This partnership work would not be possible if we did not make time to meet, collaborate, and grow on the Developmental Progressions together.

CONCLUDING THOUGHTS

As we reflect on what has facilitated the successful launch of the FCPS–GMU iLEAD partnership, we also are reminded of times when we have activated our IS toolkit to respond to challenges along the way. Not only are we teaching others to be user-centered when defining problems of practice and their solutions, but we are also user–centered in our work. The COVID-19 pandemic has tested some of our partnership initiatives, especially the SIIP NIC. We were coming to the end of Year 1 of the SIIP NIC pilot in spring 2020, and, at first, we mostly continued the SIIP NIC work as planned. We had a virtual convening of leadership from SIIP NIC schools in June 2020 and continued virtual convenings that looked very similar to the in-person convenings throughout the 2020–21 school year. The challenges really began, however, with the 2021–22 school year at which point FCPS started the year in person despite the emergence of the Delta variant of the virus. While it was actually easier to have virtual convenings than the in-person convenings in the 2020–21 school year because of built in asynchronous learning days, FCPS put a moratorium on all non-essential professional learning for a significant portion of the fall and winter of the 2021–22 school year.

In spite of these challenges, we were able to continue the SIIP NIC work. Because our work with the SIIP NIC schools persisted across two school years, these SIIP teams had come to value our support and the IS tools we instilled through our collaborations. This led us to transition from full–day sessions teaching IS with time for the SIIP teams to plan to a one-on-one coaching model. The partnership offered options that ranged from 30-minute coaching calls, an office hour, three-hour workshops, or full-day workshops. All SIIP NIC schools continued their engagement despite the operational challenges presented by the pandemic. Currently, the partnership is exploring options for scaling the SIIP NIC to additional schools across all five regions in FCPS.

ATTENDING TO THE MISSION OF OUR PARTNERSHIP WORK

Our eagerness to collaborate notwithstanding, we are well attuned to the necessity of consistently engaging in conversations about the purpose of our partnership work. We hold regular retreats to discuss our mission, driver diagram, and progress on the Developmental Progressions. Each retreat produces illuminating teachable moments that help to accelerate our work together. For instance, upon reflection on the Developmental Progressions, we noted our lack of progress on (24) Public Communication could undermine our work if others did not know about it. We launched several working groups on strategies to better communicate our work and build an understanding of how our efforts led to the integration of IS in FCPS. As mentioned, part of these efforts includes planning a public-facing conference, our Learning to Improve conference, to showcase the IS efforts in FCPS leadership induction and EDLE Master's students. This attentiveness to our mission is critical to keep all parties active and involved in our iLEAD work.

Building a meaningful partnership takes time and commitment. The GMU/FCPS partnership has been fortunate to have senior leaders who value recognizing the power of inter-institution collaboration. While on our individual improvement journeys, each institution implemented meaningful change. Together, though, we are shifting minds and actions on how complex systems can work on problems of practice to better educational communities for students.

Questions for Discussion

1. Like some of the other cases in this volume, the FCPS/GMU partnership grew out of existing relationships between the school district and university. This narrative makes a good case for that past history being important to subsequent success,

and at one point they refer to it as "essential." Do you think it's possible for an improvement partnership to be successfully initiated and sustained without such a past history—and if so, how might that be done?
2. In the concluding pages of the case, the authors write that, "we saw very little resistance to change, which is often a significant barrier to improvement efforts." Given that higher education and school districts are notoriously difficult to change, what factors seem to explain why the authors encountered something different in their partnership?
3. More than most chapters in this section, the Development Progressions are described as playing a key role in helping the two institutions (school district and university) work together toward common ends (as boundary objects do). Do you see this as a potentially generalizable strategy—and what are some of the conditions that would have to be put in place to make it work in other contexts?

References

Bryk, A. S., Gomez, L. M., Grunow, A., & LeMahieu, P. G. (2015). *Learning to improve: How America's schools can get better at getting better*. Harvard Education Press.

George Mason University School of Education. (2022). *Education leadership program*. https://education.gmu.edu/education-leadership/

Indiana University Center for Postsecondary Research. (2021). *Graduate instructional program classification*. The Carnegie Classifications of Institutions of Higher Education. https://carnegieclassifications.iu.edu/classification_descriptions/grad_program.php

CHAPTER 4

Using Improvement Science Principles for New-Teacher Support

HIGH TECH HIGH AND HIGH TECH HIGH GRADUATE SCHOOL OF EDUCATION

Julia Jacobsen and Diana Cornejo-Sanchez

In 2016, High Tech High (HTH) and the High Tech High Graduate School of Education (HTH GSE) redesigned the HTH new-teacher induction program to improve novice teacher support and development by integrating principles of improvement science. In the new design, teams of teachers focused on a common problem of practice with coaching from a content expert. The program's curriculum drew from improvement science tools in order to support the learning. Participants report a strong sense of belonging and value the learning in their teams. The teacher induction program has been a rich learning space for both facilitating continuous improvement and developing a partnership for improvement.

Context

HIGH TECH HIGH & THE HIGH TECH HIGH GRADUATE SCHOOL OF EDUCATION

High Tech High (HTH) is a charter network of 16 K–12 schools in San Diego, California.[1] Founded in 2000, High Tech High schools strive to embody the design principles of equity, personalization, authentic work, and collaborative design through project-based learning. At High Tech High, students in kindergarten through twelfth grade engage in real-world projects while teachers at High Tech High schools have to be continuous learners in order to hone their craft as facilitators of deeper learning.

The High Tech High Graduate School of Education (HTH GSE) was founded in 2007 by K–12 educators from High Tech High with the goal of empowering

---

[1] See HTH and GSE websites: https://www.hightechhigh.org and https://hthgse.edu. In addition, see online Appendix for additional documentation of this partnership work at https://textbooks.rowman.com/gomez-improving.

educators within and beyond the High Tech High network to lead for equitable deeper learning. As practitioners themselves, the founders recognized that adults—just like K–12 students—learn best through hands-on, personalized learning. Thus, the HTH GSE was established to give adult learners the opportunity to apply their learning in an authentic context. HTH GSE strives to develop leaders to have the capacity to shift our systems so that students are collaborative designers of their experience.

High Tech High and the HTH GSE have a unique relationship. Over half of the HTH GSE faculty are former High Tech High teachers and leaders, including the president and the dean. At its best, this relationship allows for the graduate school and the K–12 to be learning with and from one another in service of creating equitable deeper learning for both kids and adults.

Although HTH and HTH GSE have a close relationship, we are still in the early stages of developing a partnership for *improvement*. The iLEAD Developmental Progressions (see Introduction to this volume) describe how higher education institutions, K–12 institutions, and their collaborative partnerships can grow over time in service of systemic improvement (table 4.1).

New-teacher induction is a HTH Teacher Center (K–12) responsibility that provides a strong example of Teacher Center/GSE collaboration to serve K–12 schools. Increasingly, it has also become a strong example of the collaborative use of improvement methods to achieve shared aims.

Problems

Xavier is a first-year teacher. He spent his student teaching practicum online during distance learning. When he entered his teacher preparation program, he had no idea that his first experiences as a teacher would be in front of a computer screen seeing his students only on *Zoom*, never actually meeting them in person. When the 2021–2022 school year kicked off, he was pumped to have his own classroom and eager to meet students face-to-face for the first time. As he welcomed masked students on the first day of school, the butterflies in his stomach were going wild; finally students were here! The first day jitters and joy were quickly replaced with fear and anxiety. He noticed attendance diminishing as students and his colleagues were exposed to the new Omicron variant. Thoughts ran through Xavier's head: Do I continue with the project? How will I catch students up? Are they ok? Do they have any high-risk family members at home? Will I get sick next? Who will cover my classes? Should I make sub plans now in case I go down? Seeing teachers around him begin to crumble with the pressure and submit their resignations, he wondered: Will I make it?

Since the pandemic began in 2020, teachers nationwide have been experiencing a spike in stress and burnout. A 2022 survey by the NEA identified burnout as the top issue facing educators right now, with 90% of teachers saying that burnout is a serious problem (GBAO, 2022). Although longitudinal studies are not yet available about the impact of the pandemic on teacher retention, 86% of teachers said they have seen more educators leaving the profession or retiring early since the beginning of the pandemic (GBAO, 2022).

Table 4.1 Description of the Developmental Progressions Category Learning to Improve

Domain	Area of Work	"Exploring Change Ideas"	"Small Change Implementation"	"Integrating IS/NICs into the Core Work"	"Institutionalizing and Sustaining the Work"
Partnership	Learning to Improve	Partnership members are exploring how to work together using IS/NICs to improve their respective and joint efforts	The LEA and IHE have initiated new structures to consolidate their learnings about the use of IS/NICs	The partnership is developing a continuous quality improvement system that includes regular data feedback from program participants during and after the program	The LEA and IHE are jointly reviewing evidence from a quality improvement system and using this to plan the next set of improvement cycles for the partnership. The partnership can document learnings from capstones that have advanced local improvements

Even before the pandemic, teachers were leaving the profession in high numbers. A 2018 study indicated that 44% of teachers were leaving the profession within the first 5 years (Ingersoll et al., 2018). Generally, pre-service teachers have relatively brief opportunities to take ownership of a classroom (e.g., 12 weeks), so new teachers face a steep learning curve upon entering their first year. Understandably, many new teachers feel overwhelmed by the demands of the classroom.

INDUCTION AS A LEVER FOR TEACHER RETENTION

The challenges of effective new-teacher support existed long before the current pandemic, and HTH GSE has collaborated with HTH schools for a number of years to address these challenges. The HTH GSE hosts two master's programs, preparing pre-service teachers and developing school leaders. Together with the K–12 schools they have continuously pondered, how can we support new teachers so that they feel a sense of belonging and feel empowered to make positive changes in their classroom? Teacher retention data—including empathy interviews with teachers—has been collected, analyzed, and discussed to help HTH develop levers to address this problem of practice. One collaborative system in place is that of teacher induction. Teacher induction is a formalized program of support for new teachers with the goal of developing high-quality teachers who remain in the profession. Induction programs for new teachers can create an on-ramp to the profession.

If designed well, induction programs can nearly double the retention rate of new teachers (Podolsky et al., 2016). Moreover, "a mentor in the early years of a teaching career increases teacher retention, improves pedagogical practice, and enhances teacher work satisfaction" (Bartlett & Johnson, 2010, p. 849). Intensive mentor models consist of opportunities to engage in frequent conversations about instructional practices, observations of experienced teachers, opportunities to receive feedback from the mentor on classroom observations of the novice teacher, and even the analysis of data, including student work, to inform instructional design.

In 1992, the California Department of Education and the California Commission on Teacher Credentialing set out to address teacher attrition by instituting the Beginning Teacher Support and Assessment (BTSA) program (Lovo et al., 2006, p. 64). With the support of a mentor, novice teachers reflected on and worked to develop within the California Standards for the Teaching Profession (CSTPs). The program proved to be successful with "84% of beginning teachers remaining in teaching for five years while 50% of those who did not participate in BTSA left the profession within the first two years of teaching" (Lovo et al., 2006, p. 56). This success led to the passing of SB 2042 in 1998, creating a two-level credential program. California teachers now begin with a preliminary credential and must complete a teacher induction program in order to receive a professional clear credential.

To create coherence within the trajectory of a novice teacher, induction programs required districts to provide the novice teacher with job-embedded professional learning support and mentorship through a two-year induction program. Most induction programs required novice teachers to create portfolios as their summative assessment, demonstrating their competency in the CSTPs. For many educators—novice teachers and their mentors included—the onerous documentation process felt like a compliance exercise that did little to support the novice teacher. Rather than developing high-quality teachers, induction programs were adding additional burden to teachers in their first years as they navigated their way through the paperwork required for documentation.

In response to these challenges, the California Teacher Credentialing Commission took a sharp turn in 2016, giving teacher induction programs around the state the autonomy to design more authentic learning experiences for new teachers with a few clear requirements. The Commission on Teacher Credentialing allowed for school districts to have autonomy over the design of their induction program as long as:

1. The novice teacher is connected with a qualified mentor through weekly meetings of at least an hour of mentorship.
2. The individuals have an opportunity to set goals within the context of an Individual Learning Plan (ILP) for their two-year induction experience within the CSTP for the sole purpose of growth and not performance evaluation.

Other than that, programs had the freedom to design a program that would best meet the goals of increasing teacher effectiveness and retention.

EXPERIMENTING WITH IMPROVEMENT IN TEACHER INDUCTION

High Tech High has hosted its own induction program since 2007 through the HTH Teacher Center, a center housed under the umbrella of the HTH K–12 schools. The program originally offered a menu of workshops that teachers could choose from each month, and culminated in the state-required portfolio. While we were meeting state requirements, the workshops insufficiently addressed the need for learning in community and in context and were not consistent with HTH design principles.

With the freedom to design our own program granted by California Commission on Teacher Credentialing in 2016, HTH teacher induction had an opportunity to create a program that supported new teachers' efficacy and ultimately their desire to stay in the teaching profession. Ideally, the redesign would embody the design principles of High Tech High, creating a space where new teachers work collaboratively toward equity; personalizing their learning in order to apply it authentically in their context, something the previous program design did not have—it had been an experience that happened outside of their teaching context.

Coincidentally, High Tech High and the High Tech High GSE joined the iLEAD cohort in 2016, creating space for program leaders to collaborate on this new challenge. Janie Griswold, the director of the HTH Teacher Center at the time, joined a team from the HTH Graduate School of Education at a Carnegie event focused on supporting improvement in school systems. Stacey Caillier, the Director of the Center for Research on Equity and Innovation at the HTH GSE and Ryan Gallagher, the Director of Continuous Improvement at the HTH GSE collaborated with Griswold to reimagine how improvement processes might elevate the teacher induction program's goals and ultimately teacher retention. Others who would contribute to the redesign process included Julie Holmes, Dr. Diana Cornejo-Sanchez, Sarah Barnes, and Julia Jacobsen. The initiative was broadly owned on both sides of the collaboration.

The redesign began with empathy interviews with induction participants. These conversations uncovered that novice teachers did not just have one mentor, but instead they had built connections with many educators who served them in different purposes—they had learned to establish a network of support. Aware of the power of mentorship and supportive relationships for new teachers, Gallagher, Caillier, and Griswold sought to create an induction experience that would foster connections between participants and provide a supportive experienced teacher (in this case an induction improvement coach) in addition to their school-based mentor. The graduate school and K–12's early introduction to continuous improvement showed promise in supporting teachers and increasing outcomes for students.

In the new program, participants met monthly with an improvement team to dive deeply into one topic over time with the guidance of an improvement coach. The topics for improvement groups emerged from the California Standards of Teaching Practice and the needs at K–12 schools and evolved based on the expertise of coaches and participant interest. These improvement teams focused on problems of practice such as Supporting Emergent Bilingual Learners, Classroom Structures of Success, Authentic Assessments, and Culturally Responsive Pedagogy in Math. Knowing that belonging, connection, and personalization are critical to fostering efficacy within novice teachers, the improvement groups are all capped at groups no larger than 15. We also worked to integrate mentor support into the program, so that participants could have a personalized experience while working toward their collective goal on their improvement team.

The first of the Six Core Principles of Improvement is to "make the work problem-specific and user-centered" (Bryk et al. 2015).[2] To better understand the problem they were working to improve, induction participants conducted empathy interviews with their students early in the program. Empathy interviews use open-ended questions to invite stories that help the interviewer more deeply understand how the interviewee experiences a problem. When induction participants conducted interviews with their students, it encouraged improvement teams to look at their problem through the eyes of a student and see possible levers they have as a teacher to make improvements in the students' experience. The empathy interviews build relationships with students—a critical component to establishing a positive classroom culture that supports the novice teachers' efficacy. Empathy interviews center equity by elevating student voices and working to replace deficit thinking with teacher agency to make improvements.

Teachers then collaborated to explore the root causes of the problem they wanted to improve, and to select and adapt change ideas to their individual context. Ideally, teachers would complete the program with an increased capacity to make improvements to the systems and practices within their own classroom. In the long term, with all new teachers at High Tech High practicing continuous improvement through induction, we also hoped to build our organizational capacity for improvement for equity (table 4.2).

---

[2] Also The Six Core Principles of Improvement Carnegie Foundation for the Advancement of Teaching https://www.carnegiefoundation.org/our-ideas/six-core-principles-improvement/

Table 4.2 HTH Teacher Center Directors and GSE Collaborators, 2016–22

	Redesign #1: Improvement Science as a curricular frame for Induction					Redesign #2: Moving online & supporting coach development		
	2016	2017	2018	2019	2020	2021	2022
Director of the HTH Teacher Center	Janie Griswold (Now Chief Learning Officer of HTH)			Diana Cornejo-Sanchez (Now Director of Instructional Leadership & Development at HTH)			Sarah Barnes
Improvement Coach Support	Ryan Gallagher Director of Continuous Improvement HTH GSE			Julia Jacobsen Improvement Specialist, IExD HTH GSE			

Note: Over the seven years since the initial redesign of induction, the director of the HTH Teacher Center has collaborated with HTH GSE faculty members on program design and coach support.

The new design had positive results, connecting teachers together in a way that induction had not in the past. In the feedback, teachers often shared positive experiences about the connections they were making with other teachers and their induction coaches. By learning collectively, teachers could not only learn from each others' successes but support one another through their failures, making a safe space for learning that the previous structure did not facilitate; one participant described this experience on the feedback form: "Now that I am getting to know my colleagues more, I truly am enjoying getting time to talk with them and share ideas, ask questions, etc."

As a result of the small group design, participants reported a strong sense of belonging and connection as novice teachers—and valued the learning in their induction sessions. On a five-point scale separately indicating participants' sense of "belonging" as well as their evaluation of their "learning" in the session, participant responses increased during the year to an average rating of 4.5 or above on both measures over the last three sessions surveyed. A participant shared on the session feedback form, "I really appreciate the time to talk with other new HTH teachers," and another talked about the immediate impact: "The class allowed me to view restorative practices in a way that can be applied to my advisory. For me, this will develop into meaningful work."

Another participant shared how their experience with their improvement team surpassed their expectations for what they imagined induction would be:

> I was pleasantly surprised that it was incredibly practical. The PDSA cycles were simple and useful, and something that I think I will continue to do in the future…. Overall, this was a great experience where I took an area (group work) that I was very weak in as a teacher and I got to experiment, learn, and actually implement something in my classroom.
>
> (Participant Feedback Form, May 27, 2017)

One of the core principles of improvement is to accelerate improvements through networked communities. "Embrace the wisdom of crowds. We can accomplish more together than even the best of us can accomplish alone" (The Six Core Principles of Improvement). Continuous improvement is a promising curricular framework for the teacher induction program because of the power of learning in community.

Challenges, Solutions, and Evidence

As we sought to create an authentic learning experience with improvement science as the foundation for the curriculum, we learned how to create a welcoming entry to improvement science, and how to better support coaches to interrupt deficit thinking and build a learning community. It is worth noting that this has been in itself a continuous improvement project, consistently recognizing the challenges to design solutions based on data. And as we are encouraged by our progress, we also recognize that there is work yet to do, with problems of practice yet to address.

CHALLENGE #1: ENTRY PLANNING THAT INCORPORATES CONTINUOUS IMPROVEMENT

Participants in the induction program sign up because it's a state requirement. They often choose our program over others because they are teaching in a HTH school, or their school has a relationship with HTH (and their schools fund their tuition). They are not opting into the program because of their enthusiasm for improvement science. One of our primary challenges was to design a program that built on the strengths of improvement science as a tool for collaborative learning while creating an experience that is engaging and relevant for participants, with the ultimate aim of improving K–12 student outcomes.

The induction team had learned that emphasizing content over cultivating relationships, including overemphasizing expertise in improvement tools, could detract from the learning goals of the program. In 2017, having just been introduced to continuous improvement, the program focused very much on the continuous improvement process as the content for induction versus the novice teacher's experience as the text. Dr. Michelle Pledger, an improvement coach in the induction program, concluded, "the goal is not to learn first and then practice improvement; the goal is to practice improvement so we can learn" (Pledger, 2020). As a result, we have shifted the ways that we engage with several of the tools and practices of improvement science within the induction program.

Root Cause Analysis

In service of the first core principle of improvement is "Make the work problem-specific and user-centered" (The Six Core Principles of Improvement). Improvement teams used a series of protocols to get clear on the problem they were hoping to solve. They collaborate to identify the root cause they will address in order to work toward improvement. Over time we have simplified these processes to increase collaboration and relevance for participants.

In 2016, participants co-constructed a driver diagram to represent the theory of action of their group. This process proved to be too abstract to be meaningful to most participants' practice. At the end of the protocol, participants were unclear as to what they might try next in their classrooms. While we still use driver diagrams to represent our theory of action as a program, participants are no longer constructing them in their improvement teams.

One of the sessions that got strong reviews from participants was the one in which participants created a fishbone diagram to capture possible root causes of their problem of practice, and an interrelationship digraph in order to converge on a root cause that the group saw as the most central to the problem. As one teacher reflected after a root cause analysis session in 2019, "I enjoyed the fishbone and diagraph, it was an activity that was collaborative and truly helped me see and communicate insight of causes to the problem statement." These processes made the collective thinking of the group visible and provided the team a space to reflect before acting. It also helped participants to see the commonalities between their experiences with the problem they hoped to address, creating a sense of common purpose.

As we moved online due to the pandemic, even the fishbone diagram protocol and interrelationship diagraph protocol became more onerous than they were worth for most coaches and participants. When moved online, the protocols focused the team's energy on maneuvering the online collaboration tools rather than facilitating conversations about teacher practice and student outcomes as it had in person.

Coaches began to explore other ways of helping participants identify the root causes of the problem. In Dr. Curtis Taylor's induction team, empathy interviews and student surveys helped focus teachers' attention on the possible root causes of equity issues in the math classroom. Dr. Taylor described how he facilitated the group to use data to focus their work:

> For lesson study, we utilize data as a way for us to identify equity themes for each lesson study team. The teachers were asked to conduct empathy interviews with 2–3 focal students about their math experience and who they are as young people. Then, teachers were asked to administer a math agency survey to their students. Based on these two data points, the lesson study teams went through a process of notice and wonder about the data to highlight any major themes that were rising for them. (Personal correspondence with authors, June 27, 2022)

In Dr. Kristin Komatsubara's induction team, teachers asked a chain of "whys" to identify the root causes of the problem they were exploring. Komatsubara shared how she refocused the group when deficit thinking arose, and how she would like to improve this process in the upcoming year:

> I then had our teachers look at our causes and adjust any that felt deficit-based to an asset-based lens. This seemed to work well but I think what I would have liked to do is start with this at the beginning of the year and then return to it at different points along our journey. (Personal correspondence with authors, June 28, 2022)

Plan-Do-Study-Act Cycles

Another principle of improvement is to "Anchor practice improvement in disciplined inquiry" (The Six Core Principles of Improvement). In order to keep track of the inquiry process around the ideas that participants were testing in their classrooms, we assigned Plan-Do-Study-Act forms as homework after the sessions. Participants tested out a change idea in their classrooms in between sessions, capturing data in order to determine whether the idea resulted in improvement.

In the first few years after program redesign, some participants struggled with PDSA cycles, sometimes procrastinating until the end of the year, at which point their completion was inauthentic and perfunctory. By the end of the program, some participants still didn't understand their purpose. In response, coaches began to build the PDSA process into sessions rather than assigning the forms as homework. Coaches facilitated collaborative protocols to share ideas, dig deeper into the problem and understand its root causes, or learn from experts through modeling. Each session concluded with the selection of a new change idea based on the group's learning and time to plan that idea with a learning partner.

The collaborative experience contributed to a sense of belonging and common purpose in the group, having a greater impact than when the forms were completed in isolation. After creating time to collaboratively reflect and plan in a session, 80% of participants felt prepared to conduct their next PDSA cycle, even amid the challenges of Omicron. As one participant shared, reflecting on the value of paired partnership teams working together in "squads": "The time that we spent with our squads was really helpful to establish my next course of action" (Participant Feedback Form, January 10, 2022).

By engaging in PDSA cycles, participants learn that (1) data comes in many forms (attendance, assessments, student work, etc.) and (2) collecting data is imperative to understand the impact of the change ideas on student learning and behaviors to inform their next steps. Teachers are encouraged to identify and collect data that will authentically inform their understanding of the problem. In a context where data collection in schools can be related to compliance and accountability, understanding data as a tool for learning can be a mindset shift for some.

During the third session, teachers reflect together on their first PDSA cycle by looking at the data together. In the feedback from the session, participants celebrated the ways that looking at data together from their first PDSA cycle deepened their learning. Below are some reflections from the feedback after that session that highlight the value that participants got from looking at data from their classroom:

What are two (2) take-aways or strategies that you learned about tonight?

- As an educator, I must use data in intentional ways to set measurable goals in teaching.
- (1) Looking at the data from your class with colleagues is super helpful! and (2) Getting to a hypothesis of why things are occurring in your class in order to find impactful solutions.
- I learned that the PDSA cycle can be very diverse and that there is not one correct thing to do. I also learned that ensuring equity in data is quite challenging.

What supported your connection with colleagues today?

- A lot of time in breakout rooms, looking at each other's data, and getting to speak on our own ideas about that data.
- Working together in small learning groups, sharing our data, experiences in education, and goals for the next learning cycle.

(Participant Feedback Form, November 15, 2021)

Even the constructive, critical feedback from participants after that session indicated an investment in learning from data to improve their practice. Comments such as the following gave us program feedback to help us support a more authentic learning experience:

What could have better supported your learning in today's session?

> I would have loved to have a link to a resource doc of several different ways/examples of data collection. I would love to branch out in how I collect data for my PDSA and examples of what other teachers have already done would be helpful (looking at what other teachers did last time wasn't helpful, because we all were directed to conduct an Empathy Interview as our data).
>
> (Participant Feedback Form, November 15, 2021)

Although looking at data publicly can be intimidating, collaboratively engaging in identifying shared problems of practice and pursuing Plan-Do-Study-Act cycles in a safe space allows novice teachers to recognize that they are not alone. One participant shared that their favorite part of the session was "Meeting other teachers and learning that we share the same fears and struggles." The solidarity in this common issue and the small improvement group size help establish the relational trust that contributes to a novice teacher's sense of belonging and feeling of support.

Sharing Learning

Another principle of improvement is to "Accelerate improvements through networked communities" (The Six Core Principles of Improvement). Improvement teams learned from each other throughout the year, and our hope was for their learning to carry over from year to year. In order to share learning with future cohorts and other improvers, teams created "change packages" at the end of their year of investigation and improvement, showcasing the most promising change ideas they had tested.

The first iteration of the change package was a collection of three- to five-page papers about the most promising change ideas identified by each individual on the team, which were then posted on a website. In theory, these papers could support other teachers who were looking to improve in the area of the team's focus. However in practice, a three- to five-page paper was not an inviting way to share ideas with other teachers. As a result, the final papers felt inauthentic for many participants. If the goal was to create a change package that would inform the practice of other teachers, teams would need to be more disciplined about evaluating the effectiveness of the ideas that were shared, and find a way to share them in a way that would support their adoption.

The goal of induction, however, is not to share promising change ideas with other teachers, but to support the learning and retention of the participants. In 2021 we shifted the final product to be a Celebration of Learning, a powerful summative assessment our K–12 students go through at the end of each semester. We had a hunch that if it was powerful for our students, it would be for adults as well.

During this final session, participants share their learning journey, highlighting "aha moments" and celebrating the people who supported them along the way. Since one of the main contributors to teachers leaving the profession within the first five years is teacher efficacy, we decided to integrate a reflection on belonging, networks, and connections to the presentation, rather than just focus on the content participants learned (Ingersoll et al., 2018). The culminating experience focused on the learning journey and support network, which better aligns with the goals of the program.

The novice teachers gather with their improvement teams, and also invite their mentors and colleagues who have made an impact on their experience as a teacher to be recognized, taking a moment to focus on the learning and the community that will help them to be resilient in a challenging profession.

Rather than relying on individual participants to share their ideas with future improvers, coaches now play an active role in identifying and sharing promising change ideas. Chris Wakefield, an induction improvement coach since 2016, emphasizes the importance of providing models in order to support high-quality work. Building on Chris's feedback, coaches now look at previous participants' PDSAs and Celebrations of Learning in order to identify strong examples to share with the new cohort. With this practice, participants can build on the learning of previous groups in a more organic way.

CHALLENGE #2: OPERATING IN A ONE-YEAR TIME FRAME

In the HTH induction program, teachers meet eight times over the course of the year in a one- or two-year program (those entering with significant teaching experience have a one-year induction program). All share a one-year frame for collaboratively defining and understanding a problem, and iterating on change ideas to work toward improvement—and one year might not be enough.

In the first iterations of the new induction program, the sessions were largely constructivist, drawing from participants' ideas and experience to identify potential change ideas to test. When participants selected a topic of interest and then attempted to co-construct an aim, groups often were unable to agree on a common aim and therefore struggled to translate group activities to their own improvement work.

Coaches now establish an aim and measures before the groups launch, so that participants sign up for an improvement group with knowledge of the aim they'll be working for rather than a general topic. When we made this shift, we were concerned that narrowing the focus of an improvement group would make it more challenging for participants to find a group that met their specific needs. We had historically sought to offer broad categories in order to increase the likelihood that participants could find a group to match the goals they identified in their Individual Learning Plan. However, we found that having a clear goal from the start reduced participants' confusion about the process and how it would apply in their classroom.

As the program evolved, we also encouraged coaches to guide participants toward best practices rather than rely solely on constructivist idea generation. Instead of spending the first few sessions digging into the problem, and the subsequent sessions testing change ideas, induction groups now work to understand the problem and test change ideas throughout the entire year. Coaches provide a high-leverage change idea for participants to test early in the program as a way for the team to understand the process of a PDSA cycle and how they might adapt change ideas to their own setting.

Coaches now also curate learning about relevant research on the topic. Originally, one of the homework assignments for participants was to look for research about their area of improvement to inform a change idea. This task did not yield high-quality ideas, in part because the quality of teaching ideas published on the internet varies widely. Since the goal of the program was not necessarily to teach participants how to comb through educational research, we instead asked coaches to identify a high-leverage change idea supported by research, and design a session in which participants could become familiar with the research behind the idea. As veteran teachers, induction coaches had lots of ideas about how they might facilitate meaningful learning of the applicable research. They embraced the autonomy that this innovation afforded.

All of these shifts combined have allowed participants to develop fluency with and ownership of the PDSA process during the eight sessions, and to more consistently share meaningful reflections on their learning and on the improvements in their classroom by the end of the program.

CHALLENGE #3: DEVELOPING THE CAPACITY OF IMPROVEMENT COACHES

All of the coaches in the induction program have full-time jobs in addition to their role as improvement coaches. Most are teachers in HTH K–12 schools, and some work at the HTH GSE, creating its own professional community of collaboration across the two organizations. Induction coaches have a tall order—to facilitate the development of improvement and teaching capacity among a team of novice teachers over only eight sessions. In the 2016 program redesign, Ryan Gallagher, the Director of Continuous Improvement at the HTH GSE, supported the induction coaching team. Gallagher recalled thinking in the design, "How do I design something so that folks who have varied needs feel the most comfortable facilitating?" (personal correspondence with authors, June 15, 2021). In order for the coaching work to be sustainable, he wanted to build structures that would support coaches to create a valuable learning experience for participants.

Coaches attended a half-day introductory course on improvement science, where they experienced some of the protocols they would use with their teams. In order to minimize the demands on their time, for the first several years of the improvement-science-focused program, coaches met just before the session with a coach lead who would brief them on the agenda for the day. While this allowed coaches to facilitate with minimal time investment, it limited their capacity to truly coach their teams.

Coaches also met for a 45-minute debrief after each session to look at participant feedback, share what worked, and reflect on challenges together. This routine allowed coaches to learn from each other, creating a mini networked-improvement community of their own, focused on improving the learning experience of participants.

Despite the high expectations and limited time for coach development, we were seeing some promising results. In the second year of the redesign, participants reported that they felt supported in their practice and 83% said they were excited about using improvement science (Figure 4.1: Participant Feedback Forms, 2017-18).

While participants felt supported, coaches had higher hopes for the learning that could happen in their groups. Coaches were also struggling with shifting deficit

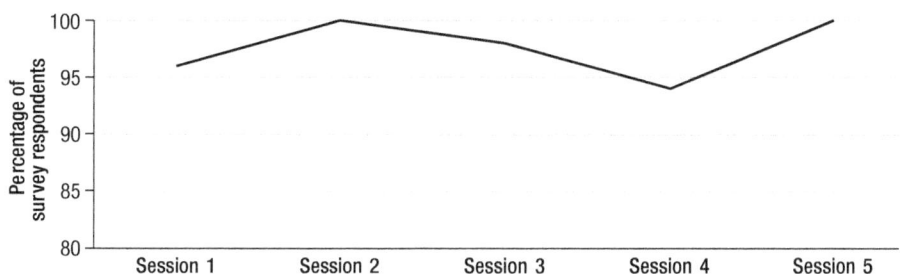

Figure 4.1 Percentage of 2017-2018 survey respondents who agree or strongly agree with the statement "I feel supported in improving my practice."

thinking in their teams, and in coaching participants toward a learning mindset rather than a compliance mindset.

Deficit Thinking

In early iterations of the program, we saw persistent deficit thinking throughout the improvement process, from the root causes analysis through the conversations about data after the test of a change idea. For example, although the fishbone protocol received positive feedback from participants, we noticed deficit thinking in their ideation about root causes. We had tried integrating a step into the protocol where participants would step back to identify "we vs. they" thinking, and to focus only on ideas within their own locus of control. However, even after this shift, participants identified the following as the root causes of their problem:

- I have families that are hard to reach.
- Students don't understand expectations.
- Adults in the home setting can be distractions.
- Lack of in-person social experience.
- Students may be behind from previous semesters.
- Learned helplessness.
- Not having the skills to keep up or participate; having a fixed mindset; and/or being complacent.

After seeing that the protocol alone would not interrupt deficit thinking, we wanted to empower coaches to interrupt deficit thinking in their groups in real time. Dr. Michelle Pledger developed a practice of interrupting deficit thinking in her induction group. In 2019, Dr. Pledger conducted a study with her induction group in which she sought to develop Culturally Responsive–Sustaining Pedagogy in novice teachers. As part of her study, she added extra sessions and offered Continuing Education Units (CEUs) to participating teachers to compensate them for their additional commitment. This space allowed her to build the relational trust required to make deep changes in teachers' mindsets and practices.

As a result of consciously interrupting deficit thinking, she saw a marked decrease in the occurrence of deficit thinking among participants in her group. In an article about her research project, she shared how her group revised the deficit thinking in their problem statement—written in their first week together—to create a problem statement that elevated their own agency:

> One inductee noticed that the way their group had phrased their problem statement—"Too few students are carrying the cognitive load in the classroom"—placed the onus of change and the blame on the students rather than placing the change practice on the teacher. The group worked together to revise the problem statement so that the teacher became the unit of change: "Teachers are providing too few opportunities for culturally and linguistically diverse students to carry the cognitive load effectively."
>
> (Pledger, 2020)

The HTH GSE produced a video of Dr. Luke Wood describing the norm of "We, not they," which outlines "acceptable language" and "unacceptable language" in root cause analysis, drawing a line between blaming and language of ownership (Wood, 2020). Gallagher reflected on the value of this clear norm setting: "Sometimes coaches noticed deficit language, but didn't feel equipped to address it. If you set norms or show the Luke Wood video, and then notice deficit language, you can refer to that. If you didn't set norms or show the video and then point out deficit language, people feel caught rather than reminded" (Gallagher, personal correspondence, June 15, 2021). Coaches reflected on the power of focusing on that norm, describing moments when participants were able to interrupt deficit thinking with each other.

Compliance Orientation

Despite our efforts to remove barriers and focus the work on authentic learning, several of the questions we were getting from participants were still about what they "had" to do. Participants were not the only ones approaching the work with a compliance mindset—coaches also felt little ownership of the process at times. The kinds of questions that we fielded from coaches were often logistical or compliance–oriented, starting with "When do we need to…" or "Are we supposed to…" The tools of improvement seemed to be creating more confusion than learning in some instances. Bethany Tipton, who has coached the Universal Design for Learning induction group for four years, described the first two years of her work as an induction coach as prescriptive. "It was like, 'Here is what you need to do, get it done.' And sometimes I didn't even have the explanation of why things needed to be completed. I just knew that they needed to be completed" (personal correspondence with authors, March 11, 2022).

We wanted induction coaches to have the skills and the agency to make decisions about how to organize and facilitate their improvement teams in order to achieve the goals.

Improving Coach Development

In 2021, the HTH GSE formed a team dedicated to developing improvement capacity. Improvement for Equity by Design (IExD) primarily served external audiences, but like other GSE teams, also collaborated informally with High Tech High programs. Gallagher passed the role of supporting improvement coaches to Julia Jacobsen, a former induction coach who now works as an improvement specialist for IExD, and is a co-author of this chapter.

IExD strives to create transformational learning experiences that support the development of effective improvement teams. In order to achieve this goal, IExD brings together cohorts of improvers to push on the learning edge of improvement teams. They also develop artifacts to support improvement for equity that are easy to adopt.

The team itself engages in a process of continuous improvement, regularly looking at feedback data and participants' work to evaluate the effectiveness of artifacts and program design. The problems that IExD sought to address in their own improvement work mirrored those that were emerging in the induction program.

Facilitating Continuous Improvement for Equity

In the spring of 2021, IExD offered a new workshop, Facilitating Continuous Improvement for Equity, designed to address how to build a team, interrupt deficit thinking, and foster ownership of the problem. All induction coaches were required to attend after completing Continuous Improvement 101. In this workshop, participants learned to facilitate specific protocols with the goal of upholding an equitable process in service of an equitable outcome.

Each participant had an opportunity to facilitate a protocol in a "lab" with their small group, and to receive feedback on their facilitation. Through this experience, coaches deepened their capacity to effectively facilitate the goals of a protocol. As one participant reflected in a feedback form after the workshop, "I appreciated the opportunity to practice some protocols with the same group over the course of the last three days. I learned that there is an immense amount of work that has to go into facilitating an effective protocol."

Induction Improvement Coach Summit

Coaches also attended a team planning summit, designed to support coaches in having greater ownership over the learning arc for the year. During the summit, coaches started by conducting empathy interviews with former induction participants. Coaches co-designed interview questions that would help them understand what created a meaningful experience for participants and what got in the way. Next, coaches looked over the arc of the year and considered how the learning map could better meet the program goals. They shared their ideas for revision with a learning partner and thought about the supports they would need in order to be effective coaches throughout the year. In addition, coaches reviewed PDSA forms from previous years and began tailoring the curriculum collaboratively to meet equity goals.

The feedback from other coaches was a valuable source of inspiration and support. One coach celebrated her learning partner by saying, "Thanks for your ideas around best practices to structure surveys for students. Thank you for being an awesome thought partner! I have such a better understanding of my aim—couldn't have sorted that without your suggestions!"

Impact

During the 2021–2022 school year, induction coaches were more likely to experiment with new agendas and bring in different protocols to meet the needs of their group. Empowered to support their teams as improvers, coaches developed other ways of cultivating improvement mindsets within their teams. Andres Perez, a new improvement coach in the 2021–2022 school year, led a team focused on Elevating Student Voice. Perez used a Success Analysis Protocol with participants in which they unpacked a success to understand the factors that led to it. Tipton partnered with Meg Hassey, another new improvement coach, to try out a "squad" structure for PDSA check-ins. Participants were paired with consistent learning partners for the year, and partnerships were paired to create a group of four, or "squad" that met regularly to discuss the results of their tests of change, and to plan new change ideas together.

The Improvement Coach Summit is a space where we can continue to learn from the collective genius of the coaching team, and to integrate new effective ideas into the regular structures of the program.

Conclusions and Lessons Learned

We have learned a great deal over the last seven years about the induction of novice teachers through a continuous improvement approach.

CI CAN BE AN EFFECTIVE FRAMEWORK FOR ADAPTIVE LEARNING

Utilizing continuous improvement in induction in HTH schools has supported the development of novice teachers' disposition that teaching in itself is a learning experience in which you dive into a problem of practice, research, design, implement change and collect data to evaluate the impact on student learning and experience. It aims to debunk the idea that teachers have all the answers and should perform as experts once given their own classroom; instead, teachers should constantly work together to understand, create, test, and apply, in order to improve teaching and learning. The HTH induction program served as a lightning rod at school sites as the novice teachers not only worked with their mentors to discuss their problems of practice and generate change ideas that could support their aim statement but expanded the process and conversation to other colleagues at their site.

The collective learning experience modeled for novice teachers that teaching should not be in isolation. Instead, networks are crucial to one's development and sustainability in the profession, and contribute to a sense of belonging—an essential element to remaining in the profession. The idea of building teacher capacity through continuous improvement also built novice teachers' efficacy, giving them a methodology to identify problems, study them, plan out change ideas, act and evaluate them through data collection and analysis—reiterating that teachers are continuously improving.

THE IMPORTANCE OF IMPROVEMENT SCIENCE IN OUR OWN PROGRAM PROCESSES

While our initial focus was integrating continuous improvement into the curriculum of the new-teacher induction program, we have since recognized the importance of using improvement science to reach our aims as a program. Since the launch of the new design, the program directors have continued to capture data, reflect and revise to create an authentic and impactful program for our teachers. However, this learning was held mostly by the individuals on the team, and much of that learning was lost through leadership transitions.

To progress in our development as an improvement partnership, we have recognized the importance of routinizing our own collaborative continuous improvement processes. How can we build in opportunities for stakeholders from HTH and the HTH GSE to look at evidence together, capture our learning and offer feedback for improvement? While we have created a more robust improvement experience for induction participants, we still have room to grow our own program improvement practices, as suggested by the Developmental Progressionsas indicated in Table 4.3.

In the spring of 2022, we participated in our first improvement review as a program, sharing our theory of action, improvement efforts, and resulting data with a team of improvement coaches from the HTH GSE, induction coaches, and HTH leadership in order to get feedback on our next steps. While induction is an important lever for teacher retention, it is not the only factor influencing whether teachers stay in the profession. We plan to continue improvement reviews, which offer a promising path to building cross–system partnerships to support teacher retention. In the upcoming year, we plan to better integrate mentors into the participants' improvement journey and into our program's improvement efforts.

DEVELOPING NEW ORGANIZATIONAL CAPACITY FOR CONTINUOUS IMPROVEMENT

One of the surprise take-aways was the organizational improvement capacity that has been developed through the induction redesign. We had a hazy idea that introducing continuous improvement to new teachers would over time make continuous improvement part of the regular vocabulary at High Tech High. We can see this happening with former induction participants like Rebecca Maldonado. Maldonado completed the induction program at HTH in 2020 and is now a mentor of a participant in the program. Having gone through the program herself, she is able to support her mentee with selecting powerful change ideas, identifying types of data to collect and reflecting on whether change ideas were successful.

The surprise was the degree to which improvement coaches have been a key source of improvement capacity for our organization. In 2020 the HTH GSE was forming the CARE Network and looking to hire improvement coaches. The internal applicants for the role with the most improvement experience were induction coaches.

We now see induction as a space for developing improvement faculty both within HTH and the HTH GSE. Of the six team members on IExD, the team at the HTH

Table 4.3 Description of the Developmental Progressions Category Learning to Improve

Domain	Area of Work	"Exploring Change Ideas"	"Small Change Implementation"	"Integrating IS/NICs into the Core Work"	"Institutionalizing and Sustaining the Work"
Partnership	Learning to Improve	Partnership members are exploring how to work together using IS/NICs to improve their respective and joint efforts	The LEA and IHE have initiated new structures to consolidate their learnings about the use of IS/NICs	The partnership is developing a continuous quality improvement system that includes regular data feedback from program participants during and after the program	The LEA and IHE are jointly reviewing evidence from a quality improvement system and using this to plan the next set of improvement cycles for the partnership. The partnership can document learnings from capstones that have advanced local improvements

GSE that supports improvement capacity, five have been involved with High Tech High's teacher induction program, including three former induction coaches. The teacher induction program continues to be a space where IExD can experiment with improvement facilitation and developing facilitators, as well as testing new protocols and materials.

Teachable Moments

Participating teachers report a high sense of belonging and value the learning in their improvement teams. However, we are not sure if this is contributing to teacher retention. With several other external factors including the pandemic and high inflation in California leading to high attrition, it's unclear to what degree induction has an impact on teachers' commitment to the profession. To address a systemic challenge like teacher retention, it will be important to partner across the system, continuing to collect and analyze data collaboratively.

The induction program has been a fruitful ground for experimentation and learning. As we think about how the partnership between HTH and the HTH GSE might grow along the Developmental Progressions, there are some teachable moments that give us insight into key questions.

HOW MIGHT IMPROVEMENT PROCESSES FOSTER CONNECTION AND BELONGING?

It is no surprise that new teachers need to have opportunities to connect with other novice teachers as well as veteran teachers. The sense of connection that novice teachers experienced throughout our induction program showcased for us the need for the collective; the understanding that they are not alone in their challenges was critical. Opportunities to connect with other novice teachers allowed them to experience safety and not feel like total failures. While opportunities were integrated into each session to allow for this sense of belonging to occur, it is important to also recognize that one cannot simply sit in the woe. Improvement coaches and mentors, as well as peers and experienced teachers, have proved important.

Having the improvement coach facilitate moments to move forward, co-design solutions based on research, and implement the change ideas was important because it began to build their capacity. As one induction participant said in 2017, "PDSA cycles are simple, direct, and can fit into what I am already doing in my classroom. They just provide a bridge where I can connect what I am already doing with a strategy to improve." These moments of gathering provided them with strategies that they so desperately wanted in order to make it another day in the classroom.

While improvement coaches are a valuable resource throughout the monthly sessions, the site-based mentors for the majority of the participants function as an intravenous line for novice teachers. They are the ones who meet weekly with the novice teachers and sit in their classes to observe them and provide them with feedback

Table 4.4 Description of the Developmental Progressions Category Faculty Development and Promotion

Domain	Area of Work	"Exploring Change Ideas"	"Small Change Implementation"	"Integrating IS/NICs into the Core Work"	"Institutionalizing and Sustaining the Work"
Institution of Higher Education	Faculty Development and Promotion	Discussions begin about the possible need for faculty development, since IS/NICs will be new work for many. Faculty explore support options available through the Higher Education Network (HEN), as well as other resources that iLEAD may subsequently develop	Professional development supports for faculty in teaching and coaching IS/NICs have been identified and discussions are underway as to how to strengthen IHE capabilities	Opportunities for faculty development exist and resources are in place to respond	New promotion and tenure policies are in place, acknowledging IS/NICs contributions as a significant criterion in these processes. One or more junior faculty have successfully engaged with these new criteria

for improvement. Because mentors are a necessary lever for novice teacher success, the development of the mentors is equally as important. As a result, mentors attend workshops to develop their capacity as a mentor to another adult—we know some may assume that a great classroom teacher makes a great adult educator/mentor; this is simply not always true. Trust, listening, and leading facilitative and directive coaching conversations are some of the skills that mentors of novice teachers in this induction program learn. Through this process, we acknowledge that their experience needs to also include an understanding of continuous improvement.

This is our biggest teachable moment: build mentors to be leaders of continuous improvement. This way, their work with their mentee is aligned with this framework of plan, do, study, act. Going forward, having a shared language and understanding will allow the development of the novice teacher to go through cycles of improvement on a daily basis—it would no longer live solely through their induction work. This will also build the mentor's capacity to serve as a catalyst for continuous improvement at their sites, in this case, schools all throughout California. Mentors are improvers, they take on the role knowing their role is to support and develop novice teachers, the continuous improvement model would provide them with the framework to ensure that development is occurring (table 4.4).

HOW CAN BOTH THE PROCESS AND THE OUTCOME OF IMPROVEMENT EFFORTS SUPPORT EQUITY?

One of our other major "aha moments" came when we checked ourselves on our vision and our principles, specifically equity. How were we ensuring that equity was central to our support of new teachers? We needed to ensure that we were disrupting deficit thinking and consistently upholding a standard of collective accountability. We need strong improvement coaches to model and foster this norm so that ultimately the team will hold one another accountable to shift their language, disposition, and practices in support of equity.

By fostering collective ownership of a norm to disrupt deficit thinking, rather than relying on coaches and protocols, participants can bring that equity lens into their practice (Hinnant-Crawford, 2020). One participant reflected on this shift:

> I felt overwhelmed by classroom management at the beginning of the year, and now I feel more confident in figuring out what works for me. Chris helped us change our mindset from it being "the kids' fault" to creatively thinking of ways to shift the culture in our classroom so students were more engaged in the work. I feel like a better teacher at the end of this year.
>
> (Participant Feedback Form, May 14, 2018)

HOW CAN WE DEVELOP SUSTAINABLE IMPROVEMENT EFFORTS?

The teacher induction improvement project has continued to grow since the original redesign in 2016. What can we learn from it that might be applied to improvement efforts across our organization? One key to the sustainability of this project is that it is operating within an existing structure at HTH. Teacher induction is a program that already seeks to support teachers to learn. It has an existing funding source, and an existing time commitment required for participating teachers and their mentors. Rather than creating a new structure to support improvement, the new-teacher induction program shifted existing structures to align with the practices of improvement science. No additional funding or time commitment is required for participants or mentors, which means that the improvement project can continue as long as the program is in operation. Where else in our system might we be able to make shifts in existing programs to better align with what we have learned about the practice of improvement?

Within our program, we also have opportunities to reconsider our design for sustainability. While mentors and participants were existing roles prior to the redesign, the role of the induction coach was newly added. Our induction program relies on the skill and expertise of coaches, most of whom also work full time as teachers. While we have worked to integrate improvement into the curriculum of induction to positive effect, our coaching structure is still designed with improvement coaching as an "add on" responsibility for the coaches themselves. While they get paid a stipend for this work, they have to balance this commitment with the demands of their full-time job, so we continue to grapple with how we ensure this "add on" role is sustainable. If schools can integrate these additional responsibilities in existing structures, these "add-ons" can be a source of sustainability for the partnership.

HOW CAN IMPROVEMENT SCIENCE HELP ORGANIZATIONS GROW TOWARD A COMMON MISSION AND DEVELOP CONCRETE UNDERSTANDINGS?

As we continue to understand the needs of novice teachers and as we sit in the middle of a teacher shortage, we must work harder to ensure that teachers remain in the profession because attrition impacts student learning and school culture.[3] As we have continued to improve our program, we recognize that it is drawing great parallels to our High Tech High design principles—equity, personalization, authentic work, and collaborative design. In this evolution, we see how these design principles not only benefit our K–12 students' sense of belonging and purpose in education but that of our K–12 educators as well.

Continuous improvement has the potential to provide a framework for elevating our community's voices, and soliciting ideas and feedback from all levels of the system to solve problems. With a norm of continuous improvement mindsets and fluency in the tools across a community, we have the potential to co-create a system of schooling where all students will thrive.

---

[3] Caprara et al., 2006

Questions for Discussion

1. One distinguishing feature of this chapter, and the work it documents, is its integration of The Six Core Principles of Improvement. To what extent do these Core Principles offer leverage for improving learning outcomes in the school system or systems of most interest in your own work?
2. Another distinguishing feature of this chapter is that it focuses much less on leadership development than on providing systemic supports for novice teachers. To what extent is the concept of teacher leadership implicit in this narrative, and how do you see such leadership being systemically developed in the partnership?
3. This chapter describes an organizationally unusual improvement partnership: High Tech High and the High Tech Graduate School of Education. Yet there are potentially significant lessons for improvement that can be useful to more traditional LEA/IHE partnerships. Apart from The Six Core Principles of Improvement discussed above, what other dimensions of improvement work are salient in your own school improvement context—and how are they salient?

References

Bartlett, L., & Johnson, L. (2010). The evolution of new teacher induction policy: Support, specificity, and autonomy. *Educational Policy*, *24*(6), 847–871.

Bryk, A. S., Gomez, L. M., Grunow, A., & LeMahieu, P. G. (2015). *Learning to improve: How America's schools can get better at getting better.* Harvard Education Press.

Caprara, G., Barbaranelli, C., Steca, P., & Malone, P. (2006). Teachers' self-efficacy beliefs as determinants of job satisfaction and students' academic achievement: A study at the school level. *Journal of School Psychology*, *44*(6), 473–490.

Carnegie Foundation for the Advancement of Teaching. (2015). *The six core principles of improvement.* https://www.carnegiefoundation.org/our-ideas/six-core-principles-improvement/

GBAO Research & Strategy. (2022, February 28). *Poll results: Stress and burnout pose threat of educator shortages.* GBAO Memo. https://www.nea.org/sites/default/files/2022-02/NEA%20Member%20COVID-19%20Survey%20Summary.pdf

Hinnant-Crawford, B. (2020). *Improvement science in education: A primer.* Meyers Education Press.

Ingersoll, R., Merrill, E., Stuckey, D., & Collins, G. (2018). *Seven trends: The transformation of the teaching force.* Consortium for Policy Research in Education.

Lovo, P., Cavazzos, L., & Simmons, D. (2006). From BTSA to induction: The changing role of school districts in teacher credentialing. *Issues in Teacher Education*, *15*(1), 53–68.

Pledger, M. (2020). *Culturally responsive continuous improvement.* HTH Unboxed. https://hthunboxed.org/unboxed_posts/culturally-responsive-continuous-improvement/

Podolsky, A., Kini, T., Bishop, J., & Darling-Hammond, L. (2016). *Solving the teacher shortage: How to attract and retain excellent educators.* Learning Policy Institute.

Wood, L. (2002, February 3). *Dr Luke Wood—We, not they.* High Tech High Unboxed. https://www.youtube.com/watch?v=XZoE-U8d6O8

SECTION II

A New Kind of Partnership
CONTINUOUS IMPROVEMENT AS AN ANIMATING FORCE

David G. Imig

This section includes four cases in which universities reached out to their school districts to ask, "how can we be of help?" Each district responded by identifying a problem of practice that was compelling for which they saw benefit in enlisting the help of the university. Many fishbones, driver diagrams, and PDSAs later, these partnerships reached agreement on a set of activities to be pursued. In some cases, this was included in memoranda of understanding but in other cases with a partner handshake. Along the way, there were shifts and turns, but five years later all four partnerships show progress toward the institutionalization of these efforts. In all cases, the Developmental Progressions framework guided some or all of this work.

The four cases in this section have striking similarities but also some important differences. All four universities are located within or adjacent to their partner school districts, and all have a history of partnering together to serve the needs of the universities for internship and apprenticeship placements and for the districts as sites for graduate degrees, research expertise, and professional development. Some engage in research-practice partnerships with the districts, and others have professional development school collaborations with partnership learning. Most of these arrangements are transactional in nature based on exchange relationships that have existed for several decades. The universities are major "producers" of talent for their respective district schools—teachers, principals, and counselors. Substantial numbers of program graduates either teach or lead in those districts, which creates forms of connectedness as the partnership evolves.

Each of the four partnerships engages a public university with a public school district, but the cases offer some contextual dissimilarities: two describe very large districts (Portland Public Schools and Prince Georges County Public Schools), and two are relatively small districts (Avondale and Oxford); three of the four are K–12 districts, and Avondale is K–8. Across these four settings, key boundary spanners, operating across the divides between schools and universities, play different roles in the formation of the four partnerships. These roles range from district superintendents to untenured professors, representing differences in access to power, resources, and authority, leading to variations in change strategies and the pace of progress.

In all cases, there is a legacy of prior Carnegie Foundation for the Advancement of Teaching efforts with the universities—University of Maryland, Portland State, University of Mississippi, and Arizona State—and some sustained work with at least two of the districts. All four of the universities had at least a decade of deep engagement in the Carnegie Project on the Education Doctorate (CPED). At least three of the four universities were in various stages of development of new EdD programs when invited to join iLEAD; hence, efforts to engage district leaders in EdD program design work were already underway when they became part of iLEAD. Deans and faculty at some of the universities were at various stages of using improvement science (IS) to guide this development and to shape courses, internships, and other field experiences. Capstone work at all four universities was underway, which had already produced a basis for their embrace of a common IS language. The education deans of the four university programs had already interacted with one another, which helped to reinforce their efforts. As a result, leadership already had a fix on what was possible and had experience in both intra-partner and inter-partner collaboration.

The Prince Georges County–University of Maryland partnership is a story of senior leadership from the university and school district taking action to reframe a longstanding but frayed relationship between a predominantly African-American community/county and the university. This case is about bending some rules in the creation of a designated center for the work, situating the center's responsibilities away from program faculty and with the dean, and engaging an array of boundary spanners to ensure its success. New systems and structures for collaborative work emerged in both the university and the district.

The Portland State–Portland Public Schools (PPS) partnership is a story of the university moving to form a partnership with a new district partner after several years of working with a different district. This is a story of re-engagement, with a clear focus on the racial gaps in literacy scores in PPS and the need to reframe and refocus university leadership preparation and professional development to address this problem. Three leaders—two from the university and one from the district—built a compelling partnership and achieved great success—yet all were somewhat removed from the sources of power in their respective institutions.

The Oxford Public Schools–University partnership is another case of senior leadership—a dean and a superintendent—working together to create change across institutional boundaries. It begins with a focus on racialized achievement differences and leads to consideration of chronic absenteeism as the compelling problem of practice. It shows the importance of an outside catalyst from the Carnegie Foundation in fostering IS practices in the two institutions. The case documents the impact in terms of program redesign and increased faculty engagement as well as successes in both institutions attributable to the partnership. The Avondale Public Schools–Arizona State partnership is one of two cases in this volume (together with High Tech High) that focuses primarily on teacher development as opposed to school leader development. Here again, the importance of strong leadership provides direction and stability on the part of both the university and the district. This case highlights the importance of identifying a shared problem of practice with an innovative district response and the university sponsoring a new clinical residency model. The case shows ways the partnership leveraged networked improvement communities and plan-do-study-act (PDSA) cycles to introduce and sustain new ways of onboarding and supporting teacher residents.

We invite district leaders, university leaders, and researchers alike to consider a number of questions that emerge from these four cases. For example: what is the importance of prior long-term partnership experiences in the formation of the partnerships that emerged from the iLEAD initiative? Is geographical proximity an asset for boundary spanning yet a possible barrier for research faculty interested in a national audience? What tensions exist within a higher education faculty with the engagement of clinical faculty to lead such initiatives and dean strategies that bypass obstacles by creating alternative reward systems, structures, and staffing?

CHAPTER 5

From a Transactional Relationship to a Transformational Partnership
UNIVERSITY OF MARYLAND COLLEGE PARK AND PRINCE GEORGE'S COUNTY PUBLIC SCHOOLS

Primary authors: Segun Eubanks and Jean Snell
Additional contributors: Douglas W. Anthony, Charoscar Coleman, Felice Desouza, Kara Miley-Libby, and Christine M. Neumerski

This case study tells the story of a partnership journey between one of the nation's largest and most diverse school districts and the flagship, Research 1 higher education institution, that resides within its borders. The case exemplifies how the principles and promise of improvement science, meaningful and trusting personal relationships, and institutional commitment and collaboration combined together to create a sustainable and mutually beneficial partnership focused on addressing the most significant and difficult problems of equity and student learning.

Context

The University of Maryland College Park (UMD) sits in the heart of Prince George's County, Maryland, but hasn't always been at the heart of the Prince George's County community. Relationships were good between and among individuals at UMD and Prince George's County Public Schools (PGCPS), and many projects flourished (mostly in teacher preparation)—but there was no real institutional partnership, no shared commitment to solving problems together, and no shared vision for advancing and supporting students in the community.

UMD is the flagship institution of the State of Maryland and one of the original land-grant institutions in America. Founded in 1856, UMD is "consistently recognized as one of the preeminent public research universities in the United States" (University of Maryland, n.d.). PGCPS is one of the nation's top 20 largest public-school systems that over the last 30 years has shifted from predominantly white to predominantly Black, with a substantial increase in Latino students in more recent years. While PGCPS is nationally recognized for its innovative academic programs, it is also critiqued for having among the lowest student achievement rates in the state of

Table 5.1 PGCPS and UMD Demographics

About PGCPS	About UMD
Annual budget: $2.3 billion	Colleges: 12
Schools and centers: 208	Majors: 100+
Student enrollment: 131,657	Student-to-teacher ratio: 18:1
Employees: 22,000	Campus clubs and organizations: 800+
STUDENT DEMOGRAPHICS:	Undergraduate enrollment: 30,922
Hispanic: 36%	STUDENT DEMOGRAPHICS
Black or African American: 55%	Maryland residents: 75%
White: 4%	Non-Maryland residents: 25%
Asian: 3%	Hispanic: 10%
Free and reduced meals: 66%	Black or African American: 12%
Special education: 11%	White: 45%
English language learners: 21%	Asian: 20%

Maryland (Prince George's County Public Schools, n.d.). These two institutions share the same geographic location and similar educational missions; however, as demonstrated in the table 5.1, they have very different demographics.

Despite these historical and contextual challenges, UMD and PGCPS have now formed a productive and mutually beneficial partnership, working together around the development of leaders, researching pressing problems of practice, strategizing around equity, and transforming from good relationships to meaningful partnerships. Their collaboration had helped to revitalize an EdD in School System Leadership, create new efforts to address inequitable student outcomes through ambitious improvement networks, and build a foundation of mutual trust and respect among leaders at both institutions that has led to a formalized institutional and sustainable partnership. Together, the partners have worked on numerous projects associated with problems of practice centered around the student learning needs of PGCPS. Yet, the core problem of practice that centered our recent partnership work was the problem of partnership building itself. As such, our aim is to "develop a deep institutional partnership that within three years will have a measurable impact on student learning and educational equity."

NOT YOUR FATHER'S MOU

A key milestone in our institutional partnership aim was a memorandum of understanding (MOU) signed by Prince George's County Public Schools and the University of Maryland College Park in January of 2020[1] (Appendix, https://textbooks.rowman.com/gomez-improving). This MOU was newsworthy, but not for the reasons one

---

[1] PGCPS/UMD MOU Announcement: https://education.umd.edu/news/01-28-20-university-maryland-and-prince-george%E2%80%99s-county-public-schools-announce-broad

might think. The partners did not announce a huge new grant by a big foundation or corporation. In fact, there were no grants or outside financial resources directly associated with the agreement. Nor did the partners announce a new project, research, or program for implementation. What made this MOU different than many other school district/college agreements—and certainly different from the dozens of prior agreements between PGCPS and UMD—was a focus not on projects but on a partnership; not on fundraising but on sharing resources; not on individual relationships but on a mutually beneficial, long-term *institutional* partnership centered on improving outcomes for the students of Prince George's County Public Schools. The MOU committed to establishing the "PGCPS/UMD Improvement Science Collaborative" to use principles of improvement science (Bryk et al., 2015) and principles of school/university partnership formation (Penuel & Gallagher, 2017) in order to support academic programs, improvement communities, research activities and professional learning opportunities centered on student-centered problems of practice identified by PGCPS and UMD leaders.

The partnership guided a coordinated and mutually beneficial response to the COVID-19 pandemic crisis with UMD and PGCPS working together to help support teaching in virtual and hybrid classrooms and launching new ambitious efforts to use technology to support PGCPS high school students make the successful transition to college through an online dual-enrollment program. Coming out of the worst of the pandemic, the partnership launched its largest school improvement effort with two district-wide Networked Improvement Communities focused on school improvement planning and learning recovery (more on that later). What has been established over the past few years is a sustainable partnership that has grown stronger through the tenure of two university presidents, two district superintendents, and three College of Education deans.

What caused such a radical change? How did these two, seemingly separate institutions develop a deep partnership that has already changed each institution and aims to make a real impact on students and their learning? What were the catalysts for moving each forward in ways that were mutually beneficial and anchored around a collective vision of equity, improvement, and leadership? What key challenges remain that could stifle partnership progress or prevent it from having a meaningful impact? If it wasn't just luck, and it wasn't just hard work, then what was the secret to its success? This case study will examine how this long relationship has grown into a deeper, more meaningful, more sustainable, and transformational institutional partnership. In particular, this chapter will examine how both partners leveraged the principles and tools of improvement science (along with membership in the iLEAD project) to design and implement strategies to improve educational outcomes for the school district.

THE BACK STORY: PEOPLE BUILDING TRUST, INSTITUTIONS LEADING CHANGE

A Change in Perspective

During speeches on and off campus, Dr. Wallace Loh, the president of UMD from 2010 to 2020, often cited an experience he had early in his university tenure. At an introductory dinner soon after his arrival in College Park with the sitting and former County Executives of Prince George's County, Dr. Loh guessed that the evening would be a relatively easy and pleasant affair; it turned out quite different. For several hours (according to Dr. Loh's telling) county leaders chastised the university president. They flat out told him that the University of Maryland was sitting in the midst of an urban, high-poverty county and ignoring it, not even trying to connect or acknowledge its needs. The leaders challenged Dr. Loh to expand the university's commitment to economic revitalization and to be a better, more proactive leader for the county's public schools. In particular, they reminded Dr. Loh that Black and Latino students in general, and PGCPS graduates in particular, were significantly underrepresented on the state's flagship campus.

Dr. Loh often spoke emotionally about the impact of this evening on him personally and on his leadership of the university; he also talked about the enduring friendships between the county leaders and him that subsequently developed. Throughout his tenure, Dr. Loh publicly and proactively addressed the challenge of improving engagement with the local Prince George's County community in general, and with PGCPS in particular, including launching a public PGCPS charter school located on the UMD Campus.

PGCPS Initiates a Catalyst for Change—the EdD in School System Leadership

The challenge of building an effective partnership wasn't solely an issue for UMD. Leaders in Prince George's County Public Schools often acknowledged the challenges of working to improve their large and complex school system. While some laud the achievements of a district serving so many high-needs students, by and large PGCPS suffered from a relatively negative reputation, buffered by its long-standing position as the second-lowest performing district in Maryland (behind only Baltimore City). This combination of complexity, size, and reputation made it challenging for PGCPS to engage university partners. In fact, PGCPS's own internal research investigation found that universities were reluctant to engage with the district even when there were available resources to support the work. As such, when PGCPS secured a substantial multi-year leadership grant from the Wallace Foundation, in 2011, one of their goals was to address their university partnership challenge.

The Wallace grant was pursued by then PGCPS Superintendent, Dr. William (Bill) Hite, who was concerned about leadership development in the district. In particular, he was concerned that school district leaders were not prepared to identify and analyze problems facing the district or to lead change efforts without extensive support. Dr. Hite and then Director of Talent Development, Dr. Doug Anthony, agreed that this extensive training should be coupled with the EdD credential from a respected university. While they knew that UMD had recently begun offering an EdD program in school leadership, Dr. Hite was skeptical about UMD's interest in or commitment to developing a special EdD cohort program with PGCPS (for all the reasons outlined above). Nonetheless, in the spring of 2012, they decided to meet with then COE Dean Dr. Donna Wiseman to explore leadership development opportunities. Fortunately, Dr. Wiseman and COE leaders were both excited about and prepared for the opportunity to strengthen ties with PGCPS and support a program of great value to the COE.

Dr. Wiseman had already been supporting professors David Imig and Willis Hawley in creating new strategies to revitalize a then dormant EdD program. Dr. Imig had situated the Carnegie Project on the Education Doctorate (CPED), a national network of universities committed to expanding and transforming a practitioner-centered EdD, on the Maryland campus in 2007. That initiative helped to reshape UMD's transformation of the EdD. Using lessons learned from a pilot program in the District of Columbia, efforts were made to establish a similar program in PGCPS. Establishing the EdD with PGCPS did not come without challenges. In fact, when the COE department that was (by design) supposed to host leadership degree programs, declined to support the new EdD, Dr. Wiseman took the almost unprecedented step of running the program directly out of the Dean's office. With the leadership of Associate Dean, Dr. Margaret McLaughlin and Dr. Imig, the first PGCPS cohort was launched later that year. Since its inception, more than 46 PGCPS administrators have enrolled; 35 have completed EdD degrees.

Through engagement with CPED and iLEAD, the principles of improvement science began to be more explicitly embedded into coursework and expectations within the dissertation in practice and became the signature pedagogy of the EdD program (Perry et al., 2020). The program has become the only one in Maryland to weave National Educational Leadership Preparation (NELP) standards and improvement science throughout its coursework while leading to superintendency certification.

The successful launch of the EdD program, along with a growing emphasis on improvement science, helped to establish a broader set of personal, professional, and institutional connections between UMD and PGCPS (Eubanks et al., 2021, pp. 141–163). While the EdD program has expanded to serve leaders in districts across the state of Maryland, it maintains a very close connection to PGCPS. In fact, Dr. Doug Anthony, a UMD EdD alum and former PGCPS associate superintendent, was recently appointed as a professor and director of the program.

UMD Initiates a Catalyst for Change: The CEii

As the EdD program continued to flourish along with other ongoing, collaborative efforts around research and teacher education, there was a growing recognition by Dr. Wiseman and colleagues that the College of Education needed to be more proactive in growing partnerships with surrounding school districts and most specifically, with PGCPS. For this reason, the COE was motivated to address at least two challenges: (1) to leverage the skills, knowledge, and capacity of its faculty to help school districts solve tough student learning and educational equity problems; and (2) to better support faculty in doing high-quality research in local districts and to engage in mutually beneficial research–practice partnerships. The College of Education needed both system and college leaders to help span the boundaries of two large institutions (Weerts & Sandmann, 2010). To address these challenges, the College of Education established the Center for Educational Innovation and Improvement (CEii) in 2017. In its founding charter, the Center's mission was to develop and maintain collaborative partnerships among faculty and local, state, regional, and national educational agencies and organizations for the purpose of promoting advancements in professional education, developing innovative solutions for current thorny problems of practice in education and supporting collaborative research designed to improve teaching, leadership, equity, and student learning in public schools.[2]

---

[2] CEii Homepage: https://education.umd.edu/research/centers/ceii

Dr. Wiseman and her leadership team began to confer with Dr. Segun Eubanks, who had received his degree in the pilot version of the EdD program and was the Chair of the Board of Education for PGCPS. Dr. Eubanks' experience and his access to top leadership in local, state, and national organizations helped to position both the COE and CEii as credible brokers and facilitators for engaging the university in authentic partnership work that supports school priorities and goals. Shortly after the CEii was launched with Dr. Eubanks as inaugural director, Dr. Jean Snell joined as an associate director bringing significant experience as a former COE faculty member and program director. Dr. Eubanks and Dr. Snell built and then expanded the work of CEii to provide leadership development and improvement science services to districts across the state of Maryland while maintaining its core partnership with PGCPS.

The launch of CEii coincided with the initiation of the Carnegie Foundation for the Advancement of Teaching's (Carnegie) Improvement Leadership Education and Development (iLEAD) initiative. With both the EdD program and CEii having embraced continuous improvement and in particular, the principles of improvement science, joining iLEAD was both timely and opportunistic. iLEAD's aim to further the capacities of IHEs and their LEA partners to enact systematic improvement efforts within their organizations and in partnership with one another, was well aligned with the direction of the growing collaboration between UMD and PGCPS. Joining the iLEAD network proved to be a key driver for growing a good relationship into a great partnership.

Importantly, participation in the iLEAD network and engagement in improvement science received significant support from leadership in both PGCPS and UMD. Dr. Kevin Maxwell, then CEO of PGCPS, was a staunch advocate and regular participant in UMD/PGCPS partnership activities, including the iLEAD network. When Dr. Monica Goldson became CEO in 2018, she continued the PGCPS commitment to the partnership, becoming an active and regular participant in the partnership activities and ultimately embracing the tools and principles of improvement science as the district's strategic approach to school improvement.

iLEAD Initiates a Catalyst for Change: Getting to the Work of Improvement

PGCPS and UMD actively participated in the iLEAD initiative, forming a team with equal representation from both partners serving on iLEAD teams and attending iLEAD convenings. Membership in iLEAD provided the PGCPS/UMD team with three essential support and learning services that guided and expedited partnership development. The first was time and expert facilitation. iLEAD provided an incredibly important opportunity for partners to disconnect from daily work challenges and spend time creatively and intellectually engaging with one another to develop ideas and strategies. Even more important, Carnegie leaders masterfully organized iLEAD sessions to allow for cross-partnership learning and to think about and explore challenges.

The second was a shared narrative and strategic framework. Prior to engagement in iLEAD, several UMD faculty had studied improvement science and incorporated it into classes and leadership programs, but few had ever engaged directly with districts in the design and implementation of improvement science strategies. For PGCPS, most leaders had little knowledge of or exposure to improvement science prior to iLEAD. Through learning, studying, and doing improvement work together, improvement science became the glue and the organizing framework of the partnership. Through this work, the partners developed a shared aim and Partnership Driver Diagram (see figure 5.1). The driver diagram provided a shared sense of goals and strategies. And while the partnership definitely considers it to be *Possibly Wrong and Definitely Incomplete* (there is still debate about the measure of student learning outcomes and the unacknowledged importance of the changes in systems practice and adult behaviors), it continues to guide the work across a wide spectrum of partnership activities and initiatives.

The third iLEAD support was a structure and roadmap for monitoring, measuring, and advancing the partnership: The iLEAD Developmental Progressions was seen as a valuable tool to help focus, understand and grow this unique improvement-centered partnership. The PGCPS/UMD team used the developmental progressions first as an assessment tool and later as a guiding tool to help focus the IS and partnership work. The tool helped to assess where the partnership stood, how each institution engaged with and implemented improvement science tools, and which particular areas of focus might garner the most leverage. UMD focused its developmental progressions efforts on embedding IS as the signature pedagogy for its EdD program; PGCPS focused on the professional development of district staff and significantly expanding IS knowledge and capacity, particularly to its over 200 principals.

Getting to Work: Our First Problem of Practice

In addition to the incredible learning resources described above, iLEAD engagement helped the UMD/PGCPS partnership to put discussions into action by implementing small-scale change efforts that helped to build capacity and implement improvement strategies. One of the very first iLEAD-generated partnership goals was to engage the over 30 recent EdD graduates serving as principals, principal supervisors, associate superintendents, and other positions of leadership within the school district through a post-doctoral network called the *Post-Doctoral Improvement Science Action Network* (PDISAN). "Improvement Science" was an essential element of the name, in that a central goal of the network was to spread and scale the theoretical constructs and practical tools of the improvement science paradigm. "Action" was also essential in its implication that the network was committed to enacting real change and not simply engaging in the academic exercises of exploration and study. PDISAN invited graduates from the UMD/PGCPS EdD cohort program, along with PGCPS school leaders and UMD faculty to examine school improvement research, promote evidence-based practices, and lead improvement networks across the districts that aim to solve tough problems and improve student outcomes.

At its first summer retreat, the post-doctoral fellows engaged with PGCPS CEO, Dr. Monica Goldson, to develop a systemic problem of practice that would become the first collective effort of the partnership to launch a networked improvement community. Dr. Goldson expressed concern that while the district was focused on improving achievement in literacy, math achievement across the district was low, with Black and Latinx students scoring significantly lower than their white peers. Network members invited UMD mathematics faculty and PGCPS mathematics curriculum staff to PDISAN meetings to study student test score results more deeply. This analysis led to a clear and focused problem of practice identified as "students of color in grades 3–8 are not demonstrating effective numeracy skills as measured by PARCC and PSAT."

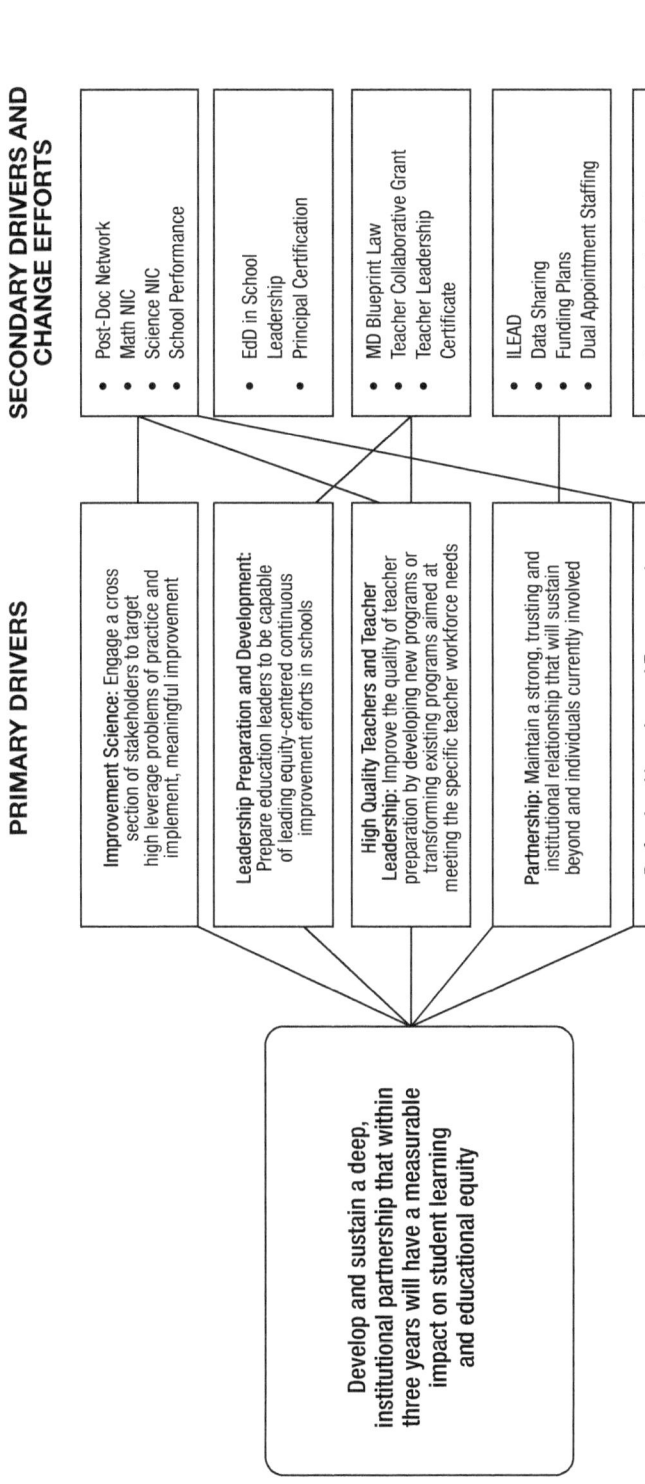

Figure 5.1 Partnership driver diagram.

PDISAN met with UMD faculty to do a causal systems analysis, plan and conduct math learning walks in six schools, and develop a driver diagram with several change ideas. Though circumstances related to the COVID-19 pandemic suspended the work of both PDISAN and the Mathematics NIC, the lessons learned from these change efforts proved valuable and laid the foundation for deeper engagement with a shared problem of practice and with the implementation and engagement of improvement science. The story of this work follows below.

Problems

A SHARED PROBLEM OF PRACTICE: PUTTING THE "IMPROVEMENT" IN THE SCHOOL IMPROVEMENT PROCESS

Prince George's County Public School's student achievement has lagged behind its district peers for many years.[3] Over the last ten years, the percentage of students who are English Learners has grown steadily from less than 20% of students to close to one-third of all students, and the concentration of students who live in poverty has also notably increased over the last decade. From 2015–2019, the percentage of students who did not demonstrate proficiency in ELA in grades 3, 5, and 8 was over 70%, and the percentage of students who did not meet or exceed standards in mathematics in grades 3, 5, and 8 trended downward from 75% in 3rd grade to below 90% in 8th grade. Given the overall performance of the district on state and national assessments as well as the shifting demographics of the school system, district leaders were fueled by a sense of urgency to boost student learning across the district.

PGCPS district leadership keenly understands how much is at stake if educators do not change the recent learning trajectory for students. For many years it had employed a range of school improvement strategies designed to help leaders use data and evidence to understand student learning and achievement gaps and employ evidence-based strategies to address them. However, school improvement processes had led to significant planning and accountability measures, but little effective school improvement and student learning gains. Through the collaborative work of the UMD/PGCPS partnership and under the auspices of the iLEAD program, collaborators engaged with each other to better understand and articulate the problem.

In Prince George's County Public Schools, the School Performance Plan (SPP) is designed to support school leaders and stakeholders with the collection and analysis of data that drive school improvement. The goal is for school teams to plan and implement strategies that increase student achievement. Ostensibly, the SPP allows for a transparent school improvement process that engages students, families, school and district staff, and other community stakeholders in collaborative efforts that foster positive relationships and eventually yield changes in adult practice. Over the past three years, the SPP has become a compliance-driven activity that school leaders reluctantly complete in order to meet performance evaluation criteria. During the 2021–22 school year, only 48% of schools completed their SPP by documenting three

---

[3] Maryland Report Card PGCPS Page: https://reportcard.msde.maryland.gov/Graphs/#/AtaGlance/Index/3/17/6/16/XXXX

short-cycle tests of change and their impacts on teacher practice. This challenge was magnified by new federal requirements in the "Every Student Succeeds Act" (ESSA), with districts in Maryland having been required to support Title 1 and other low-performing schools with more intensive school improvement planning.

The team struggled with the notion of the School Performance Plan having become mostly a compliance instrument and found that principals saw little or no value. Based on this analysis, the team identified and articulated a shared problem of practice: "School Leaders use the PGCPS School Performance Plan to address compliance and evaluation rather than to drive improvement or student learning."

LEVERAGING THE NEW STRATEGIC PLAN

In the district's newest strategic plan: "Transformation 2026, Equity and Excellence," the goal of educational excellence was defined as <u>both</u> improving educational outcomes <u>and</u> narrowing achievement gaps in mathematics and ELA across all grade levels.[4] Moreover, in the district's local ESSA Consolidated Strategic Plan Report, the number one prioritized academic goal was to significantly increase aggregate student performance and, thereby "reverse the decline" in mathematics across all grade bands, with the second priority being to increase the percentage of students who meet or exceed the state standard in mathematics and ELA testing. These explicit priorities reflect the long-standing challenge this district faced in promoting high levels of student learning in core academic subject areas. The leadership challenges this raised for the district were around how to build momentum in learning and achievement for all students and how to promote high levels of learning which result in sustained high levels of achievement, particularly in mathematics.

The strategic plan explicitly linked the district's accountability for meeting state/national achievement indicators through its annual ESSA reporting to its school-level performance planning processes and outcomes. For example, in the "PGCPS Planning and Monitoring Structure," school performance planning was positioned as "enabling" the district to work towards meeting its overall performance targets in mathematics and English/Language Arts.[5] So while the district leadership laid out its vision for how to move forward to reverse historic achievement gaps and trends in the new strategic plan, the pressure to change the district's academic profile rested much more directly with the results that localized school performance planning can and must yield.

The renewed district strategic plan reinforced the bridge between school performance planning and continuous improvement through the identification of five "Strategic Imperatives." One plank of the District's vision was "Academic Innovation." The Plan described how

> PGCPS must re-imagine teaching and learning in non-traditional ways to meet and inspire the needs of a dynamically changing community of learners—continuing to set high expectations and ensuring every student, in every grade, receives rigorous, engaging and relevant instruction that prepares students to be college-, career-, and life-engaged.

---

[4] PGCPS Strategic Plan Homepage: https://www.pgcps.org/about-pgcps/strategic-plan
[5] PGCPS Accountability Page: https://www.pgcps.org/about-pgcps/strategic-plan/holding-ourselves-accountable

Thus, the challenge for district leadership was how to simultaneously support school leaders and classroom-based educators in engaging in the mandated school performance planning implementation and reporting, while at the same time, encouraging their educators to embrace the transformative paradigms of innovation, inquiry, and improvement.

While the new school performance planning (SPP) template aligned closely with the core components of the federal guidance, what appeared to be missing was a framework that conveyed how school improvement was more than a technical process. The district had introduced a new SPP template that was aligned with ESSA requirements. The new template was very technical, and while all schools were required to utilize a School Performance Plan, these plans inhibited schools from reaching a deeper level of thinking and examination of practice to move schools meaningfully.

Challenges, Solutions, and Evidence

IMPROVEMENT SCIENCE AS A SHARED METHODOLOGY AND "SOLUTION"

UMD and PGCPS were able to leverage improvement science (IS) as a methodology and focal point for the partnership, and as a kind of answer to the problem of compliance-driven school performance planning and under-developed partnership learning. For PGCPS, IS was seen as a path away from the seemingly endless cycle of failed reforms toward a strategic mindset that puts the power of change into the hands of educators and school leaders. For UMD, IS was seen as an effective way to teach, research, and support educational improvement, equity, and school leadership.

This grounding in improvement science was spurred through the partners' membership/participation in the iLEAD network. A large combined team of district leaders and UMD faculty attended the spring 2018 and 2019 Carnegie Improvement Summits, the two institutions applied for (but did not receive) a Gates Foundation "Networks for School Improvement" grant, and the two organizations co-hosted a two-day "Greater Impact" Conference on Partnerships, Leadership, and School Improvement in 2020. Furthermore, *the Post-Doctoral Improvement Science Action Network* (PDISAN), described previously, provided UMD faculty and district leaders with a forum through which to explore shared problems of practice and to learn together about the framework and tools of improvement science. Importantly, PGCPS CEO Monica Goldson became an active participant in PDISAN meetings.

Dr. Goldson was simultaneously energized by the possibilities of improvement science, and also concerned that despite the concerted efforts of school teams across the district to engage with the new SPP template, there was not yet a consistent connection between school performance planning and improved outcomes. To address these concerns, and to chart an enhanced improvement course, at the 2019 Summer Leadership Institute Dr. Goldson introduced the PDSA cycle into the "Coherence Framework"[6] and initiated the integration of improvement science into school performance plans as a way of revitalizing continuous improvement across the system.

---

[6] PGCPS Accountability Page: https://www.pgcps.org/about-pgcps/strategic-plan/holding-ourselves-accountable

In addition to the incorporation of the IS Framework and PDSA cycles into the district's school performance planning template, district leadership more recently signaled the influence of this shared methodology in identifying Organizational Learning Culture as one of the five key Strategic Imperatives in the updated strategic plan. Calling for the district to transform into an active learning organization and to prioritize the implementation of systemic learning initiatives, the plan spotlights the vital importance of creating conditions that foster continuous learning, knowledge application, structured evaluation, and routine reflection for continuous improvement.

The Partnership "Solution" to the Challenge of District Capacity Building with SPPing

The UMD–PGCPS partnership helped provide district leadership with the resourcing needed to build capacity across all 200+ schools for renewed school performance planning. PGCPS leadership realized that the SPP was a "viable way" to impact all schools through the principles of improvement science, and a way to move beyond compliance to strong performance. At the PGCPS Summer Leadership Institute in July 2019, the superintendent formally introduced improvement science by incorporating PDSAs as an anchor in the district coherence framework, and since that time with the support of UMD, the central office staff and school-based teams have been engaged in ongoing training in the principles of improvement science.

The Office of Monitoring and Accountability collaborated with UMD faculty to co-develop and co-lead a customized training series for all Instructional Directors (principal supervisors) and Improvement Specialists on the principles and tools of improvement science, and in particular, causal systems analysis and disciplined inquiry cycles, in the spring of 2020. These trainings were designed to equip central office leaders to support principals in infusing their school performance planning with the components of improvement science. As a result of these collaborative sessions, district leaders were able to shift the emphasis of goals and aims in the SPP from solely student outcomes to how to change to adult practice in schools and central offices. This shift was captured in a revised school performance planning addendum which reflected this dual emphasis on improved student outcomes and changes to adult practice.

One aspect of improvement science which was embedded in all school performance plans was causal systems analysis. All schools across the system invited teams of local stakeholders to undertake site-based Fishbone analysis exercises, through which every school team identified their leading problems of practice. UMD faculty collaborated directly with the district to facilitate the next set of customized training series for school-level leaders on the tools of improvement science. These professional learning opportunities provided district mentors, school principals, and teacher leaders from a network of high-needs schools, with the opportunity to apply the tools of improvement science, such as problem identification and causal systems analysis, to the implementation of their own school performance plans. As a result of this second round of collaborative training, participating school leaders reported increased confidence in engaging their teachers and parents in improvement planning and a commitment to engaging more deeply with their continuous improvement efforts.

One additional resource which some PGCPS schools were able to deploy to accelerate their performance planning efforts was the teacher leaders who had been enrolled in UMD's "School Improvement Leadership" Post-Baccalaureate Certificate program. Two cohorts of Prince George's County teacher leaders (30 teachers in total) completed this four-course certificate based on improvement science and designed for the partnership. Teacher leaders all selected a site-based problem of practice as a focus of their program course of study. Their culminating project was to develop a proposal for a networked improvement community to engage a broader array of stakeholders in addressing their selected problem of practice. Moreover, half of these teacher leaders extended their Certificates to complete the internship requirement for their Maryland Administrator 1 certification. As part of their internship in the fall of 2020, these aspiring leaders helped to guide their school improvement team colleagues through problem selection, root cause analysis, and evidence-based strategy selection.

LOOKING FORWARD TO FUTURE WORK: THE LAUNCH OF 2 PARTNERSHIP NETWORKED IMPROVEMENT COMMUNITIES

The strong foundation laid by partnership development work enabled the UMD CEii Director, Dr. Segun Eubanks, and the PGCPS CEO, Dr. Monica Goldson, to seize the unprecedented opportunity offered through the American Rescue Act funding (ESSER) to launch two new systemwide Networked Improvement Communities (NICs) in 2022. These two NICs were designed to leverage shared expertise between the two partners and to use improvement science principles to address the learning continuity needs of PGCPS. Each NIC has a central focus, namely: (1) how can we embed school and classroom practices into the everyday work of practitioners to address the learning recovery needs that have been identified as a result of the COVID-19 pandemic? and (2) how can we better utilize School Performance Planning as an effective process to close achievement and opportunity gaps for students most in need?

The SI–NIC was organized around a group of 15 schools from across the district that share a problem of practice focused on lagging mathematics learning and achievement. This network was intended to support and extend localized continuous improvement work already underway in these schools by providing resourcing, professional learning, and coaching through quarterly short-cycle testing. These two NICS are staffed by a team which draws from both UMD faculty and PGCPS leaders. Additionally, current PGCPS doctoral students enrolled in the university EdD program for School Systems Leaders will participate in both NICs and will be positioned to contribute their combined district and improvement leadership capacity to network learning.

SHOWING EVIDENCE OF PARTNERSHIP IMPACT

As outlined in partnership Driver Diagram (figure 5.1), the partnership aims to impact student outcomes and close equity gaps, while at the same time, recognizing that success starts with strong proximal evidence about change in systems and adult practice. As such, when partners examine the work done and assess progress along the developmental progressions they have seen that the partnership has made considerable progress and has set the foundation for effective improvement, research and collaboration that is likely to impact student learning and educational equity. This evidence is based on a Theory of

Improvement, which posits that to make the SPP a true improvement process it must: (a) change the problem of practice and aim focus to include clearly articulated and measurable changes in adult practice; (b) shift the principal accountability for school improvement from "stand and deliver" to "learn and grow"; and (c) embed the principles and practices of improvement science directly into the school performance process.

Through engaging in this work, partners have seen the developing evidence of progress in several key dimensions:

Evidence of Engagement and Commitment Is Strong and Growing

Colleagues from both partner institutions are actively engaging in the "productive struggle" of improvement work. The common language of improvement science is becoming more embedded and accepted. This can be particularly evidenced in the fact that the partnership and improvement work continued, if even in a significantly modified process, throughout the most trying times of the COVID-19 pandemic.

Growth in the iLEAD Developmental Progressions

The iLEAD team decided to focus on three key dimensions of the Developmental Progressions which were deemed essential to partnership development: Learning to Improve; Curriculum/Program Development; and Professional Development of District Staff. Through annual self-assessments efforts have matured from small-scale change to institutionalized practice over the course of three years.

Emerging Data of Change in Systems Practice

As one of the PGCPS district iLEAD leaders said about the change in practice regarding the SPP process, "I don't know yet if I can prove it, but I can *feel* it." Along with this feeling of change is documented evidence of the work of improvement: Over a dozen UMD-led trainings and engagement with key leaders across PGCPS departments; systemic training on improvement science tools led by PGCPS Instructional Directors for all 200+ principals at two Summer Leaders Institutes; ongoing training, coaching and technical assistance on PDSA cycles for school leadership teams provided by the PGCPS Office of Monitoring and Accountability; a PDSA planning template embedded in every School Performance Plan co-developed by PGCPS and UMD staff; an evolving change of the PGCPS quarterly reporting and supervision meetings with principals to reflect a new emphasis on learning and improving; over 200 schools engaging in some form of quarterly PDSA. Measuring long-term impact on schools and students is still a work in process, however. PGCPS leaders characterized the shifts in practice and perspective in table 5.2.

In the framework of improvement science, the partnership continues to grapple with the challenges of how to measure what changes in capacity, routines, or district practices are leading to any improvement and how to measure and attribute changes to student learning given its distance from work being done on systems change and adult practice. The next phase of the UMD/PGCPS partnership has included engaging with UMD researchers and faculty members to develop a research agenda and more robust and practical improvement-centered measurement to examine both the impact of the partnership and the impact of our collective improvement work.

Table 5.2 PGCPS SPP Process Transformation

Former SPP Process	Improvement-Centered SPP Process
Technical	Adaptive
Goals	Problems of practice
Activities	Targeted strategies
Student outcomes	Adult practice that impacts student outcomes
Focused on problems of outcome	Focused on problems of practice
"Stand and Deliver" presentations	Learning and collaboration sessions
End-of-year outcomes review	PDSA short-cycle tests

Lessons Learned

KEY LEARNING #1: BUILDING STRONG RELATIONSHIPS IS THE STARTING POINT

Effective relationships are essential to any great partnership, which is true for the story of the UMD–PGCPS partnership. The development of this partnership revealed both *why* relationships matter to shared improvement work and *how* great relationships can be forged. Senior leaders from both organizations, including three deans, three CEO/superintendents, and two university presidents, shared a vision of the importance of forging a stronger alliance between the two institutions, an optimism about the potential for good that could be generated through such a partnership, and a commitment to identifying the kinds of work that could be accomplished together.

These leaders provided support and resources, including time and funding, to mid-level leadership—faculty from the UMD Center for Educational Innovation and Improvement and Cabinet members from several central office teams—to explore what kinds of work could become the glue of the partnership. Participation in the iLEAD network provided a safe and consistent space to facilitate such exploration, and this exploration, in turn, helped to deepen the trust and relationships between faculty and leaders from the two organizations. As such, the partnership discovered that its members enjoyed listening to and learning from one another. And they learned that they could uncover shared priorities, with the university following the lead of their district partners in identifying the greatest needs and responding in kind.

KEY LEARNING #2: FOCUS ON PROBLEMS OF PRACTICE AND STAY PREPARED FOR CHANGE

The architects of improvement science suggest that the Problem of Practice is the starting point for continuous improvement (Bryk et al., 2015). For the UMD–PGCPS partnership, it was an iterative journey to locate and identify the primary shared problem of practice. And yet as each (potential) problem has emerged, the partnership has grown deeper and stronger.

The first NIC that the partnership attempted was focused on mathematical reasoning for middle school students. This NIC was spurred by the needs assessment which was the foundation for a collaborative grant submission to the Gates Foundation in 2018, and by the simultaneous urging of the CEO/superintendent to bring our shared focus to boosting mathematics achievement in the district. This focus also played to one of the areas of deep expertise in the College of Education by engaging with a team of internationally-recognized faculty at the COE's Center for Math Education. The NIC was making progress toward a shared aim and preparing to test innovative change ideas when the work came to a screeching halt in March of 2020 and our partnership efforts needed to shift in response to the pandemic, school closings, and a move to virtual learning.

With the support and initiative of the new UMD president, Dr. Darryll Pines, the math focus remained but the focus was shifted with an initiative to offer an online dual-enrollment Calculus course for over 80 PGCPS high school students who had limited access through their schools. As the pandemic has shifted and the unprecedented challenges of reopening schools have deluged district colleagues, the focus of the partnership continues to evolve. When determining how to best use the district's Elementary and Secondary School Emergency Relief (ESSER) federal funds, the PGCPS CEO/superintendent committed a significant funding stream to enable the partnership to continue building district capacity around continuous improvement and school performance planning through the new NIC work explained previously.

Teachable Moments

These Teachable "Moments" are a reflection on key events, circumstances, or times and what they taught partners about moving from transactional relationships to mutually beneficial partnerships.

YOU'RE NOT REALLY MARRIED IF YOU DON'T HAVE THE PAPER

In Lessons Learned, the importance of relationships is highlighted, but a relationship without a formal commitment is always on shaky grounds. For the first three years of the iLEAD partnership, the idea of formalizing a memorandum of understanding was taken very seriously. It is often assumed that if there is no formal program or specific grant there is no need for a formal agreement. Yet, the MOU signed in January 2020 ended up being an essentially important step. Like most marriage licenses, it may not even be all that important what the particular words say. What is important is knowing that there is a mutual commitment and that the personal relationships and trust are being sustained by a long-term institutional partnership.

ADAPT, DON'T ABANDON

Good partnerships need to respond to crises. Less than three months after signing the MOU between UMD and PGCPS, the COVID-19 pandemic changed everything. Most of the work was suspended. However, with the commitment as strong as ever, the partnership shifted to the work that was most important for the time and came back to what was planned only after collaboratively supporting the needs of both partners during the crisis.

SHIFTS HAPPEN

In far too many cases, a change in leadership at either partner can have a significant impact on the nature, relevance, or sustainability of a partnership. During the five-year course of the UMD/PGCPS partnership, there have been two presidents at UMD, three deans at the College of Education, and two CEO/superintendents at PGCPS. Anticipating these changes and engaging new leadership deeply and early on in their tenure proved to be critically important. It takes a bit of luck to have leaders who share the broader vision and purpose of the work, but it needs to be an intentional effort to engage leaders in the strategy and implementation work.

JUST DO SOMETHING

Improvement and equity work are complex, and the learning curve is significant. Early on in the partnership, debates abounded as to whether it would be best to be sure everyone is "on the same page" and to first do an extensive professional development and learning process so that the effort wouldn't fail. Instead, the partnership decided to get to work by gathering some friends—about 25 PGCPS leaders who had graduated from the UMD EdD program over the course of the previous five years. Getting started with improvement work and "learning while doing" helped us to identify a small group of improvement champions. The partnership experienced some failures, but more importantly built momentum for the work.

References

Bryk, A., Gomez, L., Grunow, A., & LeMahieu, P. (2015). *Learning to improve: How America's schools can get better at getting better.* Harvard Education Press.

Eubanks, S., McLaughlin, M., Snell, J. L., & Coleman, C. (2021). From learning to leading: Teaching leaders to apply improvement science through a school-university partnership. In D. T. Spaulding, R. Crow, & B. N. Hinnant-Crawford (Eds.), *Teaching improvement science in educational leadership* (pp. 141–162). Myers Education Press.

Penuel, W., & Gallagher, D. (2017). *Creating research-practice partnerships in education.* Harvard University Press.

Perry, J., Zambo, D., & Crow R. (2020). *The improvement science dissertation in practice.* Myers Education Press.

Prince George's County Public Schools. (n.d.). *About PGCPS.* Retrieved August 29, 2022, from https://www.pgcps.org/about-pgcps

University of Maryland. (n.d.). *About UMD.* Retrieved August 29, 2022, from https://www.admissions.umd.edu/explore/about-umd

Weerts, D. J., & Sandmann, L. R. (2010). Community engagement and boundary-spanning roles at research universities. *The Journal of Higher Education, 81*(6), 632–657. https://doi.org/10.1080/00221546.2010.11779075

APPENDIX 5.1: MEMORANDUM OF UNDERSTANDING BETWEEN PRINCE GEORGE'S COUNTY BOARD OF EDUCATION AND THE UNIVERSITY OF MARYLAND, COLLEGE PARK ON BEHALF OF THE COLLEGE OF EDUCATION'S CENTER OF INNOVATION AND IMPROVEMENT

THIS MEMORANDUM OF UNDERSTANDING ("MOU"), effective as of the date of final Party signature below, is entered into by and between the Board of Education of Prince George's County (the "Board") and the University of Maryland, College Park ("UMD"), a public agency and instrumentality of the State of Maryland, on behalf of the UMD College of Education's (the "College('s)") Center for Innovation and Improvement (each a "Party" hereto and collectively the "Parties").

WHEREAS, the Board embraces the "Six Essential Elements of Effective Partnerships" as outlined by Prince George's County Public Schools ("PGCPS") leaders based on years of experience developing partnerships, which include:

1. Foster meaningful relationships;
2. Understand your partner;
3. Establish strong systems and structures;
4. Create clear points of contact;
5. Solve problems in mutually beneficial ways; and
6. Work through challenges together.

WHEREAS, the College has developed a comprehensive five-year strategic plan which identified the development of and engagement in strategic partnerships as one of three pillars of planned work, based upon the following principles of effective partnerships:

- Strategic partnerships should be long-term institutional relationships strategically designed to address persistent problems of practice and policy that are amenable to scholarly insight and study;
- Strategic partnerships should be expected to be of mutual benefit to both partners;
- Strategic partnerships should require partners to commit resources they control, share governance of the partnership, and engage in time-bound projects of mutual benefit, including the ongoing evaluation of these efforts; and
- Strategic partnerships should seek to build the capacity of local school systems and UMD to achieve sustainability in addressing problems of practice.

WHEREAS, the Parties have a long and proud history of partnership and collaboration on a wide array of educator development, research, school/program improvement, and policy projects and are committed to developing long-term, institutional partnerships that include mutual commitments, mutual benefit, and shared governance.

WHEREAS, in November 2017, colleagues from Prince George's County Public Schools and UMD met at the first iSchool Leadership, Entrepreneurship, Advocacy, and Development ("iLEAD") Council and developed a vision of potential collaborative work organized around the following strategies:

- The Center for Educational Innovation and Improvement at UMD is to serve as the organizing hub of the collaborative and leads planning and development efforts;
- UMD faculty are to be engaged in collaborative activities, including teaching in leadership programs, participating in Networked Improvement Communities ("NIC(s)"), and other improvement activities. One key component of this engagement will be Faculty Fellowships in the Center for Educational Innovation and Improvement.
- Administrators in the PGCPS are to be offered career growth opportunities by participating in leadership programs to be offered by UMD, including the Doctor of Education ("Ed.D.") program, an Admin Certification program, and other professional learning opportunities.
- PGCPS and UMD are to engage in numerous NICs addressing problems of practice in the PGCPS district.
- Graduates from the PGCPS cohorts of the UMD Ed.D. program are expected to become active leaders and participants in NICs and other collaborative improvement efforts.

WHEREAS, the College offers graduate coursework that advances leadership development through continuous improvement ("Improvement Science" coursework) which, among other activities, may involve work in (a) the PGCPS system, (b) the PGCPS Teachers, Schools, and Leaders ("TSL") Incentive Program, (c) the intentional collaboration through the iLEAD Council, and (d) the Post Doctorate Improvement Science Network;

WHEREAS, the Board has a goal of creating and sustaining a pipeline of highly effective leaders within PGCPS who will work to solve problems germane to the PGCPS district, particularly through solutions that will impact and improve student achievement by leveraging Improvement Science methodology;

NOW THEREFORE, in consideration of the mutual promises set forth herein and other good and valuable consideration, the receipt and sufficiency of which is hereby acknowledged, the Parties, intending to be legally bound, have agreed as follows:

I. PGCPS/UMD Improvement Science Collaborative

The Parties shall collaborate on a regular basis to leverage Improvement Science to address certain PGCPS-identified problems of practice. The Parties agree to participate regularly (endeavoring to do so at least once per month) and contribute to the overall and on-going effort to solve the identified problems of practice. Moreover, the Dean of the College and the Chief Executive Officer of PGCPS will participate at regular meetings but will also afford their respective staff the opportunity to engage regularly in the meetings and to engage in the work necessary to address the problems of practice.

II. Projects Include:

A. **School Improvement Leadership Certificate Program.** The Parties will collaborate to offer a series of four (4) courses designed to advance the goal of the Board, to PGCPS teachers who qualify for the program. The program will be made available for two cohorts of fifteen (15) PGCPS teachers selected by the Board (the "Participants" or individually, a "Participant"). The College will designate appropriate staff to meet with the PGCPS Talent Development Office no less that one time each quarter during the term of the MOU to design and evaluate the program.

At the conclusion of a one-year certificate program, program Participants will have the opportunity to complete two (2) additional courses to obtain a Maryland Administrator I certification, in accordance with the Memorandum of Understanding entered into by and between Prince George's County Board of Education) and University of Maryland College Park on 05/03/2019.

B. **Doctorate of Education in School System Leadership.** The Parties agree that within the next 12 months the program will start a new cohort available for PGCPS leaders with PGCPS helping to identify and support promising candidate program participants. The Parties agree that absent additional outside funding, programs and offerings shall be paid for by the PGCPS participants, not by UMD. The Parties also agree to plan for the next PGCPS cohort program (either open to school leaders from other counties or closed to only PGCPS leaders) to launch within the initial Term of this MOU.

C. **Carnegie Foundation for the Advancement of Teaching Project.** The Parties commit to participate within and contribute to the Carnegie Foundation's iLEAD project (Improvement Leadership Education and Development). This commitment will be maintained until at least July, 2020 which represents the current iLEAD funding cycle. The Parties' participation in iLEAD hereunder shall include:
   1) both Parties assigning staff to serve on the iLEAD core leadership team which meets monthly to coordinate all activities;
   2) both Parties sending at least two representatives to each of the three annual iLEAD meetings (conditioned upon the Carnegie Foundation's agreement to pay for all related expenses);
   3) both Parties sending at least two representatives to the annual Improvement Science Summit in April (with expenses paid by the Parties for their respective representatives); and
   4) to the extent practicable, both Parties agree to engage in local improvement projects, activities, and professional learning developed from the iLEAD convenings and coaching sessions.

D. **Professional Learning and Engagement:** The Parties agree to design and execute a professional learning agenda aimed to improve the capacity of both PGCPS staff and UMD faculty to design, plan, execute, research, and scale continuous improvement efforts focused on equity and student learning. The professional learning agenda may include workshops, conferences, courses, online seminars, and other learning opportunities, and may include both the study of and practice of Improvement Science principles and tools.
E. **The Post Doctorate Improvement Science Action Network (PDISAN).**
   1. The Parties agree to develop, support, and expand the PDISAN launched by the Parties in June 2018. The PDISAN shall endeavor to bring together graduates from the UMD/PGCPS Ed.D. Cohort program along with PGCPS school leaders, UMD faculty, and other outside experts to examine school improvement research, promote evidence-based practices, publish quality research, and lead improvement networks across the PGCPS districts in an effort to solve identified practice-related problems and improve student outcomes. Through the PDISAN the Parties will create at least two active NICs focused on problems of practice identified by PGCPS in concert with network fellows (PGCPS staff). The first NIC shall be focused on math achievement in PGCPS.
   2. To dive deeply into this problem of practice, the Parties agree in principle to share the costs of the UMD faculty member to co-lead the NIC work with a designated PGCPS staff member, subject to the terms of an employment appointment developed in collaboration with UMD's Office of Faculty Affairs. The Parties further agree upon the following principles:
      - UMD's College of Education, Department of Teaching and Learning, Policy and Leadership may hire a new lecturer or assistant clinical professor in math education and at least 50% of the faculty members time will be committed to PDISAN and the math achievement NIC;
      - PGCPS will support this position by supporting 33% percent of the faculty member's salary over the three years of this MOU.
      - This MOU will represent agreement in principle with a more detailed agreement to be completed within six months of this MOU start date.

III. Dual Appointment Liaison

The Parties agree to consider options for dual appointment. One option Parties will consider is that a member of each organization will have dual appointments in the respective organization. The PGCPS appointment would serve as adjunct faculty to the College and Senior Fellow to the Center for Educational Innovation and Improvement. The UMD appointment will serve as the district coordinator for improvement science or other appropriate title. Appointees will commit a minimum of 20% time and commitment to the secondary appointment. Another option could be one dual appointment sharing time evenly (50/50) between the two organizations. While considering options, the dual appointment would serve the following purposes and work functions:

- To influence, monitor, champion and support the scale, spread and sustainability of Improvement Science work in both partner organizations.
- To organize and facilitate Networked Improvement Communities.
- To serve as a key conduit and spokesperson to the partnership and to leverage the Center for Educational Innovation and Improvement and PGCPS to expand improvement and leadership work and partner with other organizations.

This MOU will represent agreement in principle to the creation of dual appointments with a more detailed agreement to be completed within six months of this MOU start date.

IV. High Quality Teachers and Leaders

The Parties agree to collaborate hereunder to support the purposes of the Kirwin Commission and to support the purposes of the 2019 Blueprint for Maryland's Future Act. In particular, the Parties will work together to improve the quality of teacher preparation by developing new programs or transforming existing programs aimed at meeting the specific teacher workforce needs of PGCPS. In addition, Parties agree to pursue funding through the new Teacher Collaborative Grant Program, which is designed to "provide funds for collaboratives to develop state-of-the-art professional education for prospective and current teachers that reflects international and national best practices."[7]

V. Data Sharing

The Parties agree to make good faith efforts, to the extent permitted by law and institutional policies, (1) to share data of both the College and PGCPS in service of intervention projects and research related to the problems of practice developed by this partnership, and (2) further, to the extent practical and reasonable, provide PGCPS school and district data, artifacts, historical materials, and policy documents for the benefit of NICs and UMD Ed.D. students working on PGCPS district-approved problems of practice.

VI. Joint Publication

The Parties agree to work with PGCPS staff and UMD faculty to document and publish the learning, processes, and outcomes of this partnership. Publications efforts may include scholarly journals, broader education and education policy publications, and/or independently published reports.

---

[7] Md. Code, ED § 6-123(b)(2)(i).

VII. Financial Commitment

The Parties agree to support the work of the iLead Council and the Post Doctorate Improvement Science Network with in-kind support and to make good faith efforts to seek funding for meetings, conferences, materials, and incidentals of the Dual Appointment Liaisons and for other cost associated with the effort. Parties also agree to pursue grant and other fundraising in support of these efforts and to write a minimum of two joint grant proposals per year during the Term of this MOU.

VIII. Scope Of Work

Parties will work collaboratively to develop a comprehensive Scope of Work for each project outlined that will include goals, objectives, timelines, and resources required. This Scope of Work will be mapped to the iLEAD Developmental Progressions which will serve as a guide for the growth and development of this partnership.

IX. General Terms

Legal term and signatures not included in this document.

CHAPTER 6

Redesigning School Staffing Models through Team-Based Residencies

ARIZONA STATE UNIVERSITY AND AVONDALE ELEMENTARY SCHOOL DISTRICT

Betsy Hargrove, Christina Flesher, Nicole L. Thompson, and Carole G. Basile

As part of the *Next Education Workforce* initiative, the Mary Lou Fulton Teachers College (MLFTC) and Avondale Elementary School District (AESD) partnered to explore team-based residency models specifically focusing on how teacher candidates could serve on professional educator teams where expertise is distributed and all educators on the team share a larger roster of students. This partnership, framed by Carnegie's iLEAD initiative to apply improvement science practices within a network improvement process, led to the development of models that enhanced both the working conditions for educators and the learning environment for students. These models, which changed the default normative one-teacher/one-mentor/one-classroom models of schooling and/or student teaching, are showing positive outcomes for both educators and their students (Johns Hopkins University, 2022).

Five years ago, not unlike most school districts in Arizona, a medium size school district in the Phoenix suburbs was experiencing a shortage of teachers to meet their needs. Current teachers were leaving for other opportunities, many outside of the field of education, and the supply of new teachers was dwindling. Enrollments in teacher education programs were down and the local university was talking of discontinuing the placement of residents (student teachers) in schools in this district (Partelow, 2019). An innovative superintendent, recognizing that such trends were likely to persist, sought the help of university faculty to help design a better intern (residency) placement regime. The Superintendent of the AESD knew that having a large pool of residents each year was a proven way to meet her future staffing needs. What she needed was a new way to attract more residents to schools in her district.

At the same time, a new dean of education at Arizona State University's Mary Lou Fulton Teachers College (MLFTC), saw a new way of staffing schools for meeting the needs of an increasingly diverse student population in the greater Phoenix area.

The dean saw the problem of shortage as an opportunity to redesign the education workforce.

As the problem was better described, the university wanted to think differently about how they would prepare teachers in the future, what would the future workforce look like, and how could they reimagine the preparation and professional learning of educators given the innovations in technology, the changing demographics of the population, and the socio-political dissonance of our time. The school district wanted to maintain the "flow" of residents (and accompanying faculty) to the district and saw the "teaming" construct at the heart of the workforce design as consistent with their own staffing practices. With resources from a federal Teacher Quality Partnership award, the design for a two-year "experiment" was formed that would focus on AESD. Could the ways that teacher candidates were placed in Avondale schools help to inform the workforce design ideas being promoted by MLFTC leadership? Clinical practice seemed like a place to start (Zeichner, 2002). Hence, building on a longstanding partnership, MLFTC and AESD created a network improvement community to address Avondale's teacher vacancies as well as offer MLFTC a different approach to not only clinical practice but to provide some insight into what teaching and learning could look like for the next generation.

This chapter describes a partnership between a university and a school district to explore ways to solve both an immediate and long-term challenge—teacher shortage—the lack of people coming into the teaching profession and an increase in people leaving quickly. And while we usually define this as a recruitment and retention problem, here we define it as a workforce or staffing design problem. The partnership described here takes on that design challenge and illustrates how educators could begin to redefine themselves, their roles, and the fundamental structure of the way they work. In this case, teacher candidates also took on a pivotal role in shaping teams around a shared roster of students—the result was that these teams of adults were formed to support learners much more effectively.

The Next Education Workforce: A Growing Idea

Five years ago, MLFTC convened a broad group of constituents in and out of Arizona to identify key questions about the education workforce and began designing a systemic approach to address those questions in ways that would ultimately lead to better outcomes and experiences for PK–12 students and professional educators. The discussion included school superintendents and other administrative leaders, representatives from the Arizona Department of Education, business partners, policymakers, researchers, and people responsible for educator preparation at several colleges of education.

These convenings led to an understanding that school systems can no longer expect every educator to be all things to all students all the time. Not every educator needs to be or can be a content expert and a pedagogical rock star (and an expert in learning disabilities, classroom management, developmental psychology, and cultural context). Communities are rich in experienced adults who have significant content knowledge in science or writing or coding but who may lack the classroom skills of career teachers. Schools have professional teachers who are classroom maestros but may not be up on the latest domain knowledge in biology or the latest workforce applications of what students are being taught (or should be taught) in school. The big idea was that kids would do better if schools developed more ways to accommodate an education workforce with distributed skills and areas of expertise (Ingersoll et al., 2018; Weisberg et al., 2009). Educators need to be able to reinvent what school looks like and unshackle themselves—and their students—from the "one teacher one classroom" model of schooling. And, while the idea of teaming was certainly not new, we felt the time was right to think about it again (Cuban, 2018).

MLFTC believed that what was needed was to move beyond "teacher shortage," understand workforce design, and challenge P–12 education and teacher preparation to move beyond traditional staffing models (Darling-Hammond, 2001). As a result, we wanted to create a statement that embodied the big ambitious goal that we were aiming to achieve. We wanted an aim statement that was good for learners and good for educators. That statement was as follows: "We (MLFTC and its partners) would: a) provide students with deeper and personalized learning by building teams of educators with distributed expertise; and b) empower educators by developing better ways to enter the profession, specialize and advance." Hence, the *Next Education Workforce* was born.

MLFTC set about creating various partnerships that were capable of leveraging resources and enacting change across the system (i.e., upskilling, team-based practices, systems-centered leadership, developing more flexible pathways for entering the profession, making room for specializations in teacher preparation, providing more advancement pathways for educators, examining human resource systems, scheduling, and more). The university recognized that there were several root causes within the overall system. Exploring each component in tandem could change not only the component itself but the entire system. This type of disciplined inquiry would support a nested cycle of improvement and raise the entire system. One of those components that MLFTC thought could "ground soften" the ideas was teacher preparation, particularly clinical practice, or the placement and support of residents in schools.

Today, we continue this work understanding that there are many systems components we are reimagining and many partners locally and nationally with whom we are working closely. The partnership described here provides insight into one slice of this work—focused primarily on teacher candidates, teaming, and team-based residencies. We learned much from this early improvement-centered pilot and we wouldn't be where we are today without the strong partnership with Avondale and the feedback loop that developed along the way.

Context: MLFTC and AESD Partnership

MLFTC and AESD had engaged in multiple opportunities for exploring professional development, content engagement, and action research for more than 15 years. For most of those years, while the partnership was strong, many of the interactions were transactional in nature based on the traditional needs of an Institution of Higher

Education (IHE) and a Local Education Agency (LEA). Student-teacher or intern placements, grant and pilot opportunities, research studies, and specific data gathering were primarily the focus. This would change significantly when MLFTC and AESD came together in 2017 to design a team-based residency program that would transform the partnership into a mutual benefit relationship.

Arizona State University's MLFTC has a student population of almost 7000, with approximately 40% students of color, and is a very highly ranked research community. AESD is a medium-sized school district in a suburb southwest of Phoenix. The district serves approximately 6000 PK to 8th-grade students across nine schools. AESD serves an ethnically and racially diverse student population with over 74% of the population eligible for free and reduced lunch. Over 66% of the students are of Hispanic origin and many are eligible for sheltered English immersion support. More than half of Avondale's 700 staff are classroom educators.

When the district and the university began their exploration of a new residency model, Avondale was already recognized for its success in raising English language arts scores (+13%) and math scores (+18%) over a three-year period from 2014–2017 with its participation in Project Momentum Arizona, a state-based collaborative focused on student performance. Superintendent Hargrove attributes this success to a capacity-building effort for all staff that was team-based and led to the increase in student performance. Recognition of that success brought recognition to AESD and an invitation to work with similar districts across Arizona (Hargrove, 2019, 2022).

MLFTC and AESD came into partnership primarily through the relationship established between two deans of the College of Education and the AESD superintendent. The result of these relationships and the visibility Avondale had earned, put AESD in line to engage in various opportunities provided by MLFTC. Historically the partnership between MLFTC and AESD centered around two things: (1) professional learning and (2) teacher preparation. Opportunities for professional learning often came in the form of grants and pilot programs aimed at improving teaching and learning. Professional learning occurred over the years, typically transactional in nature with faculty providing professional development to district teachers. Teacher preparation, also transactional, provided the district with teacher candidates and served as a hiring pathway for the district.

The partnership between MLFTC and AESD that focused on teacher preparation and clinical practice was long-standing. At the start of every semester, the college would communicate with AESD seeking placements for the field experience requirements of the teacher-preparation programs. Avondale would respond by providing effective teacher mentors for a worthwhile experience. With governance structures already in place, the effort to build a new teaming model resulted in learning for college faculty, residents, mentor teachers, and AESD and MLFTC leadership. These models helped MLFTC develop more robust opportunities for their teacher candidates to learn the art and science of teaching and provided AESD with a workforce that matched their innovative approach student improvement outcomes based on a districtwide teaming approach.

Figure 6.1 illustrates the challenges that confronted both partners. The old partnership between MLFTC and AESD was fine and served its purpose for both entities but never got past early-stage changes that were exploratory or produced small

Problems faced by districts and schools	Problems faced by professional educators	Problems faced by teacher-prep programs	Problems faced by P–12 learners
Current shortage of qualified teachers	Lack of empowerment and opportunities for creativity	Challenges presented by 1:1 mentor model	Lack of individualized instruction to advance academic outcomes
Inadequate pipeline of future teachers	Lack of advancement pathways and roles that combine instructional and leadership responsibilities	Financial burdens of teacher candidates in a full-year residency	Too few adults with whom to build relationships that advance socio-emotional learning

Figure 6.1 Problems facing the education community.

incremental changes. As district and university leaders considered new avenues of cooperation, they reached agreement that what was needed was a more intentional and concentrated partnership that would help solve a number of systemic problems.

Challenges, Solutions, and Evidence-Based Teacher Preparation

The Phoenix metropolitan area has a population of almost five million people and spans over 517 square miles. Within this area, there are over 30 school districts, serving almost 700,000 PK–12 students. The outlying areas of the Phoenix valley are typically hard-pressed to find quality teachers applying in their districts. With that being said, the college students requesting field placements in conjunction with their coursework were also staying in the urban areas. The suburban area, where AESD is located, and rural school districts surrounding the greater Phoenix metropolitan area were starting to experience a teacher shortage long before the nationwide teacher shortage was realized.

CHALLENGES FOR AESD

Nothing in the field of education has ever been flawless. Over the years, education has seen many different issues and problems come and go, but one of the most persistent problems is that of teacher shortage. AESD started noticing the lack of teachers seeking jobs before other states. In a matter of 6 years, starting in 2009, AESD went from riffing staff to traveling nationwide to seek teachers to fill classrooms. Multiple factors were at play including significant reductions in school funding, a stressed economy, and an unstable district budget allocation from the state. Further, the influx of charter schools within AESD boundaries and around the state created competition for educators and school staff as well as for student enrollment. Within AESD's boundaries alone, eight charter schools were created that drew teachers away from AESD and other traditional school districts.

First looking inward, AESD considered what could be done to increase the retention of current teachers and the recruitment of additional teachers. Seeking to attract and retain teachers to AESD, a comprehensive overhaul of the compensation structure across the district was enacted. Teacher compensation, historically low relative to other professions, was a complicating factor, especially during the recession. Staff could step out of the field of education and readily get a job in other industries. As well, the recession eliminated many of the opportunities for staff to be compensated for additional duties and roles. Stipends were decreased and extracurricular experiences were reduced or eliminated to effectuate the decline in resources. In some places, entire fields of study were reduced or eliminated, such as art, music, and technology, and supplemental staffing such as for paraprofessionals was riffed. The result of these factors impacted the decision-making of college-going students, and the teacher pipeline started to decline further. Even with the long-standing partnership between MLFTC and AESD, the decline in students entering the college of education threatened the future of AESD serving as a clinical practice site.

CHANGES AND VISION AT MLFTC

In the summer of 2016, MLFTC experienced a shift in leadership. As noted above, the new dean began her tenure by meeting area superintendents and local leaders to share her vision and intended direction for the college of education. Dean Basile's vision capitalized on distributed expertise and collective efficacy (Spillane, 2005). In that vision, multiple members of the school as well as greater community members would engage in the education of students through a teaming model wherein various job and role-specific opportunities were exercised. This approach included businesspeople, volunteers, and educational and support staff in the classroom all accountable for all students' success. This model would involve training opportunities and multiple entry points for adults to support children and learning.

A RENEWED PARTNERSHIP

Superintendent Hargrove of AESD saw a possible alignment with the vision being articulated by Dean Basile. The idea of finding a long-term solution to the challenges of significant teacher shortages and educators leaving the profession for jobs outside of the field was imperative. Add a crippling recession and a decline in students enrolled in teacher education programs in Arizona and elsewhere, it was certainly a crisis that had to be addressed. As Dean Basile shared throughout those first meetings and continuously through her tenure, teaching as currently being done is untenable, inflexible, and isolating.

AESD Superintendent Hargrove attended these brainstorming sessions designed by the dean and her team. From design thinking to envisioning the Next Education Workforce, the superintendent became more and more convinced that the shift away from the "one teacher, one classroom" model had merit and needed to be explored for its possibilities. The superintendent saw this approach as building a better environment that could possibly attract young people to the profession again and keep teachers in the profession longer. She saw that the approach could also provide advancement pathways as teachers took on compensated team leader roles; decrease the financial burden of teacher candidates (as the district found ways of paying these candidates to work on teams); and begin to personalize and deepen learning for students through the use of distributed responsibility and expertise. AESD already had systems and an organizational model in place for teaming and collective responsibility and this approach could amplify that work as well. Grade-level, site-based, and cross-district levels of professional development and accountability for all children were already a focus in living the AESD mission of growing every child as a thinker, problem solver, and communicator to pursue their future without limits. Rethinking the preservice experience while at the same time further developing the in-service experience through a team-based model was easily envisioned.

In November 2017, MLFTC and AESD entered into discussions about the *Next Education Workforce* and what it could mean for MLFTC's teacher candidates and AESD's professional teachers. The energy was new, and the commitment to solving the teacher shortage conundrum challenge was strong. The partnership between MLFTC and AESD had always been strong, but this was the time the partnership would take on institutional and sustaining work commitments. Reinforcing the relationship was the acceptance of the Carnegie Foundation's invitation for MLFTC and AESD to become part of the Improvement Leadership, Education, and Development (iLEAD) initiative. The work with iLEAD would provide a structure and a framework to begin imagining what a renewed partnership could look like and it gave both partners a way to visualize continuous cycles of improvement. Having teams of educators with varying experiences and expertise working collaboratively to ensure academic success and social well-being now became a shared vision.

And so, AESD and MLFTC began working together to design a model that would leverage teacher preparation, both simultaneously renewing teacher preparation and reframing the default normative grammar of schooling (Tyack & Tobin, 1994). MLFTC had obtained a Teacher Quality Partnership grant from the US Department of Education and was in the midst of designing a much more flexible, integrated teacher-preparation program. AESD was exploring new ways of teaming professional staff to better meet student needs. The commitment to iLEAD and the idea of improvement science sat squarely at the center of the work of both partners. Both parties knew it would be iterative and cyclical as they figured out how teams would work

156 SECTION II: A NEW KIND OF PARTNERSHIP

For schools
Build teacher pipeline by filling immediate vacancies with Residents instead of substitutes or teachers hired under emergency certification.

For Residents
Relieve debt burden and reduce the need to work additional jobs.

For MLFTC
Retain students and eliminate the need to find more effective mentors than possible.

Figure 6.2 Immediate outcomes.

and what other institutional norms it would impact (i.e. schedules, planning, planning time, time for personalized and deeper learning, teacher evaluation, hiring processes, etc.). Improvement science then gave a path to follow for designing, developing, and iterating these models (Bryk et al., 2017).

SERENDIPITY AND EARLY MODELS

In 2017, in recognition of the teacher shortage conditions, Arizona began offering an intern certificate to allow teacher candidates to be in a classroom on their own in their senior year of college. There was recognition on the part of both the district and the university that simply moving teacher candidates to being full teachers of record was not the solution to filling classroom vacancies. While teacher candidates, undergraduates, and graduates, had had multiple courses in pedagogy and some internship experience, they were still underprepared to take on a classroom on their own. In addition, it was recognized that being the sole teacher in a classroom without support and guidance compounds the loneliness and overwhelming feeling expressed by teachers. And the "one teacher candidate–one mentor" model was also not sufficiently supportive and propagated a system that wasn't working. The goal was to attract teacher candidates to the district and support them in ways that would also retain them.

During the fall semester of 2017, Superintendent Hargrove was shopping at a local hardware store and recognized the cashier. He was one of the teacher residents, who was completing his student teaching at an AESD school and was working each evening after his day of student teaching was complete. After recognizing the superintendent, the resident teacher assured her that he was making time for his teacher duties (lesson planning and grading student work) but explained that he would not be able to finish his degree and student-teach if he did not have some sort of income. Seeing the teacher resident in this predicament sparked a new idea for the AESD Superintendent. Could there be a way to compensate the teacher residents during their student teaching or internship within the district and create a team-based residency model at the same time?

MLFTC had been requiring teacher candidates in their senior year of early-childhood and elementary education programs to conduct full-year teaching residencies using a 1:1 mentor model without financial support. There were several persistent challenges with that model, which MLFTC faculty sought to address. The proposed redesign focused on team-teaching experiences that would provide candidates with paid experiences (which they desperately needed) but also provide the kind of support that cannot be provided by a single mentor teacher. The team "idea" that emerged in its truest form would include multiple professional teachers and teacher candidates working in sync, distributing expertise and responsibility appropriately, and sharing a larger roster of students.

IMPROVEMENT SCIENCE: PLANNING, DOING, STUDYING, ACTING

This first iteration was a model wherein a lead teacher oversaw a team of teacher residents who would share the workload and responsibility of two classrooms of students. This would elevate the responsibility and compensation of a lead/mentor teacher as well as compensate the teacher residents using the pay that would have gone to another professional teacher. Rather than one student-teacher and one mentor teacher working in partnership to support one classroom, there emerged the idea of one lead teacher and two or three teacher residents working collaboratively to deliver instruction and support to two classrooms.

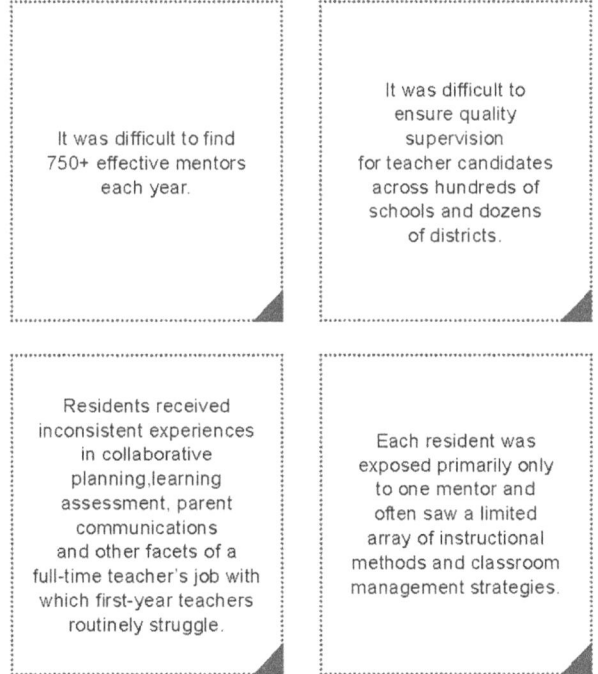

Figure 6.3 Persistent challenges.

Leadership from both organizations began envisioning and planning. While there was no formal agreement, MLFTC and AESD developed a staffing and service model founded in collaborative and collective accountability, with shared and distributed expertise using a team-based approach. The synergy and like-mindedness, as well as the long-standing partnership between the two organizations laid the groundwork for quickly transitioning to offer a paid team-based student-teacher model to 36 incoming student residents for the fall of 2018. The core features included:

Residents

Residents applied for jobs through the AESD's existing hiring processes. The district used funds they would otherwise have used to hire substitutes and emergency-certified teachers. They paid residents approximately one-third (up to $12,000) of what they would have paid a first-year teacher, essentially securing three residents for the price of one alternative FTE.

Lead Teachers

District and school administration sought educators who had a combination of the following: strong teacher evaluations; grade-level and subject-area experience; and experience as teacher-leaders either among their peers or because they had previously mentored teacher candidates.

Site Lead

MLFTC clinical faculty serving as site leads provided coaching and support to individual residents, teams of residents, and, in many cases, to lead teachers, helping to balance the learning needs of residents with the learning needs of PK–8 students.

Instructional Configurations

Teams were empowered to determine their schedules, physical learning configurations, and allocation of responsibilities to provide residents with broader exposure to instructional modes and surround learners with more adults able to deliver personalized attention and instruction.

Studying the Innovative Approach

The entire approach was a strong example of addressing a joint problem of practice. The immediate need of AESD, not having enough teachers to fill classrooms, and the MLFTC vision for change in education to a team-based approach, came alive in this effort. The improvement science process of plan, do, study, and act was a perfect match for the endeavor. The goals were: to build collective efficacy, increase job satisfaction, and ultimately, realize positive outcomes for students. The joint problem of practice was identified as a strength of the partnership. Having an aligned problem of practice provided a foundation for the improvement work (Gomez et al., 2021).

The planning led to the development of a year-long in-service opportunity for teacher candidates who would earn an income while completing the year-long residency. MLFTC teacher candidates were playing a dual role: full-time college students completing their residency requirements and part-time district employees. The teacher candidates also experienced mentorship and guidance from both district lead teachers and university faculty. The improvement science cycle helped both parties to iterate quickly and constantly. If the team felt that something wasn't working as well as it could, the cycle helped them to pivot quickly. There were certainly those times when the teaming models broke down. There was a delicate balance of relationships, understanding of what teaming was or could be and navigating the IHE student/university verse LEA employee/employer expectations including the calendar of two different organizations. The effort was moving fast and building a just-in-time model. As leaders of both organizations noted, "we didn't have the training or the infrastructure but using the frame of improvement science allowed us to recognize the concerns quickly and to act fast to resolve them."

The leadership teams from MLFTC and AESD started engaging in solutions-based conversations at the end of the fall semester in 2017. The spring semester carried a series of meetings to discuss different ideas on how both sides could make this happen as soon as possible. The launch of this new program model was scheduled to start in the fall of 2018, and both groups had a lot of planning to do. This program was brand new to the preservice teachers and they had no idea it was even an option in which to participate. The option to enter into a team-based residency teaming model had to be explained to potential teacher candidates with the full understanding they were expected to extend their school year to match that of the school district rather than an MLFTC schedule as well as adhere to policies that were different from being a college student. Mid-spring semester, the AESD superintendent attended the student-teacher placement meeting. For some candidates, this was overwhelming. MLFTC faculty and the AESD Superintendent shared the vision of the new paid teacher residency program and students were encouraged to sign up if interested. The biggest selling point was that they would be paid while having the experience of full-time work in a team with enhanced support from the district and the full-year exposure from new teacher in-service orientation to the last day of school.

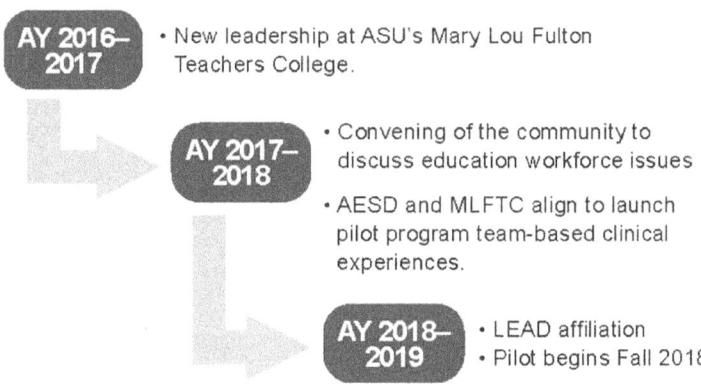

Figure 6.4 Timeline.

A new approach to hiring needed to be developed and implemented quickly within AESD as they had a compressed timeline to build the teams. In a matter of three weeks, teams of teacher residents needed to be interviewed and placed at school sites and grade levels/content areas assigned. The MLFTC faculty worked alongside the AESD staff members from the beginning, including sitting in with the district interviews to select the teacher candidates interested in being a part of this pilot program. AESD staff worked with the MLFTC team to develop the process for the teacher residents to apply for the program. The residency openings were posted on the district website where the teacher candidates were asked to apply. Interviews were set up and the selection process began. Site administrators from AESD joined the interview panel, looking for candidates to fit with their school and grade-level teams and MLFTC faculty sat on the panel to ensure that teacher candidates were able to meet all of their university program requirements while in the year-long placements. True of the new teaming model, the teacher candidates went through an actual group interview with their peers, and 36 of the 37 who interviewed were offered a team-based residency position.

There were many key players in this new model, both from MLFTC and AESD. MLFTC assigned two longtime site coordinator supervisors to oversee the implementation of this model, along with one part-time faculty member. AESD developed a job description for lead teachers and posted an internal position announcement to generate interest among the certified staff to support these team-based residency teams. Six of the ten AESD campuses were designated as team-based residency sites, based on the vacant position history and the site administrator's interest level. Site administrators interviewed and staffed the lead teacher positions at each of their campuses, typically including two classroom settings, and 11 team-based residency teams were built. All of the teacher candidate teams started out as triads, supported by one lead teacher at the same campus. The thought behind having a triad of teacher candidates, versus a pair, is while working or co-teaching with the lead teacher, none of the teacher candidates would ever be alone in the classrooms.

At MLFTC, a review of the program and coursework needed to be considered. Over the 2018 summer months, a group of about 15 MLFTC faculty members planned out the program and coursework details. They were anticipating having four different undergraduate program areas to be represented and had to ensure that all of the teacher candidates in this model were still able to master the course objectives in their remaining coursework. The planning of this was not easy. There were many different factors to consider, time constraints, multiple voices from the different programs, and a very tight deadline. After several weeks of planning, they all agreed that what was needed was to start with an iteration designed by the team, keep the lines of collaboration open, and make needed adjustments along the way. This served as a beneficial approach as modifications to scheduling and demonstration of mastery and completion of coursework shifted to maximize the opportunities and experiences of the teacher residents. Further, discussions included dialogue between university faculty and AESD district leadership to provide input and suggestions to improve the upcoming experience for all involved.

In a similar approach, prior to the start of the 2018 school year, AESD staff and leadership came together to process the next steps. Ideas shared included communication with families and colleagues, ongoing support and intentional meetings, and collaboration between lead teachers across the district to build collective efficacy and identification of share challenges and successes. MLFTC faculty participated in the meetings and provided input and suggestions for structures and solutions. All members were full participants in the development of this model. This collaborative approach continued throughout the year and ongoing informal and formal communication occurred as we navigated the messiness of something completely new.

Once the teams were assembled at each of the AESD sites, the MLFTC faculty led the welcome orientations and trainings for the lead teachers and the teacher candidate teams. Many hours went into developing the team structures, setting the team norms, getting to know each other, and distributing the expertise among the classroom team members. The MLFTC faculty members spent every day of the week at the AESD sites, visiting classrooms, providing feedback to the lead teachers and the teacher candidates, and collecting field-based data. All of the college coursework was taught on-site, after school hours, and data-driven coaching sessions were created in real time to help support the teacher candidates at the highest level. The communication flow between the MLFTC faculty, the AESD lead teachers, and the administrative teams was happening daily and organically. Around every corner, both parties were finding new ways to navigate through the distinguishing between the role of the resident as a teacher candidate and their role as a part-time district employee.

Engaging in a collective orientation meeting promoted partnership cohesion with a united team who, while they may not have had all of the answers, shared a vision of possibilities around being part of something so innovative and solution-focused. Ongoing communication was a strength of this model. A strong foundation in partnership relationships was key to our success.

As reported by one participant to iLEAD "a strong bond of trust and respect has formed and provided the basis for even difficult conversations to happen. Formal and informal conversations have occurred throughout the process." Defining the role of AESD as an employer and MLFTC as a student supporter presented some challenges. For example, if a student had an incident that rose to the level of administration, MLFTC would use it as a coachable moment, whereas AESD had to consider employment law, as well as the confidential expectations by both institutions. Both AESD and MLFTC leaders recognized that partnerships can only move at the speed of trust. In this case, Basile and Hargrove together assert that "trust was rooted in prompt responses and mutual respect and in knowing that everyone was on this journey together—all with the very best of intentions."

The MLFTC faculty assigned to the team-based residency model scheduled a revolving meeting every week to plan upcoming content, share the grading of coursework assignments, share and respond to the field data by creating data-driven coaching sessions, and discuss any celebrations or issues in the field. MLFTC and AESD continued the internal scheduled governance meetings with the larger group, once a quarter to share data, placement, and program information and collaborate on any current issues. Impromptu and informal phone conversations and emails happened throughout the weeks, as needed. Small-scale changes were being monitored at the classroom level as both partners discovered how teams function, what roles teachers take on and give up, and how teaming impacts other systems within the classroom experience.

Over time the model changed as everyone recognized that school leaders needed more support to sustain the model and grow the teaming models across the schools, with and without teacher candidates. Today, AESD continues to iterate the collective efficacy model first established through Project Momentum to grow all educators, as well as embeds the *Next Education Workforce* team-based models during their interventionist time within a grade level and in some cases across grade levels. Teacher candidates continue to be part of the instructional teams and also to work with professional educators sharing rosters of students.

Lessons Learned

There were many lessons learned through this pilot. Partnerships always seem fragile but approaching them with an improvement science mindset actually allays the friction that can happen along the way. This pilot was no different—lessons learned, pivots made quickly, moving forward.

INVESTED AND INVOLVED LEADERSHIP

Upon considering factors for success in our improvement work and implementing fundamental change in both the way teacher candidates are prepared and the way professional educators in classrooms work, the commitment and engagement of leadership from both organizations were important. The roles of the education dean and the school superintendent were essential for this work to be initiated, continued, and institutionalized. While there were no official MOUs, the fact that leadership from both MLFTC and AESD were deeply involved and operating with a common problem of practice enabled the work of the partnership to be successful. Leadership being readily available to process challenges or to assist in removing barriers allowed both organizations, at all levels, to know the value of the work and to efficiently transition with the clearly communicated goal and direction in sight. Also important to note was that as people left or leadership changed, particularly at the mid-management level, unit directors at ASU or principals at AESD, the need to re-orient was imperative if we were to continue making progress.

In partnerships where leadership changes, attention often wanes or is pulled in another direction, progress becomes stagnant and direction is unclear, partnerships can end. Being very conscious of this challenge, we constantly focused on capacity-building for our team members. As part of this process, it was continuous improvement—each day better than the one before—that takes time, attention, and focus. The ways teams functioned, the roles that teachers and teacher candidates played, the way schedules changed, and the way new teachers were hired were all part of a gradual process of constant evaluation and improvement for better effectiveness and flexibility.

Another lesson learned is the power behind a shared narrative. We worked together to deepen the vision and then provided broad strokes to teacher residents and teacher-leaders to have them get behind the vision and be participants. Once they were on board, the MLFTC/AESD team worked collaboratively and inclusively throughout the initial year to build the systems and processes as we went. Without a shared narrative and a clear vision of what we were building and wanting to see, we never would have been able to implement such a shift in approaches.

SYSTEMS AND STRUCTURES

Working with iLEAD, allowed the MLFTC/AESD team to truly focus on improvement efforts and identify areas where they were being successful and where more development was needed. While leadership commitment, partnership relationship, and shared narrative were present, full knowledge of improvement science and systems for gathering consistent data and shared agreements for necessary information were initially lacking. Having the leadership and vision of improvement allowed for significant and immediate change; however, a vision can only go so far and what had changed could have fallen apart just as quickly. Further, as reflected earlier, the holders of the vision needed to be broadened through communication, data and evidence of impact, and clear next steps. Engaging in iLEAD provided the structure necessary to formalize and systematize the work that had intuitively begun.

Success was measured in many ways, both formally and informally. Formally, the success of a school-based team was measured by classroom content data as well as student achievement markers and growth. Informally, we measured success by the team's self-reported stress levels, overall happiness, and delegation of classroom teacher duties among the team, also known as distributed expertise. Because MLFTC professors were dedicated to the success of the teacher candidates and the pilot program, faculty were on six AESD elementary campuses and in each of the classrooms every week. Organic conversations were happening at every visit and formal, academically guided conversations were happening during the two (per semester) formal evaluations of each of the teacher candidates.

The MLFTC program expectation was to provide all teacher candidates feedback through four informal, non-scheduled walk-throughs each semester. Along with the walk-through feedback, two formal performance assessments were scheduled and co-scored with every lead teacher from AESD and the MLFTC supervisor. Feedback and support were ongoing conversations with each of the lead teachers and teacher candidates. If patterns of need surfaced among our 36 teacher candidates in any area, academically or professionally, the MLFTC team was able to respond to their needs by addressing them in conversation or creating a data-driven coaching session.

In addition, when it came to systems and structures, there seemed to be strong agreement that the partners were focused on the need for public communication. Changes in practice at this scale and at this level of change needed to be communicated early and often to parents of students enrolled and community members. Throughout the pilot, we continued to agree that the process of improvement science was key to the success of the program

CHALLENGES OF TEAMS

A universal feature of teacher-prep programs that work with schools to provide clinical and professional experiences for teacher candidates is the steep learning curve interns or residents face as they transition from college coursework to working in schools. Balancing the professional learning goals of residents with those of PK–8 learners in Avondale was a challenge that all teacher-prep programs and schools face together. The pilot model introduced in AESD caused additional degrees of complexity that MLFTC, AESD, residents, supervisors, lead teachers, and site leads had to navigate. The team-teaching model was new. It was ambitious. As Superintendent Hargrove put it:

> Stakeholders need to be flexible because there's going to be some challenges. How can we be creative? How can we live in the messy and be okay with messy? A high degree of collaboration needs to be there. If it's not, it's a siloed classroom, and you're in a box. We've seen that. We experienced that.

Follow-up surveys of key stakeholders illuminated other challenges:

- Some principals and lead teachers overvalued the vacancy-filling dimension of the pilot and undervalued the learning gains and professional development benefits the team model sought to generate.
- Some residents were asked to do too much too soon with too little support. Sometimes this appears to have been a function of teacher shortage. Sometimes it appears to have been a function of school personnel not balancing the residents' roles as both paid employees and college students who are in fact pre-novices.
- A minority of lead teachers conducted themselves in accordance with a traditional mentor model. In such cases, residents received fewer of the model's intended benefits regarding the opportunity to team teach and deliver personalized instruction. Some personal friction among residents and between residents and lead teachers inhibited teams. In such cases, they ended up conducting parallel teaching rather than collaborative co-teaching or turn-taking without the intended role definition and specialization.
- And, in some cases, residents and lead teachers felt they were told to be creative without being given clear teaming models and instructional configurations to try.

AESD saw results in the first year of the new program. The immediate impact was having 11 classrooms taught collaboratively with a lead teacher and teams of teacher candidates across two classrooms. Of the 36 teacher candidates, 7 stayed on with Avondale for the following year. (Five of the seven remain employees in AESD and are entering their fifth year of teaching in August 2022.) Of the 2021–22 cohort of teacher residents, 13 of the 14 teacher residents hired by AESD are returning for their second year of teaching. Many of the original cohort are participants in leadership opportunities in our team-based professional development district-wide. Superintendent Hargrove suggests that one of the reasons the model was successful was that MLFTC faculty were assigned to the district where they taught courses, studied the process, and provided continuous support for the teacher residents. MLFTC faculty met with Avondale teachers and leaders in ongoing collaborative meetings to iterate the process throughout. The resident's yearlong experience (residency and coursework) was in the district where they were integrated into teaching teams to meet the learning needs of Avondale students.

DEVELOPMENTAL PROGRESSIONS AND GROWTH IN COLLABORATION

The relationship between the MLFTC and AESD leaders continued to grow and deepen as the work developed and expanded during 2018 and 2019. The AESD leaders and lead teachers came to multiple college faculty meetings to share their experiences in the team-based residency model. The AESD team members articulated their successes and challenges in an academic space that was important for all to hear. Authentic conversations about the parameters of each organization were continuing as shifts to policies and practices happened. Ensuring the lines remained clear for teacher candidates/employees was important. Developing collaborative solutions to challenges that occurred while remaining focused on the collective goal—development of an excellent team-based model—allowed both partners to rethink the approach to pre-service teacher education through the engagement of Avondale teachers in the transformation process. In this pilot experience, the vast majority of participating teachers contributed to and experienced success.

As a result of this pilot, MLFTC formed an office focused on Next Education Workforce wherein the team has worked with the AESD site leaders and teams to engage in the process of design thinking. (This work occurred within the time frame of the pilot but was not connected to the establishment of collective teaching teams and started before the iLEAD work began in earnest). This design thinking experience was the first engagement by AESD in such work and allowed members of the district and site leaders to have a framework and language for what was done intuitively in the continuous improvement process. This became the foundation for some of the work. However, it was not until the engagement with iLEAD that the deepening of understanding occurred. The protocols for feedback and reflection drove the shift from creating while implementing to planning with intention.

When the renewed partnership started, the AESD had a goal to fill teacher vacancies with the most qualified candidates, senior/fourth-year education majors who, hopefully, would stay and provide continuity in the classrooms. The MLFTC had a vision of changing the landscape of education from "one classroom, one teacher" to a collective team-based approach. The processing with and through the iLEAD network and using the Developmental Progressions enabled AESD and MLFTC to come together and clearly define the problem of practice and develop a shared narrative that was on-point for both.

AESD is now in year four of the team-based residency model with the MLFTC and not one year has looked the same. In the middle of the four-year span, the whole world dealt with the COVID-19 pandemic (Biag et al., 2021). As we came out of the pandemic, we realized that we needed to continue refining this work and that we needed the following:

- A system for gathering data and reflecting on our progress.
- Data sharing agreements and a process to better track both teacher candidates and PK–12 students who have experienced this model.
- Additional measures for determining the success of the team-based approach and its effectiveness.
- Further exploration of how the iLEAD Developmental Progressions and improvement science tools can be used at scale.
- Professional learning for teacher candidates, mentor teachers, lead teachers, and school leaders.

Ongoing formal and informal communication between AESD and MLFTC has been integral to the further development of the team-based residency. Central to the success and evolution of this partnership was clarifying the joint problem of practice and shared partner narrative. As discussed previously, the impetus for developing this model was not necessarily aligned. Both organizations benefited from the proposed solution in that the LEA now has more highly qualified individuals in front of their students and the IHE was able to engage the team-based approach and gauge the success of its implementation.

The work with iLEAD provided a structure and rhythm to yield a deeper level of reflection and consideration of the next steps. Having the opportunity to share our work with other iLEAD school-university partners formalized our language, clarified our definitions, and made us pause to see it from other's perspectives through structured feedback cycles. The iLEAD Developmental Progressions Framework served as a device that elevated reflection and allowed both the IHE and LEA to engage independently and in partnership systematically throughout the process. As well, it provides discussion points for areas for celebration, focus, and refinement. The probing and prompting of fellow iLEAD participants from the ten other sites and the Carnegie Senior Fellows pushed our improvement journey to deeper levels.

The MLFTC and AESD partnership and the team-based residency model set a foundation for subsequent years and enabled the expansion of the new teaming models to different districts beyond Avondale. *The Next Education Workforce* team at MLFTC continues to study and develop school models and teams of educators, in part with the work and partnership that happened in the AESD team-based residency model. This project, the use of improvement science, and support provided by Carnegie set the stage for scaling and sustaining this work across multiple partners and reimagining teacher preparation in significant and much more flexible ways.

The partnership between AESD and ASU is moving forward. AESD has remained committed to placing teacher candidates in team-based models as paid employees of the district. Through this process, AESD recognized that leadership will be key to moving innovative efforts like this one forward. We also recognize that we will need to move leaders from traditional instructional leadership responsibilities to building systems leadership and the leadership of teams. This won't diminish the work we have started; it can only strengthen it.

AESD continues to focus on teams in many of its structures, including the use of them for intervention opportunities. The value and impact of this work are demonstrated most importantly in its impact on student achievement. Students served through this model immediately showed higher than traditional classroom student achievement results. Further, student and parent feedback was positive citing stronger relationships and connections, with more adults to support learners. Parents who were initially hesitant about the process, readily shared examples of its success as well as requested that they be allowed to participate again. Teacher residents shared their reflections on being prepared and while the process was overwhelming at times, they were able to get through it together and felt ready to take on their own classroom, many of whom chose to stay in AESD after graduation. Further evidence of success is in the fact that site leaders held classroom positions open to be able to participate the following year with new teacher residents (Hargrove, 2022).

Based on a comprehensive series of interviews with superintendents, human resources administrators, principals, lead teachers, residents, and site leads, MLFTC views the pilot as a success that warrants the introduction of the team-teaching residency *model, in both paid and unpaid implementations, to additional districts. In successful* implementations of the team-based residency model, teams of educators were able to address and overcome the set of interconnected challenges that traditional residencies present to residents, teachers, schools, and learners.

In such cases, residents expressed greater degrees of satisfaction with their experiences; school administrators regarded residents as more prepared for first-year teaching positions than teacher candidates who had not participated in the pilot; and all observed gains in academic outcomes and socio-emotional development for learners. In the best cases, superintendents and principals observed significant professional growth among lead teachers. These comments reflect those sentiments:

> You're required to go to all PDs and then anything prior to school, so we went to all the new teacher orientations which I think was super beneficial. I learned a lot in my PDs and sitting with the lead teacher and asking questions during those PDs which helped me professionally develop as a teacher. —*Resident*

> There are teachers who are not in these models who are saying, 'Wait. We like this. How can we do this?' —*Superintendent*

> The Staff understood that the residents were here as 'teacher candidates' but they treated them like peers. They were here for every meeting and professional development we had—they were staff here. —*Principal*

> I was able to fill in more gaps for students that there is no way I could have done that by myself with the whole class. I was able to communicate and build better relationships with those students. —*Lead teacher*

However, the experience varied among schools and among teams within schools. From the interviews, it's possible to identify key characteristics of challenged teams and successful teams, as well as elements that need to be further refined and developed when introducing the model into additional schools and districts.

CHARACTERISTICS OF SUCCESSFUL TEAMS

When teams were successful, they were very successful. In interviews with teacher candidates, lead teachers, and principals, teams and teaming were viewed as a promising practice. Teacher candidates felt they were members of a professional community. In-service teachers viewed them as colleagues. They became embedded in school organization and culture, attending professional development events, staff meetings, and other workplace functions. They also reported a greater sense of ownership and responsibility.

Teacher candidates reported that they were exposed to more facets of the job such as learner assessment, IEPs, and parent conferences, as well as lesson planning and instruction for both large and small groups of learners. Learners developed meaningful relationships with more adults and were not dependent on having a good-fit relationship with one mentor.

Teacher candidates and lead teachers both reported engaging in deeper forms of collaborative lesson planning based on individual learner data than they did under the previous residency model. Teacher candidate teams practiced many forms of teaching such as whole-group instruction, small-group instruction, station teaching, and more. They also spoke positively of the creativity and enthusiasm they were able to generate among themselves and, consequently, among their learners.

Related to K–12 learners, teacher candidates and lead teachers reported seeing and measuring learning gains on student assessments, which they attributed to the ability of teams to provide deeper, personalized instruction. Learners received more personal and small-group instruction tailored to individual learning needs.

Leadership was also a driving factor. Lead teachers developed skills and practices characteristic of teacher-leaders such as coaching, role assignment, and schedule management. Many reported acquiring a fuller understanding of leadership skills. And, in the estimation of superintendents, principals, lead teachers, and the residents themselves, residents emerged better prepared than in typical teacher-preparation programs.

Conclusion

Today, we continue to have confounding staffing shortages, heightened teacher absences, unexpected resignations, too few substitutes, and increased teacher burnout. With team-based models and new working conditions and learning environments,

CHAPTER 6: REDESIGNING SCHOOL STAFFING MODELS   169

we have the potential for deeper and more personalized learning, whole-child supports, a more diverse workforce, and new pathways, novice teachers who are never alone, integration of community educators, and more educator autonomy and less isolation. Following MLFTC's success in partnering with AESD, in the Fall of 2021 ASU expanded its partnering efforts and was working with 5 districts, 27 schools, 86 educator teams, 268 professional educators, and impacting 6,600 students. By the fall of 2023, we project that these numbers will double.

We are seeing different kinds of models at all levels, elementary, middle, and high school. The move from a "one teacher one classroom" model to teams is to open the doors to new ways of thinking about schedules that allow for more deeper and personalized learning and planning time, teacher evaluation (from individual to teams), educator advancement (including paraprofessionals and others), compensation systems, and much more (Darling-Hammond et al., 2020). These teams are more than professional learning communities after school or a change in leadership structure. Research is showing increases in teachers' ability to promote equity for learners, greater confidence in their ability to personalize and deepen learning for students, and job satisfaction (Audrain, in preparation; Audrain et al., under review; Johns Hopkins University, 2022).

Figures 6.5, 6.6, and 6.7 illustrate how teams are beginning to form in different contexts, the roles adults could be playing as a team around a shared roster of students. So many more models are forming as more and more partners come on board. We are seeing within grade teams as shown below, but also vertical teams, and teams-based models appropriate for smaller, rural schools. Technology is prevalent in these new models, used for personalized and deeper learning but also for remote learning and instruction (Darling-Hammond, 2019). The core ideas, however, are clear: (1) there is

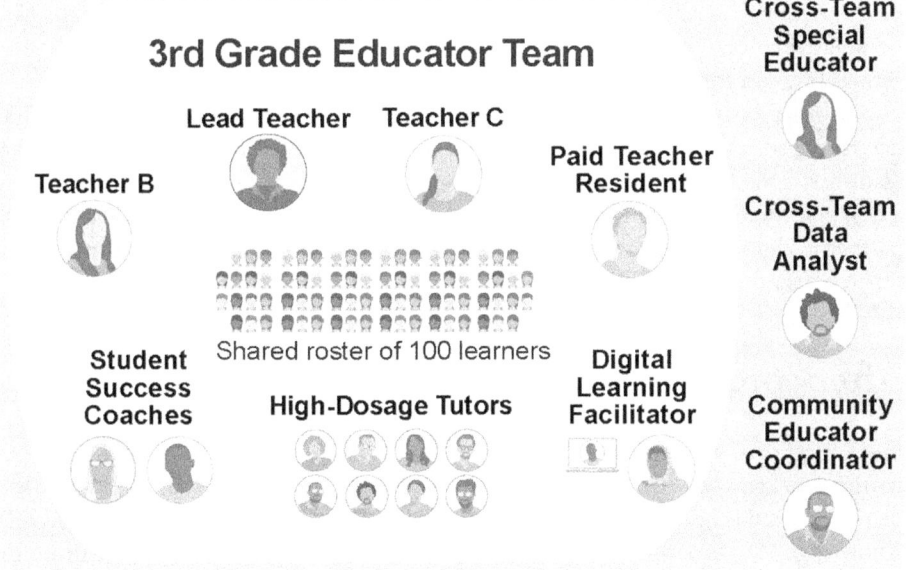

Figure 6.5 Models of teams with distributed expertise, elementary exemplar.

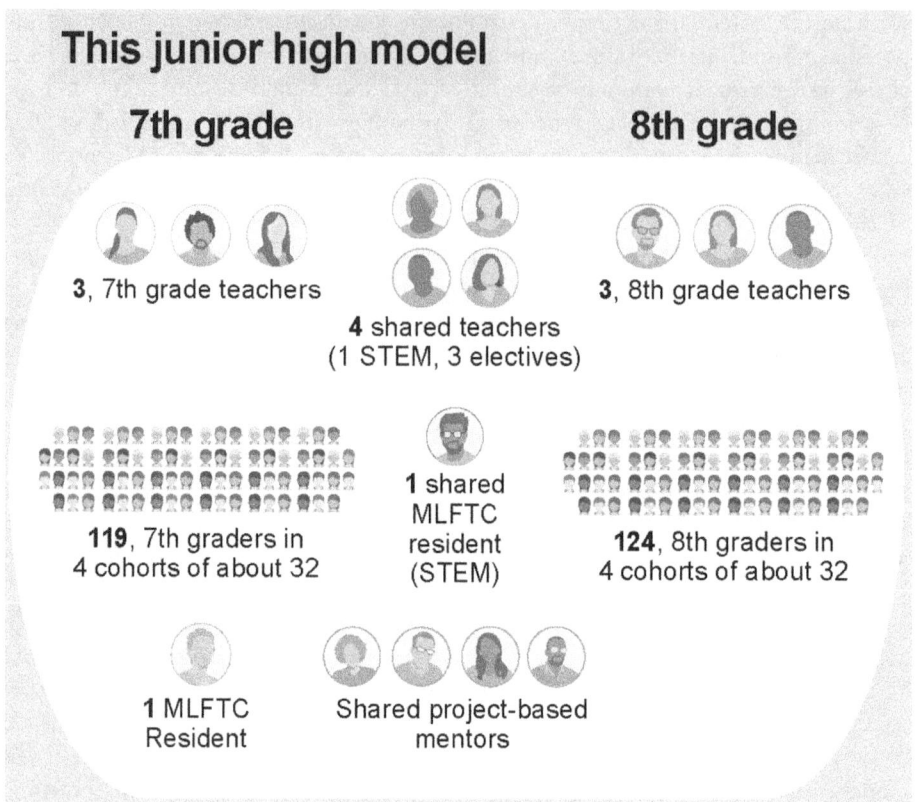

Figure 6.6 **Models of teams with distributed expertise, junior-high exemplar.**

no "one model"—school and community context determine the model; (2) this will be iterative work—healthy, lasting change moves at the speed of trust; and (3) this should be good for students, families, and educators.

Arizona and the nation are facing an unprecedented teacher shortage. MLFTC has launched a *Next Education Workforce* learning cohort and we are hopeful that team-based models will become more prevalent. We need to build new systems, form a new grammar of schooling, establish an expectation that schools and universities will partner in significant and sustaining ways, and we need to do it quickly to recruit and retain educators—our children are at stake.

Afterword: Beyond Teacher Preparation

Since this initial work with AESD, MLFTC has grown the *Next Education Workforce* partnership network with national partners such as AASA, The School Superintendents Association; the American Association of College Teacher Educators (AACTE); Knowledge Works, Communities in Schools, and other higher education institutions. By the end of the spring of 2022, over 200 school systems from across the country had visited Next Education Workforce schools. MLFTC has been honored to receive

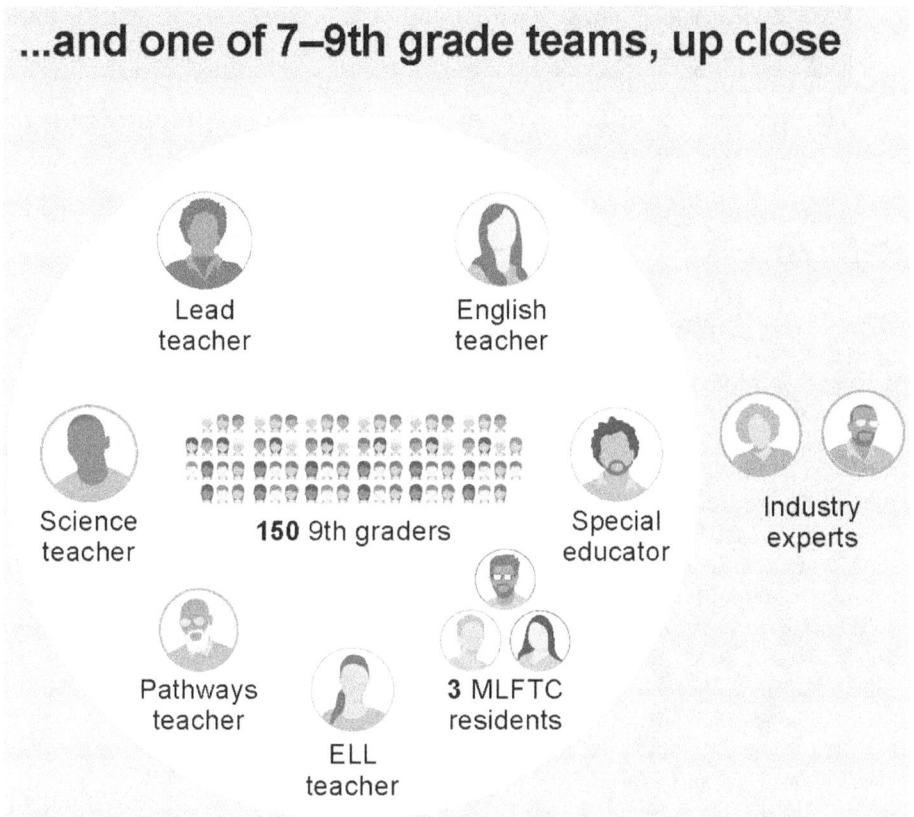

Figure 6.7 Models of teams with distributed expertise, high-school exemplar.

funding from major donors including the Walton Family Foundation, Schusterman Family Philanthropies, Overdeck Family Foundation, Gates Foundation, and the Arizona Community Foundation. A new US Department of Education TSL grant is helping us explore and change human resource systems so that district-level systems can be ready for team-based models. Much more can be found online about this work, our partners, and our research (https://workforce.education.asu.edu).

We are also collaborating with Johns Hopkins University and the Center on Reinventing Public Education on a very robust research agenda related to building and scaling *Next Education Workforce* models (essential elements, the models themselves, transformation); educator outcomes (efficacy, diversity, satisfaction, recruitment, retention); and student outcomes (academic growth, skills, mindsets, dispositions, social capital).

Questions for Discussion

1. Partnership maintenance can be an enormous problem when there are many small and intermediate districts engaged with a single university. How do you prioritize relationships and build enduring partnerships?

2. When a partner in an ongoing partnership has a big, bold, and potentially transformative idea, are there ways to effectively change the purpose of the partnership while building capacity and integrating new direction?
3. While partners can see innovation as positive, they can have disparate goals and outcomes. How do you work to satisfy both?

References

Audrain, R. L. (in preparation). *Exploring teacher working conditions in a large, southwestern school district.*

Audrain, R. L., Ruiz, E. A., Wyatt, L. G., Nailor, N., & Weinberg, A. E. (under review). Sustaining teachers through collaboration and autonomy outcomes of a professional development experience. *The New Educator.*

Basile, C. G. (2017). *Why education innovation matters.* Mary Lou Fulton Teachers College.

Basile, C. G., & Maddin, B. W. (2022). *The next education workforce: Team-based staffing models can make schools work better for both learners and educators.* American Enterprise Institute for Public Policy Research. https://www.aei.org/research-products/report/the-next-education-workforce-team-based-staffing-models-can-make-schools-work-better-for-both-learners-and-educators/

Biag, M., Gomez, L. M., Imig, D. G., & Vasudeva, A. (2021). Responding to COVID-19 with the aid of mutually beneficial partnerships in education. *Frontiers in Education, 5.* https://www.doi.org/10.3389/feduc.2020.621361

Bryk, A. S., Gomez, L. M., Grunow, A., & LeMahieu, P. G. (2015). *Learning to improve: How America's schools can get better at getting better.* Harvard Education Press.

Cuban, L. (2018, December 9). Whatever happened to team teaching? *Larry Cuban on School Reform and Classroom Practice.* Retrieved August 5, 2022, from https://www.larrycuban.wordpress.com/2018/12/09/whatever-

Darling-Hammond, L. (2001). The challenge of staffing our schools. *Educational Leadership, 58*(8), 12–17.

Darling-Hammond, L., & Oakes, J. (2019). *Preparing teachers for deeper learning.* Harvard Education Press.

Darling-Hammond, L., Schachner, A., & Edgerton, A. K. (with Badrinarayan, A., Cardichon, J., Cookson, P. W., Jr., Griffith, M., Klevan, S., Maier, A., Martinez, M., Melnick, H., Truong, N., & Wojcikiewicz, S.). (2020). *Restarting and reinventing school: Learning in the time of COVID and beyond.* Learning Policy Institute. https://restart-reinvent.learningpolicyinstitute.org/

Feiman-Nemser, S. (2020). From preparation to practice: Designing a continuum to strengthen and sustain teaching. *Teachers College Record, 103*(6), 1013–1055. https://doi.org/10.1111/0161-4681.00141

Gomez, L., Biag, M., & Imig, D. (2022). 19. Improvement science: The social glue that helps helpers help. In M. Suárez-Orozco & C. Suárez-Orozco (Eds.), *Education: A global compact for a time of crisis* (pp. 335–360). Columbia University Press. https://doi.org/10.7312/suar20434-022

Hargrove, B. (2019). *Project momentum Arizona: The Avondale ESD case study.* Avondale Elementary School District.

Hargrove, B. (2022, June 2). *How our district turned failing schools into excelling ones (and others can too).* AzCentral.

Ingersoll, R. M., Merrill, E., Stuckey, D., & Collins, G. (2018). *Seven trends: The transformation of the teaching force – Updated October 2018*. Consortium for Policy Research in Education. https://repository.upenn.edu/cpre_researchreports/108/

Johns Hopkins University. (2022). *Results from the year one survey of next education workforce (NEW) teachers*. https://education.asu.edu/sites/default/files/2022-08/ASU_NEW_Technical_Report_13July22.pdf

Partelow, L. (2019, December 3). *What to make of declining enrollment in teacher preparation programs*. Center for American Progress. https://www.americanprogress.org/issues/education-k-12/reports/2019/12/03/477311/make-declining-enrollment-teacher-preparation-programs/

Spillane, J. P. (2005). Distributed leadership. *The Educational Forum*, *69*(2), 30, 143–150. https://www.doi.org/10.1080/00131720508984678

Tyack, D., & Tobin, W. (1994). The "grammar" of schooling: Why has it been so hard to change? *American Educational Research Journal*, *31*(3), 453–479. https://www.doi.org/10.2307/1163222

Weisberg, D., Sexton, S., Mulhern, J., & Keeling, D. (2009). *The widget effect*. New Teacher Project.

Zeichner, K. (2002). Beyond traditional structures of student teaching. *Teacher Education Quarterly*, *29*(2), 59–64. https://www.jstor.org/stable/23478291

CHAPTER 7

District-University Partnerships for Continuous Improvement: How Can UM Help?
UNIVERSITY OF MISSISSIPPI AND OXFORD SCHOOL DISTRICT

Denise A. Soares, Mark E. Deschaine, W. Bradley Roberson, David Rock, Marni Herrington, and Brian Harvey

This is a story of how a School of Education dean and the district superintendent(s) worked together to build a new kind of school–university partnership based on addressing problems of practice through the use of improvement science. They built capacity and support among their respective staff. Together they increased their understanding of and ability to use improvement science in both the district and the SOE. Today they have well-established processes working within each institution and for the partnership. Improvement projects routinely take place in the schools and in the SOE. Through an MOU, the two agencies have created a scholar-in-residence position to help guide future work of the partnership and are creating a national center to promote and extend this work.

Oxford School District (OSD) is located within five miles of the University of Mississippi (UM) campus and provides excellent clinical practice sites at all levels for UM School of Education (UM-SOE) candidates. UM faculty provides professional development as needed to OSD teachers and staff. This traditional kind of partnership existed for decades before David Rock, Dean of the School of Education, and Brian Harvey, Superintendent of Oxford School District saw the possibility of creating a new kind of partnership in 2017. Using improvement science, they sought to improve schooling for all students in Oxford. As a first step, Dean Rock and Superintendent Harvey submitted a proposal to participate in the Carnegie Foundation for the Advancement of Teaching's Improvement Leadership Education and Development (iLEAD) network. At the first convening of iLEAD in San Francisco, the Mississippi partnership represented by six members drawn from OSD and the UM-SOE was formed. One significant feature of the new partnership was the active involvement of both the dean and the Superintendent in planning, implementing, and evaluating this new partnership.

Context: Beginning the Partnership Work

The OSD superintendent and UM-SOE dean saw an opportunity through iLEAD to create a new kind of partnership, one that is mutually beneficial and which focuses on addressing shared problems of practice. A partnership team was formed and attended the first iLEAD meeting in 2017. At that meeting, they thought they would try to address the large achievement gap between demographic groups in the OSD. They quickly realized that this "problem" was too broad so they focused on student absenteeism, one of the perceived drivers of the achievement gap. The partnership sponsored a project to address absenteeism which had some positive effects, but the team realized that to advance in addressing the problem of practice they needed to build capacity in both the district and the School of Education. Major progress was made when the partnership sponsored a Carnegie Explorer's Workshop where over 75 teachers, school administrators, and university faculty learned about improvement science. In the ensuing years since that workshop, over 20 problems of practice have been addressed in OSD, the SOE and by the partnership (see figure 7.1).

The Achievement Gap Project

The OSD is situated in the city of Oxford which has a population of approximately 28,000; the district serves over 4500 students. It is recognized as an "A" school district by the Mississippi Department of Education indicating that the district meets the established criteria regarding student achievement, individual student growth, graduation rate, and participation. The OSD is, in fact, the top-performing school district in the entire state. While this is a great distinction and testament to the district's commitment to education, the district also has the greatest achievement gap for the state of Mississippi in several categories (see demographics in table 7.1). Oxford's gaps are almost double the state averages. The achievement gap between white and Black students is 51.7% overall which is 23.1% greater than that of the state overall. Additionally, when comparing students not designated as economically disadvantaged to those designated as economically disadvantaged (ED) students they have a 46.5% achievement gap which is 20.0% points greater than the state.

OSD distributes resources equitably (i.e., based on need as opposed to equally) to schools, staff, and students to ensure that all students are provided the support they need to obtain a high-quality education. The district has been awarded a District of Innovation designation from the Mississippi Department of Education (MDE) which enables OSD flexibility to create non-traditional learning environments, use creative funding strategies, as well as provide multiple curriculum choices. Given the gaps in achievement, the newly formed OSD-UM partnership decided its first problem of practice would be finding ways to ameliorate those gaps.

The Mississippi Department of Education (MDE) Office of School and District Accountability (MDE, n.d.) annually reports on the percentage of students meeting or exceeding the high-water mark (Proficiency or Advanced) on Mississippi's statewide assessments. These data are used to determine how well Mississippi students gain the

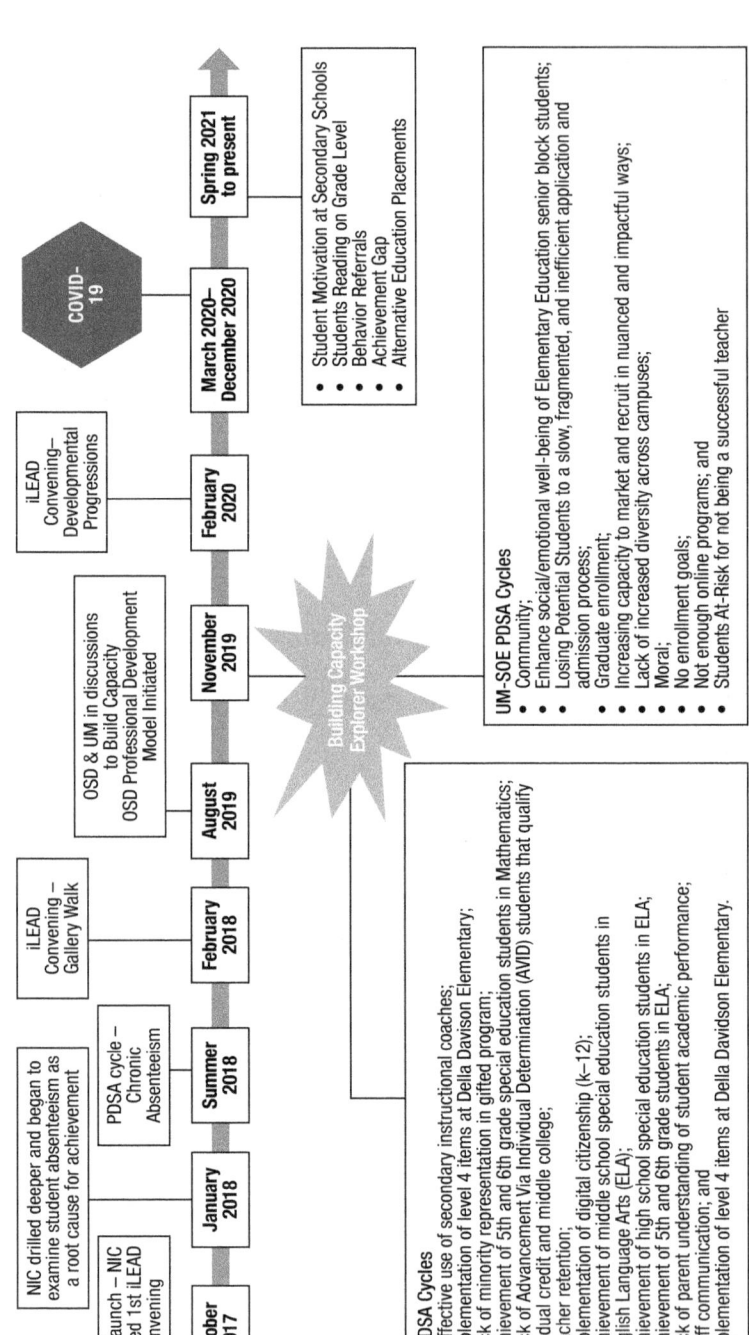

Figure 7.1 OSD and UM-SOE timeline.

Table 7.1 Demographics for OSD and UM-SOE

	Student Demographics		Faculty/Staff Demographics	
	UM-SOE	OSD	UM-SOE	OSD
White	77%	54%	84.7%	74%
African American	17%	36%	8.5%	25%
Hispanic or Latino	3%	5%	3.4%	0%
Asian	1%	3%	1.7%	1%
Other	2%	2%	1.7%	0%

knowledge to be considered fully proficient and ready for the next grade or course that requires additional understanding and application. At the time, OSD was first in the state in overall student achievement but also had the largest gap in achievement between Black and white students. Given this challenge, Dean Rock approached Superintendent Harvey with the question, "How can UM School of Education help the Oxford School District improve student achievement?"

Dean Rock and Superintendent Harvey began a series of discussions to determine what a partnership could do to address problems of practice that negatively impact student achievement. Following the initial meetings between the superintendent and dean, the members of the Oxford School District and School of Education were invited to their first iLEAD meeting in October of 2017. At the iLEAD meeting, the team determined the first problem of practice to be targeted by the newly formed partnership was the achievement gap of OSD students. They took the initial step of forming an Achievement Gap Project to address the problem. The solution they proposed was to redesign the clinical experiences for UM-SOE pre-service teachers working in OSD as well as the role of the University Supervisor. Their thought was that better equipping preservice teacher candidates to address the needs of all students could decrease the gap.

After exploring the problem of practice and solution, and gaining knowledge of the improvement science process, the team realized that the original goals were too ambitious. As such, they settled on a more realistic and focused project—addressing student attendance, one of the influences (drivers) of the achievement gap. The partnership refined the *project aim* to reduce the percentage of students with chronic absenteeism in two specific schools, Oxford High School and Della Davidson Elementary. Although chronic absenteeism lacks a standard definition within the larger policy and academic communities, the Mississippi Department of Education (MDE) identifies chronically absent students as learners who miss at least 10% of the school year (18 days) for any reason—excused or unexcused. The Partnership used this definition to guide the development of the new project and gathered evidence on the consequences of chronic absenteeism.

The National Center for Education Statistics 2009 (Snyder & Dillow, 2010) revealed that students as young as kindergarten age, who attend school regularly showed higher achievement levels when compared to students who were absent 18 or more days. OSD studied their data on attendance and found a significant number of their students missed over 10% of the school year. Approximately 11% of the students in the district in 2016–2017 were defined as chronically absent (students who missed 10% or more of the school year, including excused and unexcused absences above 18 days in a 180-day school year). As a result, the theory of improvement adopted by the partnership was that reducing the percentage of students who were chronically absent in these two schools, would decrease the achievement gap within the district.

At that time, the work of the partnership was expanded to include two Networked Improvement Communities (NICs), one at each of the two participating schools. Summer meetings were held in 2018 and the NICs developed specific strategies aimed at addressing the absentee problem. Students of 3rd grade and 9th grade with chronic absenteeism were identified from the two participating schools. Strategies were identified to reduce absenteeism as well as overcome barriers to student attendance. The UM dean joined the principals and teachers of each school team to design an intervention utilizing a Plan-Do-Study-Act (PDSA) cycle.

Chronic Absenteeism PDSA Cycle

PLAN

In the summer of 2018, the partnership team (UM-SOE and OSD) established the following Aim Statement: "By June 2019, we will reduce chronic absenteeism at our school from 16% to 8% by calling parents of students who are absent." The school NICs hypothesized that direct communication with parents at the time of absence would have a positive, significant impact on chronic absenteeism. To meet this aim and test the hypothesis, UM faculty and OSD teachers agreed that student-teachers and veteran teachers rarely dealt with absenteeism beyond their own classroom. The UM-SOE Teacher Education Department began a redesign for practicum and student teacher candidates placed in OSD. The clinical practice for student-teachers at these two schools was restructured so that all student-teachers would contact *all* parents of their absent students *daily*.

DO

The undergraduate, senior student-teachers serving Oxford High School (grades 9–12) and Della Davidson Elementary School (grades 3–4) created a morning attendance phone tree and assisted the schools in contacting parents of students who were not in school during the first 20 minutes of the school day. They followed a script when the parents answered the phone (see textbox 7.1). The script included a description of the positive qualities of the student and sought information regarding the absence. Parents were then asked if they wished to have material/work that their child missed at school sent home for completion. If parents requested the work, the student teacher electronically sent the work to the parent. The team created a Google form to document information about the contact, parent request for student work, and reflection of the pre-service teacher. The cycle began in January 2019 (spring semester) and concluded at the end of the 2018–19 school year.

TEXTBOX 7.1. PARENT CALL SCRIPT

Hello [Parent's name].

I am [caller's name] from **Della Davidson Elementary School/Oxford High School**. How are you doing today?

First, let me say it is a pleasure having [child's name] in my class at **Della/OHS**.

(include a comment about a quality the child has (e.g., [child's name] has a wonderful smile, is always willing to help other children, etc.)

I'm calling because we noticed [child's name] was absent today. Is **he/she** feeling ok?

(Wait for parent response)

I wanted to let you know what [child's name] missed at school today. We did…
….[**insert day's lesson**].

Would you like me to send his work from today's lesson via email?

(If so…get the parent's email address)

Is there anything else we can do to help [child's name]?

(Give parent time to talk.)

Please don't hesitate to let me know how we can be helpful to you and to [child's name] moving forward.

Thanks for taking time to talk today. I look forward to seeing [child's name] tomorrow!

STUDY

To test our hypothesis, UM-SOE collected data for both OSD schools for the prior academic year (fall 2017 to spring 2018) and the fall of 2018 and spring of 2019 when the project was implemented. All students who were absent were part of this study, not simply the students identified as chronically absent the previous year.

Notably, 52% of calls that went out in the spring of 2019 were answered. Thirty-six percent of the calls were answered by parents, indicating that parents *do* answer phone calls despite the prevalence of text and email communication. Controlling for parents from the sample who had proactively made contact, a total of 62% of calls were answered (43% by parents). Not only did parents tend to answer these calls, but 72% of those who answered the call requested their child's missed work. These data indicate that parents are willing to engage with schools to ensure that their children complete their assignments. After the project's conclusion, student-teachers noted that parents, overall, were "very appreciative" of the calls about the absence.

ACT

Overall, the pilot project successfully reduced absences among elementary school students. Looking year-by-year, 65 students comprise the control group (as measured by their absences during the 2017–18 school year and their absences during the spring 2019 treatment period). Of these students, 37% (n=24) saw a decrease in the number of absences during the treatment year. Among chronically absent students, all recorded a decrease in the number of absent days. The average number of days missed decreased from 24 to 13 under the pilot. Over the 2019 project, only *one* of the 65 students was chronically absent. Key outcomes of the pilot project included

- 37% of elementary school students contacted had an annual decrease in absences compared to the previous school year.
- 33% of elementary school students in the study had a decrease in absences between semesters.
- 36% of high-school students contacted had an annual decrease in absences compared to the previous school year.
- 33% of high-school students had a decrease in absences between semesters.

Seventy students in the first PDSA cycle recorded absences over both the fall 2018 and spring 2019 periods. Of this group, 28% (n=20) saw a decrease in their number of absences in the spring term. Because almost half of these students missed fewer than six days in fall 2018, the number of missed days among this cohort was already minimal; thus, it is difficult to conclude the exact impact that the pilot project had from term to term as there were fewer absences per student. High-school outcomes largely mirrored elementary school results, with a (slightly) more notable positive impact when looking year to year rather than term to term.

Forty-five students participated in the treatment group who were also absent during the 2017–18 school year. Of that cohort, 36% (n=16) recorded a decrease in the number of missed days. However, the reduction of chronic absences was not as profound among high-school students. Compared to elementary school students who were chronically absent (four in 2017–18, one in 2019), most high-school students who were chronically absent in the previous year were also chronically absent during the pilot. Of the nine chronically absent treatment students, only one had fewer absences during the treatment year. This could speak to the additional challenges associated with reengaging chronically absent high schoolers.

Within the year, 51 students were absent during both fall and spring. The first PDSA resulted in a decrease of, or no change in, absences among 33% (n=17). As with the elementary school cohort, most students who were absent in the fall had fewer than six missed days (59%). In team discussions, the partnership team decided they needed to better understand why absences occur and they agreed to use the Youth Truth Survey (2017) to get additional information.

As the partnership celebrated the success of the first PDSA cycle, the superintendent and dean assessed current needs and decided that they and their staff needed additional professional development training in improvement science (IS) in order to gain a better understanding of and support for the process. A local Explorer's Workshop with Carnegie staff was offered to build capacity in the OSD and the UM School of Education.

Parallel to the iLEAD work, the district began providing professional development to teachers two days a month in the mornings. With teacher input, they decided on the topics of the training. From August to November, professional development activities were guided by teacher "passions." This professional development initiative came together with the iLEAD work and the *Passion Professional Development PDSA cycle* emerged.

BUILDING CAPACITY

The Carnegie Explorer's Workshop (November 2019) turned out to be a significant leverage activity for building capacity that moved the partnership forward. More than 75 people including OSD teachers and leaders and UM faculty and staff attended the workshop. The two-day training focused on understanding the elements of Networked Improvement Communities (NICs), the working partnership of a NIC, the practice of using improvement tools, and the discovery of potential high–leverage problems to solve using improvement science. It was a crucial turning point for the

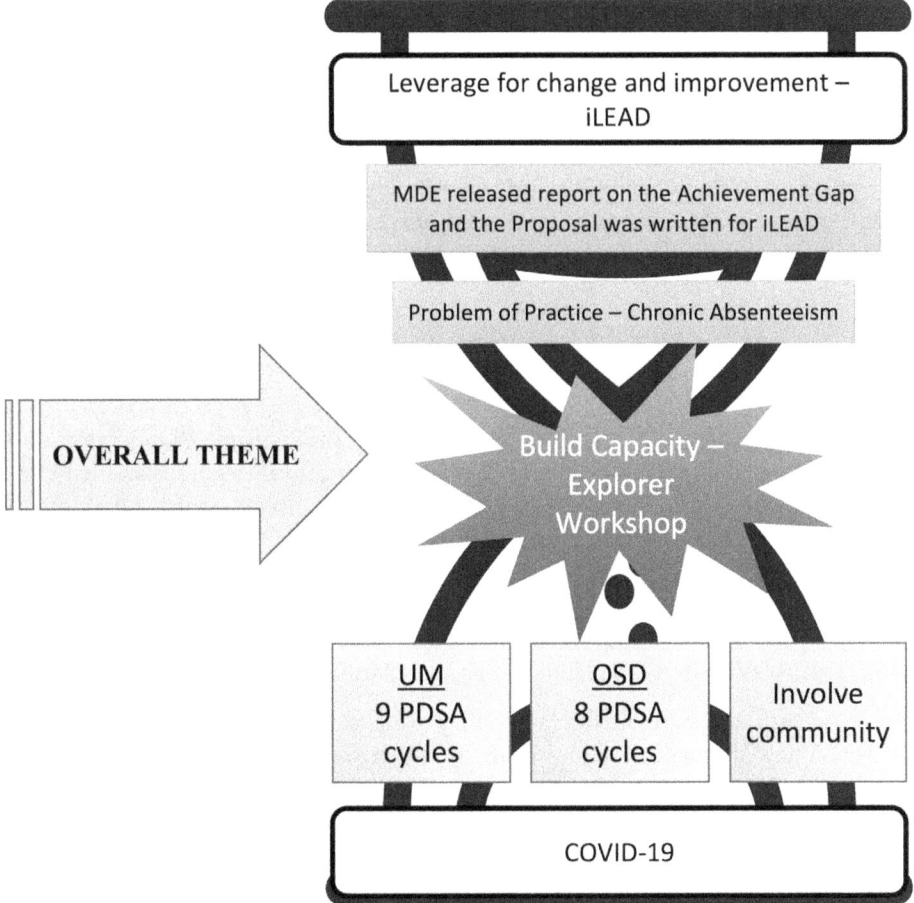

Figure 7.2 OSD and UM-SOE leverage for change.

partnership. NICs within both organizations were formed which led to the implementation of improvement science practices within the district and UM School of Education.

This workshop allowed both groups to develop momentum, strengthen their systems, and grow capacity. A larger audience was introduced to IS and several NICs were established in schools and within the SOE, which identified problems of practice to focus their efforts to improve. The superintendent and dean stimulated new PDSA cycles in both OSD and UM. The conclusion from this experience was that having a dedicated partnership that included the dean and superintendent helps to ensure the sustainability of the IS work as well as provides a level of accountability not found in other partnerships.

To be successful in this process the partnership embraced three main principles: ownership of the problems, unity and coherence about how to solve the problems, and a process that could be sustained through any changes in leadership or member participation. Additionally, the workshop propelled the OSD to continue to conduct PD for district teachers about IS and to maintain the NICs with PD offerings to a small group of teachers. The high-school teachers identified as a problem of practice the lack of high-school student motivation and relevance as noted in a then recent Youth Truth Survey (2017). They developed an aim to improve student motivation and increase the relevance of high school for these students.

At the same time, the UM-SOE faculty created ten IS groups inside the School that each identified a problem of practice. They created fishbone diagrams that recognized possible drivers. Once drivers were identified, each group began its own PDSA cycle. UM-SOE non-academic staff also created their own group and began PDSA cycles as well. Each group reported on their progress monthly at SOE faculty meetings.

SPREAD AND SCALE PROGRESS

Some specific examples of capacity–building lie in the multiple PDSA cycles happening in both the OSD and UM–SOE. Although eight OSD groups and ten UM–SOE groups originally identified problems of practice, many additional IS groups have formed to solve additional problems. Some specific PDSA cycle examples are below.

OSD IMPROVEMENT SCIENCE PROBLEMS OF PRACTICE

The then assistant superintendent, Bradley Roberson, directly supervised building principals and all curriculum and instruction personnel, so it was decided and supported that OSD would use their instructional meetings to tackle problems of practice within the district. To further build capacity, he trained each member of the instructional team in IS and guided them through the process with a problem of practice of their choice.

PASSION PROFESSIONAL DEVELOPMENT PDSA CYCLE

Plan

As noted above, in the fall of 2019, the OSD School District instituted a professional development plan based on problems of practice for which staff members were passionate.

Do

Teachers were able to select two rounds of professional development in which to participate. The PD was offered face-to-face or online. Dean Rock and Superintendent Harvey facilitated a course on improvement science principles as a major component of the OSD Passion PD Plan. Eight Oxford School District teachers enrolled in the university course for credit and participated twice a month throughout the 2019–20 school year.

Study

Round 1 of PD was held during the months of August to October, and Round 2 was from October to January. Passion PD took place every Monday morning from 7:30–10:00 am, and the school day had a delayed start. Overall teacher perception of Passion PD was positive and action was taken on what they learned and implemented in classrooms. Teachers evaluated each round on a 1 to 5 scale. The mean scores were as follows:

Overall, the face-to-face PD fared slightly higher than the online PD; however, providing PD that teachers were passionate about impacted teacher effectiveness and the classroom environments. The reality is that if the PD is meaningful for teachers there is engagement and value added for professional growth.

Act

The OSD was considering adopting Passion PD for future school years when Covid changed their plans. Due to the pandemic, the school district did not schedule the delayed start for PD, but it is a practice that is being considered for future school years.

YOUTH TRUTH SURVEY PDSA CYCLE

Research indicates student perceptions are linked to academic outcomes, so as participants assessed the data on chronic absenteeism, the partnership began to consider a PDSA cycle on student engagement and relationships.

Plan

The plan was to administer a nationally recognized survey, the Youth Truth Survey (2017), which asks students simple questions about their experiences in school including engagement, rigor, and preparedness for post-secondary life.

Table 7.2 Teacher Perceptions of Passion PD

	Round 1 Online	Round 1 Face-to-face	Round 2 Online	Round 2 Face-to-face	Total
I gained knowledge and skills to improve my practice as an educator.	4.0	4.19	4.07	4.19	4.11
My Passion PD has been closely connected to my school's priorities.	4.125	4.34	4.23	4.32	4.25
My Passion PD has provided me with strategies to better meet my students' needs.	3.85	4.17	3.88	4.23	4.03
My Passion PD has helped me progress toward my professional growth goals established with my administrator.	3.85	4.21	3.93	4.25	4.06

Do

The survey information was sent out to all high-school students and 89% of them ($n = 1080$ responses) completed the survey.

Study

Results for OSD High School in 2019 indicated that only 37% of the students agreed or strongly agreed that they enjoyed coming to school most of the time. In comparison, the national response for high-school students according to the Youth Truth Survey (2017) was 54% of the students agreed or strongly agreed that they enjoyed coming to school most of the time. Results also indicated that only 29% of the students agreed or strongly agreed that what they learned in class helps them outside of school as compared to the national average of 49%.

Act

Based on the results from the Youth Truth Survey (2017), eight teachers adapted Youth Truth metrics to a three-question probe to allow twice-weekly short-cycle testing within each classroom. Results from the short-cycle testing generated 1200 student responses; however, the process and analysis was impeded by the start of the COVID-19 pandemic.

The Oxford School District Principles of the Passion PD sessions have now established additional NICs in the OSD community. OSD identified the following list of concerns: (a) ineffective use of secondary instructional coaches; (b) implementation of enrichment activities at Della Davidson Elementary; (c) lack of minority representation in the gifted program; (d) achievement of 5th- and 6th-grade special education students in mathematics; (e) lack of Advancement Via Individual Determination (AVID) students that qualify for dual credit and middle college; (f) teacher retention; (g) implementation of digital citizenship (K–12); (h) achievement of middle school special education students in English Language Arts (ELA); (i) achievement of high-school special education students in ELA; (j) achievement of 5th- and 6th-grade students in ELA; (k) lack of parent understanding of student academic performance; and (l) staff communication.

UM-SOE Improvement Science Problems of Practice

The UM-SOE team created ten breakout teams who identified problems of practice for future PDSA cycles. Each team identified a problem and created a fishbone diagram. The problems were: (a) community engagement; (b) enhancing the social/emotional well-being of elementary education senior block students; (c) losing potential students to a slow, fragmented, and inefficient application and admission process; (d) graduate enrollment; (e) increasing capacity to market and recruit in nuanced and impactful ways; (f) lack of increased diversity across campuses; (g) morale; (h) lack of enrollment goals; (i) not enough online programs; and (j) pre-service students at risk for not being successful teachers.

GRADUATE STUDIES OFFICE PDSA CYCLE

Plan

One such example is the Graduate Studies Office (GSO) in the UM-SOE which collects admission data for the Director of Assessment. The problem of practice discovered was the lack of data or missing variables in the data set. The GSO found that 54 variables are needed for the report, but that it only collects 16 of those variables for admission. For the fall report, the GSO spent 40+ hours running five reports to try and complete the data set. To identify and organize the potential causes a fishbone diagram was completed. The branches led to many discoveries: (a) the admission process was different with each department; (b) the multiple variables that were not available in any report; (c) the amount of time needed to complete the report was significantly higher than expected; and (d) lack of systems that lead to a fragmented and inefficient application and admission process.

Do

In the assessment of the fishbone diagram, the GSO began with implementing the plan on the admission process. The group inaugurated a comparable admission process across all departments, so we had a process for which applications, references, years of teaching, test scores, etc. were collected by one office and tracked using an Excel spreadsheet. When all materials were collected and the application was completed, this information was provided to a Graduate Program Coordinator (GPC) ensuring each GPC was only reviewing complete applications. The GPC then notified the GSO of the recommendation for admission.

Study

This has lessened the fragmentation of the process and improved the collection of some previously missing variables. In addition, students receive more timely decisions about admissions.

Act

The GSO has adopted this process across all departments in the SOE.

There is intent to begin another PDSA cycle that involves the many reports needed to obtain all the variables. The goal now is to determine whether the SOE can obtain a custom university report to aid in the collection of accreditation data.

UM-SOE DEAN'S OFFICE STAFF PDSA CYCLE

Plan

After the Explorer's Workshop, the staff in the dean's office identified administrative tasks within the SOE that were not being completed. Through a fishbone diagram, they acknowledged four drivers: attitude (e.g., not my job, we have never done it that way before), roles (e.g., change in staff, unsure of roles), procedural (e.g., no clear process on how to report problems or issues), and knowledge (e.g., role changes within the office and unsure who is responsible for solving those problems).

Do

The group decided to use a "ticketing system" similar to that used for Technology and Assessment Requests and create an SOE Task Request Form. The SOE Network Administrator created and added a Wufoo Form on the SOE Website. If a task within SOE needed to be completed, then a person would complete and submit a Task Request Form. The completed form would be emailed to the assistant to the dean. The assistant to the dean would route the request to the correct person within SOE that would need to complete the task. If the assistant to the dean is unsure of where it needs to go, the task is discussed with the dean and then either the assistant completes the task herself or she forwards it to the right person.

Study

This drastically reduced the number of tasks not being completed and/or automatically being sent to the assistant to the dean to complete. Departments took more of an initiative to complete tasks and communication among the staff was improved. However, three problems arose: (a) there was not an efficient way to track or provide documentation for tasks requested or completed; (b) the system did not allow for an efficient way to collect data; and (c) the process did not provide an efficient way to prioritize tasks.

Act

The SOE staff decided to abort the existing ticketing system and use another app called Freshdesk. The Task Request Form was replaced with this new ticketing system so that all requests within SOE go through the same system. One process was implemented for all SOE assessment and administrative requests.

Additional PDSA cycles followed as they continued to refine the ticketing process.

UM Developmental Progression

THE "HOW" OF PARTNERSHIPS (PARTNERSHIP MECHANISMS)

The first task for the UM-SOE and OSD Partnership when created was to ensure understanding that everyone was seeking to improve education for all students and, although UM-SOE and OSD are separate organizations, they are interrelated in the cycle of improvement. The use of the process of the PDSA cycle to improve both units and further develop and maintain systematic effective solutions was embraced. Both groups sought to integrate change in the form of sustainable practices so any less enthusiastic faculty or staff could witness positive progress and hopefully become more engaged in the process.

EXPECTATIONS, SUSTAINABILITY, NORMS, & ROUTINES

Intentionality is one of the keywords that describe the leadership team's organization, both inter- and intra-organization. The leadership of both organizations, starting with the dean and superintendent(s), committed personal, professional, and organizational resources (especially time) to support the partnership within their own communities, as well as across the two organizations.

OSD and UM-SOE each have leadership teams that meet independently on a regular basis, two to three times per month to reflect on the successes and challenges and to strategize ways that the iLEAD processes can be improved within their organizations. They also discuss ways to enhance support for the benefit of all constituents involved. This degree of intentional collaboration has resulted in a solid partnership that continues. A key norm that pervades the interactions between both systems is the active relationship between the two organizations. There exists a level of trust that allows for open discussion of issues without judgment. For example, the initial issue that brought the two organizations together was the concern about increasing student achievement in the OSD. Open and honest collegial discussions allowed both organizations to explore the true issues without assigning blame or passing judgment. The only gain both organizations sought was an increase in OSD student achievement, both academically and through improvements in social-emotional learning (SEL). The formation of that relationship has provided both organizations with a better opportunity to effectively research issues that impact identified practice gaps.

VISION FOR THE FUTURE

The structure for tackling problems has gone through a transformation. In the future, the Partnership anticipates that IS will be the norm problem-solving approach in the community and individual organizations. There are three goals for the future: (a) to create a shared vision to drive collaboration and to involve community partners; (b) to demonstrate sensitivity and competence for understanding as participation is increased from diverse and multi-dimensional groups; and (c) to work together to build an improved community.

There is a mutual commitment to helping establish and create other partnerships through the spreading and scaling to other organizations within the sphere of influence of each organization. Partnership commitment to IS includes evolving the processes and products by getting increased awareness and acceptance. To continue evolving, the Partnership intends to offer the Carnegie Explorer's Workshop to the community, school, and institutional leaders (e.g., the mayor's office, Board of Aldermen, and school board).

The goal is to move forward with building the infrastructure to support the improvement work. Establishing and maintaining this culture of continuous improvement has proven to be a difficult task in organizations that previously relied on "hope" as a strategy for growth. Changing the mindsets and behaviors is at the core of continuous improvement and the Partnership quickly learned that primary leadership to oversee the shifting of the culture was extremely important. While both the superintendent of the Oxford School District as well as the dean of the School of Education were "all in" with instilling the improvement science principles within their respective teams and as leaders of their organizations, it was difficult to make the time to establish, track, and monitor continuous improvement projects. To address this ongoing need, as identified in the iLEAD Developmental Progressions, a new position entitled Scholar in Residence has been established. The Scholar in Residence uses information and resources from both organizations to solve problems of practice that inhibit teacher and leader development as well as student learning in the Oxford School District. The position ensures there is an authentic and true partnership between the Oxford School District and the UM School of Education to work hand in hand to create a dynamic learning experience for all parties and candidates. The current responsibilities are outlined below.

The Scholar in Residence:

- Develops organizational and cross-organizational network improvement communities to solve problems of practice.
- Spends six to eight hours per week on-site at Oxford School District.
- Meets bi-weekly with district and school leaders to discuss progress of continuous improvement projects.

- Works with school and district leaders to develop scorecards to measure success of continuous improvement projects.
- Conducts continuous improvement trainings for OSD and UM School of Education staff and students.
- Conducts leadership trainings for OSD current and prospective leaders.
- Serves as a key member of the OSD Teacher Recruitment Team.

This new MOU was designed to allocate a faculty member to monitor and report on IS projects. This is a huge and necessary step in continuing the progression of our goals into the fabric of the Partnership.

Based on our successful partnership between the UM-SOE and the Oxford School District, the UM-SOE is proposing the creation of a new research center, the National Center for School–University Partnerships (NCSUP), to study, develop and scale expertise in improvement efforts in schools, through improvement networks and partnerships between local education agencies (LEAs), institutions of higher education (IHEs), and other community-based agencies. The National Center for School–University Partnerships seeks to build a community "stronger together" to achieve vastly improved learning outcomes for every child, especially those from historically marginalized groups. Our goal is for NCSUP to become a national leader in school improvement practices through university partnerships due to the success and work of the Carnegie Foundation for the Advancement of Teaching (CFAT) pilot of the Improvement Leadership Education and Development (iLEAD) network that was comprised of 13 national district-university partnerships committed to the use of improvement science to develop leaders, address local problems of practice, and promote equitable educational opportunities and outcomes for all students. The draft mission and vision of NCSUP are as follows:

NCSUP MISSION

The National Center for School–University Partnerships seeks to build a community "stronger together" to achieve vastly improved learning outcomes for every child, especially those from historically marginalized groups. We seek to develop expertise in leading improvement efforts in schools, through improvement networks, and through mutually beneficial partnerships between local education agencies (LEAs), institutions of higher education (IHEs), and other community-based agencies.

NCSUP Vision and Objectives:

1. **Build meaningful partnerships with diverse stakeholders.** We build partnerships with a range of leaders and organizations including policymakers, philanthropic groups, community-based organizations, professional associations, and other stakeholders working to ensure that every student receives an equitable and high-quality education.
2. **Strengthen educational improvement leadership and workforce.** Working closely with institutions of higher education, local education agencies, and other community-based agencies, we support the training and career development of

leaders and educators capable of leading continuous improvement efforts that strengthen schools and school systems.
3. **Establish and support collaborative working arrangements including Networked Improvement Communities.** We establish and support collaborative scientific learning communities that leverage continuous improvement methods to address shared problems of practice.
4. **Advance knowledge.** We advance an improvement-oriented research agenda and seek to disseminate tools and resources that further knowledge in the field and enhance the practice of school leaders and educators.
5. **Create standards of practice.** We identify and elevate exemplary improvement models and practices in education. We develop training and professional development programs that support educational improvement leaders and practitioners. We provide guidance on the quality and integrity of the implementation of improvement efforts in schools and school systems.

Lessons Learned

We have learned several things that could benefit others when establishing partnerships between Universities and Local School Districts. First and foremost, the progress and sustainability of our partnership occurred because we had the two leaders (e.g., dean and superintendent) involved in and leading the partnership. In reflecting on our success, we feel that our leaders are the key to sustained success. The leaders are the engine that pulls the train. For example, having the superintendent and dean at the table allow decisions to be made on the spot. If the partnership needs something that would require financial support (i.e., Explorer's Workshop) leaders do not need to be brought up to speed and convinced of the value of the work being done. Many teams begin their partnership by engaging the worker bees rather than getting buy-in from key leaders and stakeholders. Our partnership work started with key leaders working to establish a mutually beneficial longitudinal relationship that was invested in a larger mission: the success of all PK–12 students inside and outside of the classroom in the greater Oxford community. The superintendent and dean understood the sense of urgency to build capacity in IS in their organizations to provide sustainability. Both leaders were aware of the need to provide continuing professional development on IS for new employees in their organizations.

At the OSD, the superintendent, assistant superintendent, and one building principal have been significant participants in iLEAD and the Partnership. At the UM-SOE, the dean, assistant dean, and director of graduate studies have led the overall efforts in the Partnership. Getting the right people in the right roles at the table who, in turn, can support and facilitate change is imperative. Without the involvement of this level of leadership, it is unlikely the Explorer's Workshop would have been conducted which, in turn, led to the creation of several new NICs to confront more than 20 different problems of practice. Our commitment to multi-stakeholder partnerships and moving to include community government agencies and actors will be essential to achieve goals, sustain lasting change, and scale the current level of collaboration.

The second lesson learned from the Partnership is that mutual understanding has to evolve. Through the building of the Partnership and the many hours of working together as a team, participants began to understand and accept the importance of building relationships, as success could be sustained only if we worked together. As the Partnership flourished, we were able to problem-solve, develop, and support improvement through a shared understanding of how our individual units had a greater impact on the overall community. Our commitment to IS includes evolving the processes and products by getting increased awareness and acceptance. To continue evolving, we hope to offer the Explorer's Workshop to community, school, and institutional leaders (e.g., mayor, Board of Aldermen, school board).

Questions for Discussion

1. Who are the school and university leaders that should be involved in this process?
2. How do you sustain the involvement of such leaders in the process?
3. How do you build the capacity of school and teacher leaders in the IS process?
4. How do you ensure a collaborative approach rather than a top-down approach in the IS process?

References

Mississippi Department of Education Office of District and School Performance. (n.d.). *Accountability report.* Retrieved August 29, 2022, from https://www.mdek12.org/OPR/Reporting/Accountability

Snyder, T. D., & Dillow, S. A. (2010). *Digest of education statistics 2009 (NCES 2010-013).* National Center for Education Statistics, Institute of Education Sciences, U.S. Department of Education.

Youth Truth Student Survey, A National Nonprofit. (2017). *Learning from student voice: How prepared do students feel for college and career?* Retrieved June 11, 2018, from http://youthtruthsurvey.org/college-career-readiness-2017/

CHAPTER 8

Equity-Focused Improvement Science

PORTLAND STATE UNIVERSITY AND PORTLAND PUBLIC SCHOOLS

Susan P. Carlile, Deborah S. Peterson (co-first authors), and Tania McKey

This case is about the leadership of a very small team of university and district leaders who gained expertise in improvement science (IS) and developed powerful university–school district relationships to address achievement disparities in their schools. Central to the story are three leaders who collaborated across institutions to prepare culturally proficient, anti-racist school administrators who use improvement science tools and resources to lead improvement efforts impacting educational disparities in the district. The partnership's equity-focused efforts reveal what happens when anti-racist, culturally responsive leaders maintain a district-university partnership over time, despite organizational challenges within the university and the district, through significant leadership changes in both institutions, while facing adaptation and sustainability issues, during historically tumultuous times due to the global pandemic, racial strife, elevated economic insecurity, and politically unstable times. Participating in networked improvement communities (NICs) through Improvement Leadership Education and Development (iLEAD), the Carnegie Project on the Education Doctorate (CPED), the University Council of Education Administration (UCEA) and partnering informally with other nationally known IS experts such as Sherril Gelmon, Robert Crow, Brandi Hinnant-Crawford, Jill Perry, Paul LeMahieu, and David Imig enhanced our ability to successfully implement system-wide change in our PSU principal licensure program, as well as in one of our partner districts. From 2017 through the conclusion of the 2022 academic year, over 500 educational leaders have participated in the new preparation program at the university in which the previous focus on anti-racism and culturally responsive leadership is now enhanced through the use of IS as the signature change leadership pedagogy. In addition, over 100 of the partner district administrators have participated in improvement science professional development, all of whom use improvement science to lead equity-focused change processes in their schools or departments.

To understand our case study, we first provide background information on three anti-racist, culturally responsive leaders whose deliberate actions contributed to a successful university–school district partnership. Next, we provide contextual information on the two partners in this study, Portland Public Schools (PPS) and Portland State University (PSU). We provide information on how we improved our program such that seated and future school leaders would gain hands-on, supervised clinical experiences leading equity-focused improvement science change efforts throughout our preparation program (Peterson & Carlile, 2019). We will share how our participation in networked improvement communities (NICs) (LeMahieu et al., 2017) impacted our program improvement (Peterson et al., 2020), and conclude by describing how a fledgling partnership with one small, suburban district led to a successful partnership with the largest urban school district in the state.

Key Leaders

Recognizing that in Oregon, as well as throughout the US, race and ethnicity are predictors of educational attainment, PSU Professor Susan Carlile and Professor Deborah Peterson began improvement efforts in 2012 to infuse equity into all principal licensure courses. While initially this improvement work was facilitated through small grants that would support our efforts, our small team subsequently received over 13 grants, totaling more than $2 million in a ten-year span, and we were awarded partnerships with several organizations whose work would lead to recruiting a talented and experienced school leader, Dr. Tania McKey, to the team. We subsequently embedded equity-focused IS throughout our principal preparation program and in partnerships with local districts. These successes were supported through the guidance of PSU Graduate School of Education Dean Randy Hitz, PSU School of Public Health Professor Sherril Gelmon, Chair Candyce Reynolds, PSU principal preparation faculty and advisors Dr. Pat Burk, Dr. Cass Thonstad, Dr. Paul Coakley, PPS Superintendent Guerrero and his leadership team, as well as hundreds of principal preparation students. Professor Carlile, Professor Peterson, and Dr. McKey have continued our improvement journey in the iLEAD partnership, as consultants and as faculty, using IS tools and processes to prepare seated and future school leaders to reduce educational disparities, using what we have come to believe is the most powerful and most socially just way (Bell, 2016) to improve our schools, with equitable outcomes for every child, of every background. We believe that equity-focused IS empowers families and students, in particular those whose voices have been historically ignored or silenced, as well as honors those who are closest to the work and have the greatest hope for improving our schools: the heroes working in our lunchrooms, hallways, and especially, in our classrooms (Peterson & Carlile, 2021, 2022).

To understand the experiences, values, and mission of the key leaders in PSU and PPS, we introduce you first to Professor Carlile, then to Associate Professor Emerita Peterson, and finally to Dr. McKey.

PROFESSOR OF PRACTICE SUSAN CARLILE

Professor of Practice Susan Carlile came to PSU with considerable knowledge about education, having earned degrees from the University of California, Berkeley, and the University of Oregon, having served as a teacher of English and special education, and as a middle, high, and central office school administrator positions prior to beginning a second career in the College of Education. A seminal experience in her very early career in Peace Corps community engagement work in Sierra Leone, West Africa, piqued her interest in continuous change and strengthened the belief that consistent and sustained change came about when people in the community, those closest to the work with knowledge of how the system operates, were actively engaged in solutions to problems. In West Africa, she was immersed in a community where people who often lacked food, clean water, shelter, and clothing were engaged in collective decision-making that served the well-being of all. Together they built water systems and planted improved varieties of rice, grounding her beliefs in teamwork, equity, cultural humility, resourcefulness, and adaptability. She was also intrigued by the early works of Hall and Hord (2015) on organizational development in complex systems and their appreciation of human factors, such as reducing isolation and increasing team capacity. She also was drawn to Senge's (2012) theory of five disciplines: personal mastery, mental models, building shared vision, team learning, and systems thinking, two of which directly focus on collaborative learning. As the program coordinator in the principal licensure program for ten years, Professor Carlile was instrumental in the collaborative efforts to prepare principal interns to participate in ecological, context-based, data-driven, and community-driven change processes (Peterson & Carlile, 2021). Given her early experiences, Professor Carlile was especially enticed by the foundational tenets of IS and the role of this methodology to prepare future school leaders to reduce learning disparities.

ASSOCIATE PROFESSOR EMERITA DR. DEBORAH S. PETERSON

Dr. Peterson began her equity journey as a young girl, when her best friend's family found a cross burning on their front lawn and her parents explained to her the hatred and violence behind that act. As a high schooler, her counselors wouldn't allow her to take the SAT and apply for college: "You're a cute girl who is just going to get married." Instead, she applied to and was accepted into an exchange program, *The International Cultural Youth Exchange,* a program committed to social justice and increasing understanding of others through yearlong cultural exchanges. The experience changed her life's trajectory as her new community integrated social justice into their daily lives and built a community of care among those whose language, religion, race, language, and culture were new or unknown to them or to her. Dr. Peterson entered the education profession at 18 as an assistant teacher in a newly created school that integrated preschoolers with special needs and newly arrived immigrants into neighborhood preschools, a new concept in Germany at that time. As a middle and high school teacher and elementary, middle, and high school administrator in the US, her goal was to create a place where every child thrived, in particular, the children whom our schools or society oppressed, marginalized, ignored, or harmed due to a manifestation of their diversity. Leading numerous continuous improvement efforts as an administrator caused Deborah to understand that her best work as an educational leader, with the best outcomes for children of color, was when the community, students, or teachers were empowered to identify solutions to problems that were harming children, enacted the change ideas, used data relentlessly, and were celebrated for their contributions; thus, social justice is a process and an outcome (Bell, 2016). Dr. Peterson's role was to hold sacred the community's vision, build partnerships, find resources, collect and facilitate the use of disaggregated data to make decisions, protect teacher's focus on teaching, and relentlessly cheer on the faculty, staff, and students. As a school and district leader, her work won awards and public recognition, but her biggest reward was when the humanity of children and families of every background was recognized and enhanced while in her schools' care (Gay, 2010; Peterson, 2020). After 30 years as a practitioner, Dr. Peterson joined PSU in a tenure-line position, and with the encouragement of her dean, the chair, and program coordinator, began an ad hoc process with Professor Carlile of revising the curriculum to embed equity in every lesson every week and recruiting leaders of color into the preparation program. Partnering with several districts and educational organizations, she has received or helped write over a dozen grants totaling over $2 million dollars to increase the diversity of leaders in Oregon, increase their focus on equity in their schools, and embed in their practices what she believes is the most socially just improvement strategy: *Improvement Science* (Peterson, 2022). While Professor Carlile was on sabbatical researching a forthcoming book with Professor Peterson on women in leadership, Professor Peterson temporarily assumed program coordination roles, including leading a state-required redesign of the principal licensure programs in 2019–2020, again embedding equity and IS in all 22 syllabi in the principal and district leadership programs while also following newly-approved state licensure guidelines. Co-editor of two books and author of dozens of articles on leadership for equity and IS, Dr. Peterson currently consults with superintendents and principals seeking additional support in equity-focused improvement initiatives and IS.

ASSISTANT PROFESSOR AND SENIOR DIRECTOR OF HUMANITIES DR. TANIA MCKEY

Dr. Tania McKey has deep experience as a teacher, international baccalaureate (IB) coordinator, school and district administrator, and higher education faculty, earning her doctorate in administration, supervision, and curriculum at Auburn University with her dissertation focused on the US Department of Green Ribbon School Award Winners 2012, 2013, and 2014. Her research interests include school improvement using IS, whole-school sustainability, green schools, literacy, and leadership preparation. Her background includes teaching, coordinating, and leading IB World Schools in Minnesota, Texas, Indiana, and Oregon, with significant leadership experience in the implementation of the first whole-school Middle Years Programme (MYP) of the IB in Minnesota. Dr. McKey served as Assistant Professor at PSU during 2017–2019 before transitioning to Portland Public Schools as the Senior Director of Humanities and then into a school principalship during the 2021–22 school year. She continues to share her experience and knowledge as an IB educator by facilitating workshops, leading site visits, and providing consultation for schools.

Context of the PSU–PPS Partnership

The PSU and PPS iLEAD partnership share a common cultural and economic environment, geographical location, and, most importantly, a relentless focus on reducing the alarming educational disparities between students of color and white students in schools in the Portland region, the state, and the nation. While each organization had its own organizational complexities, these unique commonalities enhanced our partnership.

PORTLAND STATE UNIVERSITY

To understand our partnership better, we'd like to first share more details about PSU, followed by details about PPS. PSU is an urban, public university serving 25,000 students situated in the downtown area of Portland, Oregon. Recognized nationally for its innovation, the PSU College of Education (COE) is also nationally ranked 153 of over 1,000 schools of education (US News, 2022) and is accredited by the Council for the Accreditation of Education Preparation, the Council for Accreditation of Counseling and Related Educational Programs, and the National Association for the Education of Young Children. As reported by the COE, it is "the first educator preparation program in Oregon, the first on the West Coast, and one of the first 10 in the nation, to be fully accredited by the Council for the Accreditation of Educator Preparation" (Accreditation Report, 2022).

The PSU COE Educational Leadership and Policy (ELP) department houses the principal preparation program, and this program prepares the highest number of principals in Oregon (2018 Oregon Equity Report) and assumes the added responsibility to ensure PSU principal licensure completers embody the characteristics of exemplary school leaders, meet, or exceed national standards for school leadership, reflect the diversity of our student population, and most importantly, are prepared to be strong leaders of change efforts that reduce educational disparities. In addition to the principal preparation program focus on social justice, a social justice focus is also embedded in PSU's Strategic Plan (Strategic Priorities, 2022), specifically PSU's focus on equity and racial justice; student success, and mobilizing engagement to strengthen the city. In addition, the COE has a focus on diversity and inclusiveness (College of Education, 2022) which is aligned with the ELP department mission to encourage democracy and social justice.

The lack of educator diversity in Oregon drives the mission and vision of PSU'S principal preparation program. In Oregon, 38% of our K–12 students are students of color, while only 10% of teachers and 11% of school leaders are people of color (Oregon Educator Equity Report, 2019). Grissom et al. (2021) make clear the value of having leaders of color in our schools. Widely known for its racist history, Oregon, like so many states in this nation, perpetuates past historical injustices when their teachers and school leaders are primarily white or when the teachers and school leaders are not fully prepared to lead improvement efforts as anti-racist, culturally responsive leaders.

Due to persistent educational disparities based on race and ethnicity in Oregon's K–12 schools and given PSU's position as the institution that prepares the largest number of school leaders in Oregon, PSU principal preparation faculty feel a responsibility to ensure that school change efforts focus on eliminating the correlation of school achievement and the race and ethnicity of the student. Children of color in Oregon cannot wait for annual standardized test results, for laborious and lengthy state improvement plans, or for large-scale improvement efforts to receive corporate, state, or federal funding for improvements to be made (Peterson & Carlile, 2021, 2022). School leaders must have the tools to begin small-scale change efforts within weeks of noticing a problem of practice in our local schools, particularly when our children of color are at risk of being suspended, expelled, ignored, and diminished by policies and practices that exclude them from educational success (Peterson & Carlile, 2021). As such, PSU's principal preparation program has embraced IS as the signature change leadership practice to eliminate educational disparities in PK–12 schools.

PSU has had a long commitment to community-engaged scholarship, thanks to former President Judith Ramaley, whose leadership in this area from 1990–1997 is nationally recognized. PSU has the motto of *Let Knowledge Serve the City*, and professors are encouraged to improve our local community through our work at PSU. Serving the city by partnering with PPS was an ideal match due to our shared commitment to equity and diversity, being located in the same urban community, sharing students and families, and focusing on a mission guided by Bell's (2016) social justice principles, believing that social justice is a process and an outcome. Further, this partnership had the potential to increase the morale of colleagues in PPS, by soliciting and enacting their recommended improvements (NEA, 2021). PSU faculty were excited to work directly with PPS teachers, administrators, district office, students, and families to address educational disparities through the use of IS.

PORTLAND PUBLIC SCHOOLS

PPS is located in the same urban center as PSU, is the largest school district in Oregon and encompasses close to 47,000 students, 54% of whom are economically disadvantaged, 17% Latinx, 9% Black, and 15% who are English learners (ELs) (Oregon Department of Education, 2021). As one indicator of educational disparities, PPS's reading outcomes reflect educational disparities in many areas related to race and ethnicity. In 2019, 68% of white 3rd-grade students in PPS were proficient at reading, 17% of Black students, 34% of Latinx students, 29% of economically disadvantaged students, and only 6% of ELs (Oregon Department of Education, 2019). Though EL status is more than a feature of language diversity, this status also represents racial diversity in PPS. A 2019 audit by Oregon's Secretary of State found that PPS's achievement gaps are *far* deeper than the statewide average (Oregon Secretary of State, 2019).

Many teachers, teacher leaders, and administrators in PPS receive their undergraduate, graduate, and educator licensure from PSU. In any given year, 50–60 principal interns complete their licensure program at PSU each year. Also important is the PPS–PSU Dual Language Teacher Residency Program, which provides alternative licensure for bilingual candidates obtaining a secondary license through coursework at PSU. Further, the Portland Teachers Program (PTP), a collaborative partnership between PPS, Portland Community College, and PSU has successfully recruited and prepared educators of color to teach in Portland for more than 30 years.

As is true in many urban areas, houselessness has been a challenging issue for the district and the city over several years, an issue exacerbated by the COVID-19 pandemic that began in March of 2020, and one that continues to be on the rise. An increase in uncollected garbage amassing on streets and parking lots, impromptu villages where unhoused residents build temporary shelters, and rampant graffiti have been a direct effect of the houseless crisis in Portland. Nightly protests related to racial justice and subsequent involvement of political groups such as the Proud Boys, who also engaged in violent protests in Washington DC on January 6, 2021 (Mesh, 2022) took place from May 2020 through the end of 2020, severely impacting downtown businesses and homes. These city-wide stressors affect the students, families, community members, teachers, and administrators and are part of what Ladson-Billings refers to as multiple pandemics (2021). Furthermore, there is a widening opportunity gap for students of color as well as students who are ELs in our schools and who are chronically stressed by these living environments (Bryk et al., 2015). Recognizing the impact of these conditions is essential to our ability to understand and influence them without faulting those who are marginalized and traumatized. We believe that engaging teachers in school solutions and ensuring the empowerment of students and families, guided by the foundational concepts of IS, contribute to the success of each child in our schools (Peterson & Carlile, 2021, 2022). The partnership between the PSU–PPS directly impacts the opportunity gap that exists between students of color and white students in PPS.

Chronology of Improvement Science Efforts

While each organization implementing IS will have its own timeline and activities that make sense in their context, our process was one that was exciting and energizing, due to the leadership of PSU Dean Randy Hitz and Chair Candyce Reynolds. They encouraged us to learn, to grow, to experiment, and to engage in new strategies that might fail—or might cause us to succeed and thrive—as we endeavored to increase social justice efforts in our schools and community. Engagement with IS in the PSU principal preparation program began in the fall of 2014 when Dean Randy Hitz inquired about faculty knowledge of IS and his curiosity regarding its use in schools. Program Coordinator Carlile, Associate Professor Peterson, and Professor Emerita Pat Burk were invited to join the Higher Education Network (HEN) from the Carnegie Foundation. As part of this involvement, the team then attended a Carnegie Foundation summit on IS. Within 18 months, in the winter of

2016, Professors Carlile and Peterson, practitioner-scholars in two of the principal preparation cohorts, enrolled in a four-credit university course from Professor Sherril Gelmon, a nationally known expert in IS in public health. Their goal was to adapt the process of learning about IS to the principal preparation courses. In the following six months, these professors adapted the existing principal preparation curriculum which already had a strong equity focus to include equity-focused IS, teaching 60 principal interns in 45 Oregon schools. Principal licensure interns led IS projects such as increasing Latinx family involvement, increasing access to district-wide counseling programs for children experiencing trauma, culturally responsive instructional practices in classrooms, anti-bullying efforts at the classroom and school level, increasing attendance among students of color, and reducing classroom discipline disparities for beginning teachers. The IS curriculum was piloted in three of the five principal preparation cohorts in 2016–17.

In the late fall of 2016, we highlighted our work to date in improvement science in the principal preparation cohorts with the Higher Education Network (HEN), describing and responding to questions from higher education representatives, including Louis Gomez and Amanda Meyer from the Carnegie Foundation. In 2016, an application to participate in the Improvement Leadership Education and Development (iLEAD) led to the first district-university partnership with Newberg Schools. We will provide more details about this initial partnership in subsequent sections of this chapter.

Next, Dean Hitz led phone conferences with the Carnegie Foundation for the Advancement of Teaching Vice President Paul LeMahieu, Program Coordinator Carlile, Associate Professor Peterson, Chair Candyce Reynolds, and leaders of a statewide education advocacy group *The Chalkboard Project*. The dean then convened a meeting comprised of LeMahieu, teachers, and administrators from several school districts employing IS, the statewide education advocacy group, *The Chalkboard Project*, and our chair, program coordinator, and principal preparation professors. Program Coordinator Carlile and Professor Peterson joined the *University Council on Education Administration* (*UCEA*) IS networked improvement community (NIC). The dean sponsored attendance at the 2017 Carnegie Summit for five members of the PSU Graduate School of Education including representatives from the dean's office, the Curriculum and Instruction Department, the assessment coordinator, Professor Peterson, and Program Coordinator Carlile. In the spring of 2017, following the 2017 Carnegie Summit, PSU, *The Chalkboard Project* and Oregon Department of Education representatives who also attended NIC met four times to identify a problem of practice, fishbone, and driver diagram to guide work for fall 2017.

While not yet experts in IS, Professors Peterson and Carlile and their interns wanted to model a learning disposition and share what they were coming to advocate for: IS as a socially just improvement method. In 2017, they presented *Latina/o Leaders Reducing Educational Disparities: Improvement Science* at the Oregon Association for Latino Administrators Conference. In addition, Peterson and Carlile presented *Preparing School Leaders to Include Student Voice: Improvement Science* at the November 2017 *UCEA* National Convention. Peterson and Carlile also presented at the 2018 Carnegie Foundation Summit: *Improvement Science in the Principal Preparation*

Program: Leadership for Equity. Professors Carlile and Peterson, as well as Dr. McKey, continued to present at local, state, and national conferences on the use of equity-infused IS and Dr. McKey and Professor Peterson also now consult with school leaders across the nation.

While progress in our partnership continued, so too did our focus on conducting research. Professor Peterson was awarded a sabbatical to conduct a replication study of Peterson and Vergara, conducting research on the experience of women leaders with Professor Carlile. During this sabbatical, Professors Carlile and McKey continued the IS work. When Professor Carlile was awarded a sabbatical to conduct research on women leaders, Professor McKey served as program coordinator and continued the iLEAD partnership. When Professor McKey joined PPS full-time, Professor Peterson assumed program coordination during the time of program revision and led the revision of 22 syllabi and two preparation programs with three additional faculty, a two-year process. Throughout the 2019–20 redesign process, and despite serious pushback from department professors who continued to believe that traditional statistical courses best serve future principals, Professors Carlile and Peterson reiterated and shared state licensure expectations, along with research from the Grissom et al. Foundation (2021) emphasizing the importance of school leaders demonstrating expertise in leading change using data in continuous improvement efforts. Ultimately, our focus on future principals using data through IS efforts prevailed, and our introductory IS course was approved by our department colleagues, the COE, as well as all governance groups in PSU. In 2020, Professor Carlile again assumed program coordination and iLEAD leadership roles.

Our partnership work reflected the research of Grissom et al. (2021) indicating that effective principals carry out four key behaviors:

1. Engaging in "high-leverage" instructional activities, such as teacher evaluation and feedback.
2. Establishing a productive climate.
3. Building collaboration and professional learning communities.
4. Managing personnel and resources strategically.

These behaviors rest on three skills

1. People skills.
2. Organizational skills.
3. Instructional skills.

Grissom et al. (2021) emphasize the necessity of principals embedding equity into leadership practices, as public schools serve growing numbers of students of color, students from low-income households, English learners, and students with disabilities. The report describes emerging research on how equity can be applied in each of the four areas through culturally responsive teaching, creating a climate that celebrates diversity, and engaging with families. A related matter is the composition of the principal workforce, which does not reflect student demographics, despite research linking principal demographic diversity to better outcomes for students of color.

Concurrent with revising the programs and syllabi, and engaging in partnership activities, Professors Carlile, Peterson, and McKey were continuing their work by presenting at state and national conferences on IS, with Peterson and Carlile writing six book chapters, editing two books (Peterson & Carlile, 2021, 2022), leading the CPED IS continuous improvement group, and being awarded the Society of Professors of Education Outstanding Book Award in 2022 for *Improvement Science: Promoting Equity in Schools* (Peterson & Carlile, 2021). Our presentations, research, publications, and partnership reflect the following characteristics:

1. Solutions reflect the expertise of families, students, and teachers.
2. Facilitate collective action.
3. Ensure efforts are ecological, context-based, and community-driven.
4. Understand variation in context and implications for change efforts.
5. Employ rapid learning cycles.

Feedback on our efforts informed our continuous improvement work. A synthesis of feedback over several years from multiple sources (program completer, consultant interviews with superintendents, and district leaders who hire PPS interns) was prepared by Professor Peterson in the winter of 2021 for PPS. The report indicated that our principal licensure completers primarily agree or strongly agree on the following: The program strengthened my ability to work with historically marginalized or oppressed groups, faculty respected intern views, even when they differed from their views; the program readings, materials, and assignments reflected non-dominant voices; and that the program prepared interns to effectively use research-based practices, strengthened interns' ability to act professionally in the field; and prepared interns to ensure students succeed and use student progress data to improve their practice. Further, the program strengthened interns' ability to engage in ongoing reflective practice for continued growth.

In addition, interns noted which experiences were the most valuable in strengthening their ability to work successfully with diverse populations:

- Engaging in IS projects as interns.
- Best practices presentations on anti-racism, culturally responsive teaching, community engagement, literacy, math, MTSS, SEL, family engagement and English learners.
- Clarifying our vision, mission, equity focus, community engagement.
- Focus on teacher growth, laws, team building, trust development, decision-making, and collaborative leadership processes.

Further, we had information regarding what our interns found the most helpful and productive in the principal preparation program. They noted the support system our program created; the equity focus in all our projects; guest lectures from seated administrators; collecting disaggregated data during classroom observations; school walkthroughs; cultural autobiographies; intensive 360-hour practicum; culturally responsive community engagement. Interns also reported what was most important in their professors: professor expertise. Interns also said:

- "Our professors have an incredible amount of combined knowledge and experience."
- "Professors could help us think through literally any situation. Amazing."

Finally, we heard comments that validated our equity focus: "I was impressed with this program and how the focus was on equity and social justice the whole time." Critically, interns reported: "Do not lose practitioner instructors," which Carlile, Peterson, and McKey are.

Networked Improvement Communities

PARTNER DISTRICTS

The concepts of IS and the support of NICs were essential to the achievement of our equity goals. Past participation over three years in multiple NICs and attendance at relevant conferences had provided opportunities to learn about IS from the experts and share our concerns and successes with colleagues from the Carnegie Foundation, CPED, *UCEA*, and professors from across the United States.

NEWBERG SCHOOL DISTRICT (NSD)

Engagement with the Newberg School District (NSD), began in the fall of 2016 when we introduced our principal preparation interns to the concepts of IS. In the fall of 2016, a four-person team from Newberg presented to our 49 interns how they use IS, why they chose IS, and the influence of IS on the work in Newberg. These practitioners were clear that teachers in the NSD were re-engaged and energized in addressing problems of practice in their schools because an organic process such as IS, a process that is respectful to teachers, was in place. In addition, NSD was one of the participating districts in the February 2016 meeting of local administrators, teachers, and the statewide advocacy organization *The Chalkboard Project* in which Paul LeMahieu shared information about IS and the work of the Carnegie Foundation for the Advancement of Teaching.

NSD committed to using improvement science as a disciplined approach to system-wide improvement in the fall of 2017 and became PSU's iLEAD partner. As a result of two years of learning, Newberg opened the school year with:

- Teacher-led workgroups leading system-wide improvement by identifying user-centered problems and testing, measuring, and scaling up ideas and initiatives in the

areas of Professional Learning & Leadership, Curriculum & Instruction, Assessment & Grading, and Student Engagement & Equity.
- Continued partnership with coaches who facilitate learning through a sharing network of like-minded districts similarly committed to improvement science (coaches were funded through a grant from the Chalkboard Project).
- Systemizing PDSA improvement cycles in our approach to teacher collaboration and professional learning.
- Two district directors having the primary role/responsibility of serving as principal coaches, coming alongside our school leaders to ensure they have the tools, skills, and practical experience to engage in short cycles of improvement aligned with their school improvement plans.
- A newly hired assistant principal whose completion of the PSU principal preparation program, which included engagement with Improvement Sciences practices, raised her skill set above and beyond other similarly experienced candidates.

CHANGES IN THE PARTNERSHIP WITH THE NEWBERG SCHOOL DISTRICT

PSU's principal licensure program and key members of the NSD shared a mutual commitment to prepare principal licensure interns of PSU's principal preparation program to become strong leaders for equity. Textbox 8.1 indicates the significant changes in the preparation of university principal interns to assume leadership roles with a focus on equity that resulted from the partnership.

TEXTBOX 8.1 OUTCOMES OF THE NEWBERG DISTRICT AND THE PSU PARTNERSHIP

Reducing Educational Disparities

- Guided principal candidates to use IS methodologies to interrupt educational disparities, with all projects focused on equity.
- Further integrated IS into the three-credit educational leadership project in fall, winter and spring terms of the yearlong principal preparation cohort experience to address educational disproportionality.

Context-Based Change Leadership

- Further integrated the IS capstone project for the principal preparation program and showcase the success of individual intern projects on local practice.
- Collaborated with teachers and students when making changes that impact them.
- Increased student voice and community engagement using IS.

The district-university partnership successfully influenced practices at the university. Data indicated that the district-university partnership successfully influenced the IS curriculum at PSU through the adoption and/or adaptation of processes successful in the field. However, the partnership focus had been centered almost exclusively on changes at the university. The partnership did not impact major change within the district. Conversations about the future of the partnership faltered, and when the key district leader who was a main liaison between iLEAD and PSU left the district, the strength of the partnership was further diminished. In addition to losing the main liaison in NSD, Professor Carlile who was the primary PSU contact with NSD went on sabbatical to conduct research. While a transition plan was successfully in place for PSU and Professor McKey assumed iLEAD and program coordination roles, the changes in leadership created an opportunity to adapt, adopt, or abandon the initial partnership with NSD.

The New District Partnership: Portland Public Schools

Professor McKey, the recently hired PSU tenure track assistant professor, had assumed program coordination responsibilities during Carlile's sabbatical and began conversations with PPS about the potential of a partnership with PPS to reduce educational disparities through the use of IS. Under Professor McKey's leadership, the partnership with NSD was ended, by mutual agreement, and a new partnership was created. In the following year, 2019, that new partnership was further strengthened when McKey left PSU and was hired to serve as the Senior Director of Humanities in PPS.

In the fall of 2018, the PSU–PPS partnership began its effort to understand "full causes," or systemic problems, by focusing on the research as suggested by Peterson and Carlile (2021) and Biag (2022) who noted "seeking to understand how leaders can intentionally configure their practice in service of equitable outcomes for marginalized children and youth" (p. 91). As a result of the multiple conversations across PSU and PPS, the mutually agreed upon problem of practice was that PPS did not have a pipeline of equity-centered leaders equipped to ensure that every single student, particularly Black, Indigenous, and other students of color, had an excellent school experience and were academically successful. The partnership recognized IS as an organizing methodology that would be intentionally configured with an equity lens, include culturally responsive practices (Peterson & Carlile, 2021, 2022), guide the specification of high-leverage problems, and test change ideas.

While Professor McKey has subsequently accepted roles outside of PPS, PPS Area Senior Director Isaac Cardona and longtime PPS principal Ben Keefer note the following about this successful iLEAD partnership:

> For the past several years, Portland Public Schools has partnered via the Carnegie Foundation's iLead initiative with PSU, the largest contributor to our district's educator pool. As one of the eleven IHE and LEA partnerships in the national iLEAD network, the strong synergy and learning

we've created between PSU and PPS has impacted numerous teachers and administrators through PSU's school of education. At the local level, our team created a course that trained and developed every single administrator in our district on the tenets of Improvement Science.

PPS leveraged PSU's Improvement Science expertise to develop a training model that ensured incoming principal candidates had elements central to the PPS Strategic Plan at the core of their initial licensure program. Embedding this level of knowledge in District and school leaders will help accelerate growth of student learning, and reduce inequities in student performance, attendance, and discipline data by identifying root causes of gaps and utilizing disciplined inquiry to address them

At the national level, our iLEAD team collaborated with other Networked Improvement Communities across the country at annual convenings. We heard about their successes, trials and tribulations, and the ways they are changing outcomes in their communities, in ways that benefit both educators and students. These NICs have allowed our iLEAD team to break out of siloed thinking and develop strong, lasting partnerships that center equity and educational outcomes for students. By focusing on our improvement cycles, we are seeing successes, and we look forward to continued growth as we address local education issues by refining interventions that address the needs of our students and school communities.

(Internal communication, July 2022)

Challenges and Solutions

A key challenge for the partnership was to develop a strategic, systematic focus for making coordinated improvements at the university and within PPS. The first step was for the team to review the improvement journey to date and help the team identify next steps (see figure 8.1).

Building on the experiences of our first partnership with Newberg, we realized that there must be a change in the work at both the district as well as the university. Though IS had been integrated into the PSU principal preparation pipeline for three years, it was not well known in PPS. Professor McKey, the program coordinator during Professor Carlile's sabbatical, was a strong liaison with PPS and was well-positioned to make that change. McKey had the experience, knowledge, and support to provide professional development in IS within PPS. Specifically, her goal was that central office and district administrators in PPS would understand that IS was not just another new program imposed on schools and teachers; there must be a change in the district's continuous improvement process—a critical aspect of change that was missing in the first partnership. Consequently, an early priority was to introduce IS as a continuous change process into the work of the district administrators. To begin that process, Professor McKey and her team considered these questions:

1. What are we trying to accomplish *and how do we ensure this improvement benefits children of all racial, ethnic, socio-economic, gender, and ability levels, especially those most under-served in our community?*

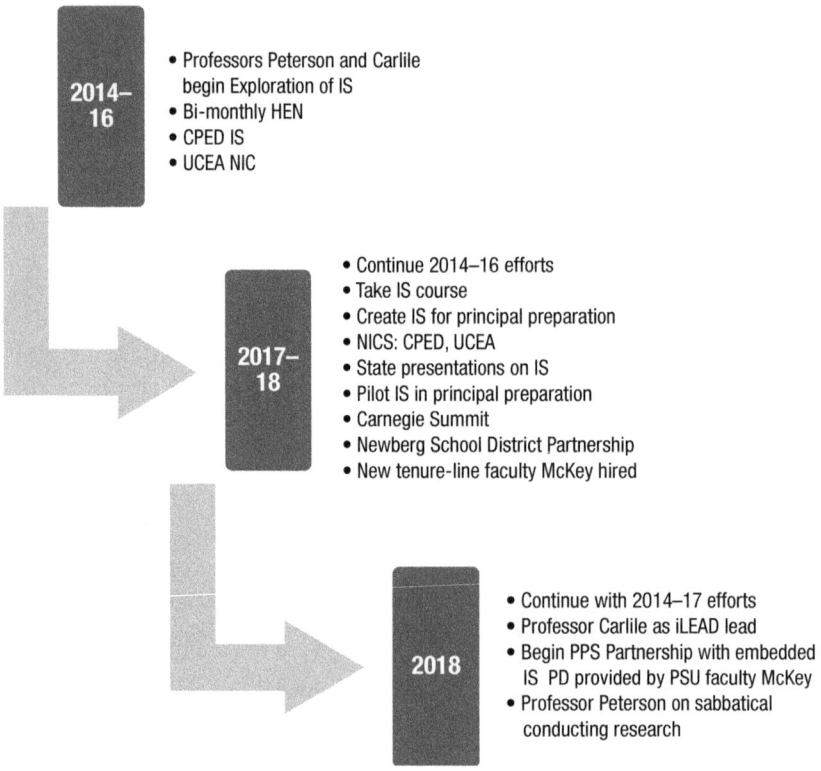

Figure 8.1 2014-2018 Chronology of IS in the PSU-PPS iLEAD partnership journey.

2. What changes can we make that will result in improvement *for children of all racial, ethnic, socio-economic, gender, and ability levels, especially those most under-served?*
3. How will we know that a change is an improvement for children *of all racial, ethnic, socio-economic, gender, and ability levels, especially those most under-served in our community?*
4. How do we ensure we include the voices of those who are most impacted by the change such that the humanity of those in our schools is enhanced? (Peterson, 2014; Peterson et al., 2022, p. 2)

Another challenge was to deepen our collective understanding and shared commitment to leadership for equity and continue to infuse equity into all aspects of our work. We used the most inclusive definition of diversity (race, ethnicity, gender, religion, gender identification sexual orientation, socio-economic status, region origin, national origin, girth, native language, and other group identification that results in advantages or disadvantages based on group identity (Gay, 2010) to inform our collaboration efforts.

Our response to a third challenge, the identification of a mutually acceptable change process, contributed to early success. The partnership recognized IS as a set of tools that would be intentionally configured with an equity lens (Carlile & Peterson, 2019).

At the same time, the Oregon Teacher Standards and Practices Commission (TSPC) revised all program and practitioner standards, requiring us to revise our licensure program. An additional challenge for the partnership was that there were no funds to conduct the redesign. Nevertheless, extensive course feedback, the results of a major stakeholder input process from 2016–2018, enabled a successful redesign. A final challenge was to use the Developmental Progressions (DP) progressions tool to articulate a shared understanding of the work in which the partnership was collectively engaged.

Tools to Identify Next Steps

The use of the DP assessment tool in 2019, created by the iLEAD community, was used to note what had been accomplished to date and guide conversations about the next steps. To begin that process, the team used the DP assessment to identify progress and challenges at the partnership and institutional levels.

PROGRESS (STRENGTHS) AT THE PARTNERSHIP LEVEL

- Cultivation of partnership relationships built around active joint work and characterized by positive attitudes and strong bonds of trust.
- Integrating IS/NICs in the core work.
- Joint development of targeted problems of practice.
- Identification of one or more problems of practice that can focus EdD and/or master students' capstones.

PROGRESS (STRENGTHS) AT PPS

- District leadership engagement active engagement of district leadership in IS.
- Networked improvement communities (NICs) and partnership work.
- Professional Development of District Staff IS/NICs training for teachers and leaders is a standard part of professional development offerings.

PROGRESS (STRENGTHS) AT THE PSU LEVEL

- Curriculum/ program development integration of IS/NICs into curriculum.
- Scholarship of improvement: An academic community is forming presentation of improvement research in scholarly venues and publications.

AREAS OF FOCUS (CHALLENGES) AT THE PARTNERSHIP LEVEL

- Formalizing partnership data agreement establishment of formal agreements around data collection and data sharing to support improvement efforts.

- Formalizing partnership data agreement establishment of formal agreements around data collection and data sharing to support improvement efforts.

AREAS OF FOCUS (CHALLENGES) IN PPS

- Implementation of IS/ NICs.
- IS/NICs are integrated into planning processes and utilized to make measurable improvements in local problems of practice.

AREA OF FOCUS (CHALLENGE) IN PSU

- Institutional and State Approvals Resolution of possible issues around institutional and state approvals on courses, programs, and accreditation.

By May 2019, the partnership had already begun development in each of the focus areas. For example, the district had made a firm decision to implement IS, beginning with the schools most in need of improvement and developing a comprehensive plan for professional development in all the district schools. NICs were integrated into the already established, school-based, professional learning communities. A redesign of PSU's principal preparation program, which included national accreditation, as well as approval from the state licensing agency and multiple PSU faculty, departments, colleges, and faculty governance bodies was underway.

The DP assessment tool provided an opportunity in 2019 for the partnership to gather baseline data in areas of strength and growth. We received an assessment of 24 variables in the categories of the partnership, the institute of higher education, and the district. Though the data guided work in the early phases and would have informed our work throughout the partnership, we did not use it again, due to timing and personnel. When the COVID-19 pandemic began and the schools closed for the remainder of the year our focus went to those students who faced enormous barriers. Despite the potential of this comprehensive tool to inform progress, minimum time and few staff were available to assess our iLEAD work.

Contextual Complexities

We learned that context matters, and we had to adjust our expectations based on the very complex context in which we were implementing our change ideas. In figure 8.2, we present the additional complexity of key personnel changes due to research sabbaticals or new roles. Professor Peterson, promoted to associate professor emerita in the spring of 2021, no longer served on the iLEAD team. Dr. McKey continued to serve in PPS at the central office or building level through the end of the 2021–22 academic year. The iLEAD team adjusted and added new members from PPS.

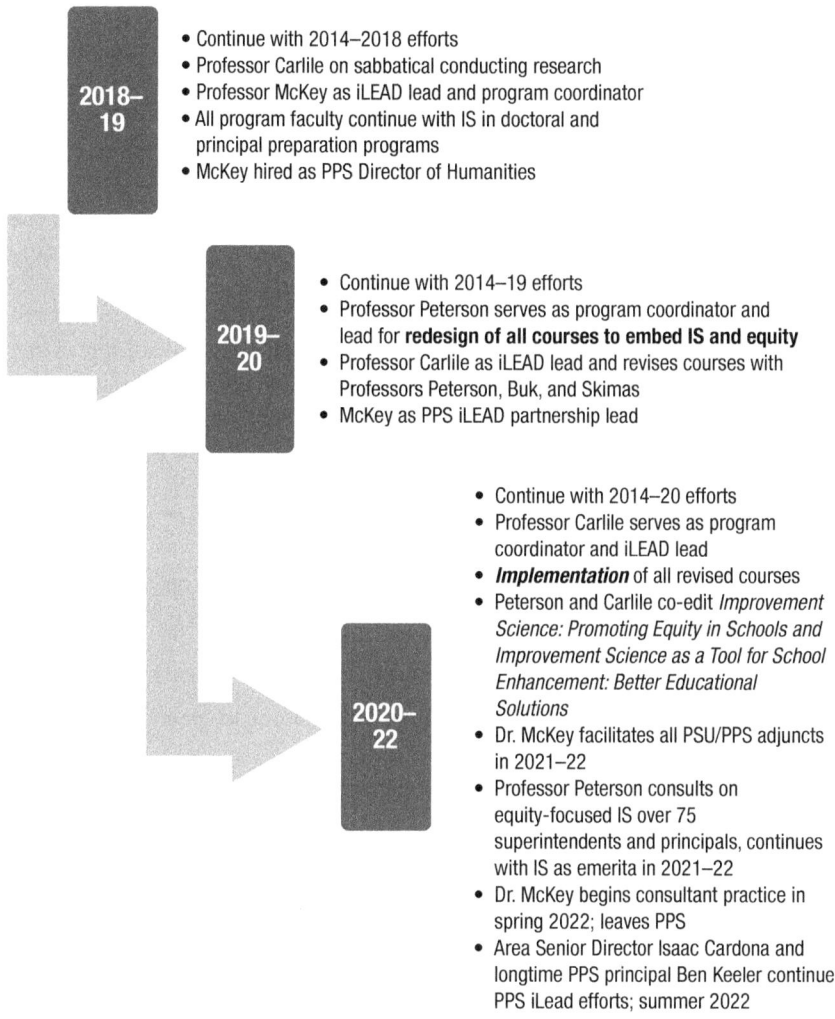

Figure 8.2 2018-2022 Chronology of IS in the PSU iLEAD partnership journey.

Theory of Improvement

PROGRAM REDESIGN

The new TSPC standards for school administrators do not specifically reference IS. For example, the scope and responsibilities of school administrators include "Support the continuous improvement and capacity of the school administrator profession" (Scope and Responsibilities of School Administrators. OAR 584-235-0010). The school administrator standards include references to "improvement" in five of the ten standards, with numerous explicit statements regarding teacher input, student voice, and family voice, with each standard tied to an equity focus. One standard focuses solely on improvement (Oregon School Administrator and English Learner License Standards 584-235-0010).

All teams revising the curriculum during 2019–22 and during the iLEAD partnership used the Oregon licensure standards to guide what current curriculum supported the development of anti-racist, culturally responsive leaders and what needed to be adapted, abandoned, or adopted system-wide. In 2019, as the initial redesign work began, the PSU faculty identified the focus of their work and the problem of practice: *PSU principal preparation curriculum needs to increase and broaden experiences and support to prepare future leaders to consistently and competently lead equity-focused change efforts that align with the new state principal licensure standards.* We analyzed root causes and identified four:

- Mapping curriculum to embed the new standards in each course, ensuring all standards are met over the course of the program and that courses and clinical practice experiences are developmentally sequenced.
- Anchoring IS throughout the program with an introductory course in IS rather than in statistics.
- Redefining the role of the supervised clinical practice experience to deepen and enhance equity-based experiences.
- Creating two new courses focusing specifically on developing expertise and experiences for supporting dual-identified English learners and students with special needs (Peterson & Carlile, 2019; Carlile & Peterson, 2019).

Our successes in implementing change ideas related to program redesign are detailed below:

- 2019–20: Modified our pilot IS project to align with new state standards; implement once approved by TSPC.
- 2019–20: Added a stand-alone introductory course in IS as part of program redesign and removed a traditional statistics course that is no longer required by TSPC standards.
- 2019–22: Determined what current PSU curriculum must be protected and what must change to prepare future anti-racist leaders.
- 2020–22: Facilitated a process where interns from PPS developed a problem of practice for their year-long IS project aligned to the PPS equity-based district mission and vision.

REDESIGN PPS PRACTICES FOR PRINCIPAL SUPPORT

Under the leadership of Dr. McKey, PPS used data from an equity audit in PPS to determine what current processes and structures must be protected and what must be changed to prepare future PPS leaders to address educational disparities. Our successes implemented in PPS include the following:

- Provided IS professional development to 50% of administrators.
- Engaged PPS administrators in IS efforts that matched the district's problem of practice and theory of action.
- Required that all school improvement plans reflect the IS methodology.

- Analyzed an "after-action review" to focus on what worked, what did not, why it worked or did not work to inform next steps.
- Create NICs to support the problems of practice in the Comprehensive Schools in need of Improvement (CSI) and Targeted Schools in need of Improvement (TSI).
- Create NICs that are reflective of the K–5 CSI schools, K–5 TSI schools. Individual schools created NICs around math, literacy, and climate.

HIRE SCHOLARLY PRACTITIONERS AS PRINCIPAL PREPARATION COHORT LEADERS

We believe that scholarly practitioners with exceptional experience and expertise leading equity-focused school improvement efforts should lead principal preparation cohorts, rather than academics with intellectual expertise but no school leadership experience. In the summer of 2021, the PSU and PSU iLEAD team members had an opportunity to reshape the instructional team. Work assignment changes for Professor Carlile, Dr. Peterson, and Dr. McKey opened instructional roles for other experienced practitioner-scholars with significant demonstrated success in reducing educational disparities. Enrollment of 100 principal interns in the 2021–22 year provided the chance to hire instructors to further adapt and deliver the TSPC-approved curriculum for these interns. We chose currently practicing administrators who were knowledgeable about leading for equity and had successfully led improvement efforts using IS in their schools or districts. Thus, in 2021–22, we hired seven PPS administrators to teach in the PSU principal preparation program, with iLEAD colleagues Professor Carlile and Dr. McKey recruiting, hiring, training, and supervising. All seven instructors were known for their culturally responsive, anti-racist leadership and three were leaders of color; each instructor had a reputation for refusing to blame teachers, students, and families when initiatives failed to create success for all students in our schools, would implement culturally relevant curriculum and would model equity-based instructional practices.

PPS HIRES PSU PRINCIPAL LICENSURE COMPLETERS

The partnership's success in hiring PPS administrators as instructional adjunct professors was significantly influenced by the history of our partnership and the trust that had developed among iLEAD partners. This trust also resulted in the iLEAD team shaping the hiring in PPS for principals, assistant principals, and district leaders throughout the partnership. For example, in the fall and winter of 2019, PPS hired 12 PSU principal licensure completers who had engaged in IS projects and two administrators who had completed their principal preparation program at PSU to serve as leaders in the PPS Humanities Department where Dr. McKey was senior director.

Lessons Learned

The success of our partnership was grounded in leadership research supporting scholarly practitioners (Carnegie Project on the Educational Doctorate, 2022), the Wallace

Foundation's continual research on principal effectiveness (Grissom et al., 2021), and the IS concepts regarding context-specific analysis of the problem, engaging those closest to the issue, collecting and analyzing data, and examining whether changes result in improvements (Peterson & Carlile, 2019). The analysis below synthesizes the focus of each concept, including full and partial implementation of IS strategies.

Co-designing the PSU administrator licensure program with former and current iLEAD members had distinct advantages for designing content-specific curricula. First, the practitioner-scholar instructors hired from the ranks of PPS were already deeply engaged in the partnership, were aware of its history and unique features, and were committed to the shared core values. As a result, the core value of equity and the focus on continuous improvement continued to be central to the work. "On-the-ground perspective" from adjunct instructors who were currently practicing administrators improved the relevance of the curriculum and credibility with students in the class, proving to be particularly valuable while teaching during multiple pandemics (Ladson-Billings, 2022).

All adjunct instructors were successful practitioners, had attended Carnegie Summits, and were knowledgeable about implementing IS and, thus, were able to anchor each of the six IS principles in the planning, including honoring the voices of the users, our principal licensure interns. This understanding allowed the PSU principal preparation faculty (comprised solely of adjuncts in 2021–22) to respond quickly to variability within and among the schools and neighboring districts, and adjust our curriculum, instruction, and assessment to meet emerging needs. We considered how to redesign our leadership preparation and pedagogy to more effectively support principal interns as they support their teachers and children in our schools, many of whom have experienced trauma-inducing events, such as those during this time of multiple pandemics (Ladson-Billings, 2021). We continue to ask the essential questions, "What do we do for the adults that changes the experience for the kids? How do we embrace solutions that regard the expertise of our students, teachers, and families?"

Next Steps

While we have made much progress in our partnership for the benefit of our schools, and we want to continue our journey of continuous improvement. As we do, we reflect on the following lessons learned.

1. It is essential to have a strong guiding vision and relentless focus on a mission that every partner and team member is committed to is critical. Neither PPS's nor PSU's commitment to equity began with the iLEAD partnership; each organization and the members of the iLEAD team had demonstrated a long commitment to social justice, culturally responsive leadership and anti-racist practices. Each partner was committed to ensuring that children of every background, of all races and ethnicities, thrive in our schools through skilled anti-racist and culturally responsive leadership.
2. Sustaining our partnership over time, with multiple leadership changes, made clear to us the need to develop leadership transition plans so that our progress is

not stymied when partnership personnel changes. A concern is that absent individuals like the three leaders in this story, future efforts won't sustain the success achieved in this partnership. Transition plans will need to address the needs of emerging leaders at PSU and PPS, as well as champion newly hired faculty to preserve the partnership, specifically in tenured-track positions such as was recently added to the PSU team.
3. Problems that emerged from sustaining a principal licensure university program staffed entirely with adjunct professors will need to be addressed. Though adjunct instructors bring recency, credibility, and enthusiasm, they earn less significantly less pay, get fewer benefits, don't have the same job security as their full-time or tenured counterparts and are not positioned to contribute to the design of long-term program term goals.
4. Key features of partnership success were strong local and national support and sufficient resources to build the effort. Moving forward, the leadership transition plan must prioritize shared resources, center on those that have the most potential to interrupt educational disparities, embrace different ways of working across the organizations and work from the premise that resource management is an ongoing process.

Conclusion

We remain committed to determining whether our principal licensure completers are impacting educational disparities in schools, and we have several tools to help us identify the next steps. First, we know that in some years we have a 90% placement rate in leadership roles. Superintendents often describe their open positions and ask us to recommend potential applicants. We use our course evaluations at the end of each term well as formative exit sheets, to inform our improvements. We need to continue reaching out to superintendents to identify why they hired who they hired, and what else we could do to prepare the best equity-focused leaders for our schools. We also believe it would be helpful to conduct empathy interviews one year after program completion and five years after program completion to inform our continuous improvement. In addition, we believe that analyzing state data on our principals' ability to reduce or close educational disparities would help us understand our effectiveness in preparing them for this critical leadership role.

As Peterson et al. (2022) noted, "Context matters. Data matter. Research matters. Empowering and enhancing the humanity of those closest to the work matters. And examining who benefits from our improvement efforts matters. Every child deserves this focus. Addressing educational disparities in our schools with urgency, commitment, and a belief that every child of every race, every ethnicity, gender, ability, and cultural identity deserves this focus. As we have shared in our partnership story, we have to increase our ability to impact schools system-wide throughout our communities. We have to find willing partners in the university and in our schools, partners who demonstrate dedication, intelligence, anti-racism, culturally responsive practices, and who are willing to adapt, adopt, or entirely discard what isn't working to make sure we serve every child with the care they deserve. We know our children can't wait."

Questions for Discussion

1. Reflect on the three shifts endured by this partnership—a change in participating districts, in state licensure requirements, and curricular redesign within the university and the district. How would you address anticipated changes in a district or university to increase the possibility that the partnership will thrive?
2. None of the three key individuals who developed and sustained the partnership currently serve in their previous position. What leadership actions should be taken to sustain and build upon accomplishments?
3. How does IS contribute to the development of unique strengths and assets within a partnership?

References

Bell, L. A. (2016). Theoretical foundations for social justice education. In M. Adams & L. A. Bell (Eds.), *Teaching for diversity and social justice* (pp. 3–16). Routledge.

Bryk, A. S., Gomez, L. M., Grunow, A., & LeMahieu, P. G. (2015). *Learning to improve: How America's schools can get better at getting better.* Harvard University Press.

Carlile, S. P., & Peterson, D. S. (2019). Improvement science in equity-based administrative practicum redesign. In R. Crowe, B. N. Hinnant-Crawford, & D. Spaulding (Eds.), *The educational leader's guide to improvement science: Data, design and cases for reflection* (pp. 197–216). Myers Education Press.

Carlile, S. P., & Peterson, D. S. (2020). Embedding improvement science in one principal licensure course: Principal leadership for equity and inclusion. In R. Crowe, B. N. Hinnant-Crawford, & D. Spaulding (Eds.), *Teaching improvement science in educational leadership: A pedagogical guide.* Myers Education Press.

Educator Advancement Council. (2019, July). *Oregon educator equity report.* https://www.oregon.gov/tspc/about/Publications_and_Reports/2019_Oregon_Educator_Equity_Report_Exec_Summary.pdf

Gay, G. (2010). *Culturally responsive teaching: Theory, research and practice.* Teachers College Press.

Grissom, J. A., Egalite, A. J., & Lindsay, C. A. (2021). *How principals affect students and schools: A systematic synthesis of two decades of research.* The Wallace Foundation. http://www.wallace-foundation.org/principalsynthesis

Hall, G., & Hord, S. (2015). *Implementing change: Patterns, principles and potholes.* Pearson.

Ladson-Billings, G. (2021). I'm here for the hard re-set: Post pandemic pedagogy to preserve our culture. *Equity & Excellence in Education, 54*(1), 68–78.

LeMahieu, P., Grunow, A., Baker, L., Nordstrum, L., & Gomez, L. (2017). Networked improvement communities: The discipline of improvement science meets the power of network. *Quality Assurance in Education, 25*(1), 5–25.

Mesh, A. (2022, June 6). Feds indict Proud Boys who paraded through Portland on seditious conspiracy charges for D.C. plot. *Willamette Week.* https://www.wweek.com/news/courts/2022/06/06/feds-indict-proud-boys-who-paraded-through-portland-on-seditious-conspiracy-charges-for-dc-plot/

Oregon Secretary of State. (2019). *ODE and PPS must do more to monitor spending and address systemic obstacles to student performance, particularly at struggling schools.* Oregon Audits Division. https://sos.oregon.gov/audits/Documents/2019-01.pdf

Peterson, D. S., & Carlile, S. P. (2019). Preparing school leaders to effectively lead school improvement efforts: Improvement science. In R. Crowe, B. N. Hinnant-Crawford, & D. Spaulding (Eds.), *The educational leader's guide to improvement science: Data, design and cases for reflection* (pp. 167–182). Myers Education Press.

Peterson, D. S., & Carlile, S. P. (2021). *Improvement science: Promoting equity in schools.* Myers Education Press.

Peterson, D. S., & Carlile, S. P. (2022). *Improvement science as a tool for school enhancement: Solutions for better educational outcomes.* Myers Education Press.

Peterson, D. S., Carlile, S. P., Olivar, M. E., & Thonstad, C. (2020). Embedding improvement science in principal licensure courses: Program redesign. In R. Crowe, B. N. Hinnant-Crawford, & D. Spaulding (Eds.), *Teaching improvement science in educational leadership: A pedagogical guide.* Myers Education Press.

Senge, P. (2012). *Schools that learn.* Random House.

The CPED Framework©. (2022). *Carnegie project on the educational doctorate.* https://www.cpedinitiative.org/the-framework#:~:text=To%20build%20an%20EdD%20program,and%20solve%20problems%20of%20practice

Walker, T. (2021, November 12). *Getting serious about teacher burnout.* NEA Today. https://www.nea.org/advocating-for-change/new-from-nea/getting-serious-about-teacher-burnout

SECTION III

Partnerships Ain't Easy
LEARNING FROM SHORT-TERM EFFORTS AND LONG-TERM SUSTAINABILITY

Randy Hitz

The work of three partnerships is presented in Section III. As is the case in Sections I and II, the partnerships are quite diverse, including two public and one private university, and two large school districts and one small one. The partnerships are in the West, Midwest, and East. They all seek to develop and sustain mutually beneficial partnerships focused on improvement and equity, but they are at various stages in that development. The South Carolina case offers insights into the challenges of beginning a new partnership. Chicago and Denver provide stories of long-standing partnerships, how they have evolved over time, and what has resulted from their work together. Documentation of the evolution of the partnerships in Chicago and Denver provides valuable insights into growing and sustaining the work over a long period of time.

The University of South Carolina has a long history of leadership with professional development schools/districts. However, in this case, they present an effort to create a different kind of mutually beneficial partnership focused on leadership for improvement. One thing that makes this case unique among others in this book is that it represents a partnership that did not do as well as they hoped despite efforts from university and district participants. The authors write, "we aim to share our partnership case with its challenges, imperfections, struggles, bright spots, and critical learnings so others might anticipate where barriers could arise to prepare for and avoid or mitigate them." Their insights will help us as we all "fail forward" and continuously learn in our work.

The University of Denver Educational Leadership and Policy Studies Department and Denver Public Schools have had a successful nationally recognized partnership for over 18 years dedicated to creating a robust principal preparation pipeline. In 2017, they built on this existing work by adding an emphasis on continuous improvement for practicing leaders and leadership teams. They have engaged over 100 schools in various degrees of networked disciplined inquiry focused on improving outcomes for marginalized groups of students. At the same time, the university revised programs to incorporate the improvement science–based continuous improvement model into the educational leadership master and doctoral programs. This is a story of work by university faculty and district mid-level leaders who served as boundary spanners and persevered over many years to gain support from college and department leadership as well as district leaders, obtaining both internal and external support for the work.

The Chicago case is also a tale of remarkable efforts by university faculty and district mid-level leaders working over long periods of time to build a nationally renowned leadership preparation program. It is a story of major across-the-board changes in the University of Illinois, Chicago (UIC) leadership preparation program and the creation of a strong mutually beneficial partnership with Chicago Public Schools (CPS). A few UIC faculty members sought to create a new kind of leadership program based on research and the unique needs of CPS. They brought in leaders from CPS to help guide and strengthen the program, and for over two decades, CPS has provided significant funding to subsidize the program. Significant external funding has also been provided and contributed to the success of the partnership. Over the last decade, CPS has demonstrably improved student outcomes, and UIC-led schools have performed better than system norms on multiple measures. Though a relatively small program, UIC graduates serve as principals in one in ten CPS schools, and one in seven has a UIC principal or assistant principal. Additional documentation of program processes and impact appears in an Appendix on the Rowman & Littlefield website linked to Appendix references in the chapter.

In the Section III cases, initial leadership to create partnerships came from university faculty. Note how individuals or small groups of faculty members built support from within their department and college and how they engaged with school and district leaders to create and sustain partnerships that are mutually beneficial and focused on improvement and equity. Note how the boundary spanners in both the university and district are invaluable in building trusting and productive relationships. Of course, not everything went well for these partnerships, and the reader will want to learn from those experiences as well. Finally, note how each partnership leveraged iLEAD's Developmental Progressions framework to guide and inform their work. The insights shared here can be useful to those seeking to create or improve their own mutually beneficial partnerships focused on continuous improvement.

When reviewing these cases, readers can consider the following questions:

1. Who, if any, are the leaders and boundary spanners in your partnership? What are they doing that makes them effective? What tools, practices, and strategies do they employ to help cross-institutional silos? With an eye toward institutionalization, what can they do to gain greater support from college and district leaders? If the dean and superintendent are the leaders, what can they do to gain support from faculty and staff?
2. What have you learned, if anything, from your challenges in a partnership?
3. How have you planned for inevitable changes in leadership and staffing?

CHAPTER 9

Shared Goals, Methods, and Learning: Partnering for Equity-Focused, Systems-Level Improvement

UNIVERSITY OF DENVER AND DENVER PUBLIC SCHOOLS

Erin Anderson and Sandra Lochhead

This chapter explores how a district and university worked in partnership to build the capacity and infrastructure to advance toward systems change for equity. Building from a partnership designed to create a robust principal preparation pipeline, currently in its 20th year, the University of Denver Educational Leadership and Policy Studies (DU-ELPS) Department and Denver Public School (DPS) added a focus on continuous improvement for practicing leaders and leadership teams in 2017. This new phase of the partnership was built from the foundation and ethos of the existing partnership, but at the same time, had a new partnership structure involving new departments in the central office and new university faculty. Figure 9.1 shows this relationship.

This expansion was not only an opportunity to support school and district leaders who were alumni of the preparation program but was also a mechanism to create conditions in schools that aligned with the shared values of the long-standing partnership, including a focus on equity and anti-racism and a continuous improvement approach to lasting change. These two partnerships have complemented each other and helped to create a strong continuum of opportunity for pre-service and in-service leaders and leadership teams. This chapter is the story of how this new partnership was built from the foundation of the preparation partnership and went beyond leadership preparation to create an ecosystem to enable systems change for continuous improvement.

Over the last five years, we have built a partnership for improvement based on shared goals (built out of common beliefs and values), shared methodology (built out of common language), and shared research (built out of common learning), which has endured numerous leadership changes. Later in the chapter, we will explore these key levers for system transformation and provide details on where we started, what happened along the way, and where we are now for each of those components. We have

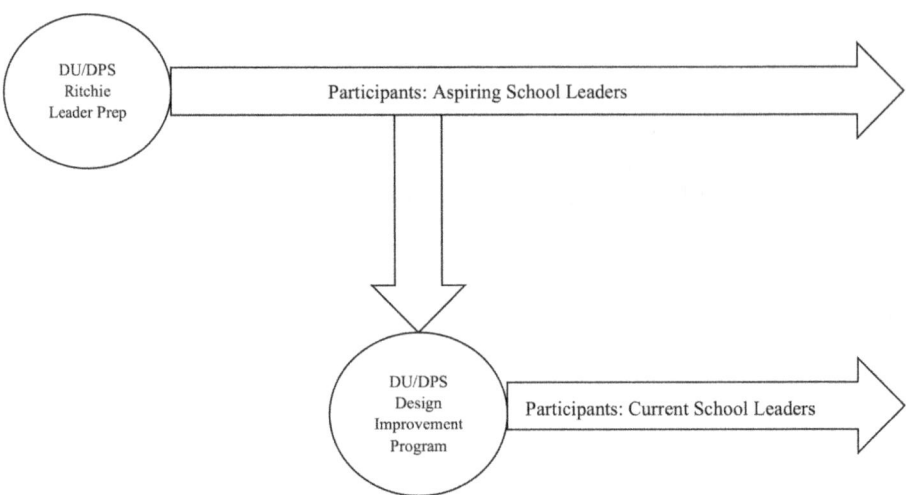

Figure 9.1 Evolution of the two partnerships.

established improvement processes in DPS schools which have (a) improved professional learning, planning, and teaching, (b) increased collaboration and distribution of leadership, (c) encouraged greater collective responsibility for improvement, (d) created intentional, focused, and targeted systems, and (e) changed mental models. Although we do not have the space to share these accomplishments in detail here, we will share four examples of how we achieved this improvement through our work as a partnership.

The principles of continuous improvement have also begun to shape district professional learning and school and district strategic planning. In fact, the work has gone from what was initially intended to be a year-long, grant-funded program serving a small group of schools to a district-wide problem-solving process, which has engaged around 110 schools in various degrees of networked disciplined inquiry focused on improving outcomes for marginalized groups of students. Additionally, the university has revised the preparation program to incorporate the improvement science-based continuous improvement model into the master and doctoral programs and continues to prepare nearly half of the current school leaders in DPS through a jointly designed program.

Context

At the start of the Improvement Leadership Education and Development (iLEAD) initiative in 2017, the DU-ELPS department and DPS had been in partnership since 2003. The partnership began as an effort to co-construct a one-year certificate program for aspiring leaders within the ELPS Department in the Morgridge College of Education (MCE) called the Ritchie Program for School Leaders (Korach et al., 2019). The partnership was created at the behest of a former DPS superintendent, who asked the university to design a model of principal preparation that would result in transformative leaders who would challenge the status quo in response to concerns that the preparation of leaders was not meeting the needs of the district. The district has a desire for leaders who were equipped with the skills and knowledge to lead change, and the Ritchie Program curriculum was uniquely aligned with these district goals.

It is significant to recognize the conditions that enabled the expansion of the partnership. This university district partnership began with jointly creating a shared vision and set of values rather than the design of program elements. The vision included an ethic of critical friends and an acknowledgement that both institutions could not obtain their goals without the partnership. The value of high expectations, courageous and effective instruction, and commitment to building learning communities became the foundation of all program development and implementation.

The team of ELPS faculty and DPS leadership co-designed a certification program that utilized a cohort model taught by a team of cohort instructors, including DU faculty and current and former district leaders. The design team for the Ritchie Program intentionally consisted of a university faculty member (Susan Korach), a district leader (Maureen Sanders) and a retired principal outside of DPS (Dick Werpy). This design team both developed and implemented all aspects of the program. Weekly meetings were held at the central office and the team also provided counsel for other district initiatives like the development of leadership standards. This tight collaboration with the same design team persisted over eight years. During this time, this process of working through problems and issues as trusted and respected partners became a standard of practice. This team approach prevented the work from becoming person dependent and the consistency and continuity enabled the partnership and the program to become institutionalized and sustained to this day.

This partnership has been successful at developing school- and district-level leaders within DPS, due to the close integration of district and department values. The preparation program aligned the competencies for effective practice stated by the district as the competencies for the program. The strength of this partnership was one reason the Ritchie Program received the University Council for Educational Administration's (UCEA's) Exemplary Educational Leadership Preparation Program (EELPP) Award in 2014. The partnership has also been featured in Wallace Foundation publications (Mitang, 2012; Turnbull et al., 2013) and used as an example to promote university program change (Crow et al., 2012).

Another measure of the success of this partnership is how entrenched Ritchie graduates are in leadership roles in the district. The district has a leadership pipeline with multiple leadership roles ranging from teacher leadership roles. As of the 2021–22 school year, there were 134 Ritchie graduates serving as DPS leaders, including 57 principals, 50 assistant principals, 17 senior team leads, three deans, and five other leadership roles. These leaders served in 95 of the schools (46%). Graduates were also in leadership and middle manager positions throughout the central office. These data are significant since there are multiple preparation programs available to aspiring leaders in the Denver metro area.

The two organizations have been able to sustain the first enduring partnership, the Ritchie Program, through shared vision, values, and norms (Korach et al., 2019). These shared visions, values, and norms ensured the partnership had mutual reciprocity, joint ownership and accountability, and interdependence. Korach and her colleagues found, "Shared vision and theory of action, as well as the systems and structures that supported joint ownership and accountability, provided the foundation for reciprocity between Ritchie and DPS" (p. 36). Furthermore, Korach and colleagues explained,

> The partnership ethos within the ELPS department has broken boundaries and blurred the lines across institutions and faculty ranks to leverage assets within contexts and empower people ... Rather than a continuum, place, or space, the partnership ethos of the ELPS department lives in the values and actions of the learning community of faculty, students, schools, and districts. Partnership is a verb and not a noun. Value and honor of partners and the relationships foster bravery and safety to challenge the status quo.
>
> (Korach et al., 2019, p. 46)

The new phase of the partnership expanded upon this partnership ethos (Korach et al., 2019) by developing shared improvement goals, a shared improvement methodology, and shared continuous learning. Together the partners iterated on the delivery, application, and enabling conditions necessary for embedding continuous improvement into the DNA of both the district and the university. In partnership, we articulated shared goals for our improvement work which was meant to (a) dig into the complex issues we face in schools, (b) create equitable and socially just spaces for children, (c) work collaboratively to solve problems and enact effective leadership, and (d) be intentional, focused, data-driven, asset-based, and systems-focused.

Problem

The existing partnership structure allowed for the two organizations to jointly recognize the opportunity to rethink approaches to supporting district schools with improvement. When the call for iLEAD came out, the partnership for leadership preparation was institutionalized; however, the desire existed to deepen and expand responses to school improvement challenges for practicing leaders, many of whom were program alumni. ELPS was in the process of developing a state-approved and state-funded professional learning "turnaround" program through which state providers work with schools and districts that have demonstrated concerning academic growth. Both institutions identified continuous improvement (e.g., Park et al., 2014), design thinking (Kelley & Kelly, 2013), and improvement science (Bryk et al., 2015; Hinnant-Crawford, 2020; Langley et al., 2009) as improvement methodologies that could bridge the preparation and practice of school leaders and support schools in "turnaround." After a few years, the team integrated the mindsets and principles of liberatory design (Anaissie et al., 2021) into the model to ensure the focus on equity throughout the improvement process.

From there, ELPS faculty and district improvement leaders committed to engaging in a partnership to support school leadership teams in priority improvement/turnaround status to utilize continuous improvement to accelerate improvement efforts leading to increased outcomes for students. The professional learning program, now known as Design Improvement (DI), was co-constructed by the university and district over five years, moving from initial familiarity with design thinking, improvement science, and liberatory design to more skilled implementation of the shared methodology, Design Improvement for Equity (DI4E). We will discuss the program and methodology in detail in this chapter. Figure 9.2 includes a timeline of the partnership with key events.

Drs. Erin Anderson and Susan Korach, along with other ELPS faculty, collaborated on the initial model for the DI program. Dr. Korach was instrumental in developing the initial principal preparation partnership, which created the relationships and conditions for DI program development. Dr. Anderson, who served as a content designer and improvement coach, became program lead in 2019. Coaches, Dr. Ellen Miller-Brown and Patty Kipp, now retired ELPS faculty and former program leads (2017–2019), supported schools on an ongoing basis and work with Dr. Anderson to develop the current programming. All ELPS faculty served in coaching roles throughout the first two years before moving to a smaller team to ensure common understanding, adaptive integration, and implementation with integrity before scaling up to a larger team (Bryk et al., 2015).

The DU team invited Amy Keltner, who was formerly the Director of Academic Projects and the Chief Impact Office; and Ann Whalen, former Associate Chief of Academics, to join the iLEAD collaboration. They were instrumental for the first two years but moved on to different positions outside the district. They also invited Sandy Lochhead, who at the time was the Director of School Leader Pipelines, Performance & Development, as well as an ELPS doctoral student who became the Senior Manager of Innovation and Improvement, to join them in the iLEAD initiative. Over the first two years, two members of Keltner's team worked closely with the DU team to iteratively develop the DI program, and then Lochhead took over that role in 2019. Currently, the iLEAD team consists of Anderson and Lochhead, but there are several additional members of both organizations who are key to the partnership. This team also works collaboratively as critical friends and has created interdependence by developing routine time together and patterns of behavior to bind the work.

District Context

As of 2022, DPS served 90,000 students and their families across 206 schools. It was the largest district in Colorado (DPS Website, 2022). Sixty-four percent of students qualified for free and reduced lunch, a proxy for students with low socioeconomic status. The student body reflected the diversity of the city with slightly over half of the students identifying as Latinx (54%). Students that identified as white numbered 25%, and 13% identified as Black. A smaller portion of students identified as more than one race (4.5%), Asian (3%), and American Indian (1%). There were 170 languages spoken among DPS students and families, and 37% of the students are English learners. Ten percent of students were gifted and talented learners, and ten percent had special needs addressed through Individualized Education Plans (IEPs). DPS, like districts throughout the state, was underfunded with Colorado ranking toward the bottom of all states for school funding (36 out of 50) (Baker et al., 2014).

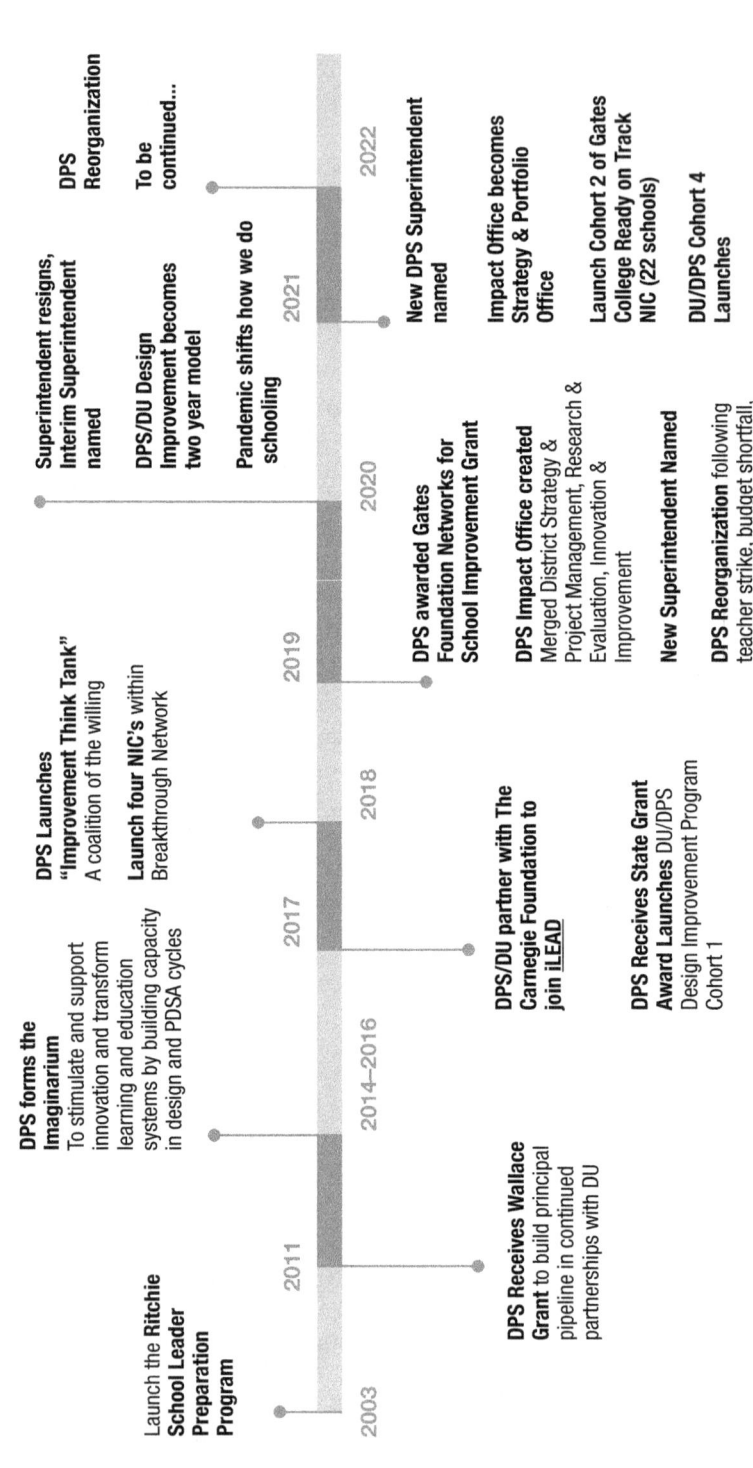

Figure 9.2 Timeline of major events in the DU-DPS partnership.

Most importantly, DPS has struggled to meet the needs of their Black, Indigenous, and people of color (BIPOC) students as measured by state test scores, an imperfect but informative measure. Sharing these disparities in student outcomes is not intended to emphasize the fact that BIPOC students were not performing at the same level as non-BIPOC students but to recognize the extent to which students were being underserved by the district. This problem can be conceptualized as an opportunity gap (e.g., Carter et al., 2013) in which the systems and structures are not set up to promote student achievement for all students. In 2017, according to the National Assessment of Educational Progress (NAEP), a test administered for the purpose of cross-district and state comparisons found that differences in 4th-grade reading scores included a gap between white and Black students that was five points wider and a gap for Latinx and white students that was 13 points wider than the national average for larger cities—Denver's comparison group. In fact, Black students' test scores were 36 points lower and Latinx students were 40 points lower than white students. These gaps in opportunity were exacerbated for Black and brown students with multiple marginalized identities, such as special education classification, emergent English language learners, LGBTQI-identification, or low socio-economic position. Opportunity gaps abounded in DPS; the district was aware of this problem and had made equity and social justice a major district priority.

More important than test scores, there had been ongoing experiences of racial inequity, and BIPOC felt disengaged from the school community. A report commissioned in 2015 by the district to understand the experiences of Black families and educators found that "African-Americans in DPS are invisible, silenced, and dehumanized, especially if you are passionate, vocal, and unapologetically black" (Bailey, 2015, p. 17). BIPOC students had been disproportionately suspended and disciplined (DPS Website, 2017). More recently in response to this report, the board passed a Black Excellence Resolution requiring all schools to have a plan to address these inequities by supporting the success of each Black student in the school.

DPS has also faced multiple transitions over the past few years. After former superintendent Tom Boasberg held the position for ten years, he left mid-year, and his former assistant superintendent Susana Cordova took over in 2019. Almost immediately, there was a teacher strike, in response to the merit pay system. The strike resulted in a massive reorganization of the central office, which included cutting 150 district positions. Cordova left during the 2020–21 school year, as the COVID-19 pandemic raged on. A new superintendent was hired and began during 2021–22. The relationship between these transitions and the partnership was also presented in figure 9.2.

Sustainable Improvement in the District

Despite numerous improvement efforts, strategies, and grant-funded initiatives to support the success and well-being of each student in the district, DPS had not yet achieved the kind of aligned, strategic, responsive change necessary to ensure impact and achieve equity. Therefore, systemic inequities remained persistent in pre-K through grade 12. Many schools within DPS participated in one or more of the popular "turnaround" programs available to schools and districts; however, despite a large investment in external providers, large opportunity gaps persisted as noted in the previous section. DPS sought the support of ELPS to help with this ongoing problem of practice to innovate and drive improvement in a more systematic and disciplined way through the grant-funded "turnaround" program tailored to the district. This funding allowed us a research and development opportunity. The grant provided resources to prototype a model and learn what works most effectively to build capacity in schools to continuously improve to create a more sustainable movement for equity.

This commitment to a different approach to school improvement was manifested in our shared theory of action:

> If we build capacity within a school or district to use the Design Improvement (DI) process to collectively and deeply examine equity-centered problems of practice, ideate potential solutions, and implement actions monitored through an improvement science framework (PDSA), then schools/districts will develop patterns of behavior, systems, strategies and tools that will be sustainable over time and adaptable to new problems.
>
> (Partnership documents, 2017)

Both the university and district were committed to improvement work to help leaders move from reactionary, quick fixes to more generative responses that addressed the underlying systems or moved the organization towards systems thinking. DI offered an integrated, strategic, and analytic approach to develop problem-solving patterns of thinking and action for schools. The co-constructed program was developed through an ongoing and iterative process to meet the needs of the schools and district.

In 2021–22, the DI program was in its fifth year. The first year began with identifying the joint problem and deciding to try a new, continuous improvement approach to supporting district schools. Using state funds, we launched the first cohort of the DI program (2017–18) with twelve schools (nine elementary, three middle/high) for one year. We worked on building our own capacity to facilitate this work. During cohort one, we learned a lot about the key levers for improving professional learning and deepened our understanding of the barriers, but we didn't reach measurable improvement in any of the schools.

The second cohort (2018–19) included seven new DPS schools (five elementary, two middle/high) as well as three schools from a neighboring suburban district, and one small rural district for eleven total design teams. We focused on building capacity and structures within the school. We began to identify our common methodology, built out the scope and sequence of the work, and developed resources. That year all the schools showed evidence of progress within at least one driver, but most were not able to track progress towards their overall aim of the project.

The third cohort (2019–20) enrolled eight new DPS schools (seven elementary, one early childhood) in what was now a two-year process. We increased the focus on conducting research and learning together by iterating on what we had learned from the first two years. We found that we had finally put some of the essential pieces together to really start improving student outcomes and spreading what worked as shared at the beginning of this presentation. Additionally in 2019, the district received

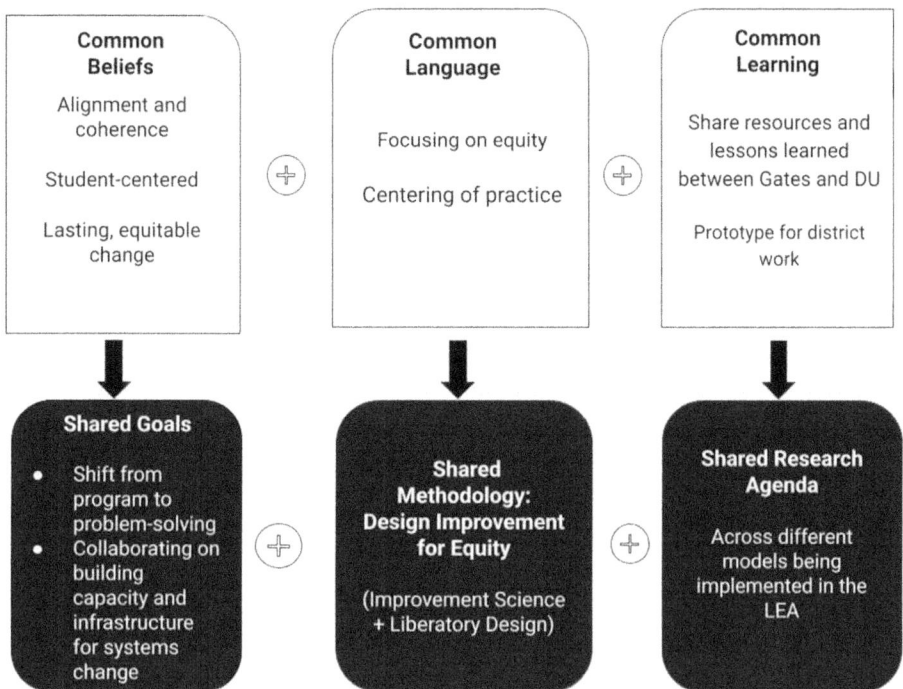

Figure 9.3 Systems and structures necessary for building capacity and infrastructure for systems change.

a Gates NSI grant to work with all high schools in DPS on math equity, which will be discussed in greater detail later in the chapter. In 2020–21, a subset of the third DI cohort (six of the eight schools) decided to stay on for a second year despite the global pandemic. We focused on building the infrastructure within their schools to sustain this work. During the current academic year (2021–22), we worked with four of the elementary schools from the previous year, who asked to participate another year, and one new alternative high school.

Challenges, Solutions, and Evidence[1]

The findings for this case explore the partnership's progress towards systems change for equity. We do not contend that we have achieved systems change, but we have

---

[1] This case is based on data, including documents, observations, and interviews, collected as part of a multi-year, multi-question research study. The documents included artifacts from the program, including documents and notes from regular university/district planning meetings (bi-weekly or monthly depending on the year) and weekly ELPS planning meetings, and documents from the schools (e.g., root cause analysis templates, empathy interview notes, driver diagrams, change idea prototypes, PDSA trackers, weekly meeting protocols, and other planning/meeting documents). Every year the researchers interviewed the faculty coaches

made promising progress over five years. Systems change can be defined as, "advancing equity by shifting the conditions that hold a problem in place" (Kania et al., 2018, p. 3) and requires "adjustments or transformations in the policies, practices, power dynamics, social norms or mindsets that underlie the societal issue at stake" (McKinsey & Company, 2021, p. 10). We will first introduce three areas in which we shifted conditions by developing systems and structures, as part of our work with the iLEAD Developmental Progressions framework, based on the partnership ethos. We will discuss where we started, the steps taken along the way, and where we are now. Then we will present a summary of the impact this work has had in schools. Lastly, we will share some ongoing challenges, lessons learned, and key questions for exploration for others interested in tackling this work.

The partnership focused on the systems and structures necessary for systems change. As the partnership went from the recognition and definition of a joint problem of practice to the development of a professional learning program to the expansion of infrastructure to support a culture of continuous improvement, the work shifted from (a) a common set of beliefs to the shared goal of emphasizing an embedded process over an external program, (b) common language around equity and centering practice in the work to a shared methodology, and (c) a belief in common learning to a shared research agenda.

SHARED GOALS: EMBEDDED PROCESS OVER EXTERNAL PROGRAM

The how and the why of the partnership for improvement shifted over time to ensure this work was institutionalized. We moved from having common beliefs, based on shared values, to shared goals. We began with the common agreement that we wanted to take a different approach to improvement. Our shared values, vision, and norms that had sustained our partnership for preparation were to be student-centered, to be focused on disrupting systems and lasting change, and to ensure alignment and coherence between the additional support that schools were engaging in and the existing improvement work in their buildings. However, when we started this work, we were still thinking of this as a program that schools would engage in for a fixed period like the types of programs we sought to replace.

---

and district leads. These interviews lasted between 30–90 minutes and asked participants to describe their connection to the improvement work, how they supported the schools, the benefits and challenges of the process, and conditions to enable the work. The researchers uploaded all documents and interviews to NVivo 12.0 and coded the data using a codebook developed during the first two years of the study. Two independent coders created the codes inductively by open-coding a subset of data. Then the research team (one faculty and two graduate students) met to agree upon the axial codes and definitions of those codes. The team created a set of deductive codes. Using those codes, a third graduate research assistant coded observation data and artifacts on an ongoing basis throughout the 2019–20, 2020–21, and 2021–22 school years. After this initial round of coding, the faculty lead completed the second cycle of coding to categorize the data into the learnings presented in this chapter.

To move towards institutionalizing, these common beliefs led to a shared goal, which was to ensure the use of DI4E was not seen as 'one more thing' or as another short-term initiative that would be the focus of the district until a new initiative replaced it. Many of our leaders talked about feeling initiative fatigue or the frustration of shifting priorities (Danielson, 2015). One DPS principal stated she no longer wanted to be "putting band-aids" on problems. We realized we needed to approach the work as a shared problem-solving process instead of a turnaround program that schools participated in for a year. We sought to empower those closest to the problems to think creatively and engage in disciplined inquiry to solve our most persistent and complex problems of equity. Systems change was dependent on this goal of shifting from a program model to the infusion of a problem-solving process, which led to spreading DI4E to different conditions throughout the district.

Where Did We Start?

The partnership began with a co-constructed approach, which was largely focused on professional development itself. The workshops were co-created by ELPS and the district. For the first two years, ELPS project leaders and faculty coaches designed the workshops and coaching sessions based on the shared project goals and common beliefs, a scope and sequence, and feedback from the stakeholders. Two ELPS faculty served as project leaders and had regular meetings with the two district leaders responsible for supporting school improvement and supervising the tiered supports available to schools. In these meetings, the ELPS project leads and district partners shared partnership goals and ideas and co-designed a scope and sequence of the work. After the development of a draft agenda and resources for the session, these were shared with all participating faculty for additional feedback, and then a final version of the workshop activities would be provided to the district leads for final approval.

This same process was used to iterate the structure and content of the workshops and to develop a joint agenda for the next workshop. Feedback from all participants was collected at the end of each session and reviewed by both DU and DPS. The planning and delivery of professional learning workshops included the stakeholders at the schools, district partners, and instructional superintendents. This alignment of district goals, each school's improvement plan, and the theory of improvement to be tested in the partnership were enriched through an iterative planning process.

What Steps Happened Along the Way?

The DI program essentially functioned as a pilot for expanding efforts within the district. A new superintendent was named, and DPS navigated a teacher strike, budget reductions, and a reorganization. As an outcome of the reorganization, a new team was formed called the Impact Office that focused on district strategy management, research and evaluation, and an innovation and improvement team. Informed by our learnings from our partnership efforts and work with iLEAD, DPS created the Innovation & Improvement team with the core function of building continuous improvement capacity within the system. DPS began to infuse improvement science principles into the approach to district strategy implementation.

After the first iLEAD convening in 2017, DPS launched several efforts simultaneously. First, DPS created a regular, optional meeting referred to as the *Improvement Science Think Tank*. The Senior Manager of the Innovation & Improvement team brought together stakeholders within DPS that were doing continuous improvement work to deepen their own understanding of continuous improvement approaches in DPS and determine ways to better align efforts. Simultaneously, one of the Instructional Superintendents (principal supervisors) launched a book study on *Learning to Improve* and created four networked improvement communities, consisting of three to five schools facilitated by a lead principal who received training and coaching support. DPS also received state grant funding to launch an exploratory project to bring a networked improvement community (NIC) of seven schools together to focus on racial disproportionality in special education.

In 2019, several aligned efforts emerged. Based on the learnings from the DI program, the district launched different models of NICs in 2019. The team launched district-wide networked improvement cohorts which consisted of 15 cohorts. At monthly two- to three-hour convenings, the team trained lead principals to facilitate these cohorts using improvement science. The cohorts met monthly for two to three hours until the pandemic hit. DPS sustained the work of the existing special education disproportionality cohort and added a cohort focused on rigorous coursework.

DPS spread the use of the DI4E methodology district-wide in 2019–2020 when the district kicked off year one of the College Ready on Track Networks for School Improvement (NSI) grant. DPS was awarded a five-year, ten-million-dollar grant from the Gates Foundation that enabled the district to launch the College Ready on Track NIC. The first cohort consisted of ten high schools whose design teams attended regular convenings and received weekly/bi-weekly coaching support. By 2023, the DPS's Gates group will use the DI4E model to work with all 38 high schools on a shared program of practice in a networked improvement community, which will be discussed in a later section.

Where Are We Now?

Starting with the third cohort (2019–20), the collaborative, co-constructed element of the work shifted from the focus on content to collaborating on how the system can create capacity for change. We are focused on DI4E becoming part of the DNA of both organizations. We integrated it into district work and leadership preparation and have tried various approaches to implementing improvement science and NICs, including (a) district-led cohorts, (b) Gates NSI, and (c) the DU/DI program. Furthermore, Lochhead is working with the Deputy Superintendent of Schools to conceptualize continuous improvement as a major improvement strategy for the district.

SHARED METHODOLOGY: THE DESIGN IMPROVEMENT FOR EQUITY (DI4E) MODEL

The partnership shared some common language around equity and centering practice in the work as well as an interest in the principles of design thinking and improvement science. The partnership evolved from distinct elements of common language around improvement being equity-centered, student-centered, and practice-centered to creating a shared model of continuous improvement that encompassed these elements and brought the shared language to life. We called our shared methodology Design Improvement for Equity (DI4E). It was created to center design methodologies on equity challenges. This model adapted the improvement science model by infusing the stages of design thinking (Kelley & Kelley, 2013) and the framework for liberatory design (Anaissie et al., 2021) to create the model (Author, 2022). Improvement science is a continuous improvement methodology designed specifically for education and for educational justice by the Carnegie Foundation for the Advancement of Teaching and liberatory design is an iteration of design thinking created by the National Equity Project and the d.school at Stanford University. The two key liberatory design practices that complemented and strengthened our original DI model were noticing and reflecting. Throughout every stage of the DI process, we "notice" by practicing self-awareness and situational awareness, and we "reflect" by pausing to reflect on our actions, our impact, emotions, and relationships—and adjusting intentions, direction, and presence. The creators explain,

> Liberatory Design generates self-awareness to liberate designers from habits that perpetuate inequality, shifts the relationship between the people who hold power to design and those impacted, fosters learning and agency for those involved in and influenced by the design work, and creates conditions for collective liberation.
>
> (Anaissie et al., 2021, np)

We had the realization that equity needed to be foundational to the work and we no longer could talk about it as equity-focus without embedding liberatory design in the process.

Where Did We Start?

The ELPS program had long included inquiry cycles in the certification, master, and doctoral programs and developed a course on design thinking for the master's program in educational leadership. The original DI program (2017–18) was based primarily on design thinking due to this familiarity with the process. The focus was more on innovation and thinking outside of the box than on measurement and disciplined inquiry.

What Steps Happened Along the Way?

Later in the first year of the partnership (2017–18), we integrated improvement science to increase the focus on measurable improvement and to give a set of core principles to frame the work. One lead faculty member was beginning to develop expertise in improvement science and helped to introduce those ideas to the work. We began year two (2018–19) with a revised model and introduced that model in its entirety at the initial training. The original model had equity implied but the partners soon realized equity needed to be explicit. In 2019–20, we merged liberatory design into the model. From there, we have been using our DI4E model and iterating on that work.

Where Are We Now?

This shared methodology has become a key piece of evidence of our impact in that it has been used within our partnership as well as within our individual organizations. We identified strengths in the existing approaches to leverage in DI4E and adapted the model for our context. Improvement science brought strong processes around building a theory of action, testing ideas, and building evidence about the theory and specific ideas. Liberatory design brought intentional focus on awareness of the mindsets and the historical context we bring to designing improvements, as well as reflection on the impact of our work throughout the improvement process. This methodology not only helped us focus on systems but on how our individual and group interactions within the system lead to impact.

Every school engaged in DI4E focused on equity and the opportunity gap. The guiding documents, protocols, and workshops had equity checkpoints or opportunities to notice and reflect embedded in them. At each phase from the pre-work of putting a team together and identifying a problem to learning more about the problem to spreading successful change ideas, there were self-reflective questions pertaining to power, bias, and outcomes that the team explores in their work. The original training uses a district-based simulation designed to activate the liberatory design mindsets and center equity. Whether in the Gates NIC or the DU/DI4E work, the schools were asked to select problems that address the needs of students in the margins, to address the opportunity gap, and to regularly ask what works, for whom, and under what conditions.

SHARED LEARNING: SHARED RESEARCH AGENDA IN A RESEARCH–PRACTICE PARTNERSHIP

As a partnership, we agreed that common learning was essential, which has expanded to a research–practice partnership. Over the five years, there has been a research agenda that has served a dual purpose: program evaluation and theory development. The shared research areas include: (a) understanding partnership design and implementation, (b) exploring school design team application, (c) identifying benefits and challenges, (d) building capacity to identify high-leverage areas for improvement, implement change, and measure stated goals, (e) prioritizing diversity, equity, and inclusion practices both internally and in work with schools and districts, and (f) creating an improvement culture of culturally responsive mindsets and practices.

We have also learned that it is important for university researchers to engage in the work alongside schools. Researchers bring a skill set to the partnership and can collect evidence and analyze the work in real time. Critical analysis and evaluation of the work, alongside doing the work, is what created change in the system and process. Through research and reflection, we have systematically identified specific challenges and then generated change ideas to test to improve our work. We continue to iterate on change ideas to achieve improvements.

Where Did We Start?

At the beginning of the partnership, we shared resources, including tools and protocols we developed for our work and resources from the Carnegie summit to recent books to help us deepen our knowledge of continuous improvement. There were also informal conversations about what worked (and what didn't) between the district-led networks and DU-led networks. DU and DPS also shared resources and books or reports to deepen learning and have conversations about those sources. We reviewed our progress using the iLEAD Developmental Progressions framework, which allowed us to calibrate on evidence, reveal opportunities for improvements and anchor our work. We jointly attended quarterly iLEAD convenings which gave us the space to study and reflect on our work and gain feedback from colleagues from other partnerships.

What Steps Happened Along the Way?

The partnership has engaged in joint learning and resource sharing to be more efficacious and sustainable. The learning from research on the DI program influenced each iteration of the model and the delivery of professional learning. This learning was integrated into a theory of improvement for the partnership as well as individual theories of improvement for each year of the program and for the Gates NSI. The leads for the Gates program met with the DU program leads to discuss best practices, tools, challenges, and lessons learned from both initiatives. Leaders of the DU and DPS work have also connected with other districts and non-profits across the state in a community of practice focused on leading NICs. Lastly, we created videos capturing the work on the 2019–20 cohort and will be holding brown bag lunches with key district personnel to discuss and debrief the videos in the future.

In the summer of 2020, a workgroup convened to consider how to help us go beyond progress monitoring our district strategy implementation to focus on learning and improving. As an outcome of this effort, there are routines, processes, and tools being utilized to amplify the voice of users in our processes and use insights from improvement work being done in schools to inform decisions about real-time adjustments to district strategy and inform the design of future strategy.

Where Are We Now?

As the partnership began the 2021–22 school year, there was a shared research agenda, leveraging learning from the DU/DPS DI program, the Gates NSI, and the district-led improvement networks to better understand how to develop the capacity for this work and how schools are making gains for equity. This shared agenda has provided several opportunities for DU and DPS iLEAD members to present at University Council for Educational Administration (UCEA), American Educational Research Association (AERA), the Carnegie Project for the Education Doctorate (CPED), and the Carnegie Foundation Summit on Improvement in Education. Lochhead and Anderson, the DPS and DU leads, co-authored a book chapter with a DPS principal and DU graduate student for a book on leading for equity using improvement science. There are additional publications based on the work under review in academic and practitioner journals.

This partnership has also led to the opportunity to partner on creating a research-based learning trajectory for the Gates network to support coaching and the development of the cabinet leadership middle-level managers, and the hub team who leads the work as well as the school leaders, facilitation leads, and other staff within the school building. Furthermore, in the spring of 2022, Anderson is collaborating with the Impact Office and other units in the central office to develop a knowledge management system. Currently, we are working together with the district lead for the Continuous Improvement Process (CIP), a process in which all schools explore data for improvement, to develop a prototype for a knowledge management system that can capture learnings and insights across the district to ensure.

Summary of Impact

We have evidence from the DU cohort that these DI4E improvement cycles resulted in better solutions and improved student outcomes, especially for historically underserved students (as measured by the individual aims) as well as (a) improved professional learning, planning, and teaching (b) increased collaboration and distribution of leadership, (c) encouraged greater collective responsibility for improvement, (d) developed intentional, focused, and targeted systems, and (e) changed mental models. We will give an example of four schools to illustrate these outcomes.

One school wanted to address early literacy. Through an exploration of their existing data and empathy interviews with students and teachers, they realized that their approach to supporting struggling readers was not working. The empathy interviews revealed that students who loved reading were becoming less enthusiastic by second grade. By pulling struggling readers out of classroom instruction to work with an interventionist, they were contributing to lower reading outcomes for students of color. When they rethought their approach and shifted the focus to providing phonics instruction for all students in the classroom, they started to see growth in their students of color that outpaced the previous years. More students were moving from Tier 2 and Tier 3 supports into Tier 1 at earlier points in the school year. Also, the gap in outcomes on benchmark literacy assessment was reduced by half between students of color and non-students of color from 22 percentage points to 11. They also saw improvement in staff culture, with teachers being more willing to admit when they needed support. The scores on the end-of-year climate surveys that asked about teachers' satisfaction with leadership were the highest the school had ever had.

Another school sought to address gaps in outcomes in math, but as they explored the problem, they realized that the teachers, whether intentionally or not, gave negative messages to marginalized students during their classroom instruction. They used empathy interviews and PDSA cycles as well as Hammond's (2015) research on culturally responsive teaching and the brain to create a protocol for teachers to intentionally monitor their positive and negative interactions with students. They tested and iterated it with a small group of teachers to ensure that it could be seamlessly embedded in instruction. They began to see more students on track to succeed on state tests in math, which they tracked by focusing on eleven target students. Of those students, eight of eleven saw progress throughout the year.

A third school began its work wanting to improve special education programming by changing the schedule. However, when they struggled to get teachers to engage in empathy interviews, they realized they seemed disinterested in the improvement focus. They took time to have open-ended conversations with teachers and students and realized that the problem was relationship building—not the schedule. By focusing on relationships between special education students and general education teachers, they saw a more inclusive culture. One leader shared, "The feedback is really telling of the mindset shift and how staff are feeling safe in sharing their fears and biases. They seem to value having the space to have these difficult conversations with one another."

Finally, another school began to explore the lack of representation in gifted education and ended up creating a model for accelerated learning for all students. This model resulted in students of color who were not identified as gifted outperforming white students who had been identified as gifted. This model pushed the school to rethink access to grade level and above instruction and to explore how school structures perpetuated inequities for students of color. This disruptive change drew the attention of parents and district leaders concerned about the lack of tailored programming for gifted students. Through the data collected in the DI process, the team was able to defend their choices and provide evidence of improved student outcomes for all students, including a 34% increase in students in Tier 1 for benchmark assessments in math.

These four schools represent the promise of a DI4E approach to school improvement as a process for interrogating systems of oppression and rethinking structures, processes, and practices that knowingly or unknowingly created inequitable opportunities, leading to a gap in student outcomes. This process relies on collaboration and a culture of trust, which is developed through shared values, vision, norms, routines, reciprocity, and interdependence. In other words, engaging in this approach to improvement can help to develop enabling conditions for change and progress toward addressing problems of practice. Furthermore, schools involved in DI, such as the first school example presented here, have been featured by the district for their gains. This school was able to make greater gains in literacy than schools involved in a two million dollar grant–funded effort. The district had this school share its learnings with the grant facilitators to help make greater strides in literacy systemwide.

We continue to iterate to improve toward a sustainable partnership committed to continuous improvement for equity in our PK–12 schools. Our district-wide NIC cohorts paused because of the pandemic. We've maintained a focus on professional learning and systems and structures but shifted our focus within those areas from design and coordination to building capacity and infrastructure. We have also committed to multi-year support for the schools, as we learned that one year was not enough time. Most importantly, we have increased our emphasis on equity and anti-racist practices.

Conclusions and Lessons Learned

The district has benefitted from having a long and strong partnership with DU-ELPS faculty serving as critical friends and key partners in helping to develop leaders committed to continuously improving. While this history of integrating continuous improvement efforts into the system helped provide a foundation for where we are today, the earlier efforts were happening in silos, in disconnected ways with varying methodologies being applied. A turning point was becoming a part of the iLEAD network because it set the expectation that senior district leaders engage in the work and allowed us to begin to learn with and from other partnerships. iLEAD helped us to recognize, we were not maximizing our potential impact because our approach was not yet strategic, coherent, or aligned.

It is important to name that our DI program targets current principals and school leadership teams. We have found that support beyond the principal pipeline is necessary to sustain our leader's capacity to lead continuous improvement for all students and redress long-standing inequities in educational opportunities and outcomes. Our current systems are inherently racist, and the energy and capacity to transform these systems require constant attention and intention. Additionally, evidence exists that continuous improvement practices are being incorporated into district leadership to help us get better at getting better as a district through this partnership.

We have not yet achieved aligned, sustained change but have the conditions in place to bring this out of the silo and into the ethos. We discovered we had to lean into our shared values, our reciprocity, and our interdependence which had been the backbone of our long partnership. It helped that the initial partnership work led to positive outcomes for both organizations creating a beneficial 'proof point' that built trust. Our shared beliefs have been that this work is about students first, and we emphasize working together to make schools better for each child disrupting systems of inequity and creating lasting change. These shared values allowed for a reciprocal relationship in which both organizations aligned their work around those shared values. We have also found our interdependence essential to our partnership. The ELPS faculty need to operate as part of the district not distinct from it, and to institutionalize change, faculty need to move beyond the surface level into deep, co-constructed work undergirded by relational trust. Additionally, we focused on not just creating a series of professional development activities but also on partnering on an emerging need and continuing to live the values.

These learnings have translated into five lessons learned that we think are valuable for institutionalizing and sustaining a partnership for continuous improvement.

LESSON 1: BE CLEAR ABOUT YOUR "WHY"—YOUR NORTH STAR GUIDES THE WAY

The goal of the work of the partnership transcends organizational boundaries. The goals are focused on improving socially just and equitable processes in schools to design conditions to improve equitable outcomes for students. To improve socially just and equitable schools, we must address gaps in opportunity, dismantle practices perpetuating racist school structures, and center the voices of teachers and families. Partnerships need to align improvement efforts around shared values. In this partnership, the shared belief is that this work is about students, and the emphasis is on working together to make schools better for each child, specifically students historically marginalized by the system. The partnership-centered practice had a common language around equity, which resulted in a shared improvement science methodology called DI4E.

LESSON 2: CREATE A SHARED THEORY OF IMPROVEMENT FOR YOUR PARTNERSHIP WORK AND USE IT AS A MAP TO REACH YOUR DESTINATION

Systems change is dependent on shared goals where the university and district create coherence and alignment through a student-centered approach to create lasting, equitable change, spreading DI4E to different conditions throughout the district—shifting from a program model to infusion into the district. The partnership created a shared theory of improvement and used it as a map to guide the work. Partnerships must be deliberate to avoid being just another initiative schools engage in, ensuring the work is institutionalized and sustained. We completed the developmental progressions together and cited evidence of improvement. Our partnership relied on this tool to help revise the theory of improvement and to identify areas for change in our partnership systems and structures and professional learning.

LESSON 3: INTERDEPENDENCE WAS ESSENTIAL TO THE PARTNERSHIP AND TO INCREASING EQUITY IN THE SYSTEM

Both partners bring diverse and critical perspectives, which are assets if leveraged strategically to accelerate the work. Specifically, university partners should operate as part of the district not distinct from it, and to institutionalize change, the university needs to move beyond the surface level into deep, co-constructed work undergirded by relational trust. This trust requires the educators in the systems to have psychological safety so that they can try new ideas without fear of repercussions or negative evaluations. Additionally, we found that partnering on a lasting initiative instead of focusing on creating a series of professional development activities could lead to more sustainable and equitable change. This work requires time and commitment to the district's outcomes. Finally, no one is positioned as the expert. Instead, we lean into our shared work and recognize that as researchers and district leaders, we should be engaged with the schools and be a part of the work—not separated from the work. What this looks like in practice is hosting weekly to monthly meetings to plan, study, and improve our approach, and university partners going into schools to see the work being applied and help tackle the barriers that arise in each unique context and condition. The role of coaches has been central to bridging multiple perspectives and to ensuring joint accountability and reciprocity between organizations.

LESSON 4: BE DISCIPLINED ABOUT A SHARED LEARNING AGENDA OR RESEARCH PLAN

Shared learning is essential. Partnerships need to be disciplined about learning by doing and working together as research–practice partners. University researchers must engage in the work alongside schools, as well as formalize collecting evidence and analyzing our work in real time. We believe the success of systems change is due to the process of critical analysis and evaluation of the work alongside all partners engaging directly in the work. This approach allowed us to capture knowledge and iterate the content, such as the DI4E methodology, and delivery of content, such as our coaching-centered model. It has also helped us to identify and write stories of success to spread the process to new schools and district leaders.

LESSON 5: DESPITE SHARED VALUES, NORMS, AND GOALS, THERE ARE STILL ORGANIZATIONAL VALUES AND CONDITIONS THAT WILL LIMIT SYSTEMS CHANGE

Over the partnership, there was some dissonance between the organizational values of higher education and K–12, including the sense of urgency that goes along with accountability. We have been able to address this tension by continuing to work together to put structures in place for us to meet regularly, clarify roles, talk through the challenges, and co-construct the next steps; however, these differences remain a challenge. Also, the complexity of this work is sometimes at odds with the myriad competing priorities being asked of schools. To ensure success, there must be an investment by district leaders, such as principal supervisors and district managers of the school improvement plan process, in supporting this work and helping to remove barriers to success. By having a co-designed onboarding plan for both district leaders and university faculty as well as the school leaders and leadership teams, it can help to mitigate some of these tensions.

Additionally, churn in both organizations, particularly at the highest levels of leadership, can be an impediment to continued progress. The work of this partnership is centered within departments and teams that are not directly connected to the priorities of the cabinet-level leadership of the district or the university. The partners must ensure that the stories of success are shared and that the cabinet leadership is aware of the progress being made. For these reasons and due to the length of time needed to make systems change, this work is vulnerable to being lost in the churn. For this work to be institutionalized and sustained, it requires active sponsorship from each organization's executives. Transforming a system demands shifts to "how we do business" and demands infrastructure and coherence. To achieve institutionalization, support is needed for removing barriers and building an improvement culture and improvement capacity not only within our schools but within our central office teams and university departments

Questions for Discussion

1. What are the equity priorities that will guide your work as your North Star? How might you create and identify the shared goals of your emerging, new, or sustained partnership based on that North Star? What would the goals be, and how can you leverage them to support students' learning experiences in schools and equitable structures and outcomes for students? What will success look like if your shared goals are achieved?
2. What values will serve as the guiding principles to anchor your work? What norms, working agreements, and routines will you establish based on those values?
3. How are you structuring learning to increase mutual reciprocity, interdependence, and learning by doing? How will you build trust and psychological safety? What systems, supports, and structures will create the conditions for your work to take root? How will you iterate to improve?

References

Anaissie, T., Cary, V., Clifford, D., Malarkey, T., & Wise, S. (2021). *Liberatory design.* National Equity Project. Retrieved June 30, 2022, from http://www.liberatorydesign.com

Bailey, S. (2016). *An examination of student and educator experiences in Denver Public Schools through the voices of African-American teachers and administrators.* Denver Public Schools Culture, Equity and Leadership Team. https://celt.dpsk12.org/wp-content/uploads/sites/52/Dr.-Bailey-Report-FULL-2.pdf

Bryk, A., Gomez, L., Grunow, A., & LeMahieu, P. (2015). *Learning to improve: How America's schools can get better at getting better.* Harvard University Press.

Carter, P., & Welner, K. (Eds.). (2013). *Closing the opportunity gap: What America must do to give every child an even chance.* Oxford University Press.

Crow, G. A., Arnold, N. R., Reed, C. J., & Shoho, A. R. (2012). The complexity of leveraging university program change. *Journal of Research on Leadership Education, 7*(2), 172–194.

Danielson, C. (2015, March 23). Helping educators overcome "initiative fatigue." *Education Week.* Retrieved June 30, 2022, from https://www.edweek.org/teaching-learning/opinion-helping-educators-overcome-initiative-fatigue/2015/03

Denver Public Schools. (2017, March 15). *DPS announces discipline reform for youngest students.* Retrieved June 30, 2022, from https://www.dpsk12.org/dps-announces-discipline-reform-for-youngest-students/

Hinnant-Crawford, B. (2020). *Improvement science in education: A primer.* Meyers Education Press.

Kania, J., Kramer, M., & Senge, P. (2018). *The water of systems change.* FSG. https://www.fsg.org/wp-content/uploads/2021/08/The-Water-of-Systems-Change_rc.pdf

Kelley, D., & Kelley, T. (2013). *Creative confidence: Unleashing the creative potential within us all.* Crown Business.

Korach, S., Anderson, E., Hesbol, K., Tabron, L., Candelarie, Doris, K., & Miller-Brown, E. (2019). Interdependence and reciprocity: Partnership ethos at the University of Denver. *Journal of Research on Leadership Education, 14*(1), 31–50. https://doi.org/10.1177/1942775118819679

Langley, G., Moen, R., Nolan, K., Thomas, N., & Provost, L. (2009). *The improvement guide: A practical approach to enhancing organizational performance.* John Wiley & Sons.

McKinsey and Company. (2021). *New allies: How governments can unlock the potential of social entrepreneurs for the common good.* Catalyst 20301. https://catalyst2030.net/wp-content/uploads/2021_New-Allies_How-governments-can-unlock-the-potential-of-social-entrepreneurs-for-the-common-good_vpublish.pdf

Mitang, L. (2012). *The making of the principal: Five lessons in leadership training.* The Wallace Foundation. https://www.wallacefoundation.org/knowledge-center/Documents/The-Making-of-the-Principal-Five-Lessons-in-Leadership-Training.pdf

Park, S., Hironaka, S., Carver, P., & Nordstrum, L. (2013) *Continuous improvement in education: Advancing teaching—Improving learning.* Carnegie Foundation for the Advancement of Teaching. https://www.carnegiefoundation.org/wp-content/uploads/2014/09/carnegie-foundation_continuous-improvement_2013.05.pdf

Turnbull, B., Riley, D., Arcaira, E., Anderson, L., & MacFarlane, J. (2013). *Six districts begin the principal pipeline initiative.* Policy Studies Associates, Inc. http://www.eric.ed.gov/contentdelivery/servlet/ERICServlet?accno=ED555867

CHAPTER 10

Organizational Changes' Impacts on University-District Partnership Development
UNIVERSITY OF SOUTH CAROLINA AND K–12 SCHOOL DISTRICT

Kathleen M. W. Cunningham, Peter Moyi, and Barnett Berry

This is a story that describes the partnership between the University of South Carolina (USC) and a South Carolina K–12 school district. With particular attention dedicated to the institution of higher education (IHE) in this case, we lean on organizational theory and two partnership frameworks to describe the progression, bright spots, and challenges the partnership experienced. In education, it feels risky for many reasons to illuminate the challenges and failures along with the successes of a new initiative. While uncomfortable, transparency is critical for our learning and contributing to the educational leadership field. We regularly ask educational professionals around us, including school building and district leaders and policymakers, to be transparent, and we expect this for ourselves as well. In this vein, we aim to share our partnership case with its bright spots, challenges, imperfections, struggles, and critical learnings so those readers embarking on their partnership journey might be able to anticipate where barriers could arise to prepare for and avoid or mitigate them.

A key tenet in improvement science is learning from and examining the conditions in the system that are leading to the current outcomes (Bryk et al., 2015). As Dr. Paul Batalden and other improvers have captured, "Every system is perfectly designed to get the results it gets."[1] In the following pages, we dissect some elements and contexts within our system design that led to the results we got. First, we offer an introduction to our case and then provide literature connected to the partnership work. Next, through describing our case's development of a new district-university partnership, including the what, why, and how of the partnership, we move to describe progress and evidence realized to different degrees. Finally, we offer lessons learned, categorized as three organizational considerations that have become instrumental in guiding our subsequent

---

[1] Paul B. Batalden, MD, is Emeritus Professor of the Dartmouth Institute. https://geiselmed.dartmouth.edu/faculty/facultydb/view.php/?uid=53

partnership work. These considerations are: (1) clearly defining goals and expectations; (2) establishing a core partnership team with consistent membership and leadership; and (3) leaning on a continuous improvement mindset to guide reflection and learning.

Context

In 2017, stakeholders at the University of South Carolina (USC) identified the Carnegie Foundation for the Advancement of Teaching's Improvement Leadership Education and Development (iLEAD) network as a promising opportunity to cultivate a meaningful district-university partnership with Myrtle Creek School District (MCSD) (pseudonym), a K–12 school district in South Carolina.

UNIVERSITY OF SOUTH CAROLINA COLLEGE OF EDUCATION

The University of South Carolina (USC) is the flagship university in the state. It is located in the capital city of Columbia and categorized as a Research I university. UCS's College of Education (CoE) houses four academic departments: Educational Leadership and Policies (EDLP), Educational Studies (Ed Studies), Instruction and Teacher Education (ITE), and Physical Education (PE). The CoE "strives to be a leader locally, regionally, nationally, and internationally by fostering an environment where diversity, equity, and inclusion are affirmed, celebrated, and vigorously pursued" (CoE, n.d.).

Our iLEAD partnership, while initially involving faculty from both the ITE and EDLP departments, shifted to involve primarily EDLP faculty. Notably, during the second year of the partnership, there were multiple personnel changes in EDLP, including one additional staff hire and three new faculty hires at the assistant professor level focused on K–12 educational leadership and policy (one being one of the authors). The hires helped bolster the capacity needed to dedicate resources (e.g., time, knowledge) towards developing the partnership and forwarding the improvement processes. In the three years that followed, EDLP lost two staff members, three faculty members to retirement, and three faculty members moved out of state to pursue other opportunities.

In addition to iLEAD, the CoE was also engaged with The Center for Teaching Quality (CTQ), a national nonprofit that works with school districts, universities, state agencies, and education associations to transform teaching, learning, and leadership. CTQ believes in the collective capacity of educators to be powerful levers for change and improvement. Therefore, CTQ collaborates with teachers, school administrators, and district leaders to create solutions to improve public education. CTQ was separately working with school districts in the state, including Myrtle Creek School District.

We, the authors, are current faculty at USC and are directly connected to this work. We are writing, reflecting on, and analyzing our experiences in the iLEAD partnership. As insiders, we are positioned to identify places of loose coupling since we know the nature of what was done and not done from the IHE role and perspective in the partnership (Weick, 1976).

Myrtle Creek School District

The Myrtle Creek School District (MCSD) is located in a community of about 75,000. The district is among the top 15 largest school districts in South Carolina and about a 90-minute drive from the university. The district consists of eight total high schools and middle schools, and 15 elementary schools, including one charter school and one magnet school (MCSD, 2022).

Like EDLP, MCSD experienced several leadership changes during the partnership initiation stage, including a new superintendent, key central office personnel, and new building leadership appointments. The improvement work began with Myrtle Creek High School (MCHS, pseudonym), which hired a new principal that year. One school was selected as the partnership planned to start small, then would scale up to include the feeder middle school and feeder elementary schools, to then eventually scale to the schools across the district. The high school involved in the partnership served over 1,500 students in grades 9–12.

THE PARTNERSHIP BETWEEN COE/EDLP AND MCSD

For the CoE, iLEAD served as the springboard to broach and navigate a brand new partnership with a local education agency (LEA). At the partnership's inception, a small group of people including administrators from the CoE and MCSD, CoE faculty members, and building principals and teachers saw promise in cultivating a new partnership. One such promising area was in line with previous research (e.g., Korach et al., 2019) that demonstrates how partnerships can include mutually beneficial co-designed programming. The CoE and MCSD representatives discussed the development of an education doctorate program (EdD) in systems leadership that would involve a cohort of leadership students from MCSD. MCSD would benefit from building the internal leadership capacity of the district, while the CoE would enroll graduate students in their EdD program.

The literature describes the structures and characteristics of strong partnerships (see King, 2014; Sanzo et al., 2011; Penuel et al., 2015; Davis, 2016; Young et al., 2022). Benefits and the elements of successful university-school district partnerships are well-documented and describe the presence of shared goals within these relationships, stakeholders from both organizations involved in carrying out these goals, and each organization gaining benefits from the relationship (e.g., King, 2014; Korach et al., 2019; Sanzo et al., 2011; Walsh & Backe, 2013). By contrast, there is less empirical research focused on the impact and outcomes of partnership. Still, scholars with long-standing preparation program–school district partnerships such as North Carolina State University's Northeast Leadership Academy (NELA) program (Fusarelli et al., 2018), University of Illinois at Chicago in their partnership with Chicago Public Schools (Cosner et al., 2015), University of Denver's long-standing relationship with Denver Public Schools (Korach et al., 2018), and University of Texas at San Antonio's work with San Antonio's Independent School District (Merchant & Garza, 2015), offer the field rich depictions of how their partnerships have resulted in mutually beneficial outcomes such as having an established educational leadership pipeline and a group of leaders familiar with the districts' pressing needs as well as consistent enrollment in the university preparation program (Cunningham et al., 2019).

Similarly, Darling-Hammond et al. (2010) describe how district-university partnerships can strengthen university preparation programming and thus bolster the leadership capacity of educational leadership candidates. Coburn and Penuel (2016) describe how these relationships can center the synergy of research with practice in beneficial ways. Literature on partnerships between universities and school districts also acknowledges the benefit of university-program relevance and the boundary-spanning roles that those involved can take (e.g., King, 2014), which invites cohesion across organizations (Howey & Zimpher, 2007) and more deliberate connections between research and practice (Penuel et al., 2015; Sanzo et al., 2011).

In relation to iLEAD participation, the CoE envisioned how the work would be anchored in the expectation of developing both teacher and school leaders, de-siloing practitioners to create more opportunities for them to observe, experience, and explore innovative practices and using improvement science to address problems of practice. One challenge that emerged as time went on was that several sets of goals or conceptualizations of what the partnership would do and offer existed simultaneously. We will revisit the point about goal articulation and cohesion later, but for example, here are some of the goals of this relationship:

1. Establish a strong partnership between the university and the school district to identify and recognize teachers to lead pedagogical reforms and principals who are effective in helping them do so.
2. Redesign graduate courses around specific competencies that provide evidence of performance and self-paced course completion.
3. Ensure that courses build on each other and are focused specifically on transforming high-need schools.

Further, and in addition to the three listed goals above, the CoE and MCSD administrators and faculty involved early in the relationship envisioned that involvement in iLEAD would result in teachers and school leaders feeling empowered to "not always take orders." District administrators sought to leverage iLEAD involvement as "a tool to change mindsets and grow leadership from within the district" (Berry, 2017, meeting notes). CoE and MCSD administrators saw an opportunity for MCSD educators to develop their leadership capacity through taking courses in the CoE. Specifically, MCSD anticipated enrolling a group of their educators in a more "personalized" graduate degree at USC (i.e., the aforementioned EdD program) that would "unfix" perceived fixed mindsets related to school leadership. In alignment with the Carnegie Foundation for the Advancement of Teaching's (hereafter referred to as Carnegie) work related to improvement science, the CoE stakeholders sought to "infuse improvement science in all of its master's and doctoral leadership programs" (Berry, 2018, field notes). It was anticipated that a district cohort would pilot the model. The online EdD would include a course in improvement science and support doctoral students in the improvement science process. The CoE and MCSD sought to develop leaders at multiple levels (e.g., classrooms, schools, districts) who use improvement science as a vehicle for inquiry into problems that connect education and social equity. In line with the nature of improvement science, the partnership leveraged the collaborative improvement network to explore preparation and school development challenges and co-constructing a model of improvement science enhanced with theories that relate societal equity with education.

In addition to the development of the EdD, other programs were also discussed. The CoE wanted to design robust graduate courses and programs while accelerating more personalization of professional learning in the context of heavy enrollment and a fully online delivery. Attention was given to developing a coherent program rather than a survey of professional literature with individual courses taught in isolation from one another. Programs were to embed improvement science research methods to address problems of practice, in the process preparing teachers and administrators to be change agents in the district. This was realized to different degrees as the partnership evolved.

Over the next few academic years, the partnership navigated a winding, but promising terrain where those closely involved experienced bursts of momentum, but also regularly traversed rocky pathways where unclear goals, challenging logistics, personnel turnover, and external challenges (e.g., COVID-19 pandemic) impacted the partnership's foundation and footing.

Developing and Sustaining a District-University Partnership

This chapter differs from others in this volume. While other chapters' articulated problems and partnership work centered on a shared problem of practice that the partnership works to address, in our chapter, we focus instead on how partners initiate and sustain a formal relationship.

In this section, we describe our trajectory in developing and sustaining the partnership. We make connections to Trubowitz's (1986) partnership stages, current literature on partnerships, and iLEAD's Developmental Progressions framework (DPs). We interpret these challenges and deepen our understanding of the partnership journey using a constellation of considerations from organizational theory (i.e., organizational coupling, Weick, 1976) with partnership frameworks (i.e., Developmental Progressions, Carnegie, 2020, and a partnership-stage model, Trubotiwz, 1986). The notion of loose and tight coupling, proposed by Weick (1976), is a helpful lens to view our partnership because he argues that in loosely coupled systems, "coupled events are responsive, but that each event also preserves its own identity and some evidence of its physical or logical separateness" (p. 3); where the maintenance of separation of events contributes to benefits of cultivating a partnership as well as reveals the weakness in the relationship structure. Weick (1976) described coupling as the degree of interdependence and connectivity between systems or organizations. He also articulates both advantages and disadvantages of loose coupling (see table 10.1). This concept contributes, from a theoretical perspective, to our sensemaking relative to how our loosely coupled organizations responded to common and unique external variables in our partnership context(s).

Table 10.1 **Advantages and Disadvantages of Loosely Coupled Systems**

Advantages	Disadvantages
• Little reaction from environmental changes • The existence of perceptive mechanisms related to changes in the organizations • Local contexts can adapt to changes • Invitations to develop creative solutions to issues and challenges • Protection from breakdowns in the system as they are insulated or disconnected from the other parts of the organization • High levels of efficacy • Autonomy and resistance • Less expensive	• Outdated systems and procedures may be perpetuated • Have fewer standardized processes established • May encounter barriers to the diffusion of ideas and/or changes for improvement • Experience unstable decision-making as it relates to funding, which can impact change efforts

Note: Adapted from Weick, 1976

TWO PARTNERSHIP FRAMEWORKS: ILEAD'S DEVELOPMENTAL PROGRESSIONS AND THE STAGE MODEL

We use Trubowitz's (1986) partnership stages with Carnegie's (2020) Developmental Progressions framework while suggesting that partnerships can also be viewed through an organizational theory lens (i.e., tight and loose coupling). These offer a framework that recognizes the challenges and bright spots at different stages of the relationship and improvement work. We will see elements of coupling that emerge in different moments by different organizational and partnership stakeholders.

Developmental Progressions (Carnegie Foundation for the Advancement of Teaching, 2020)

Carnegie outlines a schema that captures iLEAD partnership work for improvement. The Developmental Progressions (Carnegie Foundation for the Advancement of Teaching, 2020) organizes the development of three distinct organizational entities: (1) the local education agency (LEA) or K–12 School/School District (e.g., MCSD), (2) the institution of higher education (IHE) (e.g., USC), and (3) the partnership between the IHE (college/school of education) and the LEA/school district (e.g., USC-CoE + MCSD/MCHS). As a tool, the Developmental Progressions serve as a "set of shared understandings [developed] within the community and guide its ongoing improvement efforts. It is intended to offer an overview for the journey ahead and a compelling vision of the 'good' that we seek to accomplish together" (Carnegie Foundation for the Advancement of Teaching, 2020, p. 1). Organizational elements related to improvement work are described in the Developmental Progressions on a four-stage continuum that moves from "Exploring Change Ideas," to "Small Change Implementation," to "Integrating IS/NIC into the Core Work to Institutionalizing and Sustaining the Work."

Stage Model (Trubowitz, 1986)

To complement the Developmental Progressions, we also reference a framework offered by Trubowitz (1986) who cogently described a stage model of district-university partnerships arguing that these partnerships navigate a relationship terrain. He proposes eight stages that we summarize below. While arguably rigid, this framework serves as a heuristic tool to situate how the partnership evolved from initiation to eventual separation. A brief description of each stage Trubowitz (1986) proposes follows:

Stage 1—Hostility and Skepticism capture hesitation and a sense of being guarded when university faculty enter the space as there is a perception they will attempt to do or dictate things *to* their K–12 partner, rather than working collaboratively *with* their partner. Trubowitz (1986) notes that communication and relationship-building efforts—particularly on the part of the university representatives—are key during this stage.

Stage 2—Lack of Trust exists at the beginning of district-university partnerships and partially stems from the partnership origin decision since it is typically made by upper-level administrators, engendering a perception that teachers are not performing well. Continuing to build trust and nurturing relationships and seeking ways members of each organization can participate in the other's work. Trubowitz suggests having teachers as guest speakers in IHE classes as one example of participation.

Stage 3—Period of Truce is entered as negative feelings dissolve as positive experiences are shared, relationships are built, and roles and intentions gain clarity. Trubowitz specifically points out the effective actions he observed when "professors and teachers participated as equals in in-service programs, when they attended the same parties, went on trips, and played in student-faculty softball and basketball games" (p. 20).

Stage 4—Mixed Approval is a stage reached as those professors who had positive relationships with staff could successfully shepherd change and offer guidance while serving as "advocates for the [school] staff" (p. 20).

Stage 5—Acceptance is reached when it became clear who was committed to the work and who was not. The consistency of committed faculty members developed goodwill and positive partnership culture and climate.

Stage 6—Regression happens when inevitable personnel changes take place that result in changes in the partnership dynamic. The pace of work might change, the norms in work may change, and increased efforts are likely to be employed to keep the momentum moving forward until all the new people in their new roles are on board. In Trubowitz's partnership work, he noted that "collaboration could easily have foundered at this stage" (p. 21).

Stage 7—Renewal involved pushing through the regression by engaging in a recalibration and revisiting the goals of the work leaning on the members of the partnership and some external thought partners. During this time, the partnership committs to meeting regularly with deliverables. Their explicit actions to nurture the partnership resulted in renewed enthusiasm for the partnership work.

Stage 8—Continuing Progress is a stage where the partnership works through growing pains and challenges to move along the pathway of working toward their improvement.

While each partnership has its unique context and rhythm and may evolve differently (and perhaps differently from what Trubowitz (1986) posits), Barnett and colleagues (2010) argue that the common purpose of a partnership "is to form an alliance of resources and expertise between organizations aimed at achieving a mutually desired outcome, one that is not likely to be realized without the involvement of both parties" (p. 14–15). Next, we summarize our journey, capturing how the partnership progressed and where the work stalled.

PARTNERSHIP JOURNEY

The journey of this partnership takes place over the course of four years, and we will briefly outline the story from initiation to ending the partnership (Young et al., 2022). It was anticipated that the partnership between USC and MCSD members would be poised to collaboratively explore, then implement and test change ideas.

Early on there were six key stakeholders from USC and MCSD engaged in initial partnership consultations who all traveled to San Francisco to attend the 2017 Carnegie Summit together. At the Summit, the group engaged in discussion about iLEAD and improvement science and it has been reported that the conversations and interactions among the university and district partners revealed that group members held different understandings of the purposes of the partnership. Further, several people involved at these initial consultation meetings (i.e., Carnegie Summit as well as local meetings) held new or interim roles in their organization (e.g., district superintendent and USC department chair). Indeed, from the start of the partnership, two major challenges were present almost immediately: (1) undefined shared goals and (2) leadership transitions at both the MCSD and the USC. In fact, between years one and two of the partnership, the district hired a superintendent and the principal at the high school and the university hired three faculty members. These changes contributed to the decision to shift the core iLEAD partnership representatives. Despite changes in personnel (which are not unusual in school-district or university settings), the partnership work began with faculty from EDLP and teachers and a principal from one school. Rather than determining a shared problem of practice, the group came together to identify a local problem of practice that was present at one school that the partnership could collaboratively improve in that local context. The school could address the problem with support from EDLP faculty and the faculty would be able to capture the process by conducting research.

Improvement Work Begins

Until this time, the initiative was more often discussed at the district-level; not at the local school level. Year two started with our iLEAD team consisting of the high school principal, the department chair from EDLP, and several EDLP faculty members. Despite the fact that membership was fluid at this point related to representatives from the MCHS and EDLP, an overarching local problem of practice was stated: "to help fully realize the stated mission of developing world class citizens through addressing racial inequities" (MCHS, n.d.). In addition, the team identified five interrelated research/improvement science areas to explore for determining a problem of practice: societal bias, discipline, school culture/climate, policy, and curriculum/pedagogy.

During this period, EDLP faculty members began to make regular visits during the school year to MCHS to meet and learn more about the staff, spend time in the school, and discuss improvement and research areas. The authentic improvement work centered on identifying and understanding the school's problem of practice emerged after some time; we surmise this was partly due to the varying levels of familiarity with improvement science approaches to addressing problems of practice; notably, this is in alignment with the first two stages of Trubowitz's model where, because the relationship is new, trust is not yet fully developed.

Establishment of a Core Improvement Team

A key partnership turning point happened when a consistent school-based improvement team was established. Five teachers from the MCHS were involved, each teaching a different subject area. The teachers were collaborative, thoughtful, and connected to the work. University faculty members' consideration of partnership members' roles and an acute awareness of the documented history of institutions of higher education going in and doing things *to* districts and not *with* districts (Partnership Stage 1–Trubowitz, 1986) made role definitions blurry. Internalized tensions existed for EDLP faculty who did not want to "take charge" while also recognizing an opportunity to lighten the loads of the teachers and principal on the improvement team (e.g., creating shared folders to organize the partnership and improvement work, developing iLEAD meeting agendas, leading conversations surrounding group norms and improvement science approaches, organizing meeting materials such as chart paper, post-it notes). Since the MCHS team members were extremely busy, university faculty saw places where they might step in, while also remaining cognizant of perceptions of roles in the partnership. For instance, there was a period of navigating and settling upon what the partnership entailed and who was responsible for what (e.g., agenda setting and data gathering).

The improvement work progressed as the team developed. With EDLP faculty serving as facilitators and thought partners, the team co-created group norms to guide decision-making and interpersonal dynamics when building consensus. These norms were (1) listen with understanding, be an active listener; (2) disagreements are okay, but be respectful; (3) be intentional in what is being said and think about how your words will be interpreted by someone else; (4) when we come to a consensus, commit to it; (5) be willing to talk about "scary topics" because it will lead to trust; and (6) work to build cohesion. Meetings had agendas developed collaboratively and captured by a faculty member who distributed the agenda information. Spending time collaborating and gaining a better understanding of working toward improving a problem of practice, a joint public presentation opportunity, and traveling together to iLEAD convenings helped deepen the relationship and engender trust among those in the partnership because communication and understanding grew (Stages 3 and 4– Trubowitz, 1986).

The improvement team engaged in improvement science methods to deeply understand the overarching local problem. First, the MCHS improvement team started the work by naming a problem they were seeing in their school: the inequitable access to opportunities for students of color. Local data and practical expertise (Carnegie, 2020; Hinnant-Crawford, 2021) helped illuminate this problem area. A theory of action to address the problem of practice emerged; and while it was developed with our school-based partner, it also intersected with the district's priorities and mission. The theory read:

> If we use and develop capacity within the utilization of an improvement science framework with consideration of societal, cultural, historical, and philosophical dimensions of the problem, then we will be able to make observable impact on addressing racial opportunity/achievement gaps in the district.

The developed theory of action and improvement work was anticipated to be scaled to other schools in the district in the future. Over the course of multiple meetings, EDLP faculty members facilitated a brainstorming session for the MCHS improvement team to engage with a root cause analysis process. As the school-based team offered insights and suggestions related to any reasons they might think of for what might be impacting their problem, the faculty captured them for later organization into a fishbone-type diagram (see figure 10.1). This diagram does not have the shape of the "fish," like in a traditional fishbone or Ishikawa diagram, but it nonetheless captures factors and sub-factors contributing to what is preventing and contributing to the aim not being met. This organizational schema also helped the team capture factors that are cross-cutting among several elements.

The brainstorming session led the group to scan the landscape of the problem and engage in continued discussions about root causes. When reviewing the causes identified, they organized them and continued to reflect on root causes as well. The team identified which areas would have to be addressed first in order to address some of the other areas. Over many weeks, the improvement team iterated their aim statement because they determined equitable opportunities could not be achieved (aim 1.0) if the culture/climate to bring everyone on board was not addressed first (aim 2.0). But the team posited that developing a strong school climate and culture could not be realized until the staff engages in the difficult work of examining themselves, the existing school and district policies, typical practices, or their system (aim 3.0), which, because this work is relational, cannot be accomplished effectively if the disconnect that exists between teachers and teachers and between teachers and students is not addressed (aim 4.); and this work is predicated on the trust between and among the stakeholders. The team surmised that the relationships and connections students and teachers developed (or lack thereof) was likely the critical linchpin that would need direct attention to create a school system that provided equitable opportunities for all students. In other words, they hypothesized that positive relationships need to be present for equitable opportunities for students to be realized. See a team artifact that emerged from this work in figure 10.2.

Following this aim statement iteration process, the team moved to the concept of empathy interviews (Carnegie, 2020; High Tech High, n.d.) to better understand the

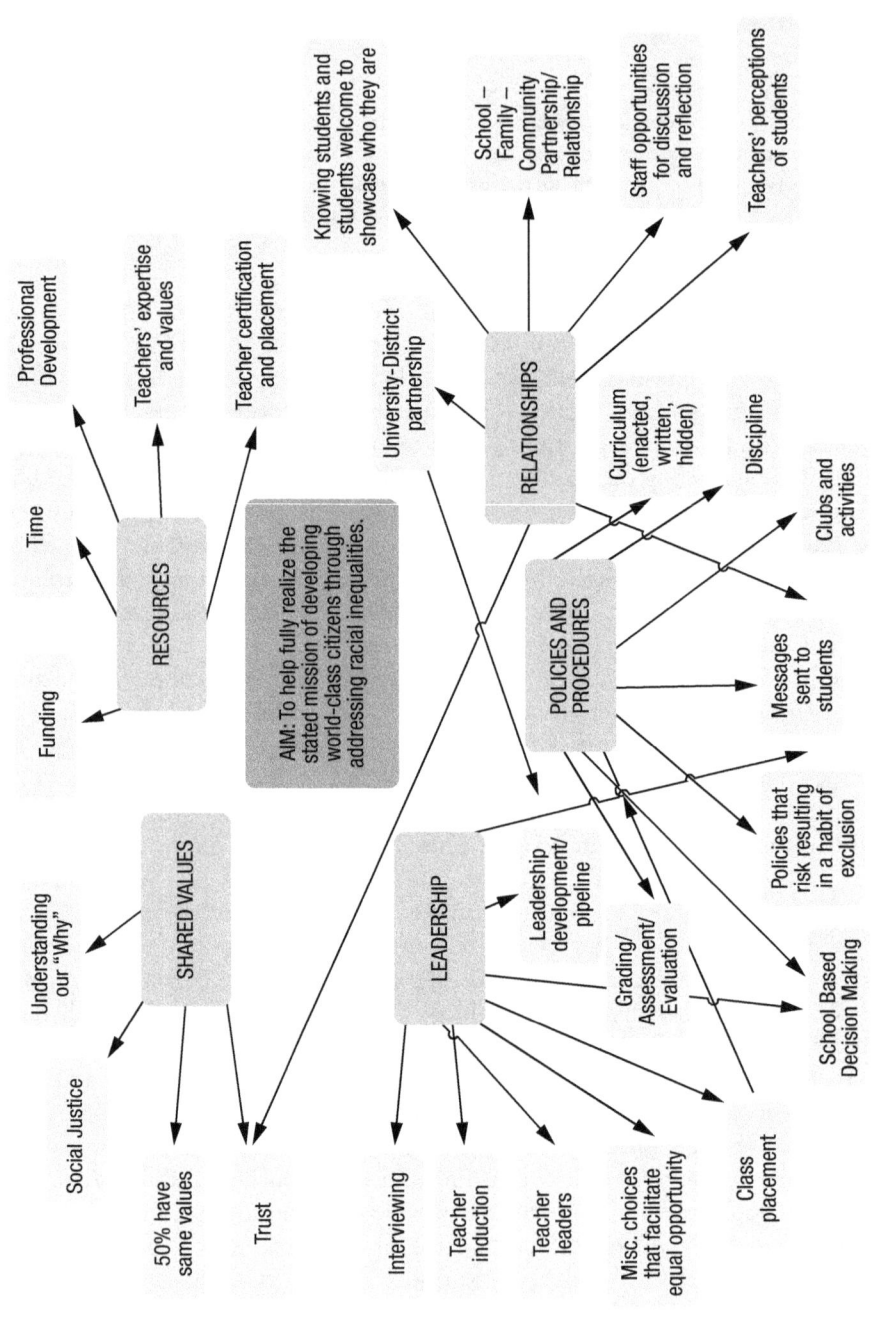

Figure 10.1 Causal systems analysis sample.

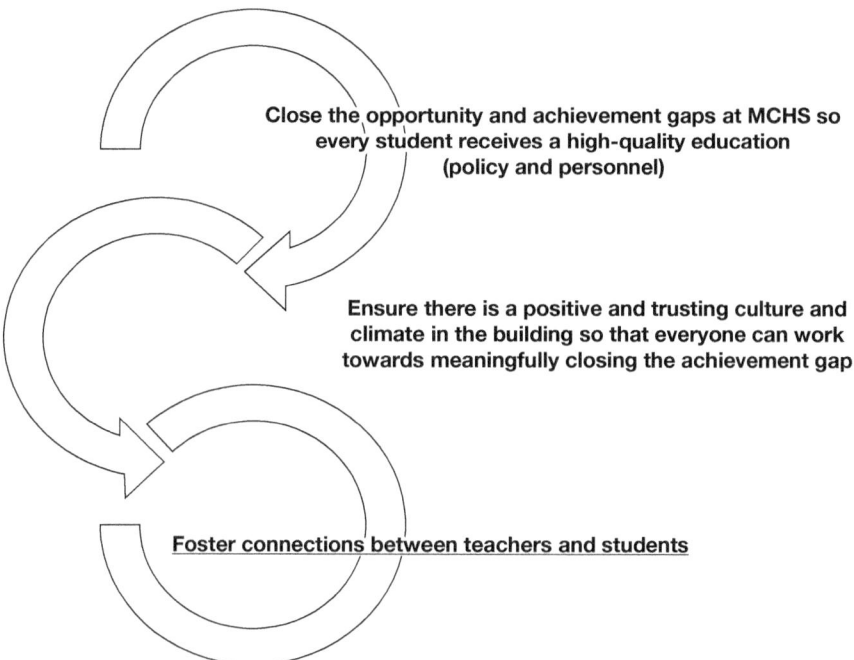

Figure 10.2 Partnership artifact: Evolution of aim statement.

stakeholder experience related to their aim. The school-based team planned to engage in a version of empathy interviews to seek insights from teachers, students, and parents and chose to do so through a structured interview protocol (Glesne, 2011) containing short, open-ended questions distributed electronically. The team was coordinating effectively with one another at this point in time and the representatives seemed to be working well together and were committed to improvement (Stage 5–Trubowitz, 1986). Then, as the empathy interview data were being gathered, the COVID-19 pandemic hit the United States, forcing students, teachers, and university professors to rapidly transition to a fully online setting and would remain fully online for the remainder of the school year. This unpredictable time led to the pause of the partnership improvement work, and the eventual stoppage of the partnership followed.

At the conclusion of the 2019–2020 school year, leadership roles at each organization turned over. The numerous stressors related to elements such as the pandemic plus the shifting in leadership pushed the partnership into the Regression stage (Stage 6–Trubowitz, 1986). As referenced above, Trubowitz (1986) warns that "collaboration could easily have floundered at this stage" (p. 21). Indeed, that is what happened, and the partnership never regained its footing.

While the partnership did not continue, we can share several bright spots of the work. The iLEAD initiative organized by Carnegie identifies three organizations or elements involved in improvement work: (1) the LEA/K–12 School (MCSD), (2) the IHE/Department (EDLP), and (3) the Partnership as its own distinct entity. Penuel et al. (2020) wrote in their article on research–practice partnerships that educational systems need to change in order to realize lasting improvement, and through some changes, progress was made in different ways. Starting with the partnership as a collective, next we briefly describe organizational, or system changes experienced by the partnership and the IHE utilizing the Developmental Progressions (Carnegie, 2020) to pinpoint progress.

ORGANIZATIONAL PROGRESS: PARTNERSHIP

As trust between and among individuals from each organization grew, the collective improvement team (i.e., USC members and MCSD members) recognized and felt pride in the progress the team was making. In fact, representatives from both organizations traveled to the iLEAD winter convening together in February 2020, which took place mere weeks before COVID-19's nationwide shut down including the transition of schools and universities to a fully virtual space.

Table 10.2 identifies which areas of the Developmental Progressions the partnership met. Unfortunately, overall, despite making promising strides, the progress of the partnership as a collective did not yield as much progress as the IHE did independently.

As illustrated in the table, the partnership never moved past the "Exploring Change Ideas" or "Small Change Implementation" categories on the Developmental Progressions (Carnegie Foundation for the Advancement of Teaching, 2020).

ORGANIZATIONAL PROGRESS: USC (I.E., COE AND EDLP)

Participation in the iLEAD partnership by EDLP faculty members benefited the IHE in several ways. Participation helped inform the design of the doctoral level (i.e., EdD) improvement science course, increased the capacity of iLEAD-participating faculty to support their graduate students in improvement work, and provided a reflective learning space to examine how the partnership was progressing and how the partnership's challenges could be addressed. iLEAD participation expanded the professional network of participating faculty members, leading to guest speakers from the iLEAD initiative visiting USC classes, sharing resources, and opportunities for professional learning, growth, and collaboration. Notably, the progress achieved at the IHE was done in a way that was relatively disconnected from the iLEAD-centric work since those actions were directed more toward the school-based problem of practice effort.

From an organizational standpoint, faculty members from EDLP found opportunities to incorporate (to different degrees) improvement science into their various degree-seeking programs. While the partnership began, so too did the EDLP Department and CoE's planning and proposing of the new strand of the College's EdD: Education Systems Improvement. Recall that an original intent of this strand was to have a full EdD cohort of MCSD students enrolled where they would use improvement science in their own settings across the district to identify problems of practice to be the topics of their dissertation in practice (DiP) work. This held the potential to more tightly couple EDLP with the MCSD since there would be increased capacity for district improvement and program design considerations. In the end, the EdD strand was approved and launched in the Fall 2020 semester and is populated with students from a variety of

Table 10.2 Partnership Development and the Developmental Progressions

Developmental Progression Objective	Developmental Progression Level	Evidence
"One or more problems of practice have been jointly identified by the local IHE-LEA partners as options for students to pursue in their coursework."	Small Change Implementation (Level 2)	School-based problem of practice identified by district and improvement team
"Regular meetings and possible other activities are occurring and provide a basis for exploring working relationships."	Small Change Implementation (Level 2)	Monthly meetings at MCHS
Identification of "key issues around which formal agreements could be established."	Exploring Change Ideas (Level 1)	iLEAD participation
University of South Carolina IRB.	Small Change Implementation (Level 2)	IRB approval received
"Partnership members are exploring how to work together using IS/NICs to improve their respective and joint efforts."	Exploring Change Ideas (Level 1)	Strategies used to understand the problem (e.g., existing data root cause analysis/fishbone, empathy interview data)
"Conversations are underway about enrolling cohorts of teacher-leaders/future principal candidates in the IHE."	Small Change Implementation (Level 2)	Informational meetings and discussion about cohort possibility
"A distinctive partnership narrative is emerging: 'What this is; Why are we doing it; Why this really matters for our educators and their students.'"	Small Change Implementation (Level 2)	Travel together, informational document created and shared with District Leadership

Note: Carnegie Foundation for the Advancement of Teaching, 2020, p. 2

school districts, institutions of higher education, and across different states and countries; notably, none are from the iLEAD partner district. Students in the EdD in Education Systems Improvement take a course dedicated to improvement science approaches in their first semester and participate in a two-day summer Improvement Science Institute after their first and second years. While MCSD was not actively involved in EDLP EdD program design discussions, the partnership work helped inform the design of these curricular opportunities. In alignment with the Developmental Progressions, table 10.3 captures a sample of elements in the IHE portion of the Developmental Progressions, and the levels attained across these selected objectives.

Table 10.3 IHE Development and the Developmental Progressions

Developmental Progression Objective	Developmental Progression Level	Evidence
IS/NICs are recognized as a departmental or divisional priority (versus just one or two interested faculty members)	Integrating IS/NIC into the core work (Level 3)	EdD students encouraged to do an IS DiP
A coherent program of study is being formulated from introductory courses to capstone projects	Integrating IS/NIC into the core work (Level 3)	EdD students required to take an improvement science course (EDLP 734); work related to DiP infused into multiple courses in the EdD
Professional development supports for faculty in teaching and coaching IS/NICs have been identified and discussions are underway as to how to strengthen IHE capabilities	Small Change Implementation (Level 2)	Resources available for all EDLP faculty to increase capacity and understanding of improvement science and improvement DiPs
iLEAD faculty are cultivating interest among their colleagues about the potential for integrating of IS/NICs in their program work	Exploring Change Ideas (Level 1)	Discussion related to how improvement science can inform internal development have taken place
IS is now publicly recognized as a signature pedagogy for the education leadership program	Integrating IS/NIC into the core work. (Level 3)	EdD program encourages DiPs design that use improvement science
Issues have been satisfactorily resolved and new program designs are now moving forward	Integrating IS/NIC into the core work (Level 3)	State permission granted for the development of the EdD strand in systems improvement

Challenges

The focus of this section of the book is centered on how to develop and sustain a partnership. We present four challenges the partnership faced. These challenges will then be reframed and expanded upon later in the Lessons Learned portion of the chapter.

CHALLENGE 1: MULTIPLE, EVOLVING GOALS

Well-defined organizational goals aim to accomplish several things. They serve as an anchor point to which work can be directed, invite clarity related to how an organization's mission and vision will be realized, and provide a consistent message throughout the organization that can eliminate confusion or convoluted interpretations of the work (McDiarmid & Caprino, 2019; Scott & Davis, 2007). As we touched on earlier (i.e., we listed three early goals), and as you may have already gleaned from reading our story up to this point, there were varying purposes and goals related to this partnership that different stakeholders held.

Reflecting on this present case, it appears that different sets of goals were developed at different times of the partnership's inception. For example, one set of goals was broad and overarching and some goals evolved as the partnership progressed. There were at least 13 goals or aims focused on partnering for the iLEAD initiative. Due to space limitations, we will not provide all the goals and purposes, as the broader take-away is not necessarily what was in the goals, but that there were simply too many goals that were not refined into an agreed-upon priority list from which to determine a partnership plan of action. The lack of cohesion and commitment to a clearly constructed and complementary set of goals likely resulted in different stakeholder groups and individual stakeholders prioritizing their own pursuits. The presence of so many goals muddied the waters of the work's direction. Prior research points out that this can easily occur in educational preparation partnerships. For example, in their study of partnering in teacher preparation, Yamagata-Lynch and Smaldino (2007) wrote:

> Individuals involved in K–12 and university partnerships do not necessarily share a clear sense of the vision, mission, or goals of their partnership or even at times of their own institution. Individuals who are involved in partnership activities are often not administrators who have direct influence on institutional goals. Consequently, partnership participants find it very challenging to clearly communicate to one another what their institutional goals are in order to build mutually beneficial relations.
>
> (p. 365)

Goals seemed to be focused more so on the work of EDLP such as research, preparation programming, learning from other IHEs, and their role in the partnership. While these aims are worthy and helpful, they provide only a partial picture of the iLEAD efforts since we do not have similarly developed lists of goals and early aims for the district or of the partnership relationship.

Reflecting on prior discussions and reviewing organizational documents (e.g., the proposal for iLEAD participation) makes evident that too many goals and expectations were held by different stakeholder groups. And while there is evidence of progress on some goals, the ability to fully realize the goals was unattainable due to a lack of clarity, lack of consensus, leadership changes, and competing priorities.

CHALLENGE 2: LOGISTICS (DISTANCE, FUNDING, TIME–COMPETING PRIORITIES)

The logistics of the partnership presented unique challenges from its start. The most basic is that the two organizations were not close in proximity. The 90-minute drive presented scheduling challenges for CoE faculty who would drive to the partner site for meetings after school. Next, the partnership was agreed upon by high-level organizational leaders with many representatives involved who had never met one another prior to iLEAD. Third, the relationship was developing at a time when CoE was experiencing financial constraints and budget cuts. While some financial elements of the initiative received financial support from Carnegie, the initiative was largely unfunded and grouped into the "service" category of the typical research, teaching, and service delineations of EDLP faculty work expectations. This is an important consideration because the categories of research and teaching receive a larger percentage of work dedication per the job description and tenure and promotion expectations. Several of the EDLP faculty involved in the partnership had the pressure of publishing to meet tenure and/or promotion requirements.

CHALLENGE 3: PERSONNEL AND LEADERSHIP TRANSITIONS

Partnership work is strengthened with supportive involvement from upper-level leadership (e.g., Merchant & Garza, 2015). Partnership members did receive explicit support to cultivate a partnership between EDLP and MCSH that utilized improvement science to address pressing problems of practice in schools. The improvement processes and actions involved were almost exclusively carried out by two mid-organizational levels: (a) school level and (b) university department level. While there are advantages that accompany local decision-making, system-level leadership involvement was limited. Further, when challenges emerge, intervention, encouragement, and creative engagement by system-level leaders could assist partnership team members in navigating them. This becomes increasingly challenging when accompanied by frequent personnel churn, which this partnership also experienced.

Leadership turnover poses challenges to educational organizations. Honig's (2004) research included turnover as a factor that challenged connections across positions and organizational levels. Snodgrass Rangel's (2018) literature review noted that principal turnover could relate to both positive and negative levels or perceptions of school culture and climate, with more of the reviewed studies indicating negative impacts. Turnover can challenge the foundation of a partnership, and both MCSD and USC underwent leadership transitions.

Trubowitz (1986) pointed out that the threat of personnel changes leads to changes in the partnership dynamic (e.g., team norms, pace of work), which calls for increased dedicated efforts to maintain momentum moving forward until all those in their new roles are on board. Farrell et al. (2018) highlight the importance of communication, coalition building, trust building, and pausing the work to ensure those with various levels of familiarity with the partnership all have consistent information and understanding of the partnership. The needed increased efforts to get everyone on board had fits and starts but it seems the efforts were not effective enough. The inability to dedicate the necessary increase in efforts was exacerbated by the next challenge, the COVID-19 pandemic.

CHALLENGE 4: COVID-19 PANDEMIC

The novel coronavirus was certainly a powerful exogenous shock to the partnership. Educational professionals in K–12 and higher education settings found themselves in a new, fluid, stressful, scary, and unpredictable space. Everyone was forced to move to a virtual environment, posing unique challenges to K–12 and university professionals. We predict that the partnership had not yet reached the point in their relationship where one organization felt they could lean on the other during tough times. Each organization instead turned inward.

The partnership and both organizations independently faced multiple challenges that undoubtedly impacted the work. Challenges related to goal clarity and agreement, logistics, leadership commitment, leadership transitions, and the COVID-19 pandemic each put this partnership, which did not yet enjoy the presence of a foundational strength yet given its newness, on even shakier ground.

Weick's (1976) conceptualizing of tight and loose coupling can aid in the sensemaking of the partnership's challenges. Our partnership was loosely coupled. This is evidenced by the independence both organizations maintained during the partnership development and work. The disadvantages of having a loosely coupled relationship emerged here. The first disadvantage Weick notes is that outdated systems and procedures are perpetuated. The partnership did not examine the innovative practices that were in place at the other's institution to explore new ways of operating and addressing improvements to educational programming. Second, Weick notes that loosely coupled organizations could each overcommit to various new initiatives. There were several competing priorities that undoubtedly diverted attention away from the iLEAD efforts. Streamlining commitments in service of the partnership work could have possibly reduced the multiple priorities (and multiple goals). The third loose coupling disadvantage points to the notion that the relationship does not have enough standardized processes within their work. The improvement team established norms and held regular meetings, but the partnership had not routinized established processes and systems to capture the progress of improvement, including a planned system for future data collection related to the improvement team's problem of practice (e.g., Plan-Do-Study-Act cycles). Time inevitably also impacted the degree to which the process could be standardized. The numerous goals present across the partnership and the maintenance of independence of each organization's work routines relate to the fourth disadvantage which posits that loosely coupled systems are not that effective in diffusing ideas across the system. The final disadvantage Weick (1976) names is funding, arguing that due to unpredictable decisions surrounding funding, it is not a reliable mechanism on which loosely coupled systems can depend.

The relatively short time that our improvement team worked together, and the parallel challenges faced by each organization (e.g., leadership considerations, COVID-19) make it difficult to pinpoint to what degree the loosely coupled nature of the relationship was actually advantageous to the efforts. One advantage of loose coupling was perhaps seen in the development of the EdD strand in systems improvement with the construction of an improvement science course and improvement science summer institutes. In other words, despite the partnership facing challenges, the IHE was still able to accomplish the organizational goal of creating the EdD program (re: Developmental Progression Objective: IHE 2. Curriculum/Program Development).

Conclusions and Lessons Learned

Our focus in this chapter was centered on developing a university–school district partnership as members of the iLEAD initiative. The journey of our initial iLEAD partnership presented challenges including goal refinement, logistics, and leadership. We were disappointed that the partnership ended, and we are reflective on why this was the case and what we can do on our end moving forward. The partnership with MCSD fizzled at Trubowitz's (1986) sixth stage (i.e., Regression) yet we continue to value partnerships between LEAs and IHEs and believe they are necessary for effective leadership preparation programs (e.g., Wang et al., 2018; Young et al., 2022). Our efforts with MCSD illuminated areas for targeted attention when embarking on subsequent partnerships. In the spirit of continuous improvement, we have examined and reflected on this partnership to learn from it. Next, we share our lessons learned so others may establish preemptive structures to help navigate successfully through Trubowitz's (1986) Regression stage to persevere, find clarity in new norms, and continue the improvement work while moving toward the last stages of partnership: Renewal (Stage 7) and Continuing Progress (Stage 8). Loose coupling "carries connotations of impermanence, dissolvability, and tacitness all of which are potentially crucial properties of the 'glue' that holds organizations together" (Weick, 1976, p. 3) so it is with care, keen awareness of past challenges, and under different circumstances, that the EDLP Department is currently nurturing a partnership with a district located close to the University. As such, we offer three considerations that stem directly from our learnings in this case that are at the forefront of our current efforts.

CONSIDERATION 1: CLEARLY DEFINED GOALS AND EXPECTATIONS

First, we suggest that partnerships engage in transparent and intentional collaboration around the development of a focused list of shared goals for the partnership that complement or supplement any IHE-specific and district-specific goals, missions, visions, and/or strategic plans. A theory of action for the partnership work could then stem directly from these intentional decisions (Young et al., 2022). Further, shared goals would serve as an anchoring tool to guide decision-making, moments of critical reflection for the partnership team members, and the development of formalized documents (e.g., Memorandum of Understand (MOU)).

CONSIDERATION 2: CORE PARTNERSHIP TEAM WITH CONSISTENT MEMBERSHIP, LEADERSHIP, AND ACTIVE COMMITMENT

The literature warns of organizational work, energy, and goals that are hinged on those in leadership positions but shifts in personnel and leadership are regular occurrences in the field of education (Snodgrass Rangel, 2017). Research describes that until the culture is inculcated by particular norms and the habits of work that transcend who specifically is at the leadership helm, the organizations are at risk of shifting cultures, priorities, and goals when leaders turnover (Snodgrass Rangel, 2017). The partnership experienced numerous—arguably an unusual amount of—shifts in personnel. Our partnership witnessed the greatest momentum in engaging in improvement processes when there was a core team in place with consistent representatives from MCHS and EDLP. Therefore, we recommend that partnerships (1) identify a core group of people who are in regular conversation, (2) dedicate deliberate efforts to engage any new members or leaders in either organization to communicate purposefully to fuel momentum and continued dedication to the work (see Trubowitz Stage 6) and (3) involve senior leadership because people serving in systems-level roles are well-positioned to interpret how the work intersects with district-, college-, and university-wide goals, missions, and visions. Further, these leaders are well-positioned to provide creative supports and resources when needed. It would be important to ensure that while district-level leaders should be involved, the work of improvement science prioritizes practical expertise and is user-centered (Bryk et al., 2015; Hinnant-Crawford, 2020). Therefore, if involved, it is critical that leaders invite school and department representatives to determine the direction of their improvement focus. In other words, high-level leaders should be actively involved but not necessarily dictating what the local—and in this case, the school-based team—should improve.

CONSIDERATION 3: LEAN ON A CONTINUOUS IMPROVEMENT MINDSET TO REFLECT AND LEARN

The work of the partnership involved using improvement science approaches to identify and understand a problem of practice at one school in the school district. The school-based site improvement team was engaged in executing the process and their IHE faculty partners served in organizing, coaching, and thought/reflective partnering roles.

Progress was made, as evidenced by the formation of a cohesive and collaborative improvement team with established group norms and regular meetings, the refinement of an MCHS-based problem of practice, the engagement in procedures to better understand the problem (e.g., fishbone-esque diagram development, empathy interview data collection) with the intention to then progress toward testing change ideas (i.e., PDSA cycles). While the work was unfortunately shortened, upon reflection we see recommendations for partners to include more systematic organizational behaviors such as adopting an improvement framework in the structuring and sensemaking processes. For instance, the IHE faculty themselves could leverage disciplined inquiry processes (Bryk et al., 2015) to continuously improve areas in their own IHE department. Future partnerships could explicitly utilize an improvement mindset and employment of improvement tools to forward the partnership work. Put another way, partners can use improvement science to improve their partnership's improvement science efforts. For example, the improvement team could focus on a goal/aim of the partnership on which to collect data and build a driver diagram to guide the team in making small tests of change to improve their own processes—all while parallel improvement work is concurrently happening on a school/district–based problem of practice.

Questions for Discussion

1. What challenges mentioned in this chapter have you encountered in your own work?
2. Look at your organization's goals, mission, vision, or other guiding frameworks. Look at your partnering organization's goals, mission, vision, or other guiding frameworks. What places of cohesion do you see? Are there areas not aligned or areas that would need special attention or consideration as the partnership progresses?
3. How are the lessons learned relevant to your current partnership status?

References

Barnett, B. G., Hall, G. E., Berg, J. H., & Camarena, M. M. (2010). A typology of partnerships for promoting innovation. *Journal of School Leadership*, *20*, 10–36. http://www.rowmaneducation.com/Journals/JSL/

Bryk, A. S., Gomez, L. M., Grunow, A., & Lemahieu, P. G. (2015). *Learning to improve: How America's schools can get better at getting better*. Harvard Education Press.

Coburn, C. E., & Penuel, W. R. (2016). Research–practice partnerships in education: Outcomes, dynamics, and open questions. *Educational Researcher*, *45*(1), 48–54. https://doi.org/10.3102/0013189X16631750

Cosner, S., Tozer, S., Zavitkovsky, P., & Whalen, S. P. (2015). Cultivating exemplary school leadership preparation at a research intensive university. *Journal of Research on Leadership Education*, *10*(1), 11–38.

Cunningham, K. M. W., VanGronigen, B. A., Tucker, P. D., & Young, M. D. (2019). Using powerful learning experiences to prepare school leaders. *Journal of Research on Leadership Education*, *14*(1), 74–97. https://doi.org/10.1177/1942775118819672

Darling-Hammond, L., Meyerson, D., LaPointe, M., & Terry Orr, M. (2010). Lessons from effective school leadership programs. *Preparing Principals for a Changing World*. https://leseprobe.buch.de/images-adb/cb/11/cb118d84-61fb-472d-b152-ba8e5bbeb234.pdf

Davis, J. (2016). *Improving university principal preparation programs: Five themes from the field*. Wallace Foundation. https://www.wallacefoundation.org/knowledge-center/Documents/Improving-University-Principal-Preparation-Programs.pdf

Glesne, C. (2011). *Becoming qualitative researchers: An introduction* (4th ed.). Pearson Education, Inc.

Honig, M. I. (2004). The new middle management: Intermediary organizations in education policy implementation. *Educational Evaluation and Policy Analysis*, *26*(1), 65–87. https://doi.org/10.3102/01623737026001065

Howey, K., & Zimpher, N. (2007). Creating p-16 urban systemic partnerships to address core structural problems in the educational pipeline. In B. Wehling (Ed.), *Building a 21st century U.S. education system*. National Commission on Teaching and America's Future.

Hulpia, H., Devos, G., & Rosseel, Y. (2009). The relationship between the perception of distributed leadership in secondary schools and teachers' and teacher leaders' job satisfaction and organizational commitment. *School Effectiveness and School Improvement*, *20*(3), 291–317. https://doi.org/10.1080/09243450902909840

iLEAD. (2021). *Carnegie foundation for the advancement of teaching.* https://www.carnegiefoundation.org/our-work/networked-improvement/ilead/
King, C. L. (2014). *Quality measures partnership effectiveness continuum.* Education Development Center, Inc.
Korach, S., Anderson, E., Hesbol, K., Tabron, L., Candelarie, D., Kipp, P., & Miller-Brown, E. (2018). Interdependence and reciprocity: Partnership ethos at the University of Denver. *Journal of Research on Leadership Education, 14*(1), 31–50. https://doi.org/10.1177/1942775118819679
McDiarmid, G.W., & Caprino, K. (2019). *Lessons from the teachers for a new era project evidence and accountability in teacher education.* Routledge.
Penuel, W. R., Allen, A. R., Coburn, C. E., & Farrell, C. (2015). Conceptualizing research–practice partnerships as joint work at boundaries. *Journal of Education for Students Placed at Risk, 20*(1–2), 182–197. https://doi.org/10.1080/10824669.2014.988334
Sanzo, K. L., Myran, S., & Clayton, J. K. (2011). Building bridges between knowledge and practice. *Journal of Educational Administration, 49*(3), 292–312. https://doi.org/10.1108/09578231111129073
Scott, W. R., & Davis, G. F. (2007). *Organizations and organizing: Rational, natural, and open system perspectives.* Pearson Education, Inc.
Snodgrass Rangel, V. (2017). A review of the literature on principal turnover. *Review of Educational Research, 88*(1), 003465431774319. https://doi.org/10.3102/0034654317743197
Trubowitz, S. (1986). Stages in the development of school-college collaboration. *Educational Leadership, 43*(5), 18–21. http://search.ebscohost.com.pallas2.tcl.sc.edu/login.aspx?direct=true&db=aph&AN=8519525&site=ehost-live
University of South Carolina College of Education. (n.d.). *About us.* https://sc.edu/study/colleges_schools/education/about/
Walsh, M. E., & Backe, S. (2013). School-university partnerships: Reflections and opportunities. *Peabody Journal of Education, 88*(5), 594–607. https://doi.org/10.1080/0161956X.2013.835158
Wang, E., Gates, S., Herman, R., Mean, M., Perera, R., Tsai, T., Whipkey, K., & Andrew, M. (2018). Executive summary. In *Launching a redesign of university principal preparation programs: Partners collaborate for change.* https://doi.org/10.7249/rr2612.1
Weick, K. E. (1976). Educational Organizations as Loosely Coupled Systems. *21*(1), 1–19.
Yamagata-Lynch, L. C., & Smaldino, S. (2007). Using activity theory to evaluate and improve K-12 school and university partnerships. *Evaluation and Program Planning, 30*(4), 364–380. https://doi.org/10.1016/j.evalprogplan.2007.08.003
Young, M. D., O'Doherty, A., & Cunningham, K. M. W. (2022). *Redesigning educational leadership preparation for equity: Strategies for innovation and improvement.* Routledge.

CHAPTER 11

Preparing Principals for Urban Schools: The Challenge of Equitable Outcomes at Scale
UNIVERSITY OF ILLINOIS CHICAGO AND CHICAGO PUBLIC SCHOOLS

Steve Tozer, Peter Martinez, Cynthia K. Barron, Shelby Cosner, Zipporah Hightower, Janice Jackson, David Mayrowetz, Sam Whalen, and Paul Zavitkovsky[1]

This is a story of continuous improvement in a 20-year partnership between Chicago Public Schools (CPS) and the University of Illinois Chicago (UIC) that has demonstrated an impact on school and system leadership in the nation's third-largest district. UIC initiated the partnership in 2002 with two core ambitions:

1. To re-design its principal preparation program to improve learning outcomes in Chicago Public Schools.
2. To *continuously improve* the program to make it possible for the partnership to improve student learning outcomes in CPS schools at scale.

The partnership began in the context of a 1988 Chicago School Reform Act that increased the autonomy of Chicago principals and the newly created Local School Councils to improve school outcomes (Bryk et al., 1999). The first decade of the partnership occurred in two waves of program re-design that were first documented in 2012 (Cosner et al.). In addition, later re-design initiatives continued to transform the partnership.

Four main areas of work have improved during the life of the partnership: (1) infrastructure development on both sides of the partnership, requiring new and real-located resources (e.g., Cosner, 2019); (2) leadership impact on the quality of CPS principals, on district policy and senior leadership, and on student outcomes (e.g., Davis & Darling-Hammond, 2012; Whalen, 2021); (3) the conception and implementation of continuous improvement (e.g., Cosner et al., 2016; Cosner, 2019); and (4) equity-focused leadership, in theory and practice (e.g., Walker, 2022; Richard & Cosner, 2022).

---

[1] The authors thank UIC colleagues Lionel Allen, Decoteau Irby, Martha Hebert, and research assistant David Ilea for their insights and contributions to this narrative.

From the district side of the local education agency/higher education (LEA/IHE) partnership, these changes could not have occurred without a sustained commitment to partnership aims, despite the frequent turnover of district leadership since 2009. From the university side, all of these continuous improvement initiatives depended on a deepening commitment to collaboration and shared ownership among academic faculty and leadership coaches—as well as the infusion of new faculty, coaches, and research staff over time, adding expertise in areas such as improvement methods and equity-focused leadership.

This is not a story of uninterrupted progress or complete success. When the partnership fell short of its own aspirations, it repeatedly made key, sometimes fundamental changes to improve. The story worth telling is how this happened. How did a large, struggling school district partner with an undistinguished leadership program in a public research university partner to achieve well-documented impact and national recognition? *And what are the places where this partnership still needs to improve to ensure that all Chicago Public School students have the learning opportunities they deserve?*

Partnership Context: Chicago School Reform and UIC's "Urban Mission"

CHICAGO SCHOOL REFORM AND STATE LEGISLATION

In 1988, led largely by activism from Chicago community organizations, philanthropic foundations, and the business community, Illinois passed the Chicago School Reform Act. This legislation dramatically reduced the size and power of the CPS central office and established the fiscal and operational authority of Local School Councils and building principals (Bryk et al., 1999). In 1995, the Act was amended to place greater power in the hands of Chicago's mayor while preserving the authority of Local School Councils to hire and fire principals and protecting the considerable budgetary and staffing autonomy of principals in a still-decentralized system.

In 1996, the Act was further amended by Senate Bill 1019 to grant CPS the right to impose principal eligibility requirements *beyond those called for by the state certificate* (Cafferty, 2010). This enabled the district to assert greater control over school leadership credentials and to pre-screen applicants that Local School Councils could consider for their schools. In 2002, CPS created a new Office of Principal Preparation and Development that would develop a competency-based process of candidate assessment that included written submissions, recommendations, and interviews before panels of CPS leaders. The state credential alone would no longer qualify applicants for a CPS principalship.

In 2002, when Congress passed No Child Left Behind, CPS was a large, under-resourced school district lagging considerably behind state and national norms in standardized achievement and high-school graduation (Zavitkovsky et al., 2016). Serving an enrollment that was 85% Black, Brown, and low-income, it was failing to realize the promise of a school reform movement that placed its bets on local school governance as well as mayoral control of schools. Chicago Mayor Richard Daley had recently installed the new leadership team of CEO Arne Duncan and Chief Education Officer Barbara Eason-Watkins, who believed that school principals would be an essential element in improving district learning outcomes. Five years later, a Harvard case study led by Richard Elmore emphasized the growing centrality of principals in CPS's theory of action, which afforded considerable autonomy to school leaders. Elmore's team captured this emphasis, writing that in CPS, "Schools are the unit of change for instructional improvement, and principals are the leaders of that change." As Chief Education Officer Eason-Watkins said at the time, "Each principal must feel empowered to drive change and receive the support that responds to the school's specific needs" (Elmore et al., 2006, p. 33).

When NCLB was passed, UIC was a public research university attempting to realize its identity as an urban-serving institution, with a College of Education Dean who urged program re-design throughout the College. The College was home to a Department of Education Policy Studies with an undistinguished record of credentialing school leaders in a master's program that resembled 30 other such programs throughout the state. Yet the Education Policy Studies Department's view was that higher education nationwide was uniquely positioned to prepare and support highly effective principals *at scale*, despite the lack of existing program models to guide us. The Department had a strong social-justice orientation, was at that time majority faculty of color, and believed, partly influenced by Edmonds's research in the 1970s, that effective principals were critical to advancing ambitious student and adult learning in under-resourced schools (Edmonds, 1978). They did not know how to do it, but they believed that partnering closely with CPS would be a necessary condition for figuring it out.

Finally, the national context included an increased public concern over "the soft bigotry of low expectations," as President George Bush said in the runup to passage of NCLB (Bush, 2000). Prevailing cultural deficit theories were being challenged. A new knowledge base for principal preparation was developing, while professional standards were emerging nationally for both teachers and principals. By 1999, influential research by Leithwood, Elmore, and others was informing a new and more sophisticated generation of research and policy discourse on the principalship as a high-leverage intervention for improving schools and addressing educational inequities (Elmore, 1999; Hallinger & Heck, 1996; Leithwood, 1999). The CPS/UIC partnership was clearly influenced by these research streams.

THE PRINCIPAL PREPARATION PROGRAM DESIGN AND RE-DESIGN: 11 KEY COMPONENTS

The program design features that emerged from this three-part context would establish the foundation for subsequent cycles of program improvement over the next two decades. These basic program design features were examined in detail in three articles in a special issue of *Planning and Changing* in 2012 as well as in subsequent publications and can be represented in 11 key components in the tables 11.1–11.3 (Davis & Darling-Hammond, 2012; Cosner et al., 2012; Shoho et al., 2012).

Table 11.1 shows the evolution of a standards-based program and degree *structure* over time. Table 11.2 emphasizes how program *content* evolved, while table 11.3

Table 11.1 Inventory of Change Over Time: Evolution of Standards-Based Vision, Structure, and Supports 2003-2022

Program Elements	Initially Implemented Design Features of the EdD Program	Evolution over Time
Vision and Goals	**Improving urban schools through leadership preparation partnership with CPS.** Programs will prepare principals to improve student learning outcomes in under-resourced urban schools: focus on K-12 students as primary clientele for program.	In light of evidence that race has been a factor in how EdD students experience and succeed in the program, together with heightened faculty attention to racism as a central source of inequity and a new CPS Equity Framework, program begins to address what equity focus implies for the racialized experience of **program candidates** and their impact on P-12.
Degree and Licensure	**Minimum three-year EdD Program with 80 credit hours.** The first year (including full-year, full-time leadership residency) led to Illinois administrative K-12 endorsement; the next two years of coursework and coached practice led to EdD, with option for **Supt. Endorsement** with added courses. *The initial plan was that **all candidates** would be coached in school leader positions following the residency.*	Extends the 80 credit hours to a 4.5-year program, inserting semester of coursework before full-year residency, so first 18 months (including full-year residency) lead to new Illinois P-12 Principal Endorsement; final 3 years integrate coursework and coaching to develop capacity to improve schools through cycles of inquiry and document the work in final capstone for EdD completion. For 19 cohorts, *95% of residency completers have taken school leader positions immediately post-residency.* Additional residency and coursework now required for IL Supt. Endorsement have helped deepen pool of graduates from that strand.
Professional Standards	**Interstate School Leader Licensure Consortium Standards** (ISLLC) are supplemented by CPS Competencies and UIC-generated "10 factors for Urban School Leadership" in early years.	Although Illinois did not pivot from ISLLC standards to PSEL standards in 2015, program has been attentive to PSEL standards as well as the refined CPS competencies which are used in eligibility assessments and all principal performance assessments in CPS. Also, CCSSO Principal Supervisor standards proved useful in strengthening Supt. Program.

(continued)

Table 11.1 (Continued)

Program Elements	Initially Implemented Design Features of the EdD Program	Evolution over Time
Structural Supports and Resources	**New faculty, coaching, and support roles** are from the beginning funded by external sources as well as by UIC. These initially include one clinical faculty position to direct coaching, an associate program coordinator for program administration, and one leadership coach. CPS creates the Office of Principal Preparation and Development so there will be an administrative team dedicated to principal quality.	CPS steadily builds its capacity for effective partnerships with Chicago Principals and Administrators Association, New Leaders, UIC, Teach for America's principal program with Harvard, etc., creating the Chicago Leadership Collaborative. Additional structures created later included the CPS Department of Principal Quality and finally the Chicago Principal Partnership with a range of external stakeholders. By 2011, UIC establishes the Center for Urban Education Leadership, which leads to increased external *and* internal funding, including elevated tuition for EdD Program candidates, all of which helps sustain a Center Director, research staff, a director of research, and six full-time leadership coaches funded by UIC and external dollars. *This chapter's co-authors represent differentiated roles in CPS and UIC.*

portrays the evolution of candidate and program *assessment, intended to serve program improvements in structure and content.* In each table, Column 2 describes the early state of each program feature in the program's first five years, which was already a radical departure from the standard MEd used to license principals at UIC and most IHEs. Column 3 describes, in brief form, how each feature then improved over a 20-year period.

Within this overall standards-based degree and professional endorsement structure, the program evolved academically and in clinical practices, as indicated in table 11.2.

The program design started with a problem of practice: how to prepare principals who could improve student learning outcomes in schools as a rule, not as an exception to the rule. We had the question, but not the answer, and we knew that our learning over time would depend on our assessing our program and our graduates' performance in leading urban schools.

Table 11.2 Inventory of Change Over Time: Evolution of Academic/Clinical Program 2003–2022

Program Elements	Initially Implemented Design Features of the EdD Program	Evolution over Time
Course Content	**80 hours of principal licensure/EdD coursework replace previous 33 hours** of licensure/MEd program with newly created or re-designed and *carefully sequenced* courses around issues of organizational leadership, change leadership, and instructional leadership in urban schools, culminating in thesis courses preparing students to write a practice-focused thesis.	By 2021, all courses re-designed and re-sequenced around three course strands: Organizational Leadership, Instructional Leadership, and Practitioner Inquiry, reflective of CPS Principal Competencies. Continuous improvement and cycles of inquiry are embedded throughout, as are (*with varying degrees of fidelity*) themes of adult learning, early childhood education, social contexts of practice, and increased emphasis on what race-conscious leadership can mean. Capstone thesis structure and coursework scaffolding are elaborately codified over time as "boundary objects" enabling faculty/coach collaboration (Gomez, Biag & Imig, 2020; Cosner, et al. 2015; Appendix of CPS/UIC artifacts, https://textbooks.rowman.com/gomez-improving).
Pedagogy	**Structured cohort experience** integrates first-year coursework with full-year, full-time, paid residency, and integrates remaining two years' coursework with practice in newly acquired leadership roles. CPS pays a full-time resident salary, assists with residency placement, and provides training for principal mentors.	The intersection of course content and fieldwork is elevated through a 2010–2012 re-design process that deepens student experience with cycles of inquiry in their residency and post-residency leadership role. Inquiry cycles—a modification of PDSA more consistent with improvement science principles—becomes program's signature pedagogy through capstone completion. Multiple boundary objects (instruments to guide collaborative practice) are created by CPS and UIC to ensure coherent collaboration in academic and clinical pedagogy (see Appendix, https://textbooks.rowman.com/gomez-improving).

(*continued*)

Table 11.2 (Continued)

Program Elements	Initially Implemented Design Features of the EdD Program	Evolution over Time
Clinical Practice	**Full-year, full-time, principal residency** in CPS schools, paid by district, mentored by selected CPS principals, and coached by full-time UIC coaches who in almost nearly all cases are proven, results-driven principals in CPS.	Coaching staff includes three program graduates or color who have demonstrated impact on schools as principals. As full-time coaching staff increases to five and then six, variability of coaching practice becomes cause for concern, leading to new cycles of inquiry around programmatic consistency of coaching dosage and quality. Coaching practices increasingly agreed on **and codified into handbooks and manuals**, while **CPS codifies similar boundary objects** such as eligibility processes, principal competencies, residency expectations, and coaching manual (see Appendix, https://textbooks.rowman.com/gomez-improving).
Academic Advising	**Academic faculty** are assigned as academic advisors.	Because full-time UIC leadership coaches communicate consistently with candidates throughout their licensure and degree programs, they are assigned as academic advisors through the completion of the capstone. Academic faculty and coaches both lead capstone thesis advising.

IMPACT OF PROGRAM DESIGN AND RE-DESIGN

From the beginning, UIC faculty believed that authentic commitment to educational equity demanded that the principal preparation program should improve. The question was how to make it better in our context. As Mayrowetz wrote to his colleagues before a department retreat on planning the new program in 2002, a year before implementation, "priorities for the educational leadership program" should include the following:

> The program must also be geared toward URBAN educational issues. I think it would be tragic if we created this program and you could just transplant it into rural Iowa and no one would bat an eye. As such, I think a slant toward social justice would be appropriate, if not imperative. Additionally, I believe that it is important for our students to gain an understanding of the communities they will serve *and themselves* in order to foster good working and respectful relationships WITH members of those communities.[1]

---

[1] Notes for the department retreat, June 6. Mayrowetz's language proved prescient. Sixteen years later, in 2018, A.J. Welton and colleagues published a research article pointing out that the organizational theory and the equity-focused, social justice leadership priorities were still operating in separate discourses that fail to inform one another (Welton, Owens, & Zamani-Gallagher, 2018).

Table 11.3 Inventory of Change Over Time: Evolution of Candidate and Program Assessment and Improvement

Program Elements	Initially Implemented Design Features of the EdD Program (2003)	Evolution over Time (2008-2022)
Recruitment and Admissions	**Candidates are recruited and selectively admitted** from pool of urban teachers with master's degrees who demonstrate strong instruction, adult leadership, and explicitly intention to lead for equity. Most admits are students of color.	Ongoing recruitment and admissions for greater numbers of Black and Brown candidates, including male candidates of color, have been helped by funded strategies in partnership with CPS and with Teach for America. Cycles of inquiry led to revision of admissions instrument to include more candidates of color while maintaining selectivity (Walker, et al., 2017).
Candidate Assessment, from Admissions to CPS Eligibility to Capstone Thesis	**Candidates are regularly assessed by UIC and CPS—and sometimes counseled out** during residency. Assessment begins with admissions, continues through internship, doctoral qualifying exams and final practitioner thesis. Mentor principals in CPS schools assess candidate readiness for eligibility. In the first several cohorts, 10% to 15% of candidates are counseled out of programs, as admissions processes are refined.	CPS revises its CPS Competency-based eligibility assessments, using interview panels; high failure rates outside of partnership programs. UIC secures funding for creating an extensive relational database to document the progress of all program candidates from background at admissions to program benchmark completion (e.g., residency, CPS eligibility, leadership roles obtained, EdD completion, etc.). New collaborative faculty assessments ("juried review") are created for post–residency performance in each subsequent year of program, including final capstone committee defense with faculty and coaches (Cosner, Tozer, et al. 2016).

(continued)

Table 11.3 (Continued)

Program Elements	Initially Implemented Design Features of the EdD Program (2003)	Evolution over Time (2008-2022)
Program Improvement	**Data are collected on each candidate's performance** in the program and in the schools to determine whether program is having its intended impact on high-need schools. External funding from philanthropic and/or federal sources is secured annually to support curriculum and coaching improvements, and funders typically insist on certain metrics being documented as benchmarks or program improvement. UIC coaches met routinely as a professional community to discuss their practice and plan improvements.	Program increasingly hires "boundary spanners" with CPS/CPS partnership experience on coaching and research staff (Gomez, et al. 2020). Nonetheless, ongoing cycles of inquiry reveal that program: a. In its first six years produced only two EdD completers. b. Appears to miss some candidates of color in admissions decisions, despite not using GPA or GRE scores as screens (Walker, et al., 2017). c. Provides possible unequal opportunities for timely program completion for Black candidates recruited disproportionately into the highest-need, more labor-intensive schools. d. Exhibits considerable variability in quality of coaching as students experience it. e. Provides student survey data showing that they believe they are not well-prepared to lead in the most challenging CPS schools. These and other findings led to collaborative planning for program improvement. E.g., while only two candidates had completed the EdD by 2010, over 130 candidates have completed since that time, increasing Black student "share" of completed doctoral degrees.

These years of continuous improvement have yielded scholarship by UIC faculty and coaches, as well as by researchers from other institutions, that documents the impact of program evolution on CPS schools (see Appendix, https://textbooks.rowman.com/gomez-improving). Early collection of data, often for purposes of securing or renewing funding from external sources such as Stone Family Foundation, Broad Foundation, the Chicago Public Education Fund, and others, enabled us to compile publicly available data on what our program was achieving or not achieving in terms of principals hired and improvement measures in those schools. That documentation led quickly to state and national recognition. From 2006 to 2013, UIC's program was formally recognized for program innovation and impact by the Illinois Board of Higher Education, the Rainwater Foundation, the University Council for Educational Administration, the Council of Great Cities Schools, and the George W. Bush Institute (see, for example, IBHE, 2006; and Cheney, 2010).

Such attention came about not just because of an ambitious, field-based, pre-service/in-service program design but because UIC began early on to collect data to drive improvement and to demonstrate impact to others. The program collected such data as the following:

- **CPS principal eligibility:** From the beginning, the program demonstrated a consistently high percent of candidates achieving CPS principal eligibility: 95%, compared to annual pass rates of 30–35% for non-CPS partnership applicants.
- **Leadership positions after residency:** UIC candidates must compete for principal positions at the Local School Council level; there is no district "placement." For 19 cohorts, approximately 95% of program completers (in some years 100%) achieved leadership positions, primarily as principals and assistant principals, immediately after residency completion.
- **Retention**: In a school system that over the past 20 years has built a principal retention rate that substantially exceeds national averages (6.4 years in position vs. 4 years), UIC leaders are slightly under district norms at 5.3 years—but 56% of principals in the first 12 cohorts were promoted to district leadership positions (the Fund, https://thefundchicago.org/wp-content/uploads/2021/03/2020-21-Chicago-Principals-Overview-1.pdf; also see UIC data in Appendix, https://textbooks.rowman.com/gomez-improving). Apart from retirements, 87% of all leaders from the first 15 cohorts (even higher in the last four cohorts) are still in *school or district* leader positions in 2022 and are publicly listed on the UIC website (The Leaders We Support, 2022).
- **Impact on CPS leadership and policy**: The partnership continues to demonstrate three kinds of leadership impact—school leaders, district leaders, and leadership policies:
  - School leaders: In a district of over 600 schools, one in ten is led by a UIC-prepared principal, and one in seven is led by a UIC principal or assistant principal (The Leaders We Support, 2022).
  - District leaders: As noted above, UIC principals often (56% of the first 12 cohorts) move to key district leader positions, from principal supervisor to Chiefs of academic units to Director of Principal Quality and CEO (see Appendix item 10, https://textbooks.rowman.com/gomez-improving).
  - District policies: UIC has played a major role in developing district leadership policies and structures from the Office of Principal Preparation and Development to the Chicago Leadership Collaborative and the Chicago Principal Partnership.
- **Closing achievement gaps:** Beginning with Davis and Darling-Hammond (2012) as well as Cosner et al. (2012), a number of publications and reports have shown UIC's impact on such CPS student learning outcomes as improved reading and mathematics scores, Freshmen-on-Track, and high-school graduation, compared to the district as a whole (see also Tozer et al., 2015; Tozer, 2018; see also competing literature on how reliable such causal claims are: e.g., Grissom, 2021; Bartanen,

2022, Young & Crow, 2016). This was in a district that a 2017 Stanford study demonstrated had risen to the top 4% of the nation in improving student learning from grades 3 to 8 (Reardon & Hinze-Pifer, 2017).

- In a 2017 internal analysis, UIC and New Leaders (also a CPS partner) found that with over 300 program graduates having led CPS schools as principals, both UIC and New Leaders graduates of full-year residency programs exceeded district norms in moving their schools up at least one level in the School Quality Rating Program, which rates all CPS schools on a range of factors from attendance to school culture and climate to achievement scores and graduation rates. This approach was but one of several that UIC personnel used to measure principal impact on student outcomes in schools. Others included the use of KNN Near Neighbors statistical algorithms, as well as longitudinal tracking of student performance before and after the arrival of a UIC principal in a given school. All of these analyses were done with publicly available data and were therefore credible to funders, the district, and state (see data displays in Appendix, https://textbooks.rowman.com/gomez-improving).

- UIC-prepared principals were just one contributor to student achievement gains in CPS, and principals overall were only a part of that story. By 2017, however, a district that in 2001 had lagged behind state norms in reading and mathematics achievement in all grade levels tested for Black, Latino, and white students, above and below the Free & Reduced Lunch (FRL) line, had caught up to or surpassed the state averages in every grade tested, for every population group. Moreover, each of the three largest population groups, Black, Latino, and white, by 2017 *exceeded* its statewide counterpart in 3rd-grade reading and mathematics. Even more impressive, by 2017 the largest enrollment group in CPS, Latinos, surpassed Illinois 3rd-graders in math and reading above and below the FRL, in effect reversing the achievement gap (Zavitkovsky & Tozer, 2017). There is little question that not just in policy but in leadership practice, UIC *helped* drive these improvements, though asserting causal relationships between school leadership and student outcomes continue to be debated (Perrone et al., 2021; Bartanen et al., 2022).

- **External impact:** The partnership has also translated local impact into state and national impact through the dissemination of practice and research in professional journals and conferences; presentations for state agencies, districts, and universities in 25 states and the U.S. Department of Education (Cosner, 2022); university-based organizations, such as CEEDAR (Collaboration for Effective Educator Development, Accountability, and Reform); and funded mentoring of other partnerships seeking to transform leadership preparation practice (Hunt & Haller, 2019; Gates et al., 2019; Wang et al., 2022).

"WE WANT TO BE AS GOOD AS PEOPLE THINK WE ARE"

The early recognition and impact that came to the CPS/UIC partnership did not convince anyone that we had reached our shared potential to improve student outcomes. There was still work to do. By 2012, UIC and Illinois State University had led a state legislative task force that resulted in Illinois "sunsetting" all principal programs with the requirement that programs would be re-approved only if they met new requirements for a partnership with a school district, selective admissions, and field-based instruction (among others).[2] In explaining why UIC, which chaired the state task force, should embrace the opportunity to make its own major program changes, Professor Shelby Cosner said in a re-design meeting, "We want to be as good as people think we are."

Despite UIC's documented impact on school outcomes as well as district and state policies, *our understanding of equity-focused leadership remained inchoate*. In 2008, as cohort 6 was beginning, UIC Professor Ward Weldon led an unpublished early study of the program "to provide opportunity for us to reflect on our progress to date and to identify both practices to continue and practices to revise" (Weldon & Barajas, 2008, p. 2). In acknowledging the program's "social justice commitment in leadership preparation," this early monograph noted:

> The College of Education in which this program is housed has noted researchers and action-practitioners that devote themselves to the study of the effects of race, native language, and class on schooling practices and student outcomes. A College leader has suggested that even more attention to these factors be given in the Ed. D. program than is presently the case.
>
> (Weldon & Barajas, p. 1)

This concern about the gap between an expressed commitment to equity and an adequate conception of how to achieve it in the program and in P–12 schools would continue to drive program changes to the present day.

Using the Developmental Progressions to Tell the CPS/UIC Partnership Story

UIC faculty first proposed a new partnership to CPS leadership in the 2001–2002 school year—two years before the first cohort began. Our organizing device for telling the partnership story will be the Developmental Progressions introduced in the Introduction and revisited throughout this volume. The Developmental Progressions were created and revised by iLEAD partners from 2017 to 2019 to serve as a maturity model for what well-developed LEA/IHE partnerships might look like if they were committed to (a) redressing persistent inequities in school systems, (b) improving through leadership development, and (c) using disciplined methods of continuous improvement—or improvement science.

The rubric is a work in progress. As the Developmental Progressions remind us, "[T]his is a framework for a local partnership to consider, not a detailed plan to be 'implemented with fidelity.'" *In that provisional spirit, we apply the Developmental*

---

[2] Hunt and Haller (2019). Tozer was asked by the heads of Illinois State Board of Education and Illinois Board of Higher Education to chair the Task Force, which was supported with Wallace Foundation funds through Illinois State University.

Progressions critically to the 20-year history of one partnership. The rubric reveals current shortcomings in the partnership efforts, which we will cast as the "next edges of growth" for the IHE, LEA, and their partnership (Bereiter & Scardamalia, 1993). We can also test the completeness and usefulness of the indicators against one case. How well does the rubric illuminate the story? Are there clear strengths or weaknesses in the UIC/CPS partnership that are not illuminated by the Developmental Progressions?

We encourage readers to pause for a moment to revisit the entire Developmental Progressions rubric: we begin with the *Partnership* section, as it sets the conditions within which the work was conducted. After using the seven Partnership objectives to present and comment on the partnership's progress, we will turn to the ten objectives that present the *IHE* change story, and then finally the seven that frame the *LEA* story of change in Chicago Public Schools.

For greater clarity, we extract just two constructs from the more complex Developmental Progressions rubric: the *Objectives* in the second column of table 11.4, and in column 3 the descriptions of mature stages of each objective, framed in the rubric as *Institutionalizing and Sustaining the Work*. The right-hand column below tells partners what the left-hand indicators can mean in mature practice. Applying the language

Table 11.4 Developmental Progressions for LEA/IHE Partnerships

	Partnership Key Objectives	Institutionalizing and Sustaining the Work
1.	Partnership Relationship	A strong bond of trust and respect has formed and provides the basis for even difficult conversations to happen.
2.	Joint Development of Targeted Problems of Practice	A regular process exists for reviewing capstone learning. The IHE and LEA are jointly planning out topical priorities going forward.
3.	Formalizing Partnership Data Agreement	Agreements are periodically revisited to ensure continuity over time and transitions in leadership.
4.	Learning to Improve	The LEA and IHE are jointly reviewing evidence from a quality improvement system and using this to plan the next set of improvement cycles for the partnership. The partnership can document learnings from capstones that have advanced local improvements.
5.	Formalizing a Joint LEA/IHE New Leaders Development Program	The local LEA–IHE partnership is now central to how the district is developing new leadership talent; it's not just "another project."
6.	A Shared Partnership Narrative	Organizational norms now operate as a forcing function on the partnership (e.g., "We need to do 'x,' because we said we are about 'y')" and they operate as a form of a moral imperative.
7.	Public Communications	The partnership improvement work is now a regular part of both IHE and LEA Communications programs.

directly from the Development Progressions, *both columns help frame the story of how well, or not, the CPS/UIC partnership instantiates each of these seven objectives and how that developed over time.*

It was over 15 years into their partnership that UIC and CPS leaders attending iLEAD convenings first examined the seven Developmental Progressions constructs above. We recognized that most partnership constructs have been embodied to a mature degree, while others clearly point to possible improvements. **The seven objectives from the rubric above appear in bold font in the narrative below.**

There is little doubt that **Partnership Relationships** have played a significant role in the partnership's history. When the UIC Department Chair approached newly appointed CPS Chief Education Officer Barbara Eason-Watkins with the partnership idea in the 2001–02 school year, she was already positively disposed to partner with UIC because of her past work with UIC Director of Leadership coaching Peter Martinez in the school reform community,[3] and more importantly because of her existing collaborative relationship with UIC College Dean Vicki Chou. Eason-Watkins and Chou had been working together for some time on aligning UIC's teacher education programs with CPS district needs.[4]

Eason-Watkins left office in 2010, and the next 12 years saw frequent turnover in the positions of CEO and Chief Education Officer. After Duncan left the CEO position for the Secretary of Education position in the Obama administration in 2009, 8 different CEOs or interim CEOs led CPS in a 12-year period, and for some CEOs, no Chief Ed Officer was appointed. A combination of factors held the partnership together during this period of rapid CEO churn. First, it was difficulty to deny that CPS needed better principals and that the partnership was producing them. Second, both CPS and UIC had built partnership infrastructure capacity, with comparative stability of personnel at levels *below* the CEO. Third, at least some of the CEOs and interim CEOs were already familiar with the CPS/UIC partnership and respected its work. Fourth, as indicated earlier, the partnership did not stand alone; it was part of a network of IHEs, not-for-profits (e.g., New Leaders), and other stakeholders supported by a substantial number of local and national foundations whose recurring investments carried the weight of credibility as well as welcome resources.[5] All of these actors had built relationships with each other over time. Finally, the mayor across

---

[3] Martinez's founding role in the program will be discussed below.

[4] Meeting in the CEdO's (Chief Education Officer) office, Tozer laid out a half-baked plan, the central idea of which was for UIC and CPS to work together on a field-intensive program to prepare principals for CPS schools. As Chief Ed Officer, Eason-Watkins immediately agreed to the idea. On the topic of relationships, it needs to be said in full disclosure that Tozer and Chou were (and are) married. This was a mixed blessing for EdD program design, because Dean Chou adhered strictly to the University's nepotism regulations and took pains not to privilege or appear to privilege the Ed Policy Department's initiatives. This hands-off stance caused occasional grumpiness in the EDPS Department, but the dean and provost did grant the Department the freedom to completely close the MEd program, replacing it with the untested EdD program, which turned out in the end to be advantageous to the College's mission as well as to the bottom line financially, which was a University concern.

[5] A representative list of external funders of the CPS/UIC partnership over time includes: Broad Foundation, Chicago Community Trust, Chase Bank Foundation, Circle of Service Foundation, Chicago Public Education Fund, Crown Family Foundation, Finnegan Family Foundation, Fry Foundation, MacArthur Foundation, McCormick Foundation, McDougal Family Foundation, OSA Foundation, Ounce of Prevention, Polk Bros. Foundation, Steans Family Foundation, W. Clement Stone and Jessie V. Stone Foundation, US Department of Education, and Wallace Foundation.

seven of the eight CEOs was Rahm Emanuel, who was himself a great supporter of the principalship as a key to improving student learning in CPS. Emanuel's tenure led also to significant stability in the CPS Board of Education, whose members the mayor appointed (Emanuel, 2016).

FROM MOU TO VENDOR CONTRACT

One unforeseen twist in the partnership did undermine the trust relationship, however. This was a shift, under Mayor Emanuel, from an MOU-based collaboration to a new partnership structure that contractually turned UIC, New Leaders, and other principal providers into vendors for CPS. UIC would annually contract to produce X number of candidates who passed eligibility (the upper end was mutually set at 20 but the target could be set lower) in exchange for Y dollars of support from CPS. CPS agreed contractually to pay a targeted number of residency salaries and provide principal mentoring in CPS schools—two enormous contributions. Moreover, for every principal and assistant principal who was hired from each cohort, CPS would again provide per-cap funding for the program.

Finally, this vendor arrangement is something that UIC—as well as other higher education providers and New Leaders—must apply for periodically when the RFP is issued. There is no guarantee that UIC nor anyone else will win a contract for a two- to three-year term, which at the very least attenuates the trust relationship.

Depending on its structure, therefore, *it is possible for a partnership to place contract-driven constraints on voice and decision-making for both university and district personnel.* Faculty and coaches have wondered aloud whether the nature of the partnership has placed the university, as a vendor, in too much of a subservient role to a massive school system that now has an $8B budget, dwarfing that of the College of Education.[6]

Returning to the Developmental Progressions, the UIC–CPS partnership was created precisely to formalize a joint **LEA/IHE Leadership Development Program** that has now produced 19 cohorts for a total of over 250 current leaders. In addition, as school leader preparation and development has become an established priority for the district, CPS has made large investments not just in UIC but in a wider infrastructure that ties UIC together with other higher education providers and with community partners in what was formalized in 2013 as the Chicago Leadership Collaborative (CLC), contracting CPS with its vendor/providers of principals. This was then supplemented in 2016 by the CPS Principal Partnership, which includes providers but also a wider community of stakeholders, described on its website as "the nation's first collaborative dedicated to making principal quality a permanent lever in a citywide school improvement strategy" https://thefundchicago.org/our-work/partnership/).

---

[6] For example, the vendor contract gives CPS formal authority to make some decisions that had previously been matters of informal agreement—such as placement of residents in schools. The UIC preference would have been to place nearly all residents with UIC-trained principals, as UIC principals in CPS quickly outnumbered the number of residents needing exemplary mentors. But CPS exercised its authority to place residents in schools and regions that would most help meet leadership needs in CPS, whether or not these were UIC leaders. This created tension within the partnership that required collaborative problem-solving over time.

UIC faculty and CEdO Janice Jackson, UIC graduate and contributor to this chapter, served on the stakeholder committee that recommended this partnership.

The lead partner for CPS in the Chicago Principal Partnership is the Fund, a unique philanthropic organization that works closely with CPS and its principal preparation partners, such as UIC, on data collection, strategic planning, securing external resources, and **Public Communications**. The Fund's website publishes annual surveys and other analyses of the state of school leadership in CPS, including principal satisfaction data (https://thefundchicago.org). UIC's forms of public communications on the EdD Program and partnership with CPS are many and varied—including scholarly research articles in refereed journals, state and national conference presentations, national podcasts done with Wallace Foundation and Education Trust, a monthly newsletter, and University outreach publications, including a prominent feature in the video that led the Chancellor's just-concluded $.75B capital campaign (see Appendix, https://textbooks.rowman.com/gomez-improving).

The CPS/UIC partnership was *not originally* framed by the **joint development of targeted problems of practice** but by the two partners independently arriving at one conclusion: CPS needed better-prepared principals. Once the district and the university agreed to partner, problems of practice were regularly identified together and discussed in quarterly meetings among the district and its principal preparation partners. One advantage of the new CLC model, led for six years by New Leaders alumna (and contributor to this chapter) Dr. Zipporah Hightower, was that the new vendor relationship enabled initial progress in building a community of professional practice among CPS partners like UIC, New Leaders, Teach for America's Harvard Leadership Residency Program, and later, Northeastern Illinois University—among others—though the full promise of that community of practice has yet to be realized, as all of its members recognize. Nonetheless, such Developmental Progressions elements as **Formalizing Partnership Data Agreement**, **Shared Partnership Narrative**, and **Learning to Improve** became baked into the collaborative network—and specifically into the CPS/UIC contractual partnership.[7] With convening support from the Fund, joint problem-solving has led to strategies to address problems identified, such as creating a new institute for assistant principals who could be groomed for high-school leadership, or providing systemic supports for sitting principals to improve retention and impact (https://thefundchicago.org/wp-content/uploads/2021/03/2020-21-Chicago-Principals-Overview-1.pdf). As discussed below, however, **Learning to Improve** could be more systemically implemented than it has been to date.

A MISSING OBJECTIVE?

A construct that does *not* appear explicitly in this section of the Progressions is that of a *network* of partnerships. UIC and CPS developed a robust partnership for leadership

---

[7] Providers and CPS meet to discuss shared data on the health of the CLC pipeline: cohort size, eligibility success, placement as AP, as principal, and retention. The group discusses supply/demand in high-need areas such as leaders of color, hard-to-staff schools, and high schools; issues are then addressed between CPS and UIC specifically.

preparation, but it became embedded in a network in which CPS would partner with other principal preparation programs, philanthropic foundations, and other stakeholders. UIC was able to leverage this wider network for program sustainability and improvement in ways that a simple one-to-one *partnership* might not afford. The wider network of partnerships was less vulnerable to rapid turnover of CPS CEOs from 2009 to 2021 than a single partnership might have been. Particularly in larger school districts, it might be important for IHEs to seek to network with other providers and stakeholders if *improvement at scale* is the aim. We have also witnessed the importance of networks in rural-environment partnerships, such as Western Kentucky University and a consortium of over 40 small districts that networked in formal ways to participate in program re-design (Gates et al., 2019; Wang et al., 2022; Leggett et al., 2022).[8]

The Chicago principal preparation community has also played a significant role in leading Illinois policy formation in principal preparation through state-agency committees and external funding. Illinois has been repeatedly recognized in the research as a leader in state policy on principal preparation (Hunt & Haller, 2019; Manna, 2015, 2021; Young et al., 2015).

PREPARATION OF CPS PRINCIPAL SUPERVISORS (NETWORK CHIEFS) AND CENTRAL OFFICE PERSONNEL

A final dimension of the CPS/UIC partnership is the extent to which it led to an increasing impact on senior leadership in CPS over time. In some cases, UIC principals were promoted to Network Chiefs, the CPS position for principal supervisors. In other cases, they became Chiefs of major CPS academic departments, such as Early Childhood Education, Language and Culture Education, and Teaching and Learning. One UIC-trained principal, Dr. Allison Tingwall succeeded Zipporah Hightower as Executive Director of the Department of Principal Quality. Another, Dr. Janice Jackson, became Chief Education Officer and then CEO, spanning a six–year period. The collective impact of UIC leaders on CPS, as documented by Dr. Sam Whalen of UIC's Center for Urban Education Leadership, has been to catalyze a shift away from an "accountability" orientation during the early post-Duncan years to a "continuous improvement" orientation that permeated senior leadership in CPS at least through the end of Dr. Jackson's tenure in 2021 (Whalen, 2021).

A NEXT EDGE OF GROWTH

Through iLEAD participation, the CPS/UIC partners located a "next edge of growth" for the partnership in the **Learning to Improve** category: "The partnership can document learnings from capstones that have advanced local improvements." While student and faculty testimony reveals that the EdD capstone studies of leading school improvement have been a profound source of learning for the program and its candidates (see Appendix, https://textbooks.rowman.com/gomez-improving), UIC had not been engaging district

---

[8] UIC was the mentoring university in Wallace Foundation-funded Western Kentucky program redesign project.

partners in that same direct learning. Capstone narratives have over time revealed problems of leadership practice—e.g., leading schools with high levels of chronic absence and student mobility—that engaged UIC and CPS in joint inquiry, problem-solving, and policy formation (Walker & Tozer, 2022; Tozer & Walker, 2021). But CPS colleagues had not been invited to participate in capstone review and collaborative dialogue about what learning might follow, and the partnership has begun to discuss how that might best be done.

SUMMARY OF *PARTNERSHIP* DEVELOPMENT

Our account of **how** the innovative CPS/UIC program design was achieved has begun with the Parj287tnership section of the Developmental Progressions. The CPS/UIC handshake agreement to form a partnership for the preparation and development of CPS principals created the riverbed through which institutional reality then flowed for both partners. Once UIC had assurances from CPS that the district was willing to fund a full-time, full-year, leadership residency, a dramatically new program structure became possible, one that embedded a full-year residency in the licensure phase of the program and then committed extended leadership coaching to three years of novice leader development post-licensure.

To support this leader development partnership and its continuous improvement, *UIC and CPS each built new institutional capacity* with new funding allocations and new professional roles. We use the Developmental Progressions to explore those developments now.

Developing Capacity as a District Partner: The UIC EdD Program

As indicated earlier, three key contexts for initiating the EdD Program at UIC were a badly struggling urban school district under new leadership, a public research university with an urban mission, and a growing knowledge base about the impact of principals on school improvement. Within that context, UIC's Education Policy Studies Department began discussions in 2000 that led to the admission of the first cohort of EdD students in the fall of 2003. Eleven key design features of the program, from admissions to curriculum to candidate/program assessment, were described above. The following section of the Developmental Progressions provides an initial heuristic for examining how these design features came about.

These ten Developmental Progressions indicators can illuminate the UIC journey as part of the CPS/UIC partnership. In re-sequencing these indicators in table 11.5, **Faculty Engagement** must assume the first position, as UIC faculty—at first tenure-line and then later professional-practice faculty—drove the internal discussion that led to our approaching CPS with the proposal to partner in an innovative program. It was also faculty such as Cosner and Smylie, as well as coaches (particularly Zavitkovsky) and Center Research Director Whalen who led successive iterations of the idea of continuous improvement (Cosner et al., 2012; Cosner et al., 2015; Cosner, 2019; Smylie,

Table 11.5 Developmental Progressions for the IHE

	IHE Key Objectives	Institutionalizing and Sustaining the Work
1.	Commitment to the Idea of Improvement	Embrace of IS/NICs is spreading to other clinical and tenured faculty throughout the IHE.
2.	Curriculum/ Program Development	A coherent program of study has been adopted. This is visible in program descriptions that link from introductory courses through to capstone projects. All aspects of these programs are now operational. These developments are impacting design conversations about other IHE program initiatives.
3.	Faculty Development and Promotion	New promotion and tenure policies are in place, acknowledging IS/NICs contributions as a significant criterion in these processes. One or more junior faculty have successfully engaged with these new criteria.
4.	Faculty Engagement	Both professional-practice and tenure-line faculty are engaged in IS/NICs. Support for these efforts is recognized as a regular part of faculty workload.
5.	Improvement Science as a Signature Pedagogy	IS is formally recognized as a signature pedagogy for the school's professional education initiatives more generally.
6.	Institutional Leadership Commitment	Dean/Dean's Cabinet continues to actively express support. University Communications recognizes this as a distinctive and "innovative" contribution.
7.	Institutional and State Approvals	These new program designs are impacting the conceptions of other IHE program initiatives.
8.	Scholarship of Improvement: An Academic Community is Forming	Faculty regularly present their improvement research at the Improvement Summit, in other scholarly venues, and publications.
9.	IHE as a Support Hub for Improvement Networks	IHE has the capacity to support multiple networks, including the possibility of inter-district networks.
10.	A New Professional Education Narrative	An institutionally recognized (and broadly owned) narrative exists about what we do and why we do it. Successes are celebrated. Student struggles are something we "own."

2009; Zavitkovsky et al., 2016; Whalen et al., 2016). Faculty, coaches, and research staff were committed to multiple rounds of wholesale as well as iterative **Curriculum & Program Development** as illustrated in table 11.2 earlier in this chapter. Faculty investment, supported by external funding from foundations as well as the DOE, was supported by **Institutional Leadership Commitment** that enabled replacing a traditional principal preparation program with a new and untested approach, including the creation of three new full-time, university-funded professional-practice (clinical) faculty lines and the founding of a new Center for Urban Education Leadership in the UIC College of Education. Institutional leadership clearly and consistently supported the **New Professional Education Narrative** that faculty put forward to establish the College's first professional doctorate, from the College Dean and Executive Committee to university administrators and Board of Trustees. While **Faculty Development and Promotion** policies at the College and campus levels have enabled all tenure-line faculty who have worked in this program to be tenured and/or promoted to associate and full professor, the intensive routines inherent in collaboration and professional preparation have placed a significant burden on those same faculty. Over time, the College has provided supports for non-tenure-line faculty have enabled leadership coaches to contribute on average over 10 years each to the program.

Leadership support also enabled the securing of **Institutional and State Approvals** for the initial program design in 2003–04, for a thorough re-design in 2010–2012, and later for the permanent approval of the Center for Urban Education Leadership, the research and development offspring of the EdD Program. Both tenure-line and clinical faculty participate regularly in the **Scholarship of Improvement, Forming an Academic Community** around the work of the EdD Program by co-authoring journal articles, webinars, and conference presentations, such as UCEA, AERA, and the Carnegie Summit. In part, because the program developed its commitment to "cycles of inquiry" as a signature pedagogy well before the vocabulary of improvement science became current in the education literature, the program continues with its established vocabulary of "cycles of inquiry" and has not pivoted to the language of **Improvement Science as a Signature Pedagogy.** It is nonetheless true that the UIC program has served as a **Support Hub for Improvement Networks** of various kinds, among other IHEs and districts as well as with school and district leaders in CPS. There are many examples, but a particularly impactful and recent one is the Networked Improvement Community (NIC) hub that the Center led to create an innovative partnership between Northern Illinois University and the state's next two largest districts after Chicago, Elgin U46 and Rockford 205. That partnership has just graduated its first cohort from a two-year, fully paid residency that results in P–12 principal licensure (*Principal residency program creates model for development of school leaders,* 2020).[9]

Elaborations and Qualifications on the IHE Narrative

VISION, SYSTEMS, AND ABOVE ALL, PEOPLE

Before turning to how the Developmental Progressions draw our attention to other potential growth areas for the EdD Program, we need to emphasize our experience of

---

[9] As Richard and Cosner point out, UIC has also participated in a substantial number of improvement networks organized by other education leadership organizations, including The Wallace Foundation, UCEA, The Carnegie Foundation for the Advancement of Teaching's ILEAD, and Learning Policy Institute's EdPrepLab (in press, 2022).

having the right people in the room—and then adding people to fill the inevitable gaps in expertise (Cosner, 2019, in Hunt & Haller). We began our change processes with the following human capital assets: (a) Department colleagues in social foundations, policy, and leadership who had a social-justice commitments; (b) leadership faculty with research interests and strengths in instruction, organization, policy, adult learning, and social contexts of schooling; (c) faculty commitment to continuous improvement in their scholarship, their teaching, and the collaborative work of change. *What we didn't have at the beginning was experienced school leaders, leadership coaches, or faculty willing to devote themselves to liasonship with the public schools or to program research.* As a department of tenure-line faculty, each of us had our own research commitments already, and they were, initially, not about studying our own program.

OUR FIRST TARGETED PROGRAM HIRE

One key example of the relationship of vision, systems, and people was hiring a faculty member specifically to help lead a yet undefined program into partnership with CPS. Once the EDPS Department had made the decision to design a new preparation program to respond to the CPS need for effective principals, we conducted a search for a clinical (practitioner) faculty member in the EDPS Department. The candidate was to have practical leadership expertise and would help build a program by devoting efforts full-time to nurturing the necessary relationships with Chicago Public Schools as well as co-leading, with the Department Chair and prospective EdD Program coordinator, the internal processes of creating faculty consensus around the design and implementation of the program. None of these activities is the traditional path to tenure or promotion in a research university.

A national search led to the hiring of Peter Martinez, who had by that time built a unique record of impact in Chicago Public Schools reform. As an Alinsky-trained community organizer, he had played a key role in bringing competing factions together to write and support the 1988 School Reform Act that was driving education reform in Chicago Public Schools. As the Education Program Officer for the MacArthur Foundation for the preceding decade, he had been in charge of a $40M portfolio and was instrumental in funding impactful and enduring school reform initiatives. Martinez's extensive work in Chicago school reform had convinced him that school principal performance was critical to improving CPS student learning outcomes at scale (Chenoweth, 2021). Whether this proven change agent could function productively as a boundary-spanner between higher education, CPS, the foundations community, and the civic community remained to be seen. We will return to the notion of boundary-spanning shortly (Gomez et al., 2020).

Martinez proved to be a linchpin in designing and executing the program. Among other contributions, he advocated strongly for a program design that would immerse candidates in leadership practice for at least 3, and what would later become closer to 5, years. His years of experience as a trainer of leaders in community organizing convinced him that intensive coaching would be necessary to transform prospective/practicing school leaders' *mindsets* into an orientation toward equity-focused change agency that was not a part of ordinary professional preparation in education. As one member of an early cohort said, "I knew this program was about transformational leadership; I just didn't know it was about transforming *me*."

BUILDING THE TEAM

The founding faculty of the program, such as Mark Smylie and David Mayrowetz in addition to Martinez, brought enormous expertise and energy to the table, without which it is hard to imagine the program being initiated. Smylie pushed early on for a clear theory of change, established an initial framing of capstone theses, and would soon publish *Continuous School Improvement*, which was used extensively in the program (2009). Mayrowetz brought expertise on equity from the government sector before turning to research on distributed leadership (Mayrowetz, 2005, 2007). Both remained committed to improvement as the program evolved, and they identified gaps that had to be filled.[10] At the time cohort 2 was completing its residency in 2005, the program hired Dr. Shelby Cosner to fill one of those gaps: the need for someone who was an experienced school leader (and in her case, also a district leader) and who had pivoted to become a leadership researcher and school-improvement activist and was therefore another kind of boundary-spanner. Cosner went on to author more leadership publications, including those specifically on this program, than any other faculty member, obtaining full professor rank in the process. More importantly from the program quality perspective, she had a profound impact on program improvement processes, curriculum content change, and on leading the codification and revision of the program's logic model, which undergirded key improvements in program coherence (see Appendix, https://textbooks.rowman.com/gomez-improving for program logic models).

Tenure-line faculty in research universities are for many reasons ill-suited to provide the leadership coaching that our residents and post-residency school leaders needed—not least of which is that they are not rewarded for such work—and our experience in multiple faculty searches over the years demonstrates that relatively few research faculty have deep experience as school leaders.[11] As a trainer of leaders, Martinez began to pilot a coaching model in the first year of the program, then each year expanded the coaching staff by hiring proven, award-winning school principals and network and district leaders as they retired from CPS (Shoho et al., 2012). Together with Martinez, expert leaders with demonstrated expertise built a community of professional practice, meeting every other week to discuss student progress, problems of coaching practice, and the differences between coaching a resident and a first- or second-year principal. Today there are six full-time coaches for the roughly 100 students enrolled in the program at any given time—from pre-service residency to third- or fourth-year leaders in their capstone phase.[12]

---

[10] Of the original founding faculty, only Mayrowetz remains, yet the program thrives, in part due to the program's continued success at attracting talent from the school system and developing leadership from within.
[11] Nor have most university faculty been change agents, as we expect principals to be. See our discussion of this problem in Tozer et al. (2015).
[12] While three of these coaches are supported by the university as clinical or professional practice faculty, three are supported by grant money, year in and year out. It is a sign of program sustainability that of these six coaches, three are graduates of the EdD program, and five are Black. In a program serving a school district

LEADERSHIP COACHES AS BOUNDARY SPANNERS

A major reason for the program's sustained impact over time has been the "boundary-spanning" role of the coaches (Gomez et al., 2020). Most UIC coaches who left public school leadership (often at retirement age) have become active and vocal participants in the academic community while spending most of their time in schools coaching pre-service and novice leaders. They also serve on admissions selection committees, plan and lead internship seminars and other courses, provide academic advising for each of their coachees, chair capstone committees, and serve as school-improvement partners to in-service leaders, among other duties. They have returned to work in the district's schools in a new capacity, representing UIC and CPS shared interest in improved schools. This work has generated recent research on the "brokering" function of coaches in the relationship between residents and their mentor principals (Cosner, Walker, et al., 2018; Cosner, et al., 2021; Cosner & De Voto, 2023; see also Appendix, https://textbooks.rowman.com/gomez-improving for *leadership coaching materials*).[13]

CREATING "BOUNDARY OBJECTS"

Gomez, et al. (2020) discuss the importance of artifacts and instruments that enable collaborators from different organizations to work together across boundaries. In the CPS/UIC partnership, prominent examples are the CPS Principal Competencies, an early-partnership CPS Coaching Manual, a Leadership Development Plan created by UIC, and the partnership contract itself, as both sides are obligated to make these instruments work in their practice (Cosner, et al., 2018; Cosner & DeVoto, 2023). But boundary objects can be important to bridge gaps within organizations, too: clinical faculty and leadership coaches come from a professional culture very different from that of most academic faculty in research institutions, and neither group can assume that the other sees leadership or leader development in the same way. Therefore, program faculty, coaches, and Center researchers have over the years codified program procedures through a number of tools and instruments to guide practice in the program's logic model, coaching, student entry planning for their first leadership positions, assessment of student work products, capstone expectations, and so on. The collaborative *manufacture* of these boundary objects creates shared understanding across professional cultures among program personnel, and the codified understandings guide program coherence. Our Appendix, https://textbooks.rowman.com/gomez-improving includes a number of representative samples of such boundary objects.

---

in which Latinos are the largest population, a current improvement goal is the hiring of Latino/a coaches. In addition to Martinez, UIC has had other outstanding Latino coaches in past years and is seeking to address this current gap.

[13] An analysis of the role of women in the UIC program—faculty, coaches, and candidates—has yet to be written, but it bears noting that women have played key leadership roles in a historically male-dominated field throughout. CPS leaders who shaped the program through serving 10 or more years as coaches and clinical faculty, for example, include Cynthia Barron, Nancy Carter-Hill, Kathleen Mayer, and Beverly LaCoste.

NEXT EDGES OF GROWTH

The Developmental Progressions surface a number of "next edges of growth" for UIC. One of these is the Development Progressions elaboration of a **New Professional Education Narrative**: "An institutionally recognized (and broadly owned) narrative exists about what we do and why we do it. Successes are celebrated. *Student struggles are something we 'own.'*" In 2022, the UIC faculty and coaches have become collectively concerned that the program has historically been much better at celebrating its successes than at owning student struggles. As Katonja Webb Walker's research has demonstrated, for example, that some Black students perceive themselves as struggling with the demands of disproportionately serving in the highest-need schools in the system while trying to complete a demanding doctoral program (Walker, 2022).[14] Program data presented in the Appendix, https://textbooks.rowman.com/gomez-improving show Black, white, and Latino students completing the program at similar rates, which is a testament to the commitment of those students. However, faculty have confirmed that Black students perceive that their experiences of the program are different from Latino and white students in a number of ways, including classroom discourse and coaching consistency, which can stem from dysconscious racism and the need to identify different needs for supports in class assignments and program completion. The EdD Program's recent Continuous Improvement meetings, led by faculty member Decoteau Irby, who has written extensively about racism and race-conscious leadership, have become explicit about "owning" these student/graduate struggles as a challenge to the conduct of the program itself (Irby, 2021; Irby et al. 2021).

Another question raised by the Developmental Progressions lies in the frequent use of the term improvement science. The UIC commitment to continuous improvement and NICs is well documented. Whether the language of improvement science will become ubiquitous in the program as "cycles of inquiry" remains to be seen.

NEED FOR NEW RESOURCES

Finally, a potential gap in the Progressions may be identification of the need for *resources* to support change processes. We are addressing this in the IHE section of the Progressions because, in the CPS/UIC case, resources for change are harder to come by in a small college of education than in a large school district with a budget roughly 1,000 times as large. The substantial investment CPS made in principal development represented less than a half percent of its budget, commensurate with Wallace Foundation findings in other districts committed to principal pipeline innovation (Gates, et al., 2019; Wang, et al., 2022).

Moreover, in research-intensive universities, it is a common expectation that faculty will have to secure external funding to support their research, but a department's instructional program is typically conducted without external funding. We saw our

---

[14] Internal Center research has also found that prevailing admissions procedures, which have resulted in admitting a larger number of Black and Brown students over time, showed statistical interviewer biases that were subsequently corrected by revising admissions procedures (Walker, Tozer, Webb, Parkinson, & Whalen, 2017; Walker, Tozer, Webb, Parkinson, & Whalen, 2018; on CUEL website).

new program design as an integration of practice and inquiry that would generate new knowledge and practices for the field, and we believed we could secure external funding from philanthropic and government resources to do so. Four areas, in particular, would need additional funding: *leadership coaches* who could supervise our candidates in the field; *administrative capacity* to handle a highly selective, field-intensive collaboration with the public schools; *data collection and analysis* to inform continuous improvement of the program; and finally, *faculty release time or summer salary* so we could engage academic faculty in working collaboratively with coaches and with each other on continuous program improvement. Due largely, at first, to our partnership with Chicago Public Schools, we were able to secure funding for all of these areas. Early program successes led to the university increasing its support in substantial ways, funding new clinical positions, new administrative positions, and the Center for Urban Education Leadership.

Our primary sources for external funding were local philanthropies, national foundations, and federal programs—*in addition to* the nearly $100,000 in salary and benefits contributed by CPS for each principal residency. Could the program operate without external funding for three additional leadership coaches? Yes. There is no one resource model that is essential. The NIU/Rockford/Elgin Public Schools two-year principal residency model, created with UIC assistance, has completed its first cohort, for example, without funds external to the district and the university (*Principal residency program creates model for development of school leaders*, 2020). In the Chicago context, the funding community seeks not just local impact but wider impact through informing research and policy influence.

How Did the District Sustain Its Share of the Partnership for 20 Years across Nine CEOs?

The *LEA Objectives* portion of the Developmental Progressions in table 11.6 are weighted toward improvement methods. Five of the seven descriptions below specify Improvement Science and Networked Improvement Communities (IS/NICs). CPS demonstrates strength in a number of these but has areas of growth if improvement methods are to permeate the culture of the system. For example, the first objective, **District Leadership Engagement,** has been reliable for school leader development across 20 years despite CEO churn, as earlier discussed. However: if the focus is instead on the "broad base of support" among senior leadership for IS/NICs, the bar for "engagement" is raised. The commitment to IS/NICS was strongest during the recent Jackson administration, as might be expected of a UIC program graduate, but the transition to a new CEO during a lingering pandemic leaves open the question of how much improvement science will be evident going forward (Whalen, 2021).

Putting aside the specific emphasis on IS/NICS, CPS demonstrates strength in a number of the Developmental Progressions categories. **District Leadership Engagement** across 9 CEOs has ensured the ongoing support and improvement of the Office of Professional Development, the Chicago Leadership Collaborative, the Department of Principal Quality, and the Chicago Principal Partnership—none of which existed

Table 11.6 Developmental Progressions for the LEA

	LEA Key Objectives	Institutionalizing and Sustaining the Work
1.	District Leadership Engagement	A broad base of expertise exists across the District's Senior Leadership Team responsible for IS/NICs. Coordination with the IHE partner is viewed as an important senior staff responsibility.
2.	Professional Development of District Staff	IS/NICs training is also integrated into the onboarding process of new hires, including teachers and leaders.
3.	Implementation of IS/NICs	IS/NICs now anchor district's current improvement efforts and planning for future work. Evidence is accumulating that working in this way has made measurable improvement for students, schools, and the district.
4.	IS and Networks as District Policy	IS/NICs are now a regular part of strategy conversations among the superintendent, other senior system leaders, and board members.
5.	Funding Support	Funding stream(s) have been secured on a continuing basis, going forward to regularize partnership participation. It is an integral part of the budget now.
6.	IS/NIC Expertise Integrated into Promotion and Hiring Decisions	Demonstrated expertise in IS/NICs has now become a highly-valued criterion in hiring, development, and promotion as part of a human capital strategy.
7.	Broadening Stakeholder Engagement	LEA has adopted formalized mechanisms for broadening stakeholder involvement.

prior to 2001. External partnerships with IHEs, New Leaders, the Fund, and other funders and civic groups have kept the ship going in the right direction even when the wheel was rapidly changing hands. As a consequence, **Funding Support** has been sustained, **Stakeholder Engagement has Broadened**, and despite the most recent leadership transitions, the Department of Principal Quality has engaged with external, intentionally non-Chicago expertise to revise the Principal Competencies for more explicit attention to equity in principal development. **Professional Development of District Staff** in the last seven years was a strength of the Jackson tenure, and initiatives have been sustained under new CEO Pedro Martinez. For example, UIC has provided sustained professional development to Network Chiefs (principal supervisors) around issues of principal supervision and continuous improvement in recent years, with the formation of a structured NIC of high-school Chiefs providing direction for a new high-school initiative. UIC and CPS are now seeking additional external funding for such work. A new "Principal University" is in the works from the Department of Principal Quality (DPQ) for accelerating assistant principal development in alignment with the new competencies. It is a sign of the strength of the partnership with UIC that the District's DPQ Executive Director and Director of School Leader Development are both UIC program graduates.

Three LEA objectives in table 11.6 are directly focused on IS/NICs and are less systemically pervasive, though observable. While CPS is experimenting with NICs in different isolated initiatives, the spirit of the indicator, **Implementation of IS/NICs,** is more ambitious, tied to measurable outcomes of IS. Similarly, it's clear that **IS/NIC Expertise is Integrated into Promotion and Hiring Decisions** in at least some cases—for example, the hiring of a Chief of Strategic Planning under Jackson—and district leaders do speak the language of continuous improvement, but evidence of IS as a "core human capital strategy" is thin. Similarly, because Continuous Improvement was a high priority in the Jackson administration, this remains a priority for leaders who have remained in key district roles. But it would not be accurate to say **IS and Networks as District Policy** "are now a regular part of strategy conversations among the superintendent, other senior system leaders, and board members."

In some iLEAD partnerships, improvement science is the defining construct that brought the partnership together. This is not what happened in Chicago 20 years ago, however. The defining construct was the improvement of school leader preparation for Chicago's schools and the recognition that neither CPS nor UIC could do this alone as well as it could be done in partnership. Continuous improvement quickly emerged as a construct from our recognition that neither the research nor prevailing practice provided sufficient guidance for us to establish a program that would **not** be in need of improvement. For improvement science, as it has emerged in recent years, to become a core construct of our partnership would require a new focus in our conversations.

Conclusions and Lessons Learned

After 20 years and 250 school leaders prepared in the partnership, we can identify a number of lessons learned. Consistent with the iLEAD theory of change, we frame this discussion around equity, partnership, leadership development, and continuous improvement. We place equity in the first position because it asserts the goals and values that the methods of partnership, leadership, and continuous improvement were intended to serve in the CPS/UIC case. There is certainly more to say about each of these four categories than we say here, but each item below was important for our learning in multiple ways.

1. *Equity*

- The CPS/UIC partnership's reason-for-being was to achieve greater equity of outcomes in urban schools, particularly CPS schools, that were persistently lagging behind state and national norms. Preparing principals to meet this challenge was and remains a central problem of practice.
- UIC principals, system leaders, and policy impact have contributed to the district's nationally recognized improvements in student learning outcomes, from achievement gains to high-school graduation and college enrollment, significantly closing

and in some cases reversing achievement gaps with comparable student populations acroos the state of Illinois.
- While our initial equity focus on CPS students was impactful, our conception of equity needed to be more deeply informed by questions about whether (a) our Black principal candidates are experiencing the program as equitable; and (b) the program is sufficiently "race conscious" in its preparation of principals for a district in which enrollment was only 10% white. UIC is now focusing on both: equity in candidate experience and equity in schools.
- While CPS has become more explicit about its own equity framework, the UIC program faculty and coaches have initiated collaborative discussions of how better to position race and racism in the EdD Program and in leading urban schools. Internal resources include new personnel, including (but not limited to) the most recently hired faculty and coaches of color, whose research and teaching foregrounds equity and race-conscious leadership.[15]

2. *Partnership*
- The partnership relationship was essential to achieving shared aims for improved leadership preparation and development that would improve school outcomes.
- Partnering effectively required new institutional capacity-building on both sides, in CPS and UIC—and **capacity-building requires resources**. CPS was willing to allocate millions of dollars annually to its multiple partnerships for principal development while UIC recognized—just as with research funding—that external resources were necessary to achieve partnership aims and leverage increased internal resources.
- Partnerships are not an unmitigated good and introduce new problems to be navigated. Part of the partnership work has been to identify problems of practice in the partnership relationship itself and seek collaborative solutions to those problems.
- Institutional leadership in both partner organizations has been essential to partnership success. The sharing of leadership *within* each organization (e.g., Martinez and Cosner leadership roles in UIC) mitigates against leadership changes becoming fatal to the partnership, as demonstrated by our partnership spanning nine district CEOs, three college deans, and three Chicago mayors in a mayoral-led school district—as well as turnover in most (or all) of the philanthropic foundations that have supported the program.
- Also critical to sustaining the CPS/UIC partnership was that the partnership did not stand alone; it was embedded collaboratively in a network of partnerships that CPS forged with other IHEs, funders, and stakeholders who invested in improving district outcomes. In addition, the foci of the UIC/CPS partnership expanded beyond principal preparation into Network Chief preparation and research–practice partnerships on high-need schools and other challenges.

---

[15] Allen (2021), Cosner & Richard (in press, 2022), Irby (2021), and Salisbury (2020) have all published recently on equity-focused and race-conscious leadership.

3. *Leadership Development: Vision, Systems, and People*

- **Vision**. From the beginning, the partnership was grounded in a vision of preparing school leaders who could learn to lead urban schools to improved student outcomes at scale—*a shared but <u>incomplete</u> vision that evolved through learning from research and practice on both sides of the partnership.*
- **Early Systems Commitments**. This partnership made three major *systems*-decisions (as in organizational systems, not *school*-system) that have endured. One is a systemic approach to **integrating pre-service and in-service leadership development**. The second is a fundamental commitment to **practice-based learning** through pre-service residency and in-service leadership coaching (e.g., Cosner et al., 2018). The third is embedding the state leadership endorsement in the first third of an **EdD architecture for implementing the first two systems**.
- **Later Systems Commitments.** The vision for effective leadership preparation grew over time in part due to the establishment of *new leadership development systems in CPS and at UIC*. CPS created a new administrative unit for the preparation and development of principals, and UIC created the new Center for Urban Education Leadership. New boundary objects were created in both organizations to facilitate collaboration across these organizations and within them. Without such systems and boundary objects on both sides, it is difficult to see how the vision could be achieved and improved over time.
- **People**. Because systems cannot be created, implemented, and sustained without people, the expertise and commitment of people in CPS and UIC have been critical to the program's success. From the beginning, faculty and coaches at UIC were hired and developed with explicit attention to program needs, and *exceptional* candidates have been recruited and competitively selected as program applicants—the majority of them candidates of color. Targeted, *boundary-spanning* hiring enabled the academic department to diversify its program faculty in race, ethnicity, gender, and field-based expertise. CPS has similarly committed highly qualified people to leadership roles in the Office of Principal Preparation and Development and the Chicago Leadership Collaborative.

4. *Continuous Improvement*

- The initial commitment to continuous improvement in the new program design was grounded in a shared recognition that we did not know how best to achieve the expressed equity aims of the program, and we would have to *learn* to improve the work of the partnership over time. As Richard and Cosner point out, a gap persisted between motivation and implementation in equity-focused strategies, and program learning would prove essential to implementation (2022).
- Fueled in part by the publication of founding faculty member Mark Smylie's *Continuous School Improvement* (2009) and Cosner's subsequent publication on continuous improvement in the UIC program (e.g., Cosner, et al., 2012, 2016; Cosner, 2019), the program had become more explicit and coherent in its systems for (a) preparing principals to use cycles of inquiry in schools, (b) using cycles of inquiry

to improve the program, and (c) holding leaders accountable to demonstrating the use of cycles of inquiry in their capstone studies of improvement practice.
- In the last eight years, from before the publication of *Learning to Improve* to 2022, both CPS and UIC have been influenced by research and practice in improvement science (Bryk, Gomez, et al., 2015). CPS has used Networked Improvement Communities in collaboration with, and independently of, UIC; and the reverse is true.
- Continuous improvement inquiry cycles are clearly embedded in the discourse and practices of the UIC program, and *Learning to Improve* (Bryk et al., 2015) has been used in the program as a course text as well as in CPS Principal Fellows program independently of UIC, though the vocabulary of improvement science is not pervasive in CPS nor in the UIC program. Program faculty are committed to inquiry cycles as central to the program's signature pedagogy and its ability to address its next edges of growth. Chief among these next edges will be the ability to prepare principals who can consistently demonstrate race-conscious leadership in their practices in schools, and the ability to address differences in how different racial/ethnic groups experience the program itself.[16]
- Finally, the partnership will have to continue to become more systematic in its measurement practices, both for continuous improvement and to inform the field. As Bryk, Gomez, et al. say, "We cannot improve at scale what we cannot measure" (2015). While data have long been collected on UIC principals' impact on such measures as student achievement, graduation rates, culture and climate, and coaching consistency, making such data collection and analysis more consistent, and more "race conscious," is the next edge of growth for the program. One significant step in that direction has been course-embedded, data-generating leadership tasks for post-residency leaders—a form of active learning that generates information for leaders as well as for program improvement (Cosner et al., 2018).

Questions for Discussion

1. One theme of this CPS/UIC case is that a partnership that set out to address inequities in student learning outcomes in urban schools did not have a well-developed sense of how the program's systems and structures needed to improve in the pursuit of equity. To what extent was that need for improvement clear in the chapter, and to what extent does this seem to be a challenge that LEA/IHE partnerships in general need to address?
2. The Developmental Progressions served as a key organizing device for telling the story of the CPS/UIC Partnership. Conversely, the chapter is intended to illuminate the value of the Developmental Progressions as a "boundary object" that can help LEAs and IHEs work effectively together on specific problems of practice. To what extent do the Developmental Progressions appear to be a boundary object that can be useful in the LEA and IHE contexts with which you are most familiar?

---

[16] For example, see UIC Associate Professor Decoteau Irby's chapter on Inquiry Cycles and Race Conscious Leadership (Irby, 2021). As noted, he currently leads professional development with UIC coaches and faculty.

3. This chapter makes the case that LEA/IHE partnerships should embrace the need to seek external resources, if necessary, as readily as researchers reach out for external resources to conduct their work. The chapter also shows how external resources in turn increased internal resource allocations over time. How promising a strategy is this likely to be in the contexts with which you are most familiar—and why?

References

Allen, L. E. (2021). How should I feel about that? Renaissance 2010 and school reform in Chicago. In I. C. Carrier & A. J. Griffin (Eds.), *Fighting the good fight: Narratives of the African American principal ship* (pp. 99–104). Word & Deed Publishing.

Anderson, E., & Reynolds, A. (2015). The state of state policies for principal preparation program approval and candidate licensure. *Journal of Research on Leadership Education, 10*(3), 193–221. https://doi.org/10.1177/1942775115614292

Bartanen, B., Husain, A. N., & Liebowitz, D. L. (2022). *Rethinking principal effects on student outcomes* (Ed Working Paper No. 22-261). Annenberg Institute at Brown University. https://doi.org/10.26300/r5sf-3918

Bereiter, C., & Scardamalia, M. (1993). *Surpassing ourselves: An inquiry into the nature and implications of expertise.* Open Court.

Bryk, A. S., Gomez, L., Grunow, A., & LeMahieu, P. (2015). *Learning to improve: How America's schools can get better at getting better.* Harvard Education Press.

Bryk, A. S., Greenberg, S., Bertani, A., et al. (2023). *How a city learned to improve its schools.* Harvard Education Press.

Bryk, A. S., Sebring, P. B., Allensworth, E., Luppescu, S., & Easton, J. Q. (2010). *Organizing schools for improvement: Lessons from Chicago.* University of Chicago Press.

Bryk, A. S., Sebring, P. B., Kerbow, D., Rollow, S., & Easton, J. Q. (1999). *Charting Chicago school reform: Democratic localism as a lever for change.* Westview Press.

Bush, G. W. (2000, July 10). *Text: George W. Bush's speech to the NAACP.* eMediaMillWorks, The Washington Post Company. Retrieved August 6, 2022, from https://www.washingtonpost.com/wp-srv/onpolitics/elections/bushtext071000.htm

Cafferty, S. M. (2010). *An historical analysis of the Chicago Public Schools policy on the requirements for the selection of principals 1983–2008* (Paper 60) [Dissertation, Loyola University EdD]. eCommons. http://ecommons.luc.edu/luc_diss/60

Cheney, G. R., Davis, J., & Garrett, K. (2010). *A new approach to principal preparation.* Rainwater Foundation.

Chenoweth, K. (2021). *Districts that succeed: Breaking the correlation between race, poverty, and achievement.* Harvard Ed Press.

Chicago Public Schools Office of Equity. (2019). *Equity framework.* https://www.cps.edu/sites/equity/equity-framework/

Chicago Public Schools Office of Principal Preparation and Development. (2007). *Leadership coach resource guide.* Chicago Public Schools Office of Principal Preparation and Development.

Cosner, S. A. (2019). Assembling the right team for implementing a continuously improving principal preparation program: Lessons learned at the university of Illinois at Chicago. In E. Hunt, A. Haller, & L. Hood (Eds.), *Reforming principal preparation at the state level: Perspectives on policy reform from Illinois* (pp. 205–206). Routledge.

Cosner, S. A. (2020). A deeper look into next generation active learning designs for educational leader preparation. *Journal of Research on Leadership Education, 15*(3), 167–173. https://doi.org/10.1177/1942775120936301

Cosner, S. (2022, July 18). *Working to strengthen the principal pipeline at the University of Illinois at Chicago* [Conference presentation]. OSEP Leadership and Project Directors' Conference.

Cosner, S., & De Voto, C. (2023). Strengthening the developmental opportunity of the clinical experience in principal preparation: Leadership coach as broker and third-party influencer. *Educational Administration Quarterly.* https://journals.sagepub.com/doi/10.1177/0013161X231153812

Cosner, S. A. (2019). What makes a leadership preparation program exemplary? *Journal of Research on Leadership Education, 14*(1), 98–115. https://journals.sagepub.com/doi/pdf/10.1177/1942775118819661

Cosner, S. A., De Voto, C., & Rah'man, A. (2018). Harnessing the school context as a learning resource in school leader development. *Journal of Research on Leadership Education, 13*(3), 238–255.

Cosner, S. A., Tozer, S., & Smylie, M. A. (2012). The Ed.D. program at the university of Illinois at Chicago: Using continuous improvement to promote school leadership preparation. *Planning and Changing, 43*(1/2), 127–148.

Cosner, S. A., Tozer, S., & Zavitkovky, P. (2016). Enacting a cycle of inquiry capstone research project in doctoral-level leadership preparation. In V. A. Storey & K. A. Hesbol (Eds.), *Contemporary approaches to dissertation development and research methods* (pp. 163–184). IGI.

Cosner, S. A., Tozer, S., Zavitkovky, P., & Whalen, S. P. (2015). Cultivating exemplary school leadership preparation in a research intensive university. *Journal of Research on Leadership Education, 10*(1), 11–38.

Cosner, S. A., Walker, L. J., Swanson, J., Hebert, M., & Whalen, S. P. (2018). Examining the architecture of leadership coaching: Considering developmental affordances from multifarious structuring. *Journal of Educational Administration, 56*(3), 364–380. https://www.emerald.com/insight/content/doi/10.1108/JEA-05-2017-0049/full/html

Darling-Hammond, L., Wechsler, M. E., Levin, S., & Tozer, S. (2022). *Developing effective principals: What kind of learning matters?* Learning Policy Institute. https://doi.org/10.54300/641.201

Davis, S. H., & Darling-Hammond, L. (2012). Innovative principal preparation programs: What works and how we know. *Planning and Changing, 43*(1/2), 25–45.

Edmonds, R. F. (1979). Effective schools for the urban poor. *Education Leadership, 37*, 15–24.

Elmore, R. F. (1999–2000). Building a new structure for school leadership (Report No. ED546618). The Albert Shanker Institute. https://files.eric.ed.gov/fulltext/ED546618.pdf

Elmore, R. F. (2004). *School reform from the inside out.* Harvard Education Press.

Elmore, R. F., Grossman, A. S., & King, C. (2006) Managing the Chicago public schools. In S. Childress, R. F. Elmore, A. S. Grossman, & S. M. Johnson (Eds.), *Managing school districts for high performance.* Harvard Ed Press.

Emanuel, R. (2016, December 16). *It's time to stop with false choices.* The Washington Post.

Finn, C. E., & Eli Broad, E. (2003) *Better leaders for America's schools: A manifesto.* The Broad Foundation and the Fordham Foundation.

Fitzpatrick, L. (2016, November 14). *CPS trying to stanch rapid turnover of principals.* Chicago Sun Times. https://chicago.suntimes.com/2016/11/14/18352057/cps-trying-to-stanch-rapid-turnover-of-principals

Gates, S. M., Baird, M. D., Master, B. K., & Chavez-Herrerias, E. R. (2019). *Principal pipelines: A feasible, affordable, and effective way for districts to improve schools.* Rand Corporation.

Gomez, L. M., Biag, M., & Imig, D. G. (2020). Learning at the boundaries: Reconsidering university-district partnerships for educational change. In N. S. Nasir, C. D. Lee, R. Pea, & M. McKinney de Royston (Eds.), *Handbook of the cultural foundations of learning* (pp. 365–384). Routledge.

Grissom, J. A., Egalite, A., & Lindsay, C. A. (2021). *How principals affect students and schools: A synthesis of two decades of research.* The Wallace Foundation. http://www.wallacefoundation.org/principalsynthesis

Grissom, J. A., Mitani, H., & Blissett, R. S. L. (2017). Principal licensure exams and future job performance: Evidence from the school leaders licensure assessment. *Education Evaluation & Policy Analysis, 39*(2), 248–280.

Hallinger, P., & Heck, R. H. (1996). Reassessing the principal's role in school effectiveness: A review of empirical research, 1980–1995. *Educational Administration Quarterly, 32*(1), 5–44.

Hunt, E., Hood, L., Haller, A., & Kincaid, M. (Eds.). (2019) *Reforming principal preparation at the state level: Perspectives on policy reform from Illinois.* Routledge.

Illinois Board of Higher Education Blue Ribbon Commission, Illinois State University. (2006). *School leader preparation: A blueprint for change.* Illinois Board of Higher Education Blue Ribbon Commission, Illinois State University. http://www.ibhe.org/Board/agendas/2007/August/Item19.pdf

Illinois School Leader Task Force, Illinois State University. (2008). *Report to the general assembly.* Illinois School Leader Task Force, Illinois State University.

Illinois State University. (2016). *Illinois school leadership advisory council final report.* https://education.illinoisstate.edu/downloads/csep/ISLAC-Final-Report.pdf

Irby, D. (2021) *Stuck improving: Inquiry-driven racial equity improvement and capacity for change.* Harvard Education Press.

Irby, D., Payne, C., & Anderson, C. (Eds.). (2021). *Somebodiness: A call for dignity-affirming education.* Teachers College Press.

Leggett, S. R., DeSander, M. K., & Stewart, T. A. (2022). Lessons learned from designing a principal preparation program: Equity, coherence, and collaboration. *Journal of Research on Leadership Education.* Advance online publication. https://doi.org/10.1177/194277512210902

Leithwood, K. (2006) Transformational school leadership for large-scale reform: Effects on students, teachers, and their classroom practices. *School Effectiveness and School Improvement, 17*(2), 201–227.

Levine, A. L. (2005). *Educating school leaders.* The Education School Project.

Manna, P. (2015). *Developing excellent principals to advance teaching and learning: Considerations for state policy.* Wallace Foundation. https://www.wallacefoundation.org/knowledge-center/pages/developing-excellent-school-principals.aspx

Manna, P. (2021). *How can state policy support local school districts as they develop comprehensive and aligned principal pipelines?* Wallace Foundation. https://www.wallacefoundation.org/knowledge-center/Documents/How-Can-State-Policy-Support-Local-School-Districts-Principal-Pipelines.pdf

Mayrowetz, D., Murphy, J., Louis, K. S., & Smylie, M. A. (2007). Distributed leadership as work redesign: Retrofitting the job characteristics model. *Leadership and Policy in Schools, 6*(1), 69–101.

Mayrowetz, D., & Price, J. P. (2005). Contested territory: Parents and teachers wrestle for power in an urban neighborhood school located within a gentrifying community. *Journal of Cases in Educational Leadership, 8*(3), 72–87.

Murphy, J., & Shipman, N. (1999). The interstate school leaders and licensure consortium: A standards-based approach to strengthening educational leadership. *Journal of Personnel Evaluation in Education, 13*(3), 205–224.

Northern Illinois University College of Education Alumni. (2020, September 28). *Principal residency program creates model for development of school leaders.* https://cedu.news.niu.edu/2020/09/28/principal-residency-program-creates-model-for-development-of-school-leaders/

O'Doherty, A., Young, M. D., & Cunningham, K. M. W. (2021). *Redesigning educational leadership preparation for equity.* Routledge.

Perrone, F., Young, M. D., & Fuller, E. J. (2021). A call for data on the principal pipeline. *Educational Researcher, 55*(6), 1–8. https://doi.org/10.3102/0013189X221075767

Reardon, S. F., & Hinze-Pifer, R. (2017). *Test score growth among public school students in Chicago, 2009–2014.* Stanford Center for Education Policy Analysis.

Richard, M., & Cosner, S. (2022). Using cycles of inquiry to drive equity-oriented curricular improvement within one leadership preparation program. In D. Fowler, J. Vasquez Heilig, S. Louganatos, & A. Johnson (Eds.), *Equity & access: An analysis of educational leadership preparation, policy & practice* (pp. 17–39). Information Age Publishing.

Richard, M., Salisbury, J., & Cosner, S. A. (2020) Examining social justice leaders in educational market contexts. In C. A. Mullen (Ed.), *Handbook of social justice interventions in education.* Springer. https://doi.org/10.1007/978-3-030-29553-0_103-1

Rutledge, D., & Tozer, S. (2019). Policy transfer from local to statewide: Scaling evidence-based principal preparation practices in Illinois. In E. Hunt, A. Haller, & L. Hood (Eds.), *Reforming principal preparation at the state level: Perspectives on policy reform from Illinois* (pp. 62–88). Routledge.

Salisbury, J. (2019). Promoting culturally relevant educational practices: Leveraging locally designed instructional artifacts as change agents. *Journal of School Leadership, 29*(5), 361–388.

Salisbury, J. (2020a). A tale of racial fortuity: Interrogating the silent covenants of a high school's definition of success for youth of color. *American Journal of Education, 126*(2), 265–291.

Salisbury, J. (2020b). Moving a school towards cultural relevance: Leveraging organizational routines and locally developed artifacts to shape social interactions. *Journal of Education for Students Placed at Risk, 25*(2), 126–145. https://doi.org/10.1080/10824669.2019.1705161

Salisbury, J., & Irby, D. (2020). Leveraging active-learning pedagogy in a scaffolded approach: Reconceptualizing instructional leadership learning. *Journal of Research on Leadership Education, 15*(3), 210–226. https://doi.org/10.1177/1942775120936

Salisbury, J., & Richard, M. (2020). Anti-racist activist leadership. In A. D. Welton, S. Diem, & D. R. Owens (Eds.), *Strengthening anti-racist leaders: Advocating for racial justice in turbulent times.* Bloomsbury.

Shoho, A. R., Barnett, B. G., & Martinez, P. (2012). Enhancing "OTJ" internships with interactive coaching. *Planning and Changing, 43*(1/2), 161–182.

Smylie, M. A. (2009). *Continuous school improvement.* Corwin.

The Chicago Public Education Fund. (2017). *Progress report.* http://thefundchicago.org/2017progressreport

The Chicago Public Education Fund. (2021). *Chicago's school leaders: 2020–2021.* https://thefundchicago.org/wp-content/uploads/2021/03/2020-21-Chicago-Principals-Overview-1.pdf

Tozer, S. (2018). Social foundations of education as an unwelcome counter-narrative and as educational praxis. *Educational Studies, 54*(1), 89–98. https://doi.org/10.1080/00131946.2017.1397518

Tozer, S. (2019). The UIC story: Starting with a question. In E. Hunt, A. Haller, & L. Hood (Eds.), *Reforming principal preparation at the state level: Perspectives on policy reform from Illinois*. Routledge.

Tozer, S., & Walker, L. J. (2021). *Reducing chronic absence: Making equity strategies specific, adaptive, and evidence-based*. University of Illinois Chicago, Center for Urban Education Leadership. https://urbanedleadership.org/wp-content/uploads/2022/02/FINALFINALChronicAbsenceDecember-2021-1.pdf

Tozer, S., Zavitkovsky, P., Whalen, S. P., & Martinez, P. (2015). Change agency in our own backyards: Meeting the challenges of next generation programs in school leader preparation. In M. Khalifa, N. Witherspoon Arnold, A. F. Osanloo, & C. M. Grant (Eds.), *Handbook of urban educational leadership* (pp. 480–495). Rowman & Littlefield.

University of Illinois Chicago College of Education. (2022). *The leaders we support*. https://education.uic.edu/academics/programs/school-leadership/schools-principals/

Walker, K. W. (2022). *"I need people": Mentoring as a strategy to support Black doctoral student success* [Unpublished doctoral dissertation]. Northeastern University.

Walker, L., & Tozer, S. (2021). *Towards the continuous improvement of Chicago Public Schools' high-churn elementary schools*. University of Illinois Chicago Center for Urban Education Leadership. https://urbanedleadership.org/wp-content/uploads/2022/02/HighChurnBrief_FINAL.pdf

Walker, L., Tozer, S., Webb, K., Parkinson, K. K., & Whalen, S. (2018). *Continuous improvement brief: Selection of school leadership candidates for UIC's EdD urban education leadership program (Part II)*. Center for Urban Education Leadership, University Illinois at Chicago. https://urbanedleadership.org/wp-content/uploads/2019/11/Selection-Brief-Part-II-Final-June-2018.pdf

Walker, L. J., Tozer, S., Webb, K., Parkinson, K. K., & Whalen, S. (2017). *Continuous improvement brief: Selection of school leadership candidates for UIC's Ed.D. urban education leadership program*. Center for Urban Education Leadership, University Illinois at Chicago. https://urbanedleadership.org/wp-content/uploads/2019/11/Selection-Brief-Part-I-Final-April-2017.pdf

Wang, E. L., Gates, S. M., & Herman, R. (2022). *District partnerships with university principal preparation programs: A summary of findings for school district leaders* (Volume 3, Part 4). RAND Corporation. https://www.rand.org/content/dam/rand/pubs/research_reports/RRA400/RRA413-6/RAND_RRA413-6.pdf

Weldon, W., & Barajas, P. (2008). *Insights achieved and challenges faced by the educational doctorate program at the University of Illinois at Chicago, 2001–2008: An historical review and self-study* [Unpublished monograph]. University of Illinois Chicago.

Welton, A. J., Owens, D. R., & Zamani-Gallagher, E. M. (2018). Anti-racist change: A conceptual framework for educational institutions to take systemic action. *Teachers College Record, 120*, 140314.

Whalen, S. P. (2021). *Transforming central office practices for equity, coherence, and continuous improvement: Chicago Public Schools under the leadership of Dr. Janice K. Jackson*. Center for Urban Education Leadership.

Whalen, S. P., Horsley, H. L., Parkinson, K. P., & Pacchiano, D. (2016). A development evaluation of a professional development initiative to strengthen organizational conditions in early education settings. *Journal of Applied Research on Children: Informing Policy for Children at Risk, 7*(2), Article 9.

Young, M. D. (2015). Effective leadership preparation: We know what it looks like and what it can do. *Journal of Research on Leadership Education, 10*(1), 3–10.

Young, M. D., & Crow, G. M. (Eds.). (2016). *Handbook of research on the education of school leaders* (2nd ed.). Routledge.

Zavitkovsky, P., Roarty, D., & Swanson, J. (2016). *How standardized test reports let us down under No Child Left Behind.* Center for Urban Education Leadership, University Illinois at Chicago. https://urbanedleadership.org/what-we-do/practice-dissemination-and-policy-advocacy/

Zavitkovsky, P., & Tozer, S. (2017). *Upstate/downstate: Changing patterns of achievement, demographics and school effectiveness in Illinois Public Schools under NCLB.* Center for Urban Education Leadership, University Illinois at Chicago. https://urbanedleadership.org/wp-content/uploads/2020/02/UPSTATE-DOWNSTATE-FINAL-w-Appendices-06.16.17.pdf

Conclusion
EVOLVING TETHERS THAT BIND SCHOOL DISTRICT TO UNIVERSITY

Louis M. Gomez and Manuelito Biag

Tightly Tethered Mutuality

After consistent quality teaching, the most critical facet of a child's education is high-quality school leadership (Grissom et al., 2021). As we close this volume, we accentuate what the preceding chapters have to say about achieving high-quality leadership in districts and schools. We take a field-level perspective on the work that contributors to this book have shared with us. In taking this field-level view on human interaction, we follow Scott (2014) and attend to iLEAD as "a collection of diverse, interdependent organizations that participate in a common meaning system" (p. 106).

Leadership at its core is coordination activity. In a school, it is leading that keeps the moving parts in view, aligned, and operating well. When the tasks of leading are spread across distinct organizations with their own institutional norms, culture, and practices, as they are here in this book, coordination is even more important. We underscore how iLEAD members leveraged their efforts to press for new field-level relationships between LEAs and IHEs. Our concluding remarks highlight how this network is working to co-construct what might become a new *common meaning system* that could exist between higher education institutions, districts, and schools. This book offers a glimpse into *how* partnerships committed to making mutuality work in a variety of settings. It details the evolution of mutuality in multiple contexts and reveals the practices of social learning that engender new common meaning systems between LEAs and IHEs. If these new meaning systems are to be sustained and institutionalized, we would learn in the years to come if the efforts described here contributed to reshaping the commerce between two historically siloed institutions.

Generally, universities and K–12 systems in the United States are loosely tethered (figure C.1). They tend to have transactional relationships based on rendering and receiving services. Moreover, LEAs and IHEs have weak connections among their constituents. Figure C.1 characterizes the normal state of relationships between universities and their school district partners. In the main, the administration in the two organizations is roughly connected around the provision of some transaction or service. In some cases, faculty are connected (as denoted by the dashed lines) to district

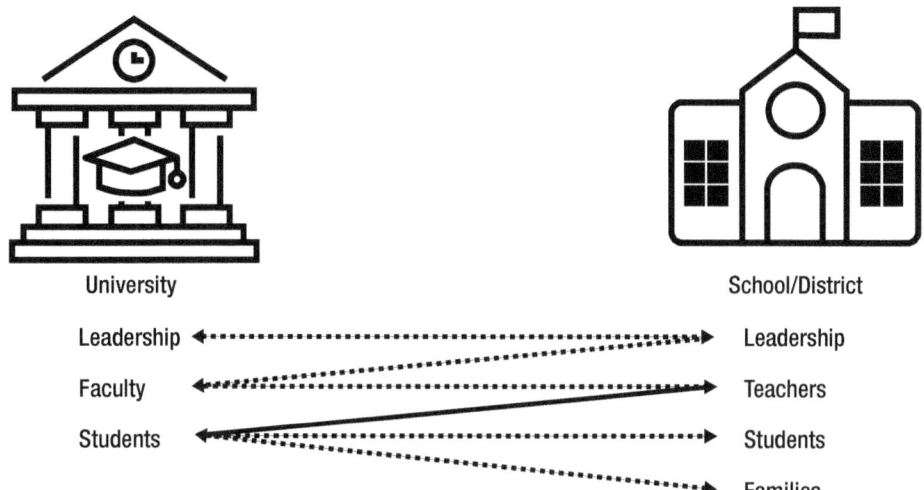

Figure C.1 Loosely tethered social arrangements between IHEs and LEAs.

leadership. Classroom teachers rarely have any sort of relationship with university leadership, and public-school students and families are generally not known beyond those university students in training to become school leaders. All of this is unfortunate as education schools and departments are an untapped resource for university community-level scholarly impact. We are in an age where postsecondary institutions are increasingly appreciating the value of community-engaged scholarship, where the evolving understanding is that scholarship deeply connected to communities leads to students' democratic citizenship, mobilizes scholarly insight into action, and hones organizational focus on improving community well-being (Gelmon et al., 2013).

The iLEAD authors conceive a more tightly coupled social arrangement between LEAs and IHEs. The contributors herein view the proper, and more meaningful, arrangement between universities, districts, and schools as much more closely tethered (as denoted by the solid lines) than the transactional relationships that have become the norm (figure C.2). Many of the efforts and lessons documented in this book represent prototypes of how these new arrangements form, operate, and sustain. As we suggest in figure C.2, this volume offers examples from diverse contexts, where multiple levels of IHEs and LEAs are firmly coupled. The authors highlight the individual, social, and organizational resources that might be required to bring about these coordinated and mutually beneficial relationships.

Educationists, including school district practitioners, researchers, and policymakers, have understood collaborative and collective action as a primary vehicle for improvement for at least the last three decades. This trend has, for instance, been reified in schools through professional learning communities that are now commonplace (Brown et al., 2018; DuFour & Eaker, 2009). Research–practice partnerships (Farrell et al., 2021) are also becoming the preferred research arrangement to achieve empirical results and produce theory as well as practice-relevant knowledge. Collaborative research is extolled for its ability to mine both relationships, building

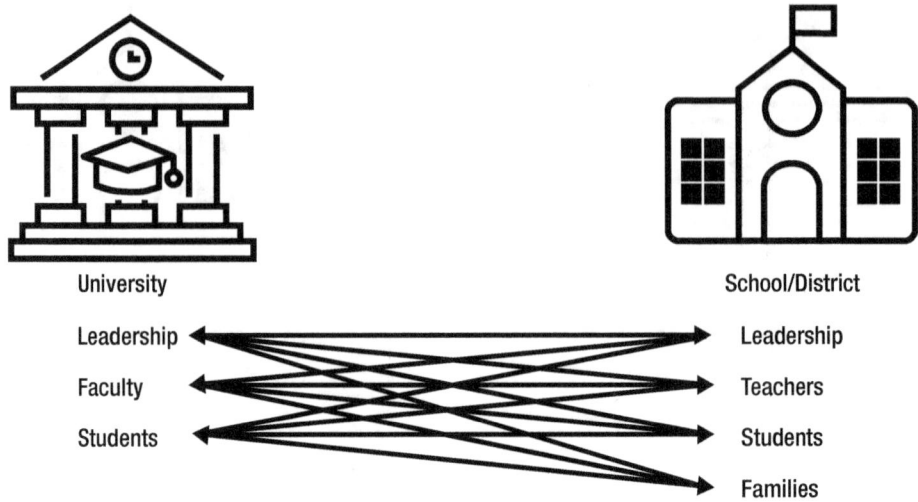

Figure C.2 Tightly tethered social arrangements between IHEs and LEAs.

interpersonal connectedness and deeper content understanding in educational practice and scholarship.

Attending to the *How* of Partnerships

While we have seen a steadily rising tide of collective activity at many levels of the education ecology, fruitful collaboration at the institutional level has been, at best, marked by fits and starts with little sustained progress (Goodlad, 1993). For example, consider undertakings like the Holmes Group (Fullan et al., 1998) and Holmes Partnership (Thurman, 2007). These efforts to reform teacher education, via collaboratives among IHEs and LEAs, leave us feeling that they could have done more to reconfigure institutional relationships between these two distinct organizations (Goodlad, 1988).

It would be hard to argue that the landscape has changed. According to some scholars (e.g., Goodlad 1988, 1993; Olson, 1987), at least part of what prevented Holmes, and perhaps other endeavors like it, from doing more was the weak attention to the specific mechanisms that might better bond LEAs and IHEs to one another. The question is how work processes and new social arrangements might change the way schools, districts, and universities work together. In each of the local contexts portrayed in this book, the authors have been stirred to action by the belief that the discovery and implementation of mutualistic work processes, disciplined by educational improvement science, would ultimately lead to better lives for the children in their charge. What distinguishes the efforts herein is that each contributor attempts to learn how to catalyze institutional-level collaboratives by doing them intensively, rather than speculating about or aspiring to them. Viewed through the lens of field building, their efforts characterize the types of actions necessary to establish a new and sustainable social contract between LEAs and IHEs that is less transactional and more for shared benefit.

Some scholars (e.g., Eddy-Spicer et al., 2020) make the case that establishing a new social contract between K–12 and postsecondary institutions can be problematic because it is a fundamentally disruptive activity. It is a contested intellectual space because some individuals are happy with things the way they are and others, like the iLEAD members, want to turn the existing social contract topsy-turvy. Disruptive change occurs in the social sector when everyday ways of doing business are challenged and fundamentally recast anew. While the activities of the present contributors do not exactly match all characteristics of disruptive social innovators offered by Christensen and colleagues (2006), there is enough of a family resemblance to conjecture that iLEAD contributors are well on their way down the road to disrupt relationships between districts and schools and their university partners.

The Role of the Carnegie Foundation for the Advancement of Teaching

Disruption requires some type of catalytic investment. The institutional changes described in this book were catalyzed by a significant organizational investment from the Carnegie Foundation for the Advancement of Teaching. From the disruption perspective, the Foundation acted as institutional entrepreneur—an actor(s) who can envision institutions breaking away from traditional patterns of behavior and establishing new patterns of action. To accomplish catalyzing new field relationships, institutional entrepreneurs must demonstrate a certain amount of institutional nonconformity (Lepoutre & Valente, 2012). Hardy and McGuire (2017) suggest that entrepreneurs catalyze because they "possess cognitive/symbolic and material immunity to dominant institutional logics" (p. 3). With a long history of innovation in education and the ability to see beyond traditional institutional logic, the Foundation, as convener and catalyst, was able to bring diverse actors together to organize a path for iLEAD to take shape.

The field-building work of iLEAD is an evolutionary tale of how these contributors sought to restructure practices that connect postsecondary and K–12 systems reciprocally. Eddy-Spicer and colleagues (2020) note that this is challenging relational work. Most complex human endeavors are launched through talk and interpersonal coordinated action. We argue that the building or recasting of a field is no different. The effort catalyzed by the Carnegie Foundation brought together school principals, teachers, university faculty, and college deans, among others, willing to fashion a new kind of relationship between their institutions. These stakeholders needed a structured and intellectually safe space to talk about complex matters. The Foundation provided this safe space. It was then the challenge of the field actors to create a relational infrastructure to sustain their interactions. The work of iLEAD is like other disruptive social innovations in that a common aspiration evolves into several models of activity and service (Christensen et al. 2006).

Building a Strong Field: Infrastructure that Recasts Partnerships

It is often impossible to essentialize complex human endeavors without disservice to human action's nuance and subtlety. We believe, however, that in this case we can extract the essence of this book. Contributors to iLEAD aimed to recraft the relationships between LEAs and IHEs to be better coordinated and mutualistic. Some nuances characterize each partnership that makes it different from its peers. Yet essentially, each partnership used the Carnegie Foundation's catalyzing energy in common ways to initiate or substantially modify their work. They each built a prototype of a new form of LEA–IHE relationality in their local context. Each chapter shows how a group of similarly intentioned people attempted to re-regulate and re-coordinate work between K–12 and postsecondary systems so that they are better positioned to improve learning outcomes for all students—especially those who are most disenfranchised.

A field, according to the James Irvine Foundation and the Bridgespan Group (2009) is a "community of organizations and individuals working together to achieve a common goal and using a common set of approaches to achieve that goal" (p. 1). The iLEAD efforts to inter-organizational regulation and coordination leads us to believe that we are observing the early days of a new field undergoing formation. One might argue that previous change efforts at the nexus of higher education and K–12, such as the Holmes Group, were suboptimal because members did not see it as essential or did not know *how*—to re-create the social bonds on the inter-organizational level. It is surely the case today that LEAs and IHEs each agree that the other is important to leader and educator preparation. Yet the field has not seen significant numbers of IHEs and LEAs develop an intentional focus on the specific inter-organizational protocols, routines, structures, and supports that enable joint work to be accomplished efficiently and effectively.

Building a field requires new specific forms of organizational interaction. The chapters in the volume make it clear the essential work is guided by a new institutional logic that shifts the architecture of the relationship between schools, districts, and universities. The traditional logic that governed their relationship, in addition to being transactional, was largely IHE-centric and guided by the individual preferences of IHE faculty and leaders—which were in turn conditioned by the norms of individual faculty success within IHEs. By contrast, the new evolving logic hews toward mutuality and shared governance. In this new logic, LEA problems of practice are the key drivers of activity, and the partnerships are not *owned* by individuals but by institutions.

As new fields evolve, the James Irvine Foundation and Bridgespan Group suggest five key characteristics that govern productive and positive evolution: shared identity, standards of practice, knowledge base, leadership and grassroots support, and funding and supporting policy. The point of these field-building elements is to construct a relational infrastructure. In table C.1, we provide a small and incomplete snapshot into how these five elements of building a strong field are enlivened in iLEAD. This table reflects how social infrastructure is developmental in nature. As such, we use the language of *first-mile* and *last-mile* activity to capture the endpoints of this evolutionary journey.

First-mile activities help to initiate the process. First-mile conversations and activities are where big ideas are introduced to a community. One example of a first-mile conversation can be found in the University of Maryland–Prince George's County case narrative. Here, the conversation about forming a new relationship between the IHE and LEA was seen as a big idea for the new president of the university. That initiating conversation strand evolved and began to enter last-mile-like territory when the LEA and IHE together crafted a new and far-reaching memorandum of understanding (MOU) that has a form of shared governance between the two organizations. Undoubtedly, there is more ground to cover including advancing system and human capability development to ensure ongoing learning and growth. Nonetheless, such conversations and activities help move a community toward sustainable implementation.

These elements of field evolution allow us to see how institutions gradually organize to become mutualistic. In the iLEAD case, infrastructure develops to accommodate the need to execute the new forms of activity by using and building boundary objects like the Developmental Progressions framework or collective problem-solving tools in improvement science (e.g., driver diagrams). The infrastructure's aim is to shape behavior. In the cases described here, we can see how institutional settings, protocols, routines, and processes collectively come together to support the development of personal relationships and joint work.

Creating Social Infrastructure for Collective Action

New fields coalesce around sturdy interpersonal activity that helps define the way diverse stakeholders come together at the boundary of their organizations, to accomplish shared aims. As relationships deepen, partnerships can withstand inevitable turbulence like shifts in the availability of resources or organizational leadership. The partnership and relationships are themselves worth sustaining even in the face of disagreements or misalignments, which are inescapable when bringing together two historically siloed institutions with distinct aims as well as organizational and cultural arrangements (Tozer et al., 2015).

We observe sustainable power in relational infrastructures in the stories of long-standing partnerships like those seen in Chicago and Denver. We see in these examples the engagement activities that engender field building, such as establishing a common vocabulary, new shared norms and narratives, proof points, and promising inter-organizational practices and professional development systems. These activities, and others like them, help foster alignment among a diverse set of actors to facilitate the shared development of norms and a propensity for collective action (Oris Impact, 2020).

Without a viable social infrastructure, any partnership would have had a hard time getting off the ground. Among other things, the underlying social infrastructure enabled iLEAD partners to co-construct and use the Developmental Progressions framework. We suspect that because the partners envisioned themselves on a path that encompassed the evolution of a new inter-institutional logic open to novel forms of

Table C.1 Examples of iLEAD First and Last-Mile Activities to Build a Strong Field (adapted from The Bridgespan Group, 2009)

Elements of a Strong Field	First-Mile Activities	Last-Mile Activities
(that allow actors to engage with one another in field building)	(initial big ideas, curating compelling examples, early adopting teams)	(sustainable implementation, understanding the details of local context. Sustained expertise)
Shared Identity	Initial informal conversations challenged the University of Maryland's lack of identity with Prince George's County Public Schools, which helped build relationships and develop a shared narrative around the need to address education equity-related problems in a coordinated manner.	An implemented MOU that details new inter-organizational personnel, structures, and process between Prince George's County and the University of Maryland that will guide coordinated work into the future.
Standards of Practice	Early on, for most partnerships, they used the Developmental Progressions as a score card after-the-fact, to document compliance in using improvement science problem-solving tools and processes (e.g., fishbone diagrams, driver diagrams, conducting empathy interviews and iterative Plan-Do-Study-Act cycles).	Later, the Developmental Progressions served as a planning and ongoing assessment tool to discipline planning conversations and guide the categories of work that organizational actors would carry out across their partnership and respective institutional levels.
Knowledge Base	Co-developing proposals and publications and co-presenting at professional conferences (e.g., American Educational Research Association, University Council on Educational Administration [UCEA]).	The University of Illinois, Chicago being reflective on where its knowledge products fall short, and how it can be more nuanced in understanding what works, for whom, and under what conditions.
Funding and supporting policy	In the beginning, most partnership funding was episodic (e.g., from RFPs).	Later, some partnerships (e.g., Chicago and Maryland) have evolved more stable institutionally coupled funding strategies.
Leadership and grassroots support	At the start, most partnerships engage in informal brainstorming-like conversations about how to create support for coordinated IHE-LEA work. The University of Maryland organized a network of leadership program alums to explore coordinated work.	Partnerships have evolved, with grassroot supports and structures more pervasive (e.g., university coursework that is driven by district problems and co-constructing improvement-centered ways to revamp existing routines like yearly School Improvement Planning processes).

cooperation like shared governance, the invention of the Developmental Progressions became a foreseeable next step.

The Progressions build upon past efforts that seek to bring IHEs and LEAs closer together in student and school-centered leadership operations (e.g., King, 2014), by identifying key areas of work that need attention not only within each organization but also within the partnership itself. The import of the Developmental Progressions rests in its attention both to the mutualistic and processual nature of inter-organizational work in education. Creating a type of boundary infrastructure to guide common work, the Progressions pays acute attention to the *how* as well as the *who*, from an organizational perspective, needs to be involved in the various individual processes that successfully get a partnership off the ground. In short, to genuinely enliven the Developmental Progressions each partnership had to re-invent local activity structures with the goal of mutualistic development.

Local invention leads to variation. While each iLEAD partnership relied on its social infrastructure to get work done, the way efforts were executed differed across the partnerships because place, local values, and history matter. The work described in this book demonstrates that partnerships, even when they are sharply focused on common leadership goals and values, are not monolithic—they are polylithic. It almost goes without saying that different contexts shape partnerships through their diversity. The partnership in New York, for example, developed district-based Academic Response Teams with the guidance of Fordham University faculty. These, and the activity systems they engendered, are shaped by the close alliance of NYCDOE Bronx staff with Fordham faculty by virtue of participation in the university's degree efforts. Similarly, tight coupling undergirds the partnership between the University of Illinois at Chicago and Chicago Public Schools. In both these cases, these partnerships rested on activity where improvement expertise flowed, at least initially from the IHE to the LEA.

From the perspective of expertise flow, the partnership in Fairfax, Virginia, illustrates an interesting contrast. Here, improvement science expertise was initially energized in the IHE by LEA staff; district and school level staff had more experience. After the LEA's initial efforts, the university deepened its experience in improvement science—integrating its methods, principles, and tools into its leadership coursework and degree programs which, in turn, are coupled to change efforts underway in the LEA.

We find that social infrastructures vary greatly across these partnerships. Different routines of collaboration were established to serve different problems of practice, and different kinds of support structures emerged in different partnerships. From this perspective, social infrastructure is creative co-invention that meets local needs, resources, and conditions. In no case was there a recipe to follow; rather, adaptive leadership was required in each case to lead processes of co-invention of solutions.

Institutional leadership is key to the success of the partnerships. Boundary-spanning leadership is particularly important if viable partnerships are to be initiated, valued, and nurtured. Such leadership can emerge around the identification of problems of practice that cuts across both institutions, such as district and school leadership that needs further development to be able to address inequities. In some cases, such as the partnership in Maryland, leadership was initiated at the very senior levels of the university. While in others, such as the partnership in Chicago, initiation was in the middle levels of both organizations but evolved to encompass senior leadership. For some, the iLEAD partnership is sufficiently new that we cannot discern the direction expertise flow will take.

Looking Forward: The Sustainability of Mutually Beneficial Partnerships for Leadership and Continuous Improvement

Sustainability is an implicit value in improvement practices that raises the bar for the implementation of change. Organizations like school districts and universities seek improvements that last, or better, provide a path to further improvement. Sustainable improvement is generally preferable to unsustainable. Lewin's (1947) classic portrayal of organizational change as unfreezing, changing, and re-freezing was not intended to describe ephemeral re-freezing, but instead something durable. It is fair to ask of the cases in this volume, given the evidence of change that has been documented, is the improvement sustainable?

Organizational change literature has for many decades grappled with the challenge of sustainability of change, and we do not expect to resolve this enduring problem in our concluding comments here. Instead, we want to affirm that the challenge of sustainability is one that is inherent in improvement work, and one that iLEAD partnerships are necessarily confronting in different ways and at different stages. *How to sustain promising changes is a good problem to have.*

The evidence of change presented in this volume is largely of two kinds: individual and organizational. We see innovations in professional practice initiated and enacted by individuals within and across organizations, and we see institutionalization of those changes as new norms of organizational practice. That difference between individuals and organizations is captured by the four progress indicators across the areas of work represented in the Developmental Progressions framework. For any element of change (e.g., faculty engagement in the university setting), the Progressions move from *Exploring Change Ideas*, to *Small Change Implementation* to *Integrating into the Core Work*, to *Institutionalizing and Sustaining the Work*. Changes in individual practice that were necessary to design and implement viable LEA–IHE partnerships have in many cases become *institutionalized*, in that they have become codified into new institutional norms and practices that are not dependent primarily on the preferences and behaviors of individuals. They have become part of the way that the institution does business.

A familiar university example of this is the difference between an elective seminar that a faculty member might wish to teach on occasion versus a university course requirement within a degree or credentialing program. In the latter case, the institution has made a commitment to offer the course, regardless of who teaches it—and in most cases has made a formal commitment to a state agency that the course will be offered in a timely manner. This example of institutionalization seems to be also a case of sustainability; universities typically would not institutionalize a course requirement unless they thought it was a sustainable change.

Yet what counts as institutionalization and sustainability in district-university partnerships is more complicated than that, if only because two (and sometimes more) organizations are engaged in the partnership. Just as changes in individual practices in a partnership might not be the same as institutionalizing change, so might institutionalization not be the same as sustainability. One can easily imagine institutional partnerships dissolving, as partnerships do, over changes in leadership, resources, or institutional priorities.

Perhaps the most intuitive measure of sustainability is the duration over time. Long-lasting innovations, or long-lasting partnerships, are said to have been sustained over time, while short-term innovations, even if institutionalized for that short period, are less likely to be characterized as sustained. Therefore, the safest way to assess whether partnerships are sustainable is to say, *time will tell.*

Most of the cases in this book are in their early stages of institutionalization. However, we see evidence of durability that makes it likely that these partnerships will be sustained for yet another year, and the year after that. One kind of evidence is positive impact. When partnerships are showing success at achieving their shared aims, it becomes more likely that they will want to continue the work rather than change course. Another kind of evidence is formal agreements, MOUs, and contracts—boundary objects that have helped create new modes of shared work that have led to the implementation of new offices, structures, roles, and routines of collaboration that are in some ways now easier to continue than to abandon.

Perhaps the most important piece of evidence is related to the learning of new methods of improvement that partnerships are increasingly sharing. Having learned new ways of working together for improvement that is guiding new routines to achieve collaborative problem identification and problem-solving, the partnering organizations in iLEAD are more resistant to going back to business as usual than if this learning had not taken place. Sustainability is thus dependent not just on agreements and structures, but on newly co-created knowledge about how to go forward from here.

At some level, institutionalization of new practices and routines creates the organizational capacity for ongoing professional learning by all those who participate in them, making sustainability an outcome that is more likely than not. While the partnerships in Denver and Chicago are examples of sustainable institutionalization through two decades each, the institutional capacity that is clearly being built in much younger iLEAD partnerships provides promising evidence of similar sustainability. To *institutionalize* change is to make sustainability more likely. Only time will tell if that perspective is warranted for the iLEAD partnerships, as there are no fully agreed-upon predictors of sustainability in the organizational change literature. In this regard, we note that, on the one hand, Kotter (2012) talks about *anchoring change* in organizational norms, and Sarason (2002), on the other hand, acknowledges the fragility of even the best of changes.

For several years, the Wallace Foundation has offered its institutional grantees, usually universities and school districts, an intriguing perspective on their own sustainability. In fact, Wallace provides a rubric for self-assessment of sustainability, which they refer to as the long-term staying power of the program, practice, organization, or tool (in funding, policy, and culture). Wallace highlights key considerations such as: (1) the "real" costs of operation have been determined so there is not a gap between expenses and revenue; (2) funding stability has been achieved, either from diversified sources or guaranteed funding for the next two years; (3) the program, practice, organization or tool has been institutionalized in supportive policies and/or procedures; (4) the program has been embedded in the culture (i.e., it is thought to have value and expected to continue); (5) the program is staffed with skilled personnel; (6) the program has been implemented in enough places to make a difference; and (7) partnerships have been established (e.g., partnerships with universities or professional associations) to ensure the work continues.

The concept of duration over time appears in the Wallace language in such phrases as *long-term staying power*, among others. Elements of institutionalization are also described. By the measures offered in the Wallace conceptualization of sustainability, the iLEAD partnerships would for the most part have to count themselves as doing the right things to achieve sustainability over time. Perhaps the most important of these *right things* will be to remain firmly committed to principles of continuous improvement that enable them to overcome obstacles to sustainability that might not otherwise be successfully identified and collaboratively addressed.

References

Brown, B. D., Horn, R. S., & King, G. (2018). The effective implementation of professional learning communities. *Alabama Journal of Educational Leadership*, 5, 53–59.

DuFour, R., & Eaker, R. (2009). *Professional learning communities at work: Best practices for enhancing students' achievement*. Solution Tree Press.

Eddy-Spicer, D., Arce-Trigatti, P., & Young, M. D. (2020). Field building through strategic bricolage: System leadership and the institutionalizing role of intermediary organizations. *Journal of Professional Capital and Community*, 6(1), 29–43.

Fullan, M., Galluzzo, G., Morris, P., & Watson, N. (1998). *The rise and stall of teacher education reform*. American Association of Colleges of Teacher Education.

Gelmon, S. B., Jordan, C., & Seifer, S. D. (2013). Community-engaged scholarship in the academy: An action agenda. *Change: The Magazine of Higher Learning*, 45(4), 58–66.

Goodlad, J. I. (1988). School-university partnerships: A social experiment. *Kappa Delta Pi Record*, 24(3), 77–80.

Goodlad, J. I. (1993). School-university partnerships and partner schools. *Educational Policy*, 7(1), 24–39.

Grissom, J. A., Egalite, A. J., & Lindsay, C. A. (2021). *How principals affect students and schools*. Wallace Foundation.

Hardy, C., & Maguire, S. (2017). Institutional entrepreneurship and change in fields. *The Sage Handbook of Organizational Institutionalism*, 2, 261–280.

King, C. L. (2014). *Quality measures partnership effectiveness continuum*. Education Development Center, Inc.

Kotter, J. P. (2012). *Leading change*. Harvard Business Press.

Lepoutre, J. M., & Valente, M. (2012). Fools breaking out: The role of symbolic and material immunity in explaining institutional nonconformity. *Academy of Management Journal*, 55(2), 285–313.

Lewin, K. (1947). Group decision and social change. *Readings in Social Psychology*, *3*(1), 197–211.
Olson, L. (1987). An overview of the Holmes Group. *The Phi Delta Kappan*, *68*(8), 619–621.
Sarason, S. B. (2002). *Education reform: A self-scrutinizing memoir*. Teachers College Press.
Scott, W. R. (2014). *Institutions and organizations: Ideas, interests, and identities* (4th ed.). Sage Publications.
Thurman, A. (2007). *The Holmes partnership trilogy: Tomorrow's teachers, tomorrow's schools, tomorrow's schools of education*. Peter Lang.

References

Akkerman, S. F., & Bakker, A. (2011). Learning at the boundary: An introduction. *International Journal of Educational Research*, *50*(1), 1–5. https://doi.org/10.1016/j.ijer.2011.04.002

Allen, L. E. (2021). How should I feel about that? Renaissance 2010 and school reform in Chicago. In I. C. Carrier & A. J. Griffin (Eds.), *Fighting the good fight: Narratives of the African American principal ship* (pp. 99–104). Word & Deed Publishing.

Anaissie, T., Cary, V., Clifford, D., Malarkey, T., & Wise, S. (2021). *Liberatory design*. National Equity Project. Retrieved June 30, 2022, from http://www.liberatorydesign.com

Anderson, E., & Reynolds, A. (2015). The state of state policies for principal preparation program approval and candidate licensure. *Journal of Research on Leadership Education*, *10*(3), 193–221. https://doi.org/10.1177/1942775115614292

Archer, M. S., & Archer, M. S. (1996). *Culture and agency: The place of culture in social theory*. Cambridge University Press.

Audrain, R. L. (in preparation). *Exploring teacher working conditions in a large, southwestern school district*.

Audrain, R. L., Ruiz, E. A., Wyatt, L. G., Nailor, N., & Weinberg, A. E. (under review). Sustaining teachers through collaboration and autonomy outcomes of a professional development experience. *The New Educator*.

Bailey, S. (2016). *An examination of student and educator experiences in Denver Public Schools through the voices of African-American teachers and administrators*. Denver Public Schools Culture, Equity and Leadership Team. https://celt.dpsk12.org/wp-content/uploads/sites/52/Dr.-Bailey-Report-FULL-2.pdf

Barakat, M., Reames, E., & Kensler, L. A. W. (2019). Leadership preparation programs: Preparing culturally competent educational leaders. *Journal of Research on Leadership Education*, *14*(3), 212–235. https://doi.org/10.1177/1942775118759070

Barnett, B. G., Hall, G. E., Berg, J. H., & Camarena, M. M. (2010). A typology of partnerships for promoting innovation. *Journal of School Leadership*, *20*(1), 10–36. https://doi.org/10.1177/105268469900900602

Bartanen, B., Husain, A. N., & Liebowitz, D. L. (2022). *Rethinking principal effects on student outcomes* (Ed Working Paper No. 22–261). Annenberg Institute at Brown University. https://doi.org/10.26300/r5sf-3918

Bartlett, L., & Johnson, L. (2010). The evolution of new teacher induction policy: Support, specificity, and autonomy. *Educational Policy*, *24*(6), 847–871.

Basile, C. G. (2017). *Why education innovation matters*. Mary Lou Fulton Teachers College.

Basile, C. G., & Maddin, B. W. (2022). *The next education workforce: Team-based staffing models can make schools work better for both learners and educators*. American Enterprise Institute for Public Policy Research. https://www.aei.org/research-products/report/the-next-education-workforce-team-based-staffing-models-can-make-schools-work-better-for-both-learners-and-educators/

Bell, L. A. (2016). Theoretical foundations for social justice education. In M. Adams & L. A. Bell (Eds.), *Teaching for diversity and social justice* (pp. 3–16). Routledge.

Bereiter, C., & Scardamalia, M. (1993). *Surpassing ourselves: An inquiry into the nature and implications of expertise*. Open Court.

Biag, M., Gomez, L. M., Imig, D. G., & Vasudeva, A. (2021). Responding to COVID-19 with the aid of mutually beneficial partnerships in education. *Frontiers in Education*, 5. https://www.doi.org/10.3389/feduc.2020.621361

Black, W. R., & Murtadha, K. (2007). Toward a signature pedagogy in educational leadership preparation and program assessment. *Journal of Research on Leadership Education*, 2(1), 1–29. https://doi.org/10.1177/194277510700200101

Bouckaert, G., Peters, B. G., & Verhoest, K. (2010). Coordination: What is it and why should we have it? In B. Peters, G. Bouckaert, & K. Verhoest (Eds.), *The coordination of public sector organizations* (pp. 13–33). Palgrave Macmillan.

Bowker, G. C., & Star, S. L. (1999). *Sorting things out: Classification and its consequences*. The MIT Press.

Brown, B. D., Horn, R. S., & King, G. (2018). The effective implementation of professional learning communities. *Alabama Journal of Educational Leadership*, 5, 53–59.

Bryk, A., Gomez, L., Grunow, A., & LeMahieu, P. (2015). *Learning to improve: How America's schools can get better at getting better*. Harvard University Press.

Bryk, A. S. (2020). *Improvement in action: Advancing quality in America's schools*. Harvard Education Press.

Bryk, A. S., & Gomez, L. M. (2008). *Reinventing a research and development capacity*. In F. M. Hess (Ed.), *The future of educational entrepreneurship: Possibilities for school reform*. Harvard Education Press.

Bryk, A. S., Gomez, L. M., & Grunow, A. (2011). Getting ideas into action: Building networked improvement communities in education. In M. T. Hallinan (Ed.), *Frontiers in sociology of education* (pp. 127–162). Springer.

Bryk, A. S., Gomez, L. M., Grunow, A., & LeMahieu, P. G. (2015). *Learning to improve: How America's schools can get better at getting better*. Harvard Education Press.

Bryk, A. S., Greenberg, S., & Bertani, A. (2023). *How a city learned to improve its schools*. Harvard Education Press.

Bryk, A. S., Sebring, P. B., Allensworth, E., Luppescu, S., & Easton, J. Q. (2010). *Organizing schools for improvement: Lessons from Chicago*. University of Chicago Press.

Bryk, A. S., Sebring, P. B., Kerbow, D., Rollow, S., & Easton, J. Q. (1999). *Charting Chicago school reform: Democratic localism as a lever for change*. Westview Press.

Bush, G. W. (2000, July 10). *Text: George W. Bush's speech to the NAACP*. eMediaMillWorks, The Washington Post Company. Retrieved August 6, 2022, from https://www.washingtonpost.com/wp-srv/onpolitics/elections/bushtext071000.htm

Byrne-Jimenez, M., & Orr, M. T. (2013). Evaluating social justice leadership preparation. In L. Tillman & J. J. Scherich (Eds.), *Handbook of research on educational leadership for equity and diversity* (pp. 688–720). Routledge.

Cafferty, S. M. (2010). *An historical analysis of the Chicago Public Schools policy on the requirements for the selection of principals 1983–2008* (Paper 60) [Dissertation, Loyola University EdD]. eCommons. http://ecommons.luc.edu/luc_diss/60

Caprara, G., Barbaranelli, C., Steca, P., & Malone, P. (2006). Teachers' self-efficacy beliefs as determinants of job satisfaction and students' academic achievement: A study at the school level. *Journal of School Psychology, 44*(6), 473–490.

Carlile, S. P., & Peterson, D. S. (2020). Embedding improvement science in one principal licensure course: Principal leadership for equity and inclusion. In R. Crowe, B. N. Hinnant-Crawford, & D. Spaulding (Eds.), *Teaching improvement science in educational leadership: A pedagogical guide*. Myers Education Press.

Carlile, S. P., & Peterson, D. S. (2019). Improvement science in equity-based administrative practicum redesign. In R. Crowe, B. N. Hinnant-Crawford, & D. Spaulding (Eds.), *The educational leader's guide to improvement science: Data, design and cases for reflection* (pp. 197–216). Myers Education Press.

Carnegie Foundation for the Advancement of Teaching. (2015). *The six core principles of improvement*. https://www.carnegiefoundation.org/our-ideas/six-core-principles-improvement/

Carnegie Project on the Education Doctorate. (2021). *The CPED framework*. https://www.cpedinitiative.org/the-framework

Carter, P., & Welner, K. (Eds.). (2013). *Closing the opportunity gap: What America must do to give every child an even chance*. Oxford University Press.

Cheney, G. R., Davis, J., & Garrett, K. (2010). *A new approach to principal preparation*. Rainwater Foundation.

Chenoweth, K. (2021). *Districts that succeed: Breaking the correlation between race, poverty, and achievement*. Harvard Ed Press.

Chesterfield County Public Schools. (2017). *2017 equity report*. https://mychesterfieldschools.com/download/195/school-board/14749/equity-report-2017.pdf

Chesterfield County Public Schools. (2019). *Imagine tomorrow: Creating a better tomorrow*. https://mychesterfieldschools.com/download/166/academics/16468/strategicplan_it_04082019.pdf

Chicago Public Schools Office of Equity. (2019). *Equity framework*. https://www.cps.edu/sites/equity/equity-framework/

Chicago Public Schools Office of Principal Preparation and Development. (2007). *Leadership coach resource guide*. Chicago Public Schools Office of Principal Preparation and Development.

Churchill, E. (2009). Introduction: Social glue. In K. S. Willis, G. Roussos, K. Chorianopoulous, & M. Struppek (Eds.), *Shared encounters: Content sharing as social glue in public places*. Springer-Verlag.

Coburn, C. E., & Penuel, W. R. (2016). Research–practice partnerships in education: Outcomes, dynamics, and open questions. *Educational Researcher, 45*(1), 48–54. https://doi.org/10.3102/0013189X16631750

Code of Virginia, Administrative Code. § 8VAC20-543-570. *State board of education-regulations governing the review and approval of education programs in Virginia-competencies for endorsement areas-administration and supervision pre K-12*. https://law.lis.virginia.gov/admincode/title8/agency20/chapter543/section570/

Collins, H., Evans, R., & Gorman, M. (2007). Trading zones and interactional expertise. *Studies in History and Philosophy of Science Part A, 38*(4), 657–666.

Cosner, S. (2019). What makes a leadership preparation program exemplary? *Journal of Research on Leadership Education, 14*(1), 98–115. https://doi.org/10.1177/1942775118819661

Cosner, S. (2020). A deeper look into next generation active learning designs for educational leader preparation. *Journal of Research on Leadership Education, 15*(3), 167–172. https://doi.org/10.1177/1942775120936301

Cosner, S. (2022, July 18). *Working to strengthen the principal pipeline at the University of Illinois at Chicago* [Conference presentation]. OSEP Leadership and Project Directors' Conference.

Cosner, S., & De Voto, C. (in press). Strengthening the developmental opportunity of the clinical experience in principal preparation: Leadership coach as broker and third-party influencer. *Educational Administration Quarterly.*

Cosner, S., De Voto, C., & Rah'man, A. (2018). Drawing in the school context as a learning resource in school leader development: Application-oriented projects in active learning designs. *Journal of Research on Leadership Education, 13*(3), 238–255. https://doi.org/10.1177/1942775118763872

Cosner, S., Tozer, S., Zavitkovsky, P., & Whalen, S. P. (2015). Cultivating exemplary school leadership preparation at a research intensive university. *Journal of Research on Leadership Education, 10*(1), 11–38.

Cosner, S. A. (2019a). Assembling the right team for implementing a continuously improving principal preparation program: Lessons learned at the university of Illinois at Chicago. In E. Hunt, A. Haller, & L. Hood (Eds.), *Reforming principal preparation at the state level: Perspectives on policy reform from Illinois* (pp. 205–206). Routledge.

Cosner, S. A. (2019b). What makes a leadership preparation program exemplary? *Journal of Research on Leadership Education, 14*(1), 98–115. https://journals.sagepub.com/doi/pdf/10.1177/1942775118819661

Cosner, S. A. (2020). A deeper look into next generation active learning designs for educational leader preparation. *Journal of Research on Leadership Education, 15*(3), 167–173. https://doi.org/10.1177/1942775120936301

Cosner, S. A., De Voto, C., & Rah'man, A. (2018). Harnessing the school context as a learning resource in school leader development. *Journal of Research on Leadership Education, 13*(3), 238–255.

Cosner, S. A., Tozer, S., & Smylie, M. A. (2012). The Ed.D. program at the university of Illinois at Chicago: Using continuous improvement to promote school leadership preparation. *Planning and Changing, 43*(1/2), 127–148.

Cosner, S. A., Tozer, S., & Zavitkovky, P. (2016). Enacting a cycle of inquiry capstone research project in doctoral-level leadership preparation. In V. A. Storey & K. A. Hesbol (Eds.), *Contemporary approaches to dissertation development and research methods* (pp. 163–184). IGI.

Cosner, S. A., Tozer, S., Zavitkovky, P., & Whalen, S. P. (2015). Cultivating exemplary school leadership preparation in a research intensive university. *Journal of Research on Leadership Education, 10*(1), 11–38.

Cosner, S. A., Walker, L. J., Swanson, J., Hebert, M., & Whalen, S. P. (2018). Examining the architecture of leadership coaching: Considering developmental affordances from multifarious structuring. *Journal of Educational Administration, 56*(3), 364–380. https://www.emerald.com/insight/content/doi/10.1108/JEA-05-2017-0049/full/html

Crow, G. A., Arnold, N. R., Reed, C. J., & Shoho, A. R. (2012). The complexity of leveraging university program change. *Journal of Research on Leadership Education, 7*(2), 172–194.

Cuban, L. (2018, December 9). *Whatever happened to team teaching? Larry Cuban on School Reform and Classroom Practice.* Retrieved August 5, 2022, from https://www.larrycuban.wordpress.com/2018/12/09/whatever-

Cunningham, K. M. W., VanGronigen, B. A., Tucker, P. D., & Young, M. D. (2019). Using powerful learning experiences to prepare school leaders. *Journal of Research on Leadership Education, 14*(1), 74–97. https://doi.org/10.1177/1942775118819672

Danielson, C. (2015, March 23). *Helping educators overcome "initiative fatigue."* Education Week. Retrieved June 30, 2022, from https://www.edweek.org/teaching-learning/opinion-helping-educators-overcome-initiative-fatigue/2015/03

Darling-Hammond, L. (2001). The challenge of staffing our schools. *Educational Leadership*, *58*(8), 12–17.

Darling-Hammond, L., Meyerson, D., LaPointe, M., & Terry Orr, M. (2010). Lessons from effective school leadership programs. *Preparing Principals for a Changing World*. https://leseprobe.buch.de/images-adb/cb/11/cb118d84-61fb-472d-b152-ba8e5bbeb234.pdf

Darling-Hammond, L., Meyerson, D., La Pointe, M. M., & Orr, M. T. (2010). *Preparing principals for a changing world*. Jossey-Bass.

Darling-Hammond, L., & Oakes, J. (2019). *Preparing teachers for deeper learning*. Harvard Education Press.

Darling-Hammond, L., Schachner, A., & Edgerton, A. K. (with Badrinarayan, A., Cardichon, J., Cookson, P. W., Jr., Griffith, M., Klevan, S., Maier, A., Martinez, M., Melnick, H., Truong, N., & Wojcikiewicz, S.). (2020). *Restarting and reinventing school: Learning in the time of COVID and beyond*. Learning Policy Institute. https://restart-reinvent.learningpolicyinstitute.org/

Darling-Hammond, L., Wechsler, M. E., Levin, S., Leung-Gagné, M., & Tozer, S. (2022). *Developing effective principals: What kind of learning matters?* Learning Policy Institute. https://doi.org/10.54300/641.201

Darling-Hammond, L., Wechsler, M. E., Levin, S., & Tozer, S. (2022). *Developing effective principals: What kind of learning matters?* Learning Policy Institute. https://doi.org/10.54300/641.201

Darling-Hammond, L., Wei, R. C., Andree, A., Richardson, N., & Orphanos, S. (2009). *Professional learning in the learning profession: A status report on teacher development in the United States and abroad*. National Staff Development Council. https://learningforward.org/docs/default-source/pdf/nsdcstudy2009.pdf

Data Quality Campaign. (2017). *From hammer to flashlight: A decade of data in education*. https://dataqualitycampaign.org/resource/from-hammer-to-flashlight-a-decade-of-data-in-education/

Davis, J. (2016). *Improving university principal preparation programs: Five themes from the field*. Wallace Foundation. https://www.wallacefoundation.org/knowledge-center/Documents/Improving-University-Principal-Preparation-Programs.pdf

Davis, S. H., & Darling-Hammond, L. (2012). Innovative principal preparation programs: What works and how we know. *Planning and Changing*, *43*(1/2), 25–45.

Dawes, S. S., Cresswell, A. M., & Pardo, T. A. (2009). From "need to know" to "need to share": Tangled problems, information boundaries, and the building of public sector knowledge networks. *Public Administration Review*, *69*(3), 392–402.

Denver Public Schools. (2017, March 15). *DPS announces discipline reform for youngest students*. Retrieved June 30, 2022, from https://www.dpsk12.org/dps-announces-discipline-reform-for-youngest-students/

Dexter, S., Clement, D., Moraguez, D., & Watson, G. S. (2020). (Inter)active learning tools and pedagogical strategies in educational leadership preparation. *Journal of Research on Leadership Education*, *15*(3), 173–191. https://doi.org/10.1177/1942775120936299

DiGiacomo, D. K., & Gutiérrez, K. D. (2016). Relational equity as a design tool within making and tinkering activities. *Mind, Culture, and Activity*, *23*(2), 141–153.

DuFour, R., & Eaker, R. (2009). *Professional learning communities at work: Best practices for enhancing students' achievement*. Solution Tree Press.

Eddy-Spicer, D., Arce-Trigatti, P., & Young, M. D. (2020). Field building through strategic bricolage: System leadership and the institutionalizing role of intermediary organizations. *Journal of Professional Capital and Community*, *6*(1), 29–43.

Eddy-Spicer, D. H., Anderson, E., & Perrone, F. (2017). Neither urban core nor rural fringe: "In-between" districts and the shifting landscape of school performance in the United States. In C. V. Meyers & M. Darwin (Eds.), *Enduring myths that inhibit school turnaround* (pp. 49–69). Information Age Publishing.

Edmonds, R. F. (1979). Effective schools for the urban poor. *Education Leadership*, *37*, 15–24.

Educator Advancement Council. (2019, July). *Oregon educator equity report*. https://www.oregon.gov/tspc/about/Publications_and_Reports/2019_Oregon_Educator_Equity_Report_Exec_Summary.pdf

Elmore, R. F. (1999–2000). Building a new structure for school leadership (Report No. ED546618). The Albert Shanker Institute. https://files.eric.ed.gov/fulltext/ED546618.pdf

Elmore, R. F. (2004). *School reform from the inside out*. Harvard Education Press.

Elmore, R. F., Grossman, A. S., & King, C. (2006). Managing the Chicago public schools. In S. Childress, R. F. Elmore, A. S. Grossman, & S. M. Johnson (Eds.), *Managing school districts for high performance*. Harvard Ed Press.

Emanuel, R. (2016, December 16). *It's time to stop with false choices*. The Washington Post.

Engeström, Y. (2009). The future of activity theory: A rough draft. In A. Sannino, H. Daniels, & K. D. Gutierrez (Eds.), *Learning and expanding with activity theory* (pp. 303–328). Cambridge University Press.

Eubanks, S., McLaughlin, M., Snell, J. L., & Coleman, C. (2021). From learning to leading: Teaching leaders to apply improvement science through a school-university partnership. In D. T. Spaulding, R. Crow, & B. N. Hinnant-Crawford (Eds.), *Teaching improvement science in educational leadership* (pp. 141–162). Myers Education Press.

Feiman-Nemser, S. (2020). From preparation to practice: Designing a continuum to strengthen and sustain teaching. *Teachers College Record*, *103*(6), 1013–1055. https://doi.org/10.1111/0161-4681.00141

Fergus, E. (2016). *Solving disproportionality and achieving equity: A leader's guide to using data to change hearts and minds*. Corwin Press, SAGE Publications, Inc.

Fine, G. A. (2012). *Tiny publics: A theory of group action and culture*. Russell Sage.

Finn, C. E., & Eli Broad, E. (2003) *Better leaders for America's schools: A manifesto*. The Broad Foundation and the Fordham Foundation.

Fitzpatrick, L. (2016, November 14). *CPS trying to stanch rapid turnover of principals*. Chicago Sun Times. https://chicago.suntimes.com/2016/11/14/18352057/cps-trying-to-stanch-rapid-turnover-of-principals

Forman, M. L., Stosich, E. L., & Bocala, C. (2017). *The internal coherence framework: Creating the conditions for continuous improvement in schools*. Harvard Education Press.

Fullan, M., Galluzzo, G., Morris, P., & Watson, N. (1998). *The rise and stall of teacher education reform*. American Association of Colleges of Teacher Education.

Galison, P. (2010). Trading with the enemy. In M. E. Gorman (Ed.), *Trading zones and interactional expertise: Creating new kinds of collaboration* (pp. 25–52). The MIT Press.

Gates, S. M., Baird, M. D., Master, B. K., & Chavez-Herrerias, E. R. (2019). *Principal pipelines: A feasible, affordable, and effective way for districts to improve schools*. Rand Corporation.

Gay, G. (2010). *Culturally responsive teaching: Theory, research and practice*. Teachers College Press.

GBAO Research & Strategy. (2022, February 28). *Poll results: Stress and burnout pose threat of educator shortages*. GBAO Memo. https://www.nea.org/sites/default/files/2022-02/NEA%20Member%20COVID-19%20Survey%20Summary.pdf

Gelmon, S. B., Jordan, C., & Seifer, S. D. (2013). Community-engaged scholarship in the academy: An action agenda. *Change: The Magazine of Higher Learning*, *45*(4), 58–66.

George Mason University School of Education. (2022). *Education leadership program.* https://education.gmu.edu/education-leadership/

Glesne, C. (2011). *Becoming qualitative researchers: An introduction* (4th ed.). Pearson Education, Inc.

Gomez, L., Biag, M., & Imig, D. (2022). 19. Improvement science: The social glue that helps helpers help. In M. Suárez-Orozco & C. Suárez-Orozco (Eds.), *Education: A global compact for a time of crisis* (pp. 335–360). Columbia University Press. https://doi.org/10.7312/suar20434-022

Gomez, L. M., Biag, M., & Imig, D. G. (2020). Learning at the boundaries: Reconsidering university-district partnerships for educational change. In N. S. Nasir, C. D. Lee, R. Pea, & M. McKinney de Royston (Eds.), *Handbook of the cultural foundations of learning* (pp. 365–384). Routledge.

Goodlad, J. I. (1988). School-university partnerships: A social experiment. *Kappa Delta Pi Record, 24*(3), 77–80.

Goodlad, J. I. (1993). School-university partnerships and partner schools. *Educational Policy, 7*(1), 24–39.

Gorman, M. E. (2002). Levels of expertise and trading zones: A framework for multidisciplinary collaboration. *Social Studies of Science, 32*(5–6), 933–938.

Gorman, M. E., Mehalik, M. M., & Werhane, P. H. (2000). *Ethical and environmental challenges to engineering.* Prentice Hall.

Grissom, J. A., Egalite, A. J., & Lindsay, C. A. (2021a). *How principals affect students and schools.* Wallace Foundation.

Grissom, J. A., Egalite, A. J., & Lindsay, C. A. (2021b). *How principals affect students and schools: A systematic synthesis of two decades of research.* The Wallace Foundation. http://www.wallacefoundation.org/principalsynthesis

Grissom, J. A., Egalite, A., & Lindsay, C. A. (2021c). *How principals affect students and schools: A synthesis of two decades of research.* The Wallace Foundation. http://www.wallacefoundation.org/principalsynthesis

Grissom, J. A., Mitani, H., & Blissett, R. S. L. (2017). Principal licensure exams and future job performance: Evidence from the school leaders licensure assessment. *Education Evaluation & Policy Analysis, 39*(2), 248–280.

Grunow, A., Hough, H., Park, S., Willis, J., & Krausen, K. (2018). *Towards a common vision of continuous improvement for California.* Stanford University Policy Analysis for California Education (PACE). https://www.edpolicyinca.org/publications/towards-common-vision-continuous-improvement-california

Gulati, R., Wohlgezogen, F., & Zhelyazkov, P. (2012). The two facets of collaboration: Cooperation and coordination in strategic alliances. *The Academy of Management Annals, 6*(1), 531–583. https://doi.org/10.1080/19416520.2012.691646

Hall, G., & Hord, S. (2015). *Implementing change: Patterns, principles and potholes.* Pearson.

Hallinger, P., & Heck, R. H. (1996). Reassessing the principal's role in school effectiveness: A review of empirical research, 1980–1995. *Educational Administration Quarterly, 32*(1), 5–44.

Hardy, C., & Maguire, S. (2017). Institutional entrepreneurship and change in fields. *The Sage Handbook of Organizational Institutionalism, 2,* 261–280.

Hargrove, B. (2019). *Project momentum Arizona: The Avondale ESD case study.* Avondale Elementary School District.

Hargrove, B. (2022, June 2). *How our district turned failing schools into excelling ones (and others can to).* AzCentral.

Hiebert, J., Gallimore, R., & Stigler, J. W. (2002). A knowledge base for the teaching profession: What would it look like and how can we get one? *Educational Researcher, 31*(5), 3–15.

Hinnant-Crawford, B. (2020). *Improvement science in education: A primer*. Meyers Education Press.

Honig, M. I. (2004). The new middle management: Intermediary organizations in education policy implementation. *Educational Evaluation and Policy Analysis, 26*(1), 65–87. https://doi.org/10.3102/01623737026001065

Honig, M. I. (2012). District central office leadership as teaching: How central office administrators support principals' development as instructional leaders. *Educational Administration Quarterly, 48*(4), 733–774. https://doi.org/10.1177/0013161x12443258

Howey, K., & Zimpher, N. (2007). Creating p-16 urban systemic partnerships to address core structural problems in the educational pipeline. In B. Wehling (Ed.), *Building a 21st century U.S. education system*. National Commission on Teaching and America's Future.

Hulpia, H., Devos, G., & Rosseel, Y. (2009). The relationship between the perception of distributed leadership in secondary schools and teachers' and teacher leaders' job satisfaction and organizational commitment. *School Effectiveness and School Improvement, 20*(3), 291–317. https://doi.org/10.1080/09243450902909840

Hunt, E., Hood, L., Haller, A., & Kincaid, M. (Eds.). (2019) *Reforming principal preparation at the state level: Perspectives on policy reform from Illinois*. Routledge.

iLEAD. (2021). *Carnegie foundation for the advancement of teaching*. https://www.carnegiefoundation.org/our-work/networked-improvement/ilead/

Illinois Board of Higher Education Blue Ribbon Commission, Illinois State University. (2006). *School leader preparation: A blueprint for change*. Illinois Board of Higher Education Blue Ribbon Commission, Illinois State University. http://www.ibhe.org/Board/agendas/2007/August/Item19.pdf

Illinois School Leader Task Force, Illinois State University. (2008). *Report to the general assembly*. Illinois School Leader Task Force, Illinois State University.

Illinois State University. (2016). *Illinois school leadership advisory council final report*. https://education.illinoisstate.edu/downloads/csep/ISLAC-Final-Report.pdf

Indiana University Center for Postsecondary Research. (2021). *Graduate instructional program classification*. The Carnegie Classifications of Institutions of Higher Education. https://carnegieclassifications.iu.edu/classification_descriptions/grad_program.php

Ingersoll, R., Merrill, E., Stuckey, D., & Collins, G. (2018). *Seven trends: The transformation of the teaching force*. Consortium for Policy Research in Education.

Ingersoll, R. M., Merrill, E., Stuckey, D., & Collins, G. (2018). *Seven trends: The transformation of the teaching force – Updated October 2018*. Consortium for Policy Research in Education. https://repository.upenn.edu/cpre_researchreports/108/

Irby, D. (2021) *Stuck improving: Inquiry-driven racial equity improvement and capacity for change*. Harvard Education Press.

Irby, D., Payne, C., & Anderson, C. (Eds.). (2021). *Somebodiness: A call for dignity-affirming education*. Teachers College Press.

Johns Hopkins University. (2022). *Results from the year one survey of next education workforce (NEW) teachers*. https://education.asu.edu/sites/default/files/2022-08/ASU_NEW_Technical_Report_13July22.pdf

Kania, J., Kramer, M., & Senge, P. (2018). *The water of systems change*. FSG. https://www.fsg.org/wp-content/uploads/2021/08/The-Water-of-Systems-Change_rc.pdf

Kelley, D., & Kelley, T. (2013). *Creative confidence: Unleashing the creative potential within us all*. Crown Business.

King, C. L. (2014). *Quality measures partnership effectiveness continuum*. Education Development Center, Inc.

Korach, S., Anderson, E., Hesbol, K., Tabron, L., Candelarie, D., Kipp, P., & Miller-Brown, E. (2018). Interdependence and reciprocity: Partnership ethos at the University of Denver. *Journal of Research on Leadership Education, 14*(1), 31–50. https://doi.org/10.1177/1942775118819679

Korach, S., Anderson, E., Hesbol, K., Tabron, L., Candelarie, D. K., & Miller-Brown, E. (2019). Interdependence and reciprocity: Partnership ethos at the University of Denver. *Journal of Research on Leadership Education, 14*(1), 31–50. https://doi.org/10.1177/1942775118819679

Kotter, J. P. (2012). *Leading change*. Harvard Business Press.

Ladson-Billings, G. (2021). I'm here for the hard re-set: Post pandemic pedagogy to preserve our culture. *Equity & Excellence in Education, 54*(1), 68–78.

Langley, G., Moen, R., Nolan, K., Thomas, N., & Provost, L. (2009). *The improvement guide: A practical approach to enhancing organizational performance*. John Wiley & Sons.

Langley, G. J., Moen, R. D., Nolan, K. M., Nolan, T. W., Norman, C. L., & Provost, L. P. (2014). *The improvement guide: A practical approach to enhancing organizational performance* (3rd ed.). Jossey-Bass.

Lave, J., & Wenger, E. (1991). *Situated learning: Legitimate peripheral participation*. Cambridge University Press.

Leggett, S. R., DeSander, M. K., & Stewart, T. A. (2022). Lessons learned from designing a principal preparation program: Equity, coherence, and collaboration. *Journal of Research on Leadership Education*. Advance online publication. https://doi.org/10.1177/19427751221090 2

Leithwood, K. (2006) Transformational school leadership for large-scale reform: Effects on students, teachers, and their classroom practices. *School Effectiveness and School Improvement, 17*(2), 201–227.

Leithwood, K. (2017). The Ontario leadership framework: Successful school leadership practices and personal leadership resources. In K. Leithwood, J. Sun, & K. Pollock (Eds.), *How school leaders contribute to student success: The four paths framework* (pp. 31–43). Springer International Publishing.

LeMahieu, P., Grunow, A., Baker, L., Nordstrum, L., & Gomez, L. (2017). Networked improvement communities: The discipline of improvement science meets the power of network. *Quality Assurance in Education, 25*(1), 5–25.

Lepoutre, J. M., & Valente, M. (2012). Fools breaking out: The role of symbolic and material immunity in explaining institutional nonconformity. *Academy of Management Journal, 55*(2), 285–313.

Levine, A. L. (2005). *Educating school leaders*. The Education School Project.

Lewin, K. (1947). Group decision and social change. *Readings in Social Psychology, 3*(1), 197–211.

Lovo, P., Cavazzos, L., & Simmons, D. (2006). From BTSA to induction: The changing role of school districts in teacher credentialing. *Issues in Teacher Education, 15*(1), 53–68.

Manna, P. (2015). *Developing excellent principals to advance teaching and learning: Considerations for state policy*. Wallace Foundation. https://www.wallacefoundation.org/knowledge-center/pages/developing-excellent-school-principals.aspx

Manna, P. (2021). *How can state policy support local school districts as they develop comprehensive and aligned principal pipelines?* Wallace Foundation. https://www.wallacefoundation.org/knowledge-center/Documents/How-Can-State-Policy-Support-Local-School-Districts-Principal-Pipelines.pdf

Mayrowetz, D., Murphy, J., Louis, K. S., & Smylie, M. A. (2007). Distributed leadership as work redesign: Retrofitting the job characteristics model. *Leadership and Policy in Schools, 6*(1), 69–101.

Mayrowetz, D., & Price, J. P. (2005). Contested territory: Parents and teachers wrestle for power in an urban neighborhood school located within a gentrifying community. *Journal of Cases in Educational Leadership, 8*(3), 72–87.

McDiarmid, G.W., & Caprino, K. (2019). *Lessons from the teachers for a new era project evidence and accountability in teacher education.* Routledge.

McKenzie, K. B., Christman, D. E., Hernandez, F., Fierro, E., Capper, C. A., Dantley, M., Gonzalex, M. L., Cambron-McCabe, N., & Scheurich, J. J. (2007). From the field: A proposal for educating leaders for social justice. *Educational Administration Quarterly, 44*(1), 111–138. https://doi.org/10.1177/0013161X07309470

McKinsey and Company. (2021). *New allies: How governments can unlock the potential of social entrepreneurs for the common good.* Catalyst 20301. https://catalyst2030.net/wp-content/uploads/2021_New-Allies_How-governments-can-unlock-the-potential-of-social-entrepreneurs-for-the-common-good_vpublish.pdf

McNamara, M. (2012). Starting to untangle the web of cooperation, coordination, and collaboration: A framework for public managers. *International Journal of Public Administration, 35*(6), 389–401.

Meadows, D. H. (1997, Winter). Places to intervene in a system. *Whole Earth.* http://www.wholeearthmag.com/ArticleBin/109.html

Mesh, A. (2022, June 6). *Feds indict proud boys who paraded through Portland on seditious conspiracy charges for D.C. plot.* Willamette Week. https://www.wweek.com/news/courts/2022/06/06/feds-indict-proud-boys-who-paraded-through-portland-on-seditious-conspiracy-charges-for-dc-plot/

Mintrop, R. (2016). *Design-based school improvement.* Harvard Education Press.

Mississippi Department of Education Office of District and School Performance. (n.d.). *Accountability report.* Retrieved August 29, 2022, from https://www.mdek12.org/OPR/Reporting/Accountability

Mitang, L. (2012). *The making of the principal: Five lessons in leadership training.* The Wallace Foundation. https://www.wallacefoundation.org/knowledge-center/Documents/The-Making-of-the-Principal-Five-Lessons-in-Leadership-Training.pdf

Muller, L., Froggett, L., & Bennett, J. (2020). Emergent knowledge in the third space of art-science. *Leonardo, 53*(3), 321–326.

Murphy, J., & Shipman, N. (1999). The interstate school leaders and licensure consortium: A standards-based approach to strengthening educational leadership. *Journal of Personnel Evaluation in Education, 13*(3), 205–224.

Ni, Y., Hollingworth, L., Rorrer, A., & Pounder, D. (2016). The evaluation of educational leadership preparation programs. In M. D. Young & G. M. Crow (Eds.), *Handbook of research on the education of school leaders* (pp. 173–201). Routledge.

Northern Illinois University College of Education Alumni. (2020, September 28). *Principal residency program creates model for development of school leaders.* https://cedu.news.niu.edu/2020/09/28/principal-residency-program-creates-model-for-development-of-school-leaders/

NPBEA. (2018). *National educational leadership preparation (NELP) program standards—Building level.* http://www.npbea.org

O'Doherty, A., Young, M. D., & Cunningham, K. M. W. (2021). *Redesigning educational leadership preparation for equity.* Routledge.

Olson, L. (1987). An overview of the Holmes Group. *The Phi Delta Kappan, 68*(8), 619–621.

Oregon Secretary of State. (2019). *ODE and PPS must do more to monitor spending and address systemic obstacles to student performance, particularly at struggling schools.* Oregon Audits Division. https://sos.oregon.gov/audits/Documents/2019-01.pdf

Orphanos, S., & Orr, M. T. (2014). Learning leadership matters: The influence of innovative school leadership preparation on teachers' experiences and outcomes. *Educational Management, Administration & Leadership, 42*(5), 680–700.

Orr, M. T. (2012). *Creating high quality internships in suburban and small city districts.* University Council for Educational Administration.

Orr, M. T. (2020). Reflections on active learning in leadership development. *Journal of Research on Leadership Education, 15*(3), 227–234. https://doi.org/10.1177/1942775120936305

Orr, M. T., & Barber, M. E. (2006). Collaborative leadership preparation: A comparative study of partnership and conventional programs and practices. *Journal of School Leadership, 16*(6), 709–739. https://doi.org/10.1177/105268460601600603

Orr, M. T., King, C., & La Pointe, M. M. (2010). *Districts developing leaders: Eight districts' lessons on strategy, program approach and organization to improve the quality of leaders for local schools.* Report prepared for The Wallace Foundation. Educational Development Center, Inc.

Orr, M. T., & Pounder, D. G. (2010). Teaching and preparing school leaders. In S. Conley & B. S. Cooper (Eds.), *Finding, preparing, and supporting school leaders: Critical issues, useful solutions.* Rowman Littlefield.

Park, S., Hironaka, S., Carver, P., & Nordstrum, L. (2013) *Continuous improvement in education: Advancing teaching—Improving learning.* Carnegie Foundation for the Advancement of Teaching. https://www.carnegiefoundation.org/wp-content/uploads/2014/09/carnegie-foundation_continuous-improvement_2013.05.pdf

Park, S., & Takahashi, S. (2013). *90-Day cycle handbook.* Carnegie Foundation for the Advancement of Teaching. https://www.carnegiefoundation.org/resources/publications/90-day-cycle-handbook/

Partelow, L. (2019, December 3). *What to make of declining enrollment in teacher preparation programs.* Center for American Progress. https://www.americanprogress.org/issues/education-k-12/reports/2019/12/03/477311/make-declining-enrollment-teacher-preparation-programs/

Penuel, W., & Gallagher, D. (2017). *Creating research-practice partnerships in education.* Harvard University Press.

Penuel, W. R., Allen, A. R., Coburn, C. E., & Farrell, C. (2015). Conceptualizing research–practice partnerships as joint work at boundaries. *Journal of Education for Students Placed at Risk, 20*(1–2), 182–197. https://doi.org/10.1080/10824669.2014.988334

Perkins, D. N. (2009). *Making learning whole: How seven principles of teaching can transform education.* Jossey-Bass.

Perrone, F., Young, M. D., & Fuller, E. J. (2021). A call for data on the principal pipeline. *Educational Researcher, 55*(6), 1–8. https://doi.org/10.3102/0013189X221075767

Perry, J., Zambo, D., & Crow R. (2020). *The improvement science dissertation in practice.* Myers Education Press.

Peterson, D. S., & Carlile, S. P. (2019). Preparing school leaders to effectively lead school improvement efforts: Improvement science. In R. Crowe, B. N. Hinnant-Crawford, & D. Spaulding (Eds.), *The educational leader's guide to improvement science: Data, design and cases for reflection* (pp. 167–182). Myers Education Press.

Peterson, D. S., & Carlile, S. P. (2021). *Improvement science: Promoting equity in schools.* Myers Education Press.

Peterson, D. S., & Carlile, S. P. (2022). *Improvement science as a tool for school enhancement: Solutions for better educational outcomes.* Myers Education Press.

Peterson, D. S., Carlile, S. P., Olivar, M. E., & Thonstad, C. (2020). Embedding improvement science in principal licensure courses: Program redesign. In R. Crowe, B. N. Hinnant-Crawford, & D. Spaulding (Eds.), *Teaching improvement science in educational leadership: A pedagogical guide*. Myers Education Press.

Pinchot, G., III. (1985). *Intrapreneuring: Why you don't have to leave the corporation to become an entrepreneur*. Harper & Row.

Pledger, M. (2020). *Culturally responsive continuous improvement*. HTH Unboxed. https://hthunboxed.org/unboxed_posts/culturally-responsive-continuous-improvement/

Podolsky, A., Kini, T., Bishop, J., & Darling-Hammond, L. (2016). *Solving the teacher shortage: How to attract and retain excellent educators*. Learning Policy Institute.

Prince George's County Public Schools. (n.d.). *About PGCPS*. Retrieved August 29, 2022, from https://www.pgcps.org/about-pgcps

Radinsky, J., Bouillon, L., Lento, E. M., & Gomez, L. M. (2001). Mutual benefit partnership: A curricular design for authenticity. *Journal of Curriculum Studies, 33*(4), 405–430.

Reardon, S. F., & Hinze-Pifer, R. (2017). *Test score growth among public school students in Chicago, 2009–2014*. Stanford Center for Education Policy Analysis.

Richard, M., & Cosner, S. (2022). Using cycles of inquiry to drive equity-oriented curricular improvement within one leadership preparation program. In D. Fowler, J. Vasquez Heilig, S. Jouganatos, & A. Johnson (Eds.), *Equity & access: An analysis of educational leadership preparation, policy & practice* (pp. 17–39). Information Age Publishing.

Richard, M., Salisbury, J., & Cosner, S. A. (2020) Examining social justice leaders in educational market contexts. In C. A. Mullen (Ed.), *Handbook of social justice interventions in education*. Springer. https://doi.org/10.1007/978-3-030-29553-0_103-1

Rutledge, D., & Tozer, S. (2019). Policy transfer from local to statewide: Scaling evidence-based principal preparation practices in Illinois. In E. Hunt, A. Haller, & L. Hood (Eds.), *Reforming principal preparation at the state level: Perspectives on policy reform from Illinois* (pp. 62–88). Routledge.

Salisbury, J. (2019). Promoting culturally relevant educational practices: Leveraging locally designed instructional artifacts as change agents. *Journal of School Leadership, 29*(5), 361–388.

Salisbury, J. (2020a). A tale of racial fortuity: Interrogating the silent covenants of a high school's definition of success for youth of color. *American Journal of Education, 126*(2), 265–291.

Salisbury, J. (2020b). Moving a school towards cultural relevance: Leveraging organizational routines and locally developed artifacts to shape social interactions. *Journal of Education for Students Placed at Risk, 25*(2), 126–145. https://doi.org/10.1080/10824669.2019.1705161

Salisbury, J., & Irby, D. (2020). Leveraging active-learning pedagogy in a scaffolded approach: Reconceptualizing instructional leadership learning. *Journal of Research on Leadership Education, 15*(3), 210–226. https://doi.org/10.1177/1942775120936

Salisbury, J., & Richard, M. (2020). Anti-racist activist leadership. In A. D. Welton, S. Diem, & D. R. Owens (Eds.), *Strengthening anti-racist leaders: Advocating for racial justice in turbulent times*. Bloomsbury.

Sanzo, K. L., Myran, S., & Clayton, J. K. (2011). Building bridges between knowledge and practice. *Journal of Educational Administration, 49*(3), 292–312. https://doi.org/10.1108/09578231111129073

Sarason, S. B. (2002). *Education reform: A self-scrutinizing memoir*. Teachers College Press.

Scott, W. R. (2014). *Institutions and organizations: Ideas, interests, and identities* (4th ed.). Sage Publications.

Scott, W. R., & Davis, G. F. (2007). *Organizations and organizing: Rational, natural, and open system perspectives*. Pearson Education, Inc.

Senge, P. (2012). *Schools that learn*. Random House.

Shoho, A. R., Barnett, B. G., & Martinez, P. (2012). Enhancing "OTJ" internships with interactive coaching. *Planning and Changing, 43*(1/2), 161–182.

Shulman, L. S. (2005). Signature pedagogies in the professions. *Daedalus, 134*(3), 52–59. https://doi.org/10.2307/20027998

Smylie, M. A. (2009). *Continuous school improvement*. Corwin.

Snodgrass Rangel, V. (2017). A review of the literature on principal turnover. *Review of Educational Research, 88*(1), 003465431774319. https://doi.org/10.3102/0034654317743197

Snyder, T. D., & Dillow, S. A. (2010). *Digest of education statistics 2009 (NCES 2010-013)*. National Center for Education Statistics, Institute of Education Sciences, U.S. Department of Education.

Spillane, J. P. (2005). Distributed leadership. *The Educational Forum, 69*(2), 30, 143–150. https://www.doi.org/10.1080/00131720508984678

Star, S. L., & Griesemer, J. R. (1989). Institutional ecology, "translations" and boundary objects: Amateurs and professionals in Berkeley's Museum of Vertebrate Zoology, 1907–39. *Social Studies of Science, 19*(3), 387–420. https://images-insite.sgp1.digitaloceanspaces.com/dunia_buku/koleksi-buku-lainnya/institutional-ecology-translations-and-boundary-objects-amateurs-pdfdrivecom-42531582402862.pdf

Stone-Johnson, C., & Hayes, S. (2021). Using improvement science to (re)design leadership preparation: Exploring curriculum change across five university programs. *Journal of Research on Leadership Education, 16*(4), 339–359. http://doi.org/10.1177/1942775120933935

Tait, M. K., & Brunson, M. W. (2021). Evaluating cooperative interactions and the roles organizations play in cross-boundary stewardship. *Society & Natural Resources, 34*(7), 925–942.

The Chicago Public Education Fund. (2017). *Progress report*. http://thefundchicago.org/2017progressreport

The Chicago Public Education Fund. (2021). *Chicago's school leaders: 2020–2021*. https://thefundchicago.org/wp-content/uploads/2021/03/2020-21-Chicago-Principals-Overview-1.pdf

The CPED Framework©. (2022). *Carnegie project on the educational doctorate*. https://www.cpedinitiative.org/the-framework#:~:text=To%20build%20an%20EdD%20program,and%20solve%20problems%20of%20practice

Thurman, A. (2007). *The Holmes partnership trilogy: Tomorrow's teachers, tomorrow's schools, tomorrow's schools of education*. Peter Lang.

Tozer, S. (2018). Social foundations of education as an unwelcome counter-narrative and as educational praxis. *Educational Studies, 54*(1), 89–98. https://doi.org/10.1080/00131946.2017.1397518

Tozer, S. (2019). The UIC story: Starting with a question. In E. Hunt, A. Haller, & L. Hood (Eds.), *Reforming principal preparation at the state level: Perspectives on policy reform from Illinois*. Routledge.

Tozer, S., & Walker, L. (2021a). *Reducing chronic absence: Making equity strategies specific, adaptive, and evidence-based*. The Center for Urban Education Leadership (CUEL). https://urbanedleadership.org/

Tozer, S., & Walker, L. J. (2021b). *Reducing chronic absence: Making equity strategies specific, adaptive, and evidence-based*. University of Illinois Chicago, Center for Urban Education Leadership. https://urbanedleadership.org/wp-content/uploads/2022/02/FINALFINALChronicAbsenceDecember-2021-1.pdf

Tozer, S., Zavitkovsky, P., Whalen, S. P., & Martinez, P. (2015). Change agency in our own backyards: Meeting the challenges of next generation programs in school leader preparation.

In M. Khalifa, N. Witherspoon Arnold, A. F. Osanloo, & C. M. Grant (Eds.), *Handbook of urban educational leadership* (pp. 480–495). Rowman & Littlefield.

Trubowitz, S. (1986). Stages in the development of school-college collaboration. *Educational Leadership*, *43*(5), 18–21. http://search.ebscohost.com.pallas2.tcl.sc.edu/login.aspx?direct=true&db=aph&AN=8519525&site=ehost-live

Turnbull, B., Riley, D., Arcaira, E., Anderson, L., & MacFarlane, J. (2013). *Six districts begin the principal pipeline initiative*. Policy Studies Associates, Inc. http://www.eric.ed.gov/contentdelivery/servlet/ERICServlet?accno=ED555867

Tyack, D., & Tobin, W. (1994). The "grammar" of schooling: Why has it been so hard to change? *American Educational Research Journal*, *31*(3), 453–479. https://www.doi.org/10.2307/1163222

University of Illinois Chicago College of Education. (2022). *The leaders we support*. https://education.uic.edu/academics/programs/school-leadership/schools-principals/

University of Maryland. (n.d.). *About UMD*. Retrieved August 29, 2022, from https://www.admissions.umd.edu/explore/about-umd

University of South Carolina College of Education. (n.d.). *About us*. https://sc.edu/study/colleges_schools/education/about/

Velásquez, C., Biag, M., Gomez, L., & Imig, D. (2019). Partnering for leadership development and continuous improvement: Carnegie's improvement leadership education and development network. *AERA Learning and Teaching in Educational Leadership Newsletter*.

Walker, K. W. (2022). *"I need people": Mentoring as a strategy to support Black doctoral student success* [Unpublished doctoral dissertation]. Northeastern University.

Walker, L., & Tozer, S. (2021). *Towards the continuous improvement of Chicago Public Schools' high-churn elementary schools*. University of Illinois Chicago Center for Urban Education Leadership. https://urbanedleadership.org/wp-content/uploads/2022/02/HighChurnBrief_FINAL.pdf

Walker, L., Tozer, S., Webb, K., Parkinson, K. K., & Whalen, S. (2018). *Continuous improvement brief: Selection of school leadership candidates for UIC's EdD urban education leadership program (Part II)*. Center for Urban Education Leadership, University Illinois at Chicago. https://urbanedleadership.org/wp-content/uploads/2019/11/Selection-Brief-Part-II-Final-June-2018.pdf

Walker, L. J., Tozer, S., Webb, K., Parkinson, K. K., & Whalen, S. (2017). *Continuous improvement brief: Selection of school leadership candidates for UIC's Ed.D. urban education leadership program*. Center for Urban Education Leadership, University Illinois at Chicago. https://urbanedleadership.org/wp-content/uploads/2019/11/Selection-Brief-Part-I-Final-April-2017.pdf

Walker, T. (2021, November 12). *Getting serious about teacher burnout*. NEA Today. https://www.nea.org/advocating-for-change/new-from-nea/getting-serious-about-teacher-burnout

Walsh, M. E., & Backe, S. (2013). School-university partnerships: Reflections and opportunities. *Peabody Journal of Education*, *88*(5), 594–607. https://doi.org/10.1080/0161956X.2013.835158

Wang, E., Gates, S., Herman, R., Mean, M., Perera, R., Tsai, T., Whipkey, K., & Andrew, M. (2018). Executive summary. In *Launching a redesign of university principal preparation programs: Partners collaborate for change*. https://doi.org/10.7249/rr2612.1

Wang, E. L., Gates, S. M., & Herman, R. (2022). *District partnerships with university principal preparation programs: A summary of findings for school district leaders* (Volume 3, Part 4). RAND Corporation. https://www.rand.org/content/dam/rand/pubs/research_reports/RRA400/RRA413-6/RAND_RRA413-6.pdf

Weerts, D. J., & Sandmann, L. R. (2010). Community engagement and boundary-spanning roles at research universities. *The Journal of Higher Education*, *81*(6), 632–657. https://doi.org/10.1080/00221546.2010.11779075

Weick, K. E. (1976). Educational Organizations as Loosely Coupled Systems. *21*(1), 1–19.

Weisberg, D., Sexton, S., Mulhern, J., & Keeling, D. (2009). *The widget effect*. New Teacher Project.

Weldon, W., & Barajas, P. (2008). *Insights achieved and challenges faced by the educational doctorate program at the University of Illinois at Chicago, 2001–2008: An historical review and self-study* [Unpublished monograph]. University of Illinois Chicago.

Welton, A. D., Owens, D. R., & Zamani-Gallaher, E. M. (2018). Anti-racist change: A conceptual framework for educational institutions to take systemic action. *Teachers College Record*, *120*(14), 1–22.

Welton, A. J., Owens, D. R., & Zamani-Gallagher, E. M. (2018). Anti-racist change: A conceptual framework for educational institutions to take systemic action. *Teachers College Record*, *120*, 140314.

Wenger, E. (1998). Communities of practice: Learning as a social system. *Systems Thinker*, *9*(5), 2–3.

Wenger, E. C., & Snyder, W. M. (2000). Communities of practice: The organizational frontier. *Harvard Business Review*, *78*(1), 139–146.

Whalen, S. P. (2021). *Transforming central office practices for equity, coherence, and continuous improvement: Chicago Public Schools under the leadership of Dr. Janice K. Jackson*. Center for Urban Education Leadership.

Whalen, S. P., Horsley, H. L., Parkinson, K. P., & Pacchiano, D. (2016). A development evaluation of a professional development initiative to strengthen organizational conditions in early education settings. *Journal of Applied Research on Children: Informing Policy for Children at Risk*, *7*(2), Article 9.

Whipple, J. M., Lynch, D. F., & Nyaga, G. N. (2010). A buyer's perspective on collaborative versus transactional relationships. *Industrial Marketing Management*, *39*(3), 507–518. https://doi.org/10.1016/j.indmarman.2008.11.008

Wood, L. (2002, February 3). *Dr Luke Wood—We, not they*. High Tech High Unboxed. https://www.youtube.com/watch?v=XZoE-U8d6O8

Worren, N. (2018). *Organization design: Simplifying complex systems*. Routledge.

Yamagata-Lynch, L. C., & Smaldino, S. (2007). Using activity theory to evaluate and improve K-12 school and university partnerships. *Evaluation and Program Planning*, *30*(4), 364–380. https://doi.org/10.1016/j.evalprogplan.2007.08.003

Young, M. D. (2015). Effective leadership preparation: We know what it looks like and what it can do. *Journal of Research on Leadership Education*, *10*(1), 3–10.

Young, M. D., & Crow, G. M. (Eds.). (2016). *Handbook of research on the education of school leaders* (2nd ed.). Routledge.

Young, M. D., & Eddy-Spicer, D. H. (2019). Bridging, brokering, bricolage: Building exemplary leadership programs from the inside out. *Journal of Research on Leadership Education*, *14*(1), 3–10. https://doi.org/10.1177/1942775118820129

Young, M. D., O'Doherty, A., & Cunningham, K. M. W. (2022). *Redesigning educational leadership preparation for equity: Strategies for innovation and improvement*. Routledge.

Youth Truth Student Survey, A National Nonprofit. (2017). *Learning from student voice: How prepared do students feel for college and career?* Retrieved June 11, 2018, from http://youthtruthsurvey.org/college-career-readiness-2017/

Zavitkovsky, P., Roarty, D., & Swanson, J. (2016). *How standardized test reports let us down under No Child Left Behind*. Center for Urban Education Leadership, University Illinois at Chicago. https://urbanedleadership.org/what-we-do/practice-dissemination-and-policy-advocacy/

Zavitkovsky, P., & Tozer, S. (2017). *Upstate/downstate: Changing patterns of achievement, demographics and school effectiveness in Illinois Public Schools under NCLB*. Center for Urban Education Leadership, University Illinois at Chicago. https://urbanedleadership.org/wp-content/uploads/2020/02/UPSTATE-DOWNSTATE-FINAL-w-Appendices-06.16.17.pdf

Zeichner, K. (2002). Beyond traditional structures of student teaching. *Teacher Education Quarterly, 29*(2), 59–64. https://www.jstor.org/stable/23478291

Index

absenteeism, 175, 177
    at CCPS, 37
    PDSA for, 178–80
Academic Response Team (ART)
    Fordham faculty guiding, 305
    NIC approach of, 69
    PoP analyzed by, 65, 68
accreditation benchmarks, 35
achievement gaps, 288–89
    CPS/UIC partnership to close, 271–72
    IS for, 192
    at OSD, 175, 177
    at PGCPS, 134, 135
    at PPS, 197
    racial disparities relation to, 200–201
Administration and Supervision M.Ed., UVA (A&S M.Ed.), 37–38
    IS integration of, 31, 46
Advancement Via Individual Determination (AVID), 185
A/E. *See* Attendance/Engagement
African American boys, *62*
American Rescue Act, 138
Anderson, Erin, 223, 233–34
Anthony, Doug, 129, 130
anti-racism
    in DU-ELPS/DPS partnership, 219
    of leadership, 192
    in PPS/PSU partnership, 212
AP. *See* assistant principals
Arizona
    Department of Education of, 150
    Phoenix, 153
    Project Momentum, 152, 162
    teacher shortage in, 149–50, 156, 170
Arizona State University (ASU). *See also* Mary Lou Fulton Teachers College
    Avondale Public Schools partnership with, 124–25
ART. *See* Academic Response Team
A&S M.Ed. *See* Administration and Supervision M.Ed., UVA
assistant principals (AP)
    DPQ for, 287–88
    NICs to train, 65–67
    SBAIP for, 86, 87
    in SIIP NICs network, 89
ASU. *See* Arizona State University
Attendance/Engagement (A/E), NICs for, 69
AVID. *See* Advancement Via Individual Determination
Avondale Elementary School District (AESD)
    collaboration at, 168
    demographics of, 152
    mentors at, 156, 157, 159, 164
    MLFTC partnership with, 149–53, *153*, 155, 156, *156*, *157*, 158–59, *159*, 160–69
    teacher shortage at, 153–55
Avondale Public Schools, Arizona State partnership with, 124–25

Basile, Carole, 154, 155
    on trust, 161
Batalden, Paul, 240
Beavers, Michelle, 39

328　INDEX

Beginning Teacher Support and Assessment (BTSA), 100
Bertani, Albert, 41
Biag, M., 204
Biggs, Regina, 80
Black, Indigenous, and people of color (BIPOC), at DPS, 225
Black Excellence Resolution, of DPS, 225
Blankenship, Beth, 80
Boasberg, Tom, 225
boundary infrastructure
　in CCPS/UVA partnership, 46–47
　for coordination, 48
boundary objects
　in CCPS/UVA partnership, 32–33
　in CPS/UIC partnership, 284
　DP for, 8, 20, 303, 305
　for sustainability, 307
　in trading zones, 2, 7–8, 20
boundary spanners, 218, 283, 284, 290, 305
Bradley, LaShel, 41
Bridgespan Group, 302
Bronx CSDs
　ART in, 67–69, 305
　Fordham University partnership with, 27–28, 52, 55–56, 59, 62, 64, 70–72
　NICs at, 65–67, 69
　teacher retention at, 53
Bryk, A. S., 291
BTSA. *See* Beginning Teacher Support and Assessment
Burk, Pat, 198
burnout, of teachers, 98
　in AESD, 168
Bush, George, 264

Caillier, Stacey, 101, 102
California, 100, 102
　Commission on Teacher Credentialing of, 101
　San Diego, 97
California Standards for the Teaching Profession (CSTP), 100
　ILP in, 101
Cardona, Isaac, 204–5
CARE Network, 115
Carlile, Susan, 193, 194, 198, 211
　Peterson relation to, 195, 199–201, 204

Carnegie Corporation, New York, 4
Carnegie Explorer's Workshop, 175, 188, 191
　for UM-SOE/OSD partnership, 180, 181, 186, 190
Carnegie Foundation for the Advancement of Teaching (CFAT)
　coordination by, 4
　Core Principles of Improvement of, 28
　Fordham/Bronx partnership relation to, 52
　HEN of, 34, 198, 199
　iLEAD of, 54
　IS of, 231, 243
　NCSUP relation to, 189
　organizational investment from, 301
　in PGCPS/UM MOU, 145
Carnegie Foundation's Improvement Summit, 41
Carnegie Project on the Education Doctorate (CPED)
　design principles in, 60
　Dissertation of the Year Award of, 62
　NICs through, 192
　Roach influenced by, 54
　university engagement in, 124
Carnegie Senior Fellows, 166
Carranza (NYC Chancellor), 53
CCPS. *See* Chesterfield County Public Schools
CEEDAR. *See* Collaboration for Effective Educator Development, Accountability, and Reform
CEHD. *See* College of Education and Human Development, of GMU
CEii. *See* Center for Educational Innovation and Improvement
Celebration of Learning, at HTH, 108
Center for Educational Innovation and Improvement (CEii)
　Eubanks as director of, 138
　founding of, 130
　as organizing hub, 144
　in PGCPS/UMD MOU, 146–47
　in PGCPS/UMD partnership, 131
Center for Math Education, of UMD COE, 141
Center for Race and Public Education in the South, 32

The Center for Teaching Quality (CTQ), 241
Center for Urban Education Leadership, of UIC, 281, 286, 290
Center on Reinventing Public Education, 171
CEU. *See* Continuing Education Units
CFAT. *See* Carnegie Foundation for the Advancement of Teaching
The Chalkboard Project
   grants from, 203
   NSD relation to, 202
   Oregon Department of Education relation to, 199
change, 40, 300–301
   co-learners for, 45
   infrastructure for, 238
   sustainability of, 306
change packages, 108
charter schools, 154
Chesterfield County Public Schools (CCPS)
   benchmarks at, 45
   Dean of Students at, 39, 40, 46–47
   Imagine Tomorrow plan of, 33–34
   IS at, 36–37
   Leadership Academy of, 42, 47
   SIIP at, 43–44
   UVA partnership with, 27, 30–35, 38, 40–43, 46–48
Chicago
   Local School Councils in, 263
   Principal Partnership of, 271, 277
   University of Illinois in, 38
Chicago Leadership Collaborative (CLC), 271, 276, 290
Chicago Public School (CPS)
   principals at, 264, 271, 275–76, 275n4, 277, 289
   UIC partnership with, 218, 262–63, *265,* 266, *266, 267,* 268–79, 276n6, 282, 283, 283n12, 284, 284n13, 285–86, 288–91, 305
Chicago School Reform Act (1988), 262, 263, 282
Chou, Vicki, 275, 275n4
CIC-NICs. *See* Curriculum, Instruction and Coherence Networked Improvement Community
CIP. *See* Continuous Improvement Process

CLC. *See* Chicago Leadership Collaborative
CNA. *See* Title I Comprehensive Needs Assessment
coaches, 109–10, 113
   as boundary spanners, 284
   in CPS/UIC partnership, 283, 283n12, 290
   deficit thinking interrupted by, 111, 112
   funding for, 286
   improvement mindset of, 114
   mentors compared to, 117
   sustainability for, 120
Coburn, C. E., 243
Code of Virginia, n.d. *See* Virginia Competencies for the Preparation of School Leaders
CoE. *See* College of Education, USC
COE. *See* College of Education
co-learners, for change, 45
collaboration, 7
   at AESD, 168
   in improvement braid, 33
   in partnerships, 251
   PDSA for, 203
Collaboration for Effective Educator Development, Accountability, and Reform (CEEDAR), 272
collective accountability, 119, 158
collective efficacy
   distributed expertise and, 154
collective orientation meeting, partnership promoted by, 161
College of Education (COE)
   of PSU, 196
   of UMD, 130, 141, 143, 144
College of Education, USC (CoE), MCSD partnership with, 241–44, 247–49, *250,* 251–53, 256–59
College of Education and Human Development, of GMU (CEHD), 77
College Ready on Track NICs, 230
community, 5
   for continuous improvement, 74
   iLEAD focus on, 6
   leadership skills for, 64
   NCSUP to build, 189
   in Six Core Principles of Improvement, 108

community school districts (CSDs)
  in New York City, 52, *53*
compliance
  accountability relation to, 45
  continuous learning compared to, 35
  mindset of, 111, 112
  SPP as instrument of, 135
Comprehensive Schools in need of
    Improvement (CSI), NICs to
    support, 211
Continuing Education Units (CEU), 111
Continuing Progress, in partnerships, 258
continuous improvement, 89, 308
  community for, 74
  conversation about, 43
  in CPS/UIC partnership, 262, 270,
    290–91
  culture of, 188
  data for, 200, 270
  in DU-ELPS/DPS partnership, 219, 220,
    222
  empathy interviews for, 213
  at HTH, 97, 102, 104–5, 114, 115, 120
  in IExD, 113
  Improvement Science Think Tank for, 230
  infrastructure for, 228
  leadership for, 38–39, 56–57, *57*, 78–79
  mentors as leaders of, 119
  middle-level leaders implementing, 48
  mindset of USC, 241
  in MLFTC/AESD partnership, 162–63,
    165
  NICs culture of, 91
  in partnerships, 20–22
  in PGCPS/UMD partnership, 144, 146
  in SIIP template, 36–37
  SI-NICs to extend, 138
  Strategic Imperatives for, 135, 137
  at UIC, 285
  in UVA Master's program redesign, 34
Continuous Improvement Process (CIP),
    234
Continuous School Improvement (Smylie),
    283, 291
conversations
  about leadership, 43
  about partnerships, 95
  for signature pedagogy, 46
coordination, 41

boundary infrastructure for, 48
by CFAT, 4
in iLEAD framework, 22
in improvement sandwich, 33
leadership as activity of, 298
Cordova, Susana, 225
Core Principles of Improvement, of CFAT,
    28
Cosner, Shelby, 273, 279, 283, 291
Council for the Accreditation of Educator
    Preparation, 196
COVID pandemic
  ART initiatives affected by, 67–68
  CoE/MCSD partnership affected by, 251,
    256–57
  DI affected by, 227
  DP affected by, 85
  ELAP affected by, 61, 64
  FCPS/GMU partnership affected by, 74
  houselessness affected by, 198
  HTH affected by, 98, 100, 106
  iLEAD partnerships affected by, 56
  inequalities caused by, 91
  opportunities from, 71–72
  OSD affected by, 183, 184
  PDISAN affected by, 134
  PGCPS/UMD partnership affected by,
    141–42
  SIIP NICs affected by, 94–95
CPED. *See* Carnegie Project on the
    Education Doctorate
CPS. *See* Chicago Public School
CRSE. *See* Culturally Responsive Sustaining
    Education
CSI. *See* Comprehensive Schools in need of
    Improvement
CSTP. *See* California Standards for the
    Teaching Profession
CTQ. *See* The Center for Teaching Quality
Culturally Responsive Sustaining Education
    (CRSE), 69–70, 111
culturally responsive teaching practices, *62*
culture
  as agentive, 6
  of continuous improvement, 188
  of improvement, 39, 64
  IS in, 84
  leadership effect on, 258–59
  teacher retention effect on school, 120

Curriculum, Instruction and Coherence Networked Improvement Community (CIC-NICs), 38
Curriculum/Program Development, of UVA, 31
cycles of inquiry
　ART relation to, 68
　for improvement, 290–91
　with improvement team, 39
　for PoP, 66
　as signature pedagogy, 281

Daley, Richard, 263–64
Darling-Hammond, L., 242–43
data
　for continuous improvement, 200, 270
　funding to gather, 286
　infrastructure for, 45
　in MLFTC/AESD partnership, 166
　partnership agreements for, 207–8
　in PDSA cycles, 107–8
　for PoPs, 257
Dawes, S. S., 2
Dean of Students, at CCPS, 39, 40, 46–47
deficit thinking
　disruption of, 119
　in HTH new-teacher induction, 111–12
DeFilippis, Kris, 65, 70
　IS integrated by, 67
DeNome, Evonne, 87
Denver Public Schools (DPS)
　diversity at, 223
　DU-ELPS partnership with, 217–19, 220, 220–22, 224, 226–30, 232–37
　NICs at, 230–31
　opportunity gaps at, 225–26
Department of Education
　of Arizona, 150
　of California, 100
　of Mississippi, 175, 177
　of Oregon, 199
　of US, 171, 272
　of Virginia, 88
Department of Principal Quality (DPQ), 287–88
Design Improvement (DI)
　co-construction of, 222–23
　COVID effect on, 227
　literacy affected by, 235

PDSA for, 226
as pilot, 229
principals targeted by, 236
research on, 233
self-awareness in, 231
Design Improvement for Equity (DI4E)
　DI relation to, 222–23
　in DU-ELPS/DPS partnership, 230
　IS in, 231, 232, 236
　for school improvement, 235
　for system change, 229
Developmental Progressions framework, of iLEAD (DP), *9–19*, 96, *274*
　for boundary objects, 8, 20, 303, 305
　in CCPS/UVA partnership, 31
　in CoE/MCSD partnership, 252–53
　in collaborative network, 277, 306
　COVID pandemic effect on, 85
　in CPS/UIC partnership, 273–75, 291
　in DU-ELPS/DPS partnership, 228, 233
　equity built by, 29
　Faculty Development and Promotion in, *118*
　in Fordham/Bronx partnership, 27–28, 55–56, 72
　in GMU/FCPS partnership, 75, 80
　in HTH program, 115, 117
　at IHEs, *254*, *280*
　improvement in, 98
　IS/NICs in, 286, 288
　LEA/IHE Leadership Development Program in, 276
　LEA in, 245, 286, 287, *287*
　Learning to Improve in, *99*, *116*, 278–79
　in MLFTC/AESD partnership, 166
　partnerships in, 244–45, *253*
　in PGCPS/UMD partnership, 132, 139
　in PPS/PSU partnership, 207, 208
　stages of, 80–84, 87–89, 92, 95, 281
　in UM-SOE/OSD partnership, 188
DI. *See* Design Improvement
DI4E. *See* Design Improvement for Equity
DiP. *See* dissertation in practice
disabilities, students with, 43
disciplinary referrals, racial disparities in
　BIPOC experiencing, 225
　Jonas focus on, 39–40
　multi-tiered systems of support for, 43
disciplined inquiry processes, at IHEs, 259

dissertation in practice (DiP), 62
    in CoE/MCSD partnership, 252
Dissertation of the Year Award, of CPED, 62
dissertations, 60, 63
    CPED award for, 62
    equity focus of, 62
dissonance, in partnerships, 238
distributed expertise, 151, 158, 163, 169–71
    collective efficacy and, 154
    MLFTC providing, 151
    success measured by, 163
    in team-based approach, 158
District of Innovation, 175
diversity
    at DPS, 223
    in gifted education, 235
    in Oregon, 196–97
Doctorate in Educational Leadership, Administration and Policy, of GSE (ELAP), 61
Doctorate of Education in School System Leadership, for PGCPS, 145
DPQ. See Department of Principal Quality
DPS. See Denver Public Schools
Dranesville Elementary, 92
DU Educational Leadership and Policy Studies Department (DU-ELPS)
    DI at, 231
    DPS partnership with, 217–19, 220, 220–22, 224, 226–30, 232–37
Duncan, Arne, 263–64, 275

Eason-Watkins, Barbara
    Chou relation to, 275
    on principals, 263–64
    Tozer relation to, 275n4
economically disadvantaged students (ED), 175
EdD. See education doctorate program
Eddy-Spicer, David, 39, 41, 301
    in CIC-NICs, 38
    T. White relation to, 34–35
EDLE. See Educational Leadership, of GMU
EDLP. See Educational Leadership and Policies, CoE
Edmonds, R. F., 264
Ed Studies. See Educational Studies, CoE
educational disparities
    IS for, 203, 204
    at PPS, 192, 193, 196, 197, 210–11
    principals to impact, 213
Educational Leadership, of GMU (EDLE)
    autonomy of, 84
    faculty meeting of, 74–75
    IS in, 78
    IS in curriculum of, 81–83, 86, 93–94
    at Learning to Improve conference, 92
    PDSA engagement of, 83
    pipeline process of, 85–86
    PoPs identified by, 79
    Shahrokhi relation to, 77
Educational Leadership and Policies, CoE (EDLP)
    goals of, 255
    in iLEAD, 252–53
    leadership transitions in, 241
    in MCSD partnership, 247–49
Educational Leadership and Policy Studies Department (ELPS), 220–21
Educational Studies, CoE (Ed Studies), 241
education doctorate programs (EdD)
    in CoE/MCSD partnership, 242, 257
    of EDLP, 253
    GSE, 60
    IS in, 124, 130
    in School System Leadership, 127
    at UIC, 279
Education Policy Studies Department, of UIC, 264, 279
Education Trust, 277
Education TSL grant, 171
EELPP. See Exemplary Educational Leadership Preparation Program
EHD. See School of Education and Human Development, UVA
ELA. See English/Language Arts
ELAP. See Doctorate in Educational Leadership, Administration and Policy, of GSE
Elementary and Secondary School Emergency Relief 3 (ESSER)
    budgeting for, 85, 92
    NICs relation to, 138
    PGCPS using, 141
Elmore, Richard, 264
ELP. See PSU COE Educational Leadership and Policy department

ELPS. *See* DU Educational Leadership and Policy Studies Department
ELs. *See* English learners
Emanuel, Rahm, 275–76
empathy interviews
  by coaches, 113
  in CoE/MCSD partnership, 249, 251
  for continuous improvement, 213
  at DPS, 234–35
  equity relation to, 106
  with induction participants, 102
English/Language Arts (ELA)
  at AESD, 152
  at OSD, 185
  at PGCPS, 135
English learners (ELs), 198
  students with disabilities as, 43
entrepreneurs, 301
equity, 39
  CCPS initiative for, 31
  in CNA process, 87
  in CPS/UIC partnership, 288–89
  DI for, 222–23
  dissertations focused on, 62
  DP to build, 29
  in DU-ELPS/DPS partnership, 219
  empathy interviews relation to, 106
  in HTH teacher induction, 101
  IExD workshop for, 112–13, 115, 117
  in iLEAD framework, 21, 22
  leadership for, 22, 85, 206, 273
  in new-teacher induction program, 119
  as North Star, 238
  partnerships for, 217
  PoP to center, 68
  at PPS, 210–11
  in principal development, 287
  at PSU, 195, 196, 201–2
  in PSU/NSD partnership, 203
  in student learning outcomes, 27
  systems change for, 227–29
  Theory of Improvement for, 138–39
  in TSPC standards, 209
  in UVA Master's program redesign, 34
Equity & Cultural Responsiveness team, of FCPS, 85
equity-focused improvement science, 60, 62, 65, 70, 75, 82, 87, 193, 199, 202, 243–44

ES. *See* executive superintendent
ESSA. *See* Every Student Succeeds Act
ESSER. *See* Elementary and Secondary School Emergency Relief 3
Eubanks, Segun, 131
  as UMD CEii Director, 138
Every Student Succeeds Act (ESSA), 135
  SPP aligned with, 136
executive superintendent (ES)
  ART collaboration with, 67
  iLEAD effect on, 71–72
Exemplary Educational Leadership Preparation Program (EELPP), 221
external funding, 292
  for research, 285–86

Facilitating Continuous Improvement for Equity workshop, 113
Fairfax County Public School (FCPS)
  CNA of, 87–88
  GMU partnership with, 8, 28, 74–75, 76, 77–78, 80–84, 88–90, 93–96
  IS used by, 77, 84–85
  leadership development at, 86
  SIIPs of, 78–79, 82–84, 88
Farrell, C., 256
FCPS. *See* Fairfax County Public School
Fergus, E., 67
field-based courses, 40
  IS in, 47–48
fields, 302
Field Transformation Strategy, iLEAD, *21*
  continuous improvement in, 22
first-mile activity, 302–3, *304*
fishbone diagram
  ART using, 69
  in CoE/MCSD partnership, 249, *250*
  in HTH new-teacher induction, 105–6
  in PGCPS/UMD partnership, 137
  SIIP NICs participation in, 92
  in UM-SOE/OSD partnership, 182, 185, 186
Fogelman, Lance, 79–80, 92
Fordham University
  Academic Response Teams guided by, 305
  Bronx CSDs partnership with, 27–28, 52, 55–56, *59*, 62, 64, 70–72
  GSE of, 54, 60, 61

Improvement Science Leadership
Proficiency survey of, 71
IS course at, 65
leadership renewal at, 54
formal commitments, for relationships, 141
Framing the SIIP from a Problem of Practice
workshop, 85
Free & Reduced Lunch (FRL), 272

Galison, P., 7
Gallagher, Ryan
on deficit language, 112
on design, 110
as Director of Continuous Improvement, 101
induction experience by, 102
Gates Foundation, grant from, 136, 141, 230
Gates NSI grant, 226, 227, 233
Gelmon, Sherril, 199
George Mason University (GMU)
EDLE of, 74–75, 77–79, 81–86, 92–94
FCPS partnership with, 8, 28, 74–75, 76, 77–78, 80–84, 88–90, 93–96
gifted education, diversity in, 235
Gil, Elizabeth, 55
Ginsberg, Mark, 77–78, 81
GMU. *See* George Mason University
goals
of ELAP, 61
in partnerships, 254–55, 258
for systems change, 237
USC partnership work defining, 241
Goldson, Monica
in PDISAN meetings, 136
as PGCPS CEO, 131, 138
on racial disparity, 132
Gomez, Louis, 199, 284, 291
Goodlad, J. I., 6
on community-centered partnerships, 22
Gorman, M. E., 6, 7
Graduate Program Coordinator, of
UM-SOE (GPC), 186
Graduate School of Education, of Fordham
University (GSE), 54
in EdD redesign, 60
ELAP of, 61
Graduate Studies Office, of UM-SOE
(GSO), 185–86

grants
from *The Chalkboard Project*, 203
for DPS, 226
Education TSL, 171
from Gates Foundation, 136, 141, 230
Gates NSI, 226, 227, 233
for PD, 152
for PSU, 193
Teacher Collaborative Grant Program
for, 147
Teacher Quality Partnership, 150, 155
from Wallace Foundation, 129
Grissom, J. A., 200
Griswold, Janie, 101, 102
GSE. *See* Graduate School of Education, of
Fordham University
GSO. *See* Graduate Studies Office, of
UM-SOE
Gulati, R., 33, 48

Hall, G., 194
Hardy, C., 301
Hargrove, Betsy
Basile relation to, 154–55
on capacity-building effort, 152
on flexibility, 164
on MLFTC success, 165
on teacher compensation, 156–57
on trust, 161
Harvey, Brian, 174, 177
Hassey, Meg, 114
Hawley, Willis, 129
Higher Education Network, of CFAT
(HEN), 34
PSU in, 198, 199
high school suspension rates, of Black males, 68, *68*
High Tech High Graduate School of
Education (HTH GSE), *103*
continuous improvement at, 102
HTH relation to, 97–98, 121
IExD at, 112–13, 115, 117
teacher retention work of, 28
High Tech High Schools (HTH), *103*
continuous improvement at, 97, 102, 104–5, 110, 115, 120
COVID pandemic effect on, 98, 100, 106
HTH GSE relation to, 97–98, 121

INDEX   335

new-teacher induction program of, 100–102, 104–12, 114, 115, 117, 119, 120
teacher retention in, 28
Hightower, Zipporah, 277
Hite, William "Bill," 129
Hitz, Randy, 198, 199
Holmes Group, 300, 302
Holmes Partnership, 300
Honig, M. I., 256
Hord, S., 194
houselessness, in Portland, 198
HTH. *See* High Tech High Schools
HTH GSE. *See* High Tech High Graduate School of Education
HTH Teacher Center, 101
Huang, Tiedan, 54

IB. *See* international baccalaureate
IB World Schools, 195
Identifying a Problem of Practice workshops, 85
IExD. *See* Improvement for Equity by Design
IHEs. *See* institutions of higher education
iLEAD. *See* Improvement Leadership Education and Development
Illinois, 273n2
Illinois State University, 272–73
ILP. *See* Individual Learning Plan
Imagine Tomorrow, CCPS, 33–34
Imig, David, 129–30
Impact Office, of DPS, 229, 234
improvement. *See specific topics*
improvement braid, 33, 47
    partnership in, 48
    sandwich evolution to, 44
Improvement for Equity by Design (IExD), at HTH GSE
    external audiences served by, 112–13
    HTH relation to, 115, 117
Improvement Leadership Education and Development (iLEAD), 3, 4, *4*, 252, 288, 302. *See also* Developmental Progressions framework, of iLEAD
    boundary objects created by, 7–8
    CCPS/UVA participation in, 30–31, 34–35, 48
    of CFAT, 54

    CoE/MCSD partnership in, 241–43, 247
    community focus of, 6
    convenings for, 57, 58, 70
    CPS/UIC partnership in, 278–79
    DU-ELPS/DPS partnership in, 229–30, 236
    EDLP in, 252–53
    EHD in, 31–32
    ELAP work by, 61
    entrepreneurs for, 301
    equity in framework of, 21, 22
    ES affected by, 71–72
    Field Transformation Strategy of, *21*, 22–23
    GMU/FCPS partnership in, 74–75, 77–78, 93, 94
    HTH/HTH GSE partnership in, 101
    MLFTC/AESD partnership in, 149, 155, 162–63
    for mutual-benefit partnerships, 5
    NICs through, 192, 205
    PGCPS/UMD partnership in, 131, 140–41, 144, 145
    PPS/PSU partnership in, 204–5, *206*, 206–7, *209*, 209–10
    PSU/NSD partnership in, 199
    UM-SOE/OSD partnership in, 174–75, 177
improvement sandwich
    assembly of, 42
    braid evolution of, 44
    in CCPS/UVA partnership, 40–41
    cooperation to coordination as, 33
    strategic planning process in, 35
    systemic learning in, 48
improvement science (IS), 35
    for achievement gaps, 192
    ART focus on, 68–69
    A&S M.Ed. using, 31, 46
    at Carnegie Explorer's Workshop, 175
    at CCPS, 36–37
    of CFAT, 231, 243
    CIC-NICs to explore, 38
    in CoE/MCSD partnership, 248–49
    for continuous improvement, 56–57
    culture in, 84
    in DI4E, 232
    in DP, 286, 288

in DU-ELPS/DPS partnership, 217–18, 222, 230
in EdD programs, 124, 130
in EDLE curriculum, 81–83, 86, 93–94
of EDLP, 252–53
for educational disparities, 203, 204
equity focused, 60, 62, 65, 70, 75, 82, 87, 193, 199, 202
FCPS using, 77, 84–85
in field-based courses, 47–48
in GMU/FCPS partnership, 80, 88
in GSE EdD redesign, 60
at HTH, 97, 104–5, 110, 115, 120
inequities redressed with, 87
in leadership development, 48, 70, 82
math performance improved by, 65–67
in MLFTC/AESD partnership, 149, 155, 156, 164, 166
outcomes examined in, 240
in partnerships, 80, 126, 162, 214, 259
PD on, 190
PDSA relation to, 75, 159
in PGCPS/UMD partnership, 128, 131–32, 136–37, 144–45, 147
PoP addressed by, 78–79, 140, 174, 259
in PPS/PSU partnership, 205–8, *209*, 210–12
for professional learning, 30
at PSU, 195, 197, 198
Saady using, 41–42
as signature pedagogy, 31, 39, 83, 132
in SIIP NICs, 89, 91
for social justice, 199
in Theory of Improvement, 139
in UM-SOE/OSD partnership, 177, 180–82, 185, 188, 191
Improvement Science (Peterson & Carlile), 201
Improvement Science in the Principal Preparation Program (presentation), 199–200
Improvement Science Leadership Proficiency survey, of Fordham, 71
Improvement Science Think Tank (meeting), 230
Improvement Summit, of Carnegie Foundation, 41
PGCPS/UMD partnership at, 136
Individual Learning Plan (ILP), 101

inequities, educational, 4, 39, 225
at CCPS, 33–34
continuous improvement to redress, 91
DP to redress, 20
at FCPS, 84–86
IS in redressing, 87
in student learning outcomes, 27–28
infrastructure
boundary, 46–48
for change, 238
for continuous improvement, 228
in CPS/UIC partnership, 262, 276
for data, 45
social, 303, 305
for systems change, *227*
Innovation & Improvement team, of DPS, 229–30
inquiry learning approaches, 39
inquiry-on-practice skills, *62*
institutions of higher education (IHEs), 4, 5, 240
disciplined inquiry processes at, 259
in DP, 8, 245
DP at, *254*, *280*
LEAs relation to, 1–3, 6, 20, 23, 31, 75, 123–24, 151–52, 159, 166, 189–90, 258, 263, *274*, 291–92, 298, 299, *299*, *300*, 300–301, 302, 305–7
Instructional Services team (FCPS), 74–75, 85
Instruction and Teacher Education, CoE (ITE), 241
intentionality, in leadership, 187
interdependence, in partnerships, 236
international baccalaureate (IB), 195–96
The International Cultural Youth Exchange, 194
intrapreneurs, middle-level leaders as, 44–45
Irby, Decoteau, 285
IS. *See* improvement science
ITE. *See* Instruction and Teacher Education, CoE

Jackson, Janice
administration of, 288
as CEO, 278
on stakeholder committee, 276–77
Jacobsen, Julia, 113
James Irvine Foundation, 302

Johns Hopkins University, 171
Jonas, Blair, 39–40

Keefer, Ben, 204–5
Keltner, Amy, 223
Kipp, Patty, 223
Kirwin Commission, 147
KNN Near Neighbors statistical algorithms, 272
Komatsubara, Kristin, 106
Korach, Susan
    principal preparation partnership developed by, 223
    on shared vision, 221–22
Kotter, J. P., 307

Ladson-Billings, G., 198
Lane, James
    disparities redressed by, 31
    T. Taylor relation to, 33
last-mile activity, 302, *304*
Latina/o Leaders Reducing Educational Disparities (presentation), 199
LCI. *See* Leadership for Continuous Improvement
LEAD. *See* Leadership Experiences, Application, and Development
leadership, 36, 121
    at AESD, 168
    anti-racism of, 192
    for community, 64
    for continuous improvement, 38–39, 56–57, *57*, 78–79
    conversations about, 43
    as coordination activity, 298
    in CPS/UIC partnership, 271, 278, 289–90
    culture affected by, 258–59
    for equity, 22, 85, 206, 273
    field-based courses to learn, 40
    at Fordham University, 54
    intentionality in, 187
    middle-level, 32–33, 44–45, 47, 48
    at MLFTC, 154
    for mutual-benefit partnerships, 1–2
    NICs to develop, 28
    partnership affected by, 1, 142, 162–63, 190, 305
    preparation programs for, 32, 47, 61
    for school improvement, 30
    transitions of, 213, 241, 242, 247, 251, 256, 263
    transparency of, 240
Leadership Academy, of CCPS, 42, 47
leadership development, 65–70
    at FCPS, 86
    IS in, 48, 70, 82
Leadership Development Program, joint LEA/IHE, 31
Leadership Experiences, Application, and Development (LEAD)
    classes for, 39
    data reviewed in, 43
    LEAD II of, 40
Leadership for Continuous Improvement (LCI), 39, 43
LEA/IHE Leadership Development Program, in DP, 276
learning, continuous
    compliance compared to, 35
    in SIIP planning process, 36
Learning to Improve
    conference for, 83, 84, 92
    in DP, *99*, *116*, 278–79
Learning to Improve (Bryk, Gomez, Grunow, & LeMahieu), 81, 94, 291
LEAs. *See* local education agencies
Leithwood, K., 264
LeMahieu, Paul, 199, 202
leverage points, 22
Lewin, K., 306
Liberatory Design, 231
Lincoln Center, Fordham EdD cohort at, 61
literacy, 124
    DI effect on, 235
    at DPS, 234
local characteristics, in organizational work, 2
local education agencies (LEAs), 71, 72
    in DP, 245, 286, 287, *287*
    DP relation to, 8
    IHEs relation to, 1–3, 6, 20, 23, 31, 75, 123–24, 151–52, 159, 166, 189–90, 258, 263, *274*, 291–92, 298, 299, *299*, *300*, 300–301, 302, 305–7
    iLEAD relation to, 4, 5
Local School Councils, in Chicago, 263
Lochhead, Sandy

Anderson relation to, 223, 233
continuous improvement work of, 230
logistics, in partnerships, 255–56
Loh, Wallace, 128–29
Lonnett, Ray, 91
loosely coupled systems, 244, *245*, 257

Maldonado, Rebecca, 115
Martinez, Pedro, 287
Martinez, Peter
  Eason-Watkins relation to, 275
  reform impact of, 282
  as trainer of leaders, 283
Maryland, 129
Mary Lou Fulton Teachers College (MLFTC)
  AESD partnership with, 149–53, *153*, 155, 156, *156*, *157*, 158–59, *159*, 160–69
  demographics of, 152
  leadership at, 154
  Next Education Workforce initiative of, 149, 151, 155, 162, 165, 166, 170–71
math performance
  at AESD, 152
  IS to improve, 65–67
  NICs for, 134
  PDSA for, 234
  at PGCPS, 135, 141
  in SI-NICs, 138
Maxwell, Kevin, 131
Mayrowetz, David, 268, 283, 283n10
MCE. *See* Morgridge College of Education
McGuire, S., 301
McKey, Tania, 193, 195–96, 199–201
  at PPS, 204, 205, 208, 210
  recruitment by, 211
McLaughlin, Margaret, 130
MCSD. *See* Myrtle Creek School District
Meadows, D. H., 22
MEd, principals licensed with, 266
memorandum of understanding (MOU), 258
  in CPS/UIC partnership, 276
  in PGCPS/UMD partnership, 127–28, 141–48, 303
  as sustainability, 307
  in UM-SOE/OSD partnership, 174, 189

Menomonee Falls School District, Wisconsin, 35–36
mentors
  at AESD, 156, 157, 159, 164
  coaches compared to, 117
  as continuous improvement leaders, 119
  in new-teacher induction program, 100–102, 109–10
Meyer, Amanda, 199
middle-level leaders, 32–33
  boundary infrastructure created by, 47
  continuous improvement integrated by, 48
  as intrapreneurs, 44–45
Middle Years Programme (MYP), 195
Miller-Brown, Ellen, 223
Mississippi Department of Education, 175, 177
MLFTC. *See* Mary Lou Fulton Teachers College
Morabito, Heather, 65, 66
Morgridge College of Education (MCE), 220–21
Motivate Lab, EHD, 31–32
MOU. *See* memorandum of understanding
MTSS. *See* multi-tiered systems of support
Muller, L., 3
multi-tiered systems of support (MTSS), 41
mutual-benefit partnerships, 23
  across organizational boundaries, 3
  equitable leaders for, 22
  iLEAD for, 5
  leadership for, 1–2
  in PGCPS/UMD MOU, 143
  transactional relationships compared to, 6, 141
MYP. *See* Middle Years Programme
Myrtle Creek School District (MCSD) (pseudonym), CoE partnership with, 241–44, 247–49, *250*, 251–53, 256–59

National Assessment of Educational Progress (NAEP), 225
The National Center for Education Statistics, 177–78
National Center for School-University Partnerships (NCSUP), 189–90
National Educational Leadership Preparation standards (NELP), 37

at UMD, 130
National Equity Project, 231
NCLB. *See* No Child Left Behind (2002)
NCSUP. *See* National Center for School-University Partnerships
NEA, on burnout, 98
NELP. *See* National Educational Leadership Preparation standards
Networked Improvement Communities (NICs)
  APs trained with, 65–67
  at Bronx CSDs, 65–67, 69
  College Ready on Track, 230
  in CPS/UIC partnership, 291
  CSI and TSI supported by, 211
  in DP, 286, 288
  for equity, 202
  equity and IS in, 70–71
  ESSER relation to, 138
  of FCPS, 77
  through iLEAD, 192, 205
  leadership developed by, 28
  mathematics, 134
  in NCSUP, 190
  online forums for, 55–56
  of PDISAN, 146
  in PGCPS/UMD partnership, 141, 144, 147
  PoPs addressed by, 69
  in PPS/PSU partnership, 207–8
  for SEL, 69–70
  SIIP joint initiative with, 84, 88–92, 94–95
  UCEA as, 38, 192, 199
  at UIC, 281, 281n9
  in UM-SOE/OSD partnership, 178, 181, 182, 184–85
networks
  DP in collaborative, 277
  of partnerships, 277–78
  of PDISAN, 132
  for teacher retention, 114
Networks for School Improvement grant, of Gates Foundation, 136
Newberg Schools District (NSD), PSU partnership with, 199, 202–5
New Leaders, 276
new-teacher induction program, 97
  continuous improvement in, 114
  deficit thinking in, 111–12
  equity in, 119
  fishbone diagram in, 105–6
  IS in, 104–5, 115, 120
  mentors in, 100–102, 109–10
  PDSA in, 106–8, 125
  teacher retention relation to, 100, 115, 117
New York
  Carnegie Corporation in, 4
  West Harrison, 61
New York City (NYC)
  CSDs in, *53*
Next Education Workforce initiative, 149, 151, 162, 171
  MLFTC/AESD partnership in, 155, 166
  office focused on, 165
  teacher shortage relation to, 170
NICs. *See* Networked Improvement Communities
NIU/Rockford/Elgin Public Schools, 286
No Child Left Behind (2002) (NCLB), 263, 264
NSD. *See* Newberg Schools District
NYC. *See* New York City

Office of Monitoring and Accountability, of UMD, 137
Office of Principal Preparation and Development, of CPS, 263, 271, 290
OLF. *See* Ontario Leadership Framework
"one teacher one classroom" model, 149, 151, 155, 165, 169
online forums, for NICs, 56
Ontario Leadership Framework (OLF), 37
opportunity gaps, 236
  at DPS, 225–26
Oregon, 198
  Department of Education of, 199
  diversity in, 196–97
Oregon Teacher Standards and Practices Commission (TSPC), 207, 209–10
Orr, Margaret Terry, 54, 64, 66–67
  Vaughan meeting with, 65
Oxford School District (OSD)
  absenteeism at, 175, 177–80
  achievement gaps at, 175, 177
  demographics of, *177*

UM-SOE partnership with, 174–75, *176*, 177, 178, 180–81, *181*, 182–91

Pamas, Roberto, 80
partnership
    work consideration of USC, 241
Partnership Driver Diagram, 132, *133*, 138
partnerships, 33, 38, *251*
    collaboration in, 251
    collective orientation meeting promoting, 161
    continuous improvement in, 20–22
    conversations about, 95
    data agreements in, 208–9
    development of, *253*
    dissonance in, 238
    in DP, 244–45, *253*
    DU-ELPS ethos of, 222
    for equity, 217
    goals in, 254–55, 258
    in improvement braid, 48
    interdependence in, 236
    IS in, 80, 126, 162, 214, 259
    leadership effect on, 1, 142, 162–63, 190, 305
    logistics in, 255–56
    NCSUP for, 189
    network of, 277–78
    relationships in, 140, 143, 171–72, 244, 246–47, 303
    sustainability in, 307–8
    trust in, 161, 237
Passion Professional Development PDSA cycle, 181, 183, *184*
PD. *See* professional development
PDISAN. *See* Post-Doctoral Improvement Science Action Network
PDSA. *See* Plan-Do-Study-Act cycles
PE. *See* Physical Education, CoE
Peace Corps, 104
Penuel, W. R., 243, 251–52
Perez, Andres, 114
persistent challenges, 157, *157*
Peterson, Deborah, 193, 194, 198, 208, 213
    Carlile relation to, 195, 199–201, 204
PGCPS. *See* Prince George's County Public Schools
PGCPS/UMD Improvement Science Collaborative, 128

Phoenix, Arizona, 153
Physical Education, CoE (PE), 241
Pines, Darryll, 141
PIP. *See* Principal Induction Programs, of EDLE
Pittsburgh, CPED in, 60
Plan-Do-Study-Act cycles (PDSA), 35–36, 114
    for absenteeism, 178–80
    of ART, 68, 69
    for collaboration, 203
    for DI, 226
    in DP, 85
    EDLE engagement in, 83
    at GSO, 185–86
    in HTH new-teacher induction, 104, 106–10, 117
    IS relation to, 75, 159
    in leadership courses, 39
    for math performance, 234
    in new-teacher induction, 106–8, 125
    Passion Professional Development, 181, 183, *184*
    in SIIP NICs, 89
    at Summer Leadership Institute, 136–37, 139
    at UM-SOE, 182, 186–87
    in UM-SOE/OSD partnership, 183, 187
    for Youth Truth Survey, 183–85
Planning and Changing (publication), 264
PLC. *See* professional learning community
Pledger, Michelle, 105, 111–12
PoP. *See* problems of practice
Porter, Meisha, 53–56, 65, 71–72
    ELAP joined by, 61
    in Fordham EdD program, 62, 64
    IS integrated by, 67
Portland, Oregon, 196
    houselessness in, 198
Portland Community College, 198
Portland Public Schools (PPS), 192
    equity at, 210–11
    McKey at, 204, 205, 208, 210
    PD at, 124
    PSU partnership with, 124, 193, 196–98, 203–5, *206*, 206–8, *209*, 209–10, 211–13
Portland State University (PSU)
    equity at, 195, 196, 201–2

NSD partnership with, 199, 202–5
PPS partnership with, 124, 193, 196–98, 203–5, *206*, 206–8, *209*, 209–10, 211–13
principal preparation program of, 196, 200–202, 208, 210, 212
Portland Teachers Program (PTP), 198
Post-Doctoral Improvement Science Action Network (PDISAN), 132, 134, 136
NICs of, 146
in PGCPS/UMD partnership, 148
PPS. *See* Portland Public Schools
PPS-PSU Dual Language Teacher Residency Program, 198
preparation programs
for leadership, 32, 47, 61
for teachers, 151, 155, 164, 166
Preparing School Leaders to Include Student Voice (presentation), 199
Presidio, Sloan, 74–75, 77–78, 81
Prince George's County Public Schools (PGCPS)
demographics of, *127*
SPP of, 134–37, *140*
Talent Development Office of, 145
UMD partnership with, 124, 126–29, 131–32, 134, 136–48, 303
Principal Induction Programs, of EDLE (PIP), 86, 87
at Learning to Improve Conference, 92
principals, 256
at CPS, 264, 271, 275–76, 275n4, 277, 289
DI targeting, 236
DU-ELPS preparation program for, 217
educational disparities impacted by, 213
equity in development of, 287
MEd to license, 266
NIU/Rockford/Elgin Public Schools residency program for, 286
PIP or, 86, 87
PSU preparation program for, 196, 200–202, 208, 210, 212
in SIIP NICs network, 89
problems of practice (PoP), 64, 72, 211
ART analyzing, 65, 68
in CoE/MCSD partnership, 247–48
in CPS/UIC partnership, 266
cycles of inquiry for, 66

data collection for, 257
dissertations addressing, 60, 61
IS to address, 78–79, 140, 174, 259
of LEAs, 302
in MLFTC/AESD partnership, 158–59, *159*, 162–63, 166
NICs addressing, 69
in PDSA, 183
in PGCPS/UMD partnership, 132, 146, 147
in PSU/PPS partnership, 210
theory of action to address, 249
in Theory of Improvement, 139
in UM-SOE/OSD partnership, 175, 177, 182, 185
professional development (PD), 28, 56, 123, 142
of CCPS staff, 31
Eddy-Spicer workshops for, 34–35
at FCPS, 77, 82, 84, 87
grants for, 152
on IS, 30, 190
in MLFTC/AESD partnership, 151–52, 155, 164, 165, 168
at PGCPS, 132
at PPS, 124
in UM-SOE/OSD partnership, 174, 180–81, 183
professional learning community (PLC), 42
Project Momentum Arizona, 152, 162
Proud Boys, 198
PSU. *See* Portland State University
PSU COE Educational Leadership and Policy department (ELP), 196
PSU Strategic Plan, 196
PTP. *See* Portland Teachers Program

racial disparities
achievement gaps relation to, 200–201
in disciplinary referrals, 39–40, 43, 225
IS to address, 192
at PGCPS, 132
in PPS literacy scores, 124
in student learning, 56
Ramalay, Judith, 197
Rangel, Snodgrass, 256
Regression, in partnerships, 258
relationships, 55–56, 301
boundary spanners building, 218

formal commitments for, 141
in partnerships, 140, 143, 171–72, 244, 246–47, 303
trust in, 187
Relative Risk Ratio, 67
Renewal, in partnerships, 258
research
 on DI, 233
 in DU-ELPS/DPS partnership, 232–34
 external funding for, 285–86
Reynolds, Candyce, 198, 199
Richmond, Virginia, 32
Ritchie Program for School Leaders, 220–22
Roach, Virginia, 54, 55
Roberson, Bradley, 182
Rock, David, 174, 177
Rodriquez, Leticia, 54
Rudolfo, Ainsley, 65–66

Saady, Kristin, 41–42
Sanders, Maureen, 221
San Diego, California, 97
Sarason, S. B., 307
SBAIP. *See* School-Based Administrator Induction Programs, of EDLE
Scholar in Residence, in UM-SOE/OSD partnership, 188–89
School-Based Administrator Induction Programs, of EDLE (SBAIP), 86, 87
 at Learning to Improve Conference, 92
School Improvement Leadership Post-Baccalaureate Certificate Program, of UMD, 137–38, 145
School Innovation and Improvement Planning (SIIP), 36–37, 40, 42, 85
 at CCPS, 43–44
 at FCPS, 78–79, 82–84, 88
 NICs joint initiative with, 84, 88–92, 94–95
School of Education and Human Development, UVA (EHD), 31–32
School Performance Plan (SPP)
 of PGCPS, 134–37, *140*
 in Theory of Improvement, 138–39
School Quality Rating Program, 272
School System Leadership, EdD program in, 127

Scott, W. R., 298
SEL. *See* Social-Emotional Learning
Senate Bill 1019, 263
Senge, P., 194
Shahrokhi, Farnoosh, 77
shared narrative, 131, 163, 165
Sherman, Harry, 54
Shulman, L. S., 34, 47
Sierra Leone, West Africa, 194
signature pedagogy, 37–38, 48
 conversations for, 46
 cycles of inquiry as, 281
 IS as, 31, 39, 83, 132
 school improvement pedagogy compared to, 47
 of UVA Master's program, 34
SIIP. *See* School Innovation and Improvement Planning
Silva, Claire, 80, 87
 SIIP NICs schools visited by, 88
SI-NICs, 138
Six Core Principles of Improvement, 102, 105, 106, 121
 communities in, 108
Smaldino, S., 255
Smylie, Mark, 279, 283, 291
Snell, Jean, 131
Social-Emotional Learning (SEL)
 NICs for, 69–70
 at OSD, 187–88
social justice, 194–95
 in GSE EdD redesign, 60
 IS for, 199
 in PPS/PSU partnership, 212
 at UIC, 264
social learning, cultural development in, 5–6
SPP. *See* School Performance Plan
staffing design problem, teacher retention as, 150
Stanford University, 231
Stosich, Elizabeth, 54, 55, 69
 NICs studied by, 65
Strategic Imperatives, for continuous improvement, 135, 137
student learning, racial disparities in, 56
student learning outcomes
 equity in, 27
 inequities in, 27–28
Success Analysis Protocol, 114

successful teams, 168
Summer Leadership Institute, PDSA at, 136–37, 139
suspension rates, high school, 68, *68*
sustainability
　of change, 306
　in HTH new-teacher induction, 120
　in partnerships, 307–8
systems change
　DI for, 229
　for equity, 227–28
　goals for, 237
　infrastructure for, *227*

Talent Development Office, of PGCPS, 145
Targeted Schools in need of Improvement (TSI), NICs to support, 211
Taylor, Curtis, 106
Taylor, Thomas, 33
Teacher Collaborative Grant Program, 147
Teacher Quality Partnership grant, 150
　MLFTC obtaining, 155
teacher retention
　at AESD, 154
　in Arizona, 156
　at Bronx CSDs, 53
　in HTH, 28
　induction programs relation to, 100, 115, 117
　networks for, 114
　at OSD, 185
　school culture affected by, 120
　as staffing design problem, 150
teachers. *See specific topics*
teacher shortage, 164
　at AESD, 153–55
　in Arizona, 149–50, 156, 170
　Next Education Workforce initiative relation to, 170
teacher strike, 225
team-based residency model, 149–50, 159–61, 165
teaming model, 152, 154, 159–60, 162, 166
team planning summit, for coaches, 113
tenure-line faculty, 283
theory of action, 249
Theory of action, drivers, and change ideas, 58–60, *59*

Theory of Improvement, 138–39
think tank, at CCPS, 41–42, 47
Tingwall, Allison, 278
Tipton, Bethany, 112
Title I Comprehensive Needs Assessment (CNA), of FCPS, 87–88
Title I schools, FCPS, 87
Tobia, Erika, 54, 64
Toler, Gina, 88
Tozer, Steve, 273n2, 275n4
trading zones
　boundary objects in, 2, 7–8, 20
　continuous improvement in, 22
　between LEAs and IHEs, 3
transactional relationships, 7
　in LEA/IHE partnerships, 123, 151–52, 298, 299
　mutual-benefit partnerships compared to, 6, 141
transition plan, for leadership, 213
Translating Equity into Practice using Improvement Science course, 84, 85
transparency, of leadership, 240
Trubowitz, S., 244–48, 258
　on collaboration, 251
　on personnel changes, 256
trust
　in partnerships, 161, 237
　in relationships, 187
TSI. *See* Targeted Schools in need of Improvement
TSPC. *See* Oregon Teacher Standards and Practices Commission
Tucker, Pamela, 37
tuition, at Fordham, 62, 64

UCEA. *See* University Council for Educational Administration
UIC. *See* University of Illinois, Chicago
UM. *See* University of Mississippi
UMD. *See* University of Maryland College Park
UM School of Education (UM-SOE)
　demographics of, *177*
　OSD partnership with, 174–75, *176*, 177, 178, 180–81, *181*, 182–91
　PDSA cycles at, 182, 186–87
United States (US), Department of Education of, 171, 272

University Council for Educational
    Administration (UCEA), 38, 192,
    199
  EELPP of, 221
University of Denver (DU). *See* DU
    Educational Leadership and Policy
    Studies Department
University of Illinois Chicago (UIC), 38
  Center for Urban Education Leadership
    of, 281, 286, 290
  coaches at, 283, 283n12
  CPS partnership with, 218, 262–63, *265*,
    266, *266*, *267*, 268–79, 276n6, 282,
    283, 283n12, 284, 284n13, 285–86,
    288–91, 305
  Education Policy Studies Department of,
    264, 279
  NICs at, 281, 281n9
  social justice at, 264
University of Maryland College Park
    (UMD)
  COE of, 130, 141, 143, 144
  demographics of, *127*
  NELP at, 130
  Office of Monitoring and Accountability
    of, 137
  PGCPS partnership with, 124, 126–29,
    131–32, 134, 136–48, 303
  School Improvement Leadership Post-
    Baccalaureate Certificate Program of,
    137–38, 145
University of Mississippi (UM), UM-SOE
    of, 174–75
University of South Carolina (USC), 217,
    240. *See also* USC College of
    Education
  CoE partnership with MCSD, 241–44,
    247–49, *250*, 251–53, 256–59
  leadership transitions at, 256
University of Virginia (UVA), 305
  A&S M.Ed. at, 31, 37–38, 46
  CCPS partnership with, 27, 30–35, 38,
    40–43, 46–48
  EHD of, 31–32
  Master's program redesign at, 34
US. *See* United States
USC. *See* University of South Carolina
Using Research to Lead School Improvement
    course, 79, 82

US News and World Report, 31
UVA. *See* University of Virginia

Vaughan, Cris, 54, 65, 66
vendor arrangement, in CPS/UIC
    partnership, 276, 276n6
Viano, Samantha, 79–80
  FCPS cohort guided by, 83
  IS experience of, 81, 82
Virginia
  Department of Education of, 88
  Richmond, 32
Virginia Competencies for the Preparation of
    School Leaders (Code of Virginia,
    n.d.), 37
vulnerable decision points, *68*

Wakefield, Chris, 109
Walker, Katonja Webb, 285
Wallace Foundation, 285
  grant from, 129
  Illinois State University relation to,
    273n2
  podcasts with, 277
  Ritchie Program featured by, 221
  on sustainability, 307–8
Weick, K. E., 244, 257, 258
Weldon, Ward, 273
Werpy, Dick, 221
West Africa, Sierra Leone, 194
Western Kentucky University, 278
West Harrison, New York, Fordham EdD
    cohort at, 61
Whalen, Ann, 223, 279
Whalen, Sam, 278
White, Courtney, 88
White, Tinkhani Ushe, 36, 41
  Eddy-Spicer relation to, 34–35
Wisconsin, Menomonee Falls School District
    in, 35–36
Wiseman, Donna, 129–30
Wood, Luke, 112

Xavier, 98

Yammagata-Lynch, L. C., 255
Young, Michelle, 38
Youth Truth Survey, 180, 182
  PDSA for, 183–85

About the Contributors

Erin Anderson is Associate Professor of Educational Leadership and Policy Studies at the University of Denver. She is the program manager of a state turnaround grant, which supports the development and facilitation of the professional learning program for leadership teams to integrate liberatory design and improvement science into school improvement work. The Design Improvement Program is co-constructed and delivered in partnership with Denver Public Schools. Anderson's research focuses on planning, leading, and implementing continuous school improvement and her work has been published widely in leading journals and books. She earned a Ph.D. in administration and supervision from the University of Virginia.

Douglas W. Anthony is Director of the Doctorate of Education in School System Leadership and Senior Fellow at the Center for Educational Innovation and Improvement at the University of Maryland. Anthony has worked with school districts, universities, and state departments of education across the country as a consultant and an executive-level coach. Prior to his work with the University of Maryland, he served as an associate superintendent for Prince George's County Public Schools (MD). Anthony served in several roles throughout his career, including as a principal; director of school leadership; and executive director for talent management. He earned an Ed.D. from the University of Maryland.

Cynthia K. Barron is Program Coordinator, Assistant Clinical Professor, and Leadership Coach with University of Illinois Chicago (UIC) Urban Education Leadership Program. In this role, Barron works collaboratively with the Center for Urban Education Leadership to strengthen the work and impact of both the Center and the Ed.D. program. She works in partnership with Chicago Public Schools on leader pipeline development, residency placement, principal eligibility processes, and development of supports for principal supervision and success. Barron also teaches graduate courses in the principal preparation and superintendent endorsement programs and has coached over 50 successful Ed.D. candidates. She earned a Ph.D. from Loyola University Chicago.

Carole G. Basile is Dean of the Mary Lou Fulton Teachers College at Arizona State University (ASU). Her work has centered on redesigning the education workforce and workplace—creating models for team-based teaching and enhancing the decision-making of educators through Principled Innovation—all to drive more equitable working and learning environments for educators and learners. She is currently working with education organizations nationally and internationally to design new systems for educators and their students to enable organizational change in this area. Basile earned an Ed.D. from the University of Houston.

Michelle M. Beavers joined the faculty at the University of Virginia in 2018 after having served Chesterfield County Public Schools as Coordinator and Assistant Coordinator of Professional Development. She is passionate about the application of theory to practice demonstrated through improvement efforts in her classes. Beavers collaborates with district and university partners teaching improvement science and implementation of practices through field-based initiatives in collaborative teaching environments. Her research interests include job-embedded adult learning and development, emotional intelligence, and continuous improvement for student learning. She earned a Ph.D. in educational leadership from Virginia Commonwealth University.

Barnett Berry is Research Professor at the University of South Carolina, where he also serves as Senior Director for Policy & Innovation. Berry's research has focused on teaching policy and teacher professionalism. His work with the National Commission on Teaching and America's Future in the 1990s led to his founding of the Center for Teaching Quality, a non-profit that paved new ground for teachers to lead efforts to transform public education. He also serves as Senior Research Fellow for the Learning Policy Institute. He earned a Ph.D. in educational administration and Policy Studies from the University of North Carolina at Chapel Hill.

Manuelito Biag currently serves as the managing director of the Center for Postsecondary Innovation at the Carnegie Foundation for the Advancement of Teaching. In this role, he leads an international portfolio of projects aimed at increasing students' social and economic mobility. He also serves as senior associate and provides instruction, coaching, and research support in the area of networked improvement science. Prior, he served as senior researcher at the John W. Gardner Center for Youth and Their Communities at the Graduate School of Education at Stanford University. Biag earned a Ph.D. in education policy from the University of California, Davis.

Regina Biggs is Associate Professor at George Mason University in the College of Education and Human Development. Biggs has served as a teacher, district leader, and managing director of an education consulting group while working across the P-20 education landscape. She teaches in the Education Leadership Program; and her interests focus on developing educators' attitudes and beliefs on issues of diversity, equity, and social justice to broaden access to excellence for all students.

Anthony S. Bryk served as the ninth president of the Carnegie Foundation for the Advancement of Teaching from 2008 through 2020, where he led the efforts to transform educational research and development, more closely joining researchers and practitioners to improve teaching and learning. Formerly, he held the Spencer Chair in Organizational Studies in the School of Education and the Graduate School of Business at Stanford University from 2004 until assuming Carnegie's presidency in September 2008. He earned an Ed.D. from the Harvard Graduate School of Education.

Susan P. Carlile has over 50 years of experience in K–12 education as a teacher, middle- and high-school principal, and director of curriculum and instruction. As a professor of practice and program lead for the Educational Leadership and Policy Program, she has facilitated the leadership development of over 600 school leaders, received 18 grants for her work, and presented and published in dozens of state, national, and international forums of leadership. Her current research focuses on continuous improvement in schools and examining the issues facing women in leadership positions and strategies for navigating the workplace to ensure gender, racial, ethnic, linguistic, and socio-economic equity in education. She earned an M.A. from the University of Oregon.

Charoscar Coleman is the Associate Superintendent for Support Services in the Prince George's County Public Schools (MD). Previously, Coleman served as an instructional director. In this role, he was responsible for supporting schools across the school district by providing direct coaching support to principals and articulating the school system's mission, goals, accomplishments, needs, and strategies to area schools and communities. During his 14 years as a principal, he was twice nominated for the *Washington Post* Principal of the Year Award. He earned an Ed.D. from the University of Maryland.

Diana Cornejo-Sanchez is a first-generation bilingual college student who started her educational journey as a high-school humanities teacher, serving as a founding teacher of High Tech High Media Arts, where she taught and mentored new teachers. After teaching, she joined the University of San Diego's Jacob's Institute for Innovation in Education. Her passion for supporting teachers brought her back to High Tech High as the director of the HTH Teacher Center, where she supported new teachers and their mentors. She currently supports High Tech High's 16 schools as the Director of Instructional Leadership and Development. She earned an Ed.D. from San Diego State University.

Shelby Cosner is Professor of Educational Organization and Leadership and Director of the Center for Urban Education Leadership at the UIC. Cosner served as co-leader for UIC's Ed.D. program, and has published widely on leadership for school improvement, the preparation and development of leaders, and the continuous improvement of leadership preparation programs. She is also engaged in leadership development in the Middle East and Global South. Her scholarly work appears in such outlets as *Educational Administration Quarterly, Leadership and Policy in Schools,* and *Journal of Educational Administration.* She earned a Ph.D. in educational leadership and policy analysis from the University of Wisconsin at Madison.

Kathleen M. W. Cunningham is an assistant professor in the Department of Educational Leadership and Policies at the University of South Carolina. Her research centers on educational leadership and includes the areas of leadership preparation programs, improvement science, program evaluation, and the intersection of science education with policy and leadership. Cunningham played a leading role in the University of South Carolina's work with iLEAD. She earned a Ph.D. in educational leadership and policy studies from the University of Iowa.

Kris DeFilippis is clinical assistant professor at New York University's Steinhardt School of Education. He began his career in education as a custodian, then became a social studies and English teacher in public schools in the Bronx, a department chairperson at a Special Act district in Westchester, and an associate principal for Warwick Valley Middle School. DeFilippis served as an executive director in New York City Department of Education, supporting school and district leaders to craft and enact equitable goals and strategies through context-specific cycles of inquiry. He earned an Ed.D. from Fordham University.

Mark E. Deschaine is Associate Professor of Educational Leadership at the University of Mississippi. Deschaine helps prepare future school and district educational leaders in the M.A., Ed.S., Ed.D., and Ph.D. degree programs. Mark is Editor of the *Journal of Contemporary Research in Education* (JCRE). He also serves as a research fellow with the Michigan Virtual Learning Research Institute (MVLRI). Deschaine earned a Ph.D. in educational leadership from Western Michigan University.

Felice Desouza is pursuing a doctorate in Education Leadership with a focus on improvement science from the University of Maryland. Currently, she serves as Supervisor of the Office of Monitoring and Accountability in Prince George's County Public Schools. Prior, she served as an instructional specialist in the Office of Monitoring and Accountability, a teacher of mathematics in grades 6–9, school improvement chairperson, girls' basketball coach, mathematics department chair, mathematics coach and specialist, turnaround specialist, and systemic improvement specialist. She earned an M.S. in education from Walden University.

David Eddy-Spicer is a professor of educational leadership in the Department of Leadership, Foundations, and Social Policy at the School of Education and Human Development at the University of Virginia (UVA). He has authored or co-authored a wide range of publications on the diffusion of innovation, professional learning, and organizational change in the public sector. He served as co-editor and one of the chapter authors of "Section One: Foundations of Improvement Research in Education" for the *Foundational Handbook on Improvement Research in Education* (Rowman & Littlefield). He earned an Ed.D. from the Harvard Graduate School of Education.

Segun Eubanks is Professor of Practice and Director of the Center for Education Innovation and Improvement at the University of Maryland, College Park where he works to bring together the shared expertise of research and practice to develop leadership, improve schools, and advance equity. Eubanks served as Chair of the Board of Education for Prince George's County Public Schools and worked in various leadership roles at the National Education Association, including as Director of Professional Educator Support and Director of Teacher Quality. He earned a Ph.D. in teaching and learning policy from the University of Maryland at College Park.

Christina Flesher is a Clinical Associate Professor and Professional Experience Strategist within the Mary Lou Fulton Teachers College of Arizona State University. She has been in the field of education since 1997 and has worked as a Gifted Education Specialist, as well as taught regular elementary and gifted students. Her research topics include gifted education, differentiated instruction, and exposing students to higher levels of cognition. She earned an M.Ed. from Northern Arizona University.

Louis M. Gomez works to help educators take a new perspective on design and educational improvement by catalyzing long-term, cooperative initiatives. The work gains its power through highly focused collaboratives called Networked Improvement Communities. He is a Professor of Education (and Information Studies) at the University of California, Los Angeles. Since 2008 he has also served as a Senior Fellow at the Carnegie Foundation for the Advancement of Teaching. Gomez earned a Ph.D. in cognitive psychology from UC Berkeley.

Betsy Hargrove has been the Superintendent of the Avondale Elementary School District (AESD) since 2012. She provides ongoing leadership and works to engage in continuous improvement by implementing and monitoring the achievement of district goals and mission for every student to grow as a thinker, problem solver, and communicator to pursue a future without limits. High-yield instructional practices in a collaborative and collective learning environment have resulted in AESD outperforming the state for growth in achievement six years in a row. Actively participating in the National Center for Education Research and Technology (NCERT), School Connect, and in other state and national venues, Hargrove collaborates and builds synergetic relationships to further educational success in her community. She earned an Ed.D. from Arizona State University.

Brian Harvey is a retired teacher-coach, principal, central office administrator, assistant superintendent, and superintendent all with the Oxford School District. During Harvey's tenure, the Oxford School District was recognized as a District of Innovation, which gives the district flexibility to create non-traditional learning environments, employ creative funding strategies, and expand curriculum choices. Under his leadership, the Oxford School District ranked first in the state for student academic proficiency in 2015–2016, and in the top five from 2016–2021.

Marni Herrington currently serves as Chief Academic Officer and Assistant Superintendent of the Oxford School District in Oxford, MS. As an educator for 20 years, she has served Oxford School District as a teacher, assistant principal, and most recently, as the principal of Della Davidson Elementary School, which received the National

Blue Ribbon of Excellence Award under her leadership. She earned an M.A. in curriculum and instruction from the University of Mississippi.

Zipporah Hightower is Superintendent of Skokie School District 73.5, where she led the creation of the district's three priorities: creating a welcoming environment, increasing the diversity of the teachers and staff to mirror their student population through hiring and retention policies and practice, and accelerating instruction with a focus on literacy. As Executive Director at Chicago Public Schools, Department of Principal Quality, she led her team in setting and achieving their outcome goals by enhancing their processes of identifying, developing, supporting, and retaining principals. During this time, she also managed the district's independent school principals. She earned an Ed.D. from National Louis University.

Randy Hitz is Dean Emeritus of the College of Education at Portland State University. His higher education administrative experience spans three decades and includes dean positions at Portland State, the University of Hawaii at Manoa, and Montana State University. He currently serves as a Senior Fellow at the Carnegie Foundation for the Advancement of Teaching where he has been part of the iLEAD project for five years. Hitz served as Chair of the American Association for Colleges of Teacher Education and Council for Accreditation of Education Professionals (CAEP) Commission as well as participating on CAEP's Board of Directors. He earned a Ph.D. from Indiana State University.

David G. Imig holds emeritus status from the Teaching and Learning, Policy and Leadership program at the University of Maryland at College Park. He served as president and chief executive officer of the American Association of Colleges for Teacher Education (AACTE) from 1980–2005. He is past chair of the National Policy Board for Educational Administration and the National Society for the Study of Education. He helped to establish the Carnegie Project on the Education Doctorate (CPED), serving as chair of the Board of Directors from 2010–2020. He serves as a senior fellow for the Carnegie Foundation for the Advancement of Teaching. He holds three academic degrees from the University of Illinois at Urbana-Champaign, and an honorary doctorate from Bridgewater State University in Massachusetts. He is the recipient of a Lifetime Achievement Award from the Universities Council for the Education of Teachers in the UK.

Janice Jackson is the CEO of Hope Chicago, a new two-generation scholarship organization that eliminates barriers to educational and economic equity by guaranteeing debt-free college and wraparound support services to Hope Scholars and their parents. Jackson began her teaching career in Chicago's South Shore High School. She went on to serve as a high-school principal, district network chief, chief education officer, and CEO of Chicago Public Schools (CPS). Under her leadership, CPS rose to record-breaking improvements in academic achievement, high-school graduation, and post-secondary completion. She earned an Ed.D. from the University of Illinois at Chicago.

Julia Jacobsen is an improvement specialist at the High Tech High Graduate School of Education. As a member of the Improvement for Equity by Design (IExD) team, she develops the capacity of organizations to build equitable systems and practices. She also supports

High Tech High's teacher induction program, developing curriculum and coaching capacity to engage new teachers in meaningful improvement. An elementary educator for ten years, Julia holds master's degrees in Technology, Innovation, and Education from Harvard and Educational Leadership from the High Tech High Graduate School of Education.

Sandra Lochhead is a principal supervisor over 11 K–8 schools in Denver Public Schools. Prior, she served as the Senior Manager of innovation and improvement, leading the team that collaborates with schools, communities, and central teams, using networked improvement and design thinking to dismantle inequitable systems and support the district and its schools to "get better at getting better." Her experiences as a special educator, general education teacher, a National Board–certified early childhood educator, assistant principal, and principal have deepened her commitment to working with school communities and students to improve outcomes. She is currently an educational doctoral candidate at the University of Denver.

Peter Martinez is a co-founder of the UIC Urban Educational Leadership Program and was its founding director of coaching. Prior to joining UIC, he was the Senior Program Officer at the MacArthur Foundation in charge of its $40 million, ten-year Chicago Education Initiative. For that work and his organizing on behalf of the passage of the 1988 Chicago School Reform Act, *Catalyst Magazine* named him one of the ten key leaders of Chicago school reform. In 2009 he was selected to serve on the National Board for Professional Teaching Standards (NBPTS) task force to develop the National Accomplished Principal Standards.

David Mayrowetz is Associate Professor in Educational Policy Studies at UIC College of Education and an original member of the team who designed the Ed.D. program. He studies how organizational and institutional forces within the educational system shape the formation and implementation of reforms such as teacher evaluation, content standards, state assessment, and special education. A teaching award recipient, Mayrowetz has chaired capstones for 15 Ed.D. graduates (and counting). His research has been published in *Educational Policy, Leadership and Policy in Schools, Educational Administration Quarterly*, and *Educational Evaluation and Policy Analysis*, among other venues. He earned an Ed.D. from Rutgers University.

Tania McKey is an educational consultant supporting schools with school/district improvement, implementation of literacy resources, training, and support. Most recently, she worked for the Portland Public School as Senior Director of Humanities and a middle-school principal. McKey's research interests include whole-school sustainability, literacy, leadership preparation, and school/district improvement. McKey's background includes teaching, coordinating, and leading International Baccalaureate (IB) World Schools in Minnesota, Texas, Indiana, Alabama, and Oregon. She earned a Ph.D. in administration, supervision, and curriculum from Auburn University.

Kara Miley-Libby is currently Strategic Initiative Officer and a part of the Executive Leadership Team for the Prince George's County Public Schools (PGCPS).

Miley-Libby has held various roles in her 37-year tenure in PGCPS from classroom teacher to social studies supervisor, K–12; director of curriculum and instruction; executive director for the division of teaching and learning; and chief academic officer. She earned an Ed.D. from Nova Southeastern University.

Peter Moyi is Associate Professor and Chair of the Department of Educational Leadership and Policies at the College of Education, University of South Carolina. His research aims to use sociological theory to understand school leadership practice and its impact on educational enrollment and attainment. He is especially interested in how past and current local, national, and international contexts influence school leadership practice. Moyi currently sits on the board of the Comparative and International Education Society and is the Associate Editor of the *International Journal of Educational Development*. He earned a Ph.D. in education policy from Pennsylvania State University.

Christine M. Neumerski is a Senior Research Fellow at the Center for Educational Innovation and Improvement in the College of Education at the University of Maryland. Her research and teaching focus on improving instruction in high-poverty, urban schools; instructional leadership; school system reform; and the relationship between public policies and classroom practices. Prior to joining UMD, Neumerski worked at Vanderbilt University and the University of Michigan, where she conducted several large-scale studies of school improvement efforts. She earned a Ph.D. in educational studies from the University of Michigan.

Margaret Terry Orr is Professor at Fordham University and Ed.D. Program Director and Chair of its division of Educational Leadership, Administration, and Policy. She has researched and published widely on leadership preparation approaches, the influence of preparation on leader practice, and school and district reform initiatives. Orr is past Division A Vice President of the American Educational Research Association and received the Edwin M. Bridges Award for Significant Contributions to the Preparation and Development of School Leaders (UCEA, 2015). She also contributed to the development of the US 2015 Professional Standards for Educational Leaders. She earned a Ph.D. in educational administration and policy from Columbia University.

Deborah S. Peterson is Associate Professor Emerita in the Educational Leadership and Policy Department at Portland State University. Peterson has prepared hundreds of anti-racist, culturally responsive school leaders at PSU. Her teaching and research focus on anti-racist, culturally responsive school leaders who empower students, faculty, and community through improvement science methodology. Her work has been published in numerous journals, including *Educational Leadership*, *Multicultural Matters*, and *School Administrator*, and she has presented at over 25 state, national, and international conferences on leadership for equity and improvement science. She earned an Ed.D. from Lewis and Clark University.

Meisha Porter has joined The Bronx Community Foundation as the inaugural President and CEO. Porter was previously chancellor of the New York City Department of Education, the nation's largest school system. She was responsible for educating 1.1 million students in over 1,800 schools. Before taking the chancellor's role, she served as The Bronx Executive Superintendent, where she invested deeply in sharpening school leaders' equity lens and building collaborative practices across schools. Porter also served as superintendent for Community School District #11 and principal of The Bronx School for Law, Government and Justice (LGJ), an Urban Assembly school. She earned an Ed.D. from Fordham University.

W. Bradley Roberson has been a public educator for 22 years serving as a mathematics teacher, coach, high-school principal, curriculum director, assistant superintendent, and currently the superintendent of the Oxford School District. Roberson led Oxford High School when Oxford School district was recognized as the #1 school district in the state of Mississippi. He was the runner-up for Mississippi Administrator of the Year in 2018. He earned an M.Ed. from the University of Mississippi.

David Rock is Dean of the School of Education at the University of Mississippi. Rock has taught mathematics in Florida and Mississippi at the middle- and high-school levels. He has conducted educational workshops and seminars at local, state, and national conferences in which his goal is to increase interest and enthusiasm for the teaching and learning of mathematics. Rock has published numerous articles and co-authored 15 books including *Teaching Secondary Mathematics* (2013) and *Scratch Your Brain Where It Itches* (2001, 2006, 2008). Rock currently serves as the chair and member of the board of directors for the Carnegie Project for the Education Doctorate (CPED). He earned an Ed.D. from the University of Central Florida.

Natasha Saunders has spent her career as a middle-school teacher, instructional coach, and disciplinary literacy specialist. Currently, Saunders supports school-based leaders, teachers, and central office staff in the Fairfax County Public Schools in their use of improvement science as a methodology for continuous improvement and disciplinary literacy. She is also a doctoral candidate at George Washington University researching leadership perspectives on the return to school following suspension for Black girls.

Farnoosh Shahrokhi is Associate Professor and Director of the Division of Education Leadership and Policy at George Mason University in Fairfax, VA. She designs and teaches graduate-level courses in the Education Leadership program, the largest such program in Virginia. Shahrokhi has been awarded multiple grants including the Teaching Excellence and Achievement Program of the US State Department from 2007 to 2018 where she served as the PI and director. She served as Academic Advisor for the Curriculum Development for Pre-service Education and School Administration Leadership for Armenia Project. She earned an Ed.D. from George Mason University.

Claire Silva taught biology and oceanography for 14 years in both high-school classrooms and online environments. She served as an instructional coach and data specialist supporting schools with using data to inform instructional decision-making. She now is a project support coach for Fairfax County Public Schools, managing strategic plan project teams. Her work includes the design and implementation of innovation and improvement efforts tackling longstanding system-wide problems of practice. Silva supports the use of continuous improvement methods including agile project management, systems thinking, and improvement science. She is currently a doctoral candidate at the University of Virginia.

Jean Snell is Senior Faculty Specialist and Associate Director for the Center for Educational Innovation and Improvement at the University of Maryland. Snell is the coordinator for the Administrator 1 certification program, and she also teaches and advises doctoral students in the School Systems Leadership program. She has dedicated the last 20 years to helping develop the next generation of school and teacher leaders and equipping them to lead continuous improvement and narrow the achievement gap in their schools and districts. She earned a Ph.D. in educational leadership and policy studies from the University of Washington.

Denise A. Soares is Assistant Dean, Director of Graduate Studies, and Associate Professor of Special Education at the University of Mississippi. Her research focuses on applied and practical experiences in academic and behavior interventions for at-risk students, as well as examining the efficacy of those interventions in classroom settings where teachers have competing time demands. Soares is involved in local school districts, where she collaborates on problems of practice and prepares educators for the complexities and demands of teaching students with exceptionalities. She earned a Ph.D. in educational psychology from Texas A&M University.

Elizabeth Leisy Stosich began her career in education as an elementary school teacher in Oakland, CA, and is now Assistant Professor and Associate Chair of the Division of Educational Leadership, Administration, and Policy at Fordham University. Stosich was awarded the 2022 Emerging Scholar Award by Division A of the American Educational Research Association. Her work has appeared in such journals as the *American Educational Research Journal* and *Educational Evaluation and Policy Analysis*. She co-authored *The Internal Coherence Framework: Creating the Conditions for Continuous Improvement in Schools* (Harvard Education Press). She earned an Ed.D. from the Harvard Graduate School of Education.

Nicole L. Thompson is a professor and vice dean of the division of teacher preparation in Mary Lou Fulton Teachers College at Arizona State University. Her work focuses on how best to prepare teachers to educate P-12 students. With a commitment to equitable and inclusive practices, her work creates, pilots, and brings to scale new roles for educators and new organizational structures for schools and systems that can better serve both learners and educators. Thompson works to create a sustainable workforce of educators prepared to work as members of collaborative teams of qualified professionals with distributed expertise who can support deeper and personalized learning for all students. She earned a Ph.D. from the University of Georgia.

Steve Tozer is Professor emeritus and past university scholar in educational policy studies at UIC, where he was the founding director of the UIC Center for Urban Education Leadership. His collaborations with colleagues from UIC and Chicago Public Schools were continuously funded for 18 years by numerous foundations and the US Department of Education. He is the lead author of a textbook, *School and Society, Historical and Contemporary Perspectives, 8th Edition* (McGraw-Hill, 2020), and lead editor of *The Handbook of Research in Social Foundations of Education* (Routledge, 2011). Tozer earned his Ph.D. in educational policy studies from the University of Illinois at Urbana-Champaign.

Samantha Viano is assistant professor in the College of Education and Human Development at George Mason University. Viano has worked in K–12 education in a variety of capacities including high-school mathematics teacher, education journalist, tutor, and organizer. Her research has been published in such peer-reviewed journals as the *American Educational Research Journal, Educational Evaluation & Policy Analysis*, and *Review of Research in Education*. Viano was a 2017 National Academy of Education/Spencer Foundation Dissertation Fellow. She earned a Ph.D. in educational leadership and policy from Vanderbilt University.

Sam Whalen is Research Director for the Center for Urban Education Leadership at the University of Illinois at Chicago. He is a quantitative and qualitative methodologist with expertise in program evaluation and the design of data infrastructures for evaluation and continuous improvement. His areas of content expertise include school leadership preparation/development, professional learning, and school–community partnerships. His work appears in several journals, book chapters, and policy/research briefs. His most recent work examines CEO leadership for continuous improvement within the context of Chicago Public Schools. He earned a Ph.D. in education from the University of Chicago.

Tinkhani Ushe White has been in education for over 20 years, having taught everything from 7th-grade mathematics to pre-calculus, mostly in schools considered "challenged." She is an associate in networked improvement science with the Carnegie Foundation for the Advancement of Teaching. Most recently, White was the Director of School Improvement in Chesterfield County Public Schools in Virginia. Her work focused on leading the school improvement efforts of the state's fifth-largest school district. There, she used her knowledge of improvement science and the state accountability system to support the revamp of the school improvement process. She earned an Ed.D. from Virginia Tech.

Paige Whitlock has taught middle- and high-school English and ESOL in seven states and supervised English departments in schools and central office for over three decades. Currently, Whitlock is Literacy Director in Residence for NoRedInk Corporation where she supports districts across the United States that seek to solve literacy problems of practice. Whitlock was the recipient of the 2021 Dissertation Award at Virginia Tech, where she earned her Ed.D.

Paul Zavitkovsky has spent most of his career as an elementary- and middle-school teacher and principal, leading Chicago's Boone Elementary School (K–8) to national recognition from the International Reading Association and the Fordham-Chase School Change Award from the National Principals' Leadership Institute during his tenure as principal (1991–2001). Zavitkovsky later served as Senior Policy Analyst for the Civic Committee of the Commercial Club of Chicago before becoming a leadership coach and assessment specialist with the Urban Education Leadership Program at UIC, where he continues to do assessment research and advocacy.

www.ingramcontent.com/pod-product-compliance
Lightning Source LLC
Chambersburg PA
CBHW060334010526
44117CB00017B/2827